THE END of
Bureaucracy
& THE RISE of the
Intelligent
Organization

THE END of
Bureaucracy
& THE RISE of the
Intelligent
Organization

Gifford & Elizabeth Pinchot

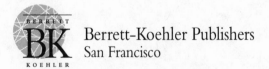

Berrett-Koehler Publishers
San Francisco

Berrett-Koehler Publishers, Inc.
155 Montgomery St.
San Francisco, CA 94104-4109
Tel: 415-288-0260 Fax: 415-362-2512

Ordering Information
Individual sales. Berrett-Koehler publications are available through most bookstores. They can also be ordered direct from Berrett-Koehler at the address above.

Quantity sales: Special discounts are available on quantity purchases by corporations, associations, and others. For details, contact the "Special Sales Department"
at the Berrett-Koehler address above.

Orders for college textbook/course adoption use. Please contact Berrett-Koehler
Publishers at the address above.

Orders by U.S. trade bookstores and wholesalers. Please contact Publishers Group West,
P.O. Box 8843, Emeryville, CA 94662; 510-658-3453; 1-800-788-3123.

Printed in the United States of America

Printed on acid-free and recycled paper that meets the strictest state and
U.S. guidelines for recycled paper (50 percent recycled waste, including 10
percent postconsumer waste).

Library of Congress Cataloging-in-Publication Data
Pinchot, Gifford
    The end of bureaucracy & the rise of the intelligent organization
    / Gifford & Elizabeth Pinchot.
    p. cm.
    Includes bibliographical references and index.
    ISBN 1-881052-34-6 (alk. paper): $24.95
    1. Bureaucracy. 2. Management. 3. Organizational sociology.
I. Pinchot, Elizabeth, 1943- . II. Title. III. Series: End of bureaucracy
and the rise of the intelligent organization.
HD38.4.P56 1993   93-40302
350-dc20   CIP

First Edition
00 99 98 97 96 95 94 93   10 9 8 7 6 5 4 3 2 1

✳ **TO OUR PARENTS**

Beulah Cain Schoonmaker

Sarah Huntington Pinchot

Gifford Bryce Pinchot

George Crossman Schoonmaker

Contents

PART III. ENSURING RESPONSIBILITY FOR THE WHOLE

APPENDICES

Foreword

GIFFORD AND ELIZABETH PINCHOT have done it again.

Their earlier book, *Intrapreneuring*, described a vital trend in corporate life today and gave it an unforgettable name. A best-seller, *Intrapreneuring* became an instant classic and deservedly so.

Their new book is even more ambitious. In it, the Pinchots tackle nothing less than the paradigm shift that is transforming the contemporary organization—changing it from an artifact of the nineteenth century to a system capable of thriving in the face of whatever the twenty-first century may bring.

In *The End of Bureaucracy and the Rise of the Intelligent Organization*, the Pinchots confront head-on the key organizational issues that have emerged over the last four decades. As early as the 1950s, a few of us who scrutinize organizations for a living looked into our crystal balls and saw the first blurred outlines of a coming revolution. In the decades following World War II, big and bureaucratic was the universal norm—in government, in business, in education. Yet a few of us were convinced, even then, that bureaucracy was a dinosaur waiting to become extinct. We did not know exactly what the successful organization of the future would look like, but we knew it had to be swifter and more flexible than what had gone before.

The Pinchots know their history and do an admirable job of summing up just why bureaucracy once worked and why it no longer does so. (Two critical factors: the dizzying acceleration of change and bureaucracy's legendary ponderousness in dealing with the new.) But what their readers will find even more useful is their description of the postbureaucratic organization, what they, with their gift for finding just the right phrase for the important phenomenon, call the *intelligent organization.*

What a lovely term! Traditional bureaucratic organizations have failed and continue to fail, in large part, because they tend to rely exclusively on the intelligence of those at the very top of the pyramid. There may have been a time—although I suspect it has always been more myth than reality—when organizations were so simple that a single man (and it was virtually always a man) could produce all the good ideas needed to sustain the operation. But the proliferation of organizations whose business is knowledge has ended that era forever. Whatever else the successful organization of the future may be, it will be a place where the intelligence of every member is treasured and allowed to bloom. It will be a place that recognizes that diversity is strength.

In recent years we have seen many popular organizational improvement programs whose essential focus is to make bureaucracy work better. We have also seen self-managing teams and other innovations to move beyond bureaucracy in particular areas of an organization. But for the most part, our organizations still depend on bureaucracy. What the Pinchots have accomplished is to offer the first clear vision of a whole organization that replaces bureaucracy with fundamentally different principles and systems for organizing work, principles that lead to greater efficiency and economic success by engaging everyone's intelligence.

I am one of those who believe that leadership is more important than ever in organizational life. But, like the Pinchots, I think the macho leaders of the past, with their command-and-control mentality, are uniquely *un*qualified to lead the organization of the future. The leaders who succeed in intelligent organizations will be the antithesis of the authoritarian leaders of our bureaucratic past. Instead of ordering, they will orchestrate. Instead of paying yes men, they will seek out and reward responsible nay-sayers.

Above all, these new leaders will be people who can articulate a vision that inspires and empowers everyone within the institution. They will be more like shamans than supervisors—people who encourage every member of the organization to dream a mutually beneficial dream.

One of the best things about this book is its essential humanism. As the Pinchots tell us, the intelligent organization is a fluid one, able to shape itself to whatever new reality presents itself. The Pinchots describe how *free intraprise*—another of their wonderfully apt coinages—can help create a successful organization. But the authors also do something rare among writers about organizations: They talk about the moral climate of success.

The Pinchots show that widespread rights, truth, equality, and community in the workplace are not merely humane options but, in fact, essential foundations for creating intelligent organizations that will succeed in today's complex and demanding world. With a hard-nosed realism combined with expansive vision that is their trademark, the Pinchots lay out in great detail how organizations that use the intelligence of every member are inherently more democratic and egalitarian than today's bureaucratic organizations. And they show how intelligent organizations effectively balance creating freedom of choice, ensuring responsibility for the whole, and maintaining economic success.

The Pinchots' is a guidebook to an organization in which fairness is understood to be as important an element of the institution's health as its efficiency. The Pinchots argue for fairness in the workplace, not simply because it is the right thing, but because it works. When individuals within an organization believe they are being treated unfairly, they often do something devastating: They withhold their energy and their ideas.

I wonder how many of the notorious corporate failures of recent years have resulted, not from market forces or other external realities, but from a kind of organizational patricide committed by members who felt badly treated by the company and its leaders. The thriving organization the Pinchots foresee is as democratic as it is intelligent.

And herein lies the ultimate gift of the Pinchots' book. It not only offers far-reaching advances in how to replace bureaucracy with more economically productive ways of organizing work, it also provides critical breakthroughs in creating more humane, democratic, and fair organizations—and shows how these "hard and soft" dimensions are, in fact, deeply intermeshed in intelligent organizations. It is not hard to see that this is destined to be a landmark book in changing how we understand, design, and lead organizations.

Warren Bennis
University Professor, University of Southern California, and author of *An Invented Life: Reflections on Leadership and Change*

Preface

THIS BOOK IS THE BEGINNING of a journey, not the end. We see a great opportunity for businesses, nonprofits, and government agencies to leave behind the bureaucratic system of organization and become more productive and more ready for the future. These new organizations will rely on systems that develop and express the intelligence, judgment, collaborative abilities, and wide-system responsibility of all their members.

Systems thinking teaches that leverage is more easily gained by changing the structure of human systems than by directly controlling events or specific behaviors. Changing the structure does not mean rearranging the organization chart in a new hierarchical pattern run from above. If we want to change a bureaucratic system, we can begin by liberating the self-organizing potential of people working in teams. Then the focus of change will be to provide the conditions in which this freedom leads to the most constructive results. Structural change of the kind needed to move beyond bureaucracy rebuilds the pattern of relationships and quality of communications in the organization on the basis of freedom and rights.

The transformation from bureaucracy to organizational intelligence is a move from relationships of dominance and submission up and down the chain of command to horizontal relationships of peers across a network of voluntary cooperation and market-based exchanges. These more open patterns of relationship are the result of thousands of voluntary alliances formed by individuals and teams as needed to get their work done. A network of numerous individuals and groups forms what is, in effect, the organization's brain.

New principles of organization are needed to produce an organizational brain that functions in a very different way from bureaucracy's vertical communications in a chain of command. A new architecture that connects laterally between specialties, geographies, products, and ways of thinking is needed. The structure of intelligent organizations is not set by those in charge during periodic restructuring; instead, order emerges as a result of everyone's voluntary connections and more democratically determined directions.

The organization of the future, to paraphrase Norman Macrae of *The Economist,* is a confederation of intrapreneurial teams.[1] Much of the discipline formerly supplied by the bureaucratic chain of command is supplied by self-management in teams and market discipline between them.

Organizations that are giving more freedom and choice to individuals and teams and reducing the control of the bureaucracy are following a pattern already established by the transformation of nations from feudal and totalitarian systems (which at their best have been bureaucratic). The newer national systems that have given people more freedom of choice and democratic responsibility tend to be high in material prosperity and closer to social equality. When most of Europe and nations such as Japan and Korea moved from feudalism to more open economies and eventually more open societies, they were making the transformation from faith in centralized power to faith in the self-organizing systems of marketplace and democratic control. A similar transformation is beginning in our workplaces.

Citizens in a free market nation with guaranteed rights are not subject to the same kind of direct hierarchical control as was imposed by the state-run economies of the former Soviet Union or is imposed on the employees of bureaucratic workplaces. In a modern nation we do not report through a chain of command stretching up to the head of state unless we work for the military or the federal government. Instead, within the boundaries created by law, the rights of others, and the practices of equal opportunity, we are theoretically free to live where we choose, seek what work we wish, form partnerships and collaborate with others of our own choice, buy from and sell to whomever we wish, and in general to make a life on our own terms.

In many industrialized nations these freedoms are a birthright, at least in theory, but the freedoms have been curtailed for many by such realities as the difficulty of making a living on one's own. Long gone are the days of the village smithy and the small farmer, when 80 percent of the adult population was self-employed, population low, and natural resources cheap and abundant. Many of us now cast our lot with bureaucratic employers who limit our freedom with more or less severity, and we are all enmeshed with numerous kinds of bureaucratic government.

Corporations and other large employers are among the last bastions of dictatorship. Within the more bureaucratic organizations, work life more closely resembles life in a totalitarian state than life in a free nation. Freedom of speech is at the sufferance of the boss. Bosses have the right to tell employees where to work and what to do. Career progress depends on pleasing but not threatening the boss. Initiative means asking for permission to do something differently.

Noticing this odd fact—that people want principles of freedom and inalienable rights recognized within their nations but choose dictatorship in the organizations where many spend most of their time—caused us to stop and think. Are today's bureaucracies, which waste the talent of the people who work in them, the best systems of coordination that can be built? We doubt it. What a cosmic joke it would be if we were given so much individual intelligence but, because of a limited conception of our ability to be both free and responsible, were doomed to work together in structures that guarantee that most of us get to use only a tiny fraction of our potential. If we consider the real needs of the future and the enormous changes our institutions will undergo in the next decades of radical change, we will see an increasingly urgent need for systems that can bring into play every ounce of our collective intelligence.

The potential intelligence of any human organization is widely distributed because the brains are widely distributed — one per person. The result of using the intelligence of a few decision makers rather than using everyone's intelligence is mediocre performance — not anarchy, but not organizational brilliance either, and definitely performance inadequate to the challenges of the twenty-first century.

In today's complex and intelligence-intensive world economy, it is becoming obvious that, in organizations as in nations, totalitarian governance and bureaucratic management are incompatible with high performance. Bureaucracy is dying because it produces organizations that lack the systems for assembling a collective intelligence to think both globally and in local detail, both near-term and long-term, and in terms of both freedom and community.

The organizations that will replace bureaucracy will grant their members more of the rights and freedoms we now consider normal for citizens in their relation to the state and to the larger society. The rights that increase organizational intelligence include freedom of speech, press, and E-mail; rights of free choice and association; rights to lateral exchange within internal markets; the right to make democratic agreements on the ways and means to promote the common good. For example, members of what we call an intelligent organization will have the right to create their own jobs if they can find other units willing to pay for their services. They will band together to form what we call "intraprises," by which we mean enterprises within a larger organization. These intraprises live or die, not by the decisions of the chain of command, but by their ability to find customers who need their services either inside or outside the organization. Given effective principles to discipline and guide self-organization, the greater the freedom of its parts, the faster the organization can learn.

Organizations composed of intraprises continually learn to function more effectively by making and breaking hundreds of voluntary connections. Our 1985 book *Intrapreneuring: Why You Don't Have to Leave the Corporation to Become an Entrepreneur* defined an "intrapreneur" as someone who fulfills the role of the entrepreneur inside a larger organization. We had a lot of adventures helping major corporations launch several hundred new ventures more cost-effectively by training and empowering intrapreneurial teams. Many succeeded — in fact, one grew to about a billion dollars in sales.

The more we worked at applying intrapreneuring, the more convinced we became that its basic principles are true. As we studied our clients' innovation successes, we found in every case a dedicated intrapreneurial team willing to buck the system. We were continually amazed by the drive, ingenuity, and courage of the intrapreneurs who emerged from the woodwork whenever the climate was even mildly hospitable. In every case we confirmed the key role of sponsors actively protecting and advising the intrapreneurial team. When a sponsor moved on to a new assignment, effective progress halted until a new sponsor worthy of the name was found.

We repeatedly found that creating an environment in which intrapreneurs could flourish created a rush of innovation. The discouragement of the last years came when watching new managers or new CEOs destroy a post-bureaucratic system that was working because they did not see the value of what their predecessors had created. We watched as successful ventures were trashed and the best intrapreneurs took early retirement. Too many of our friends were hurt.

We have come to realize that freedom at the sufferance of good bosses is not reliable enough to create lasting organizational intelligence. The tenure of bosses and management philosophies is often shorter than the cycle of major innovations or major cultural change.

Lasting freedom is based on guaranteed rights and inherently liberating forms of organization. It is not enough that a few anointed innovators be given freedom as long as the chain of command shines upon them; freedom is needed in the base businesses if the organization is to meet the multidimensional challenges of the twenty-first century.

We concluded that the intraprises that would collectively make the biggest difference to our clients were not those focused on new ventures, but rather those focused on providing services to the existing business units more innovatively and at lower cost. In the experiments with choices of internal suppliers we are beginning to see, we detect early signs of a free intraprise network replacing the monopolies of bureaucratic power.

The hallmark of an effective entrepreneurial network is the flexibility and ingenuity demanded for survival in an open market structure — the freedom and responsibility to innovate, to get rapid feedback from customers, to learn and change. Many of the virtues of the free market can be brought inside the corporation. When intrapreneurs have more of the rights, responsibilities, and challenges of entrepreneurs, the system acquires the permanent speed and adaptability of a network of entrepreneurial firms.

The paradox of market discipline is this: On the one hand, the customer gets more choice and control over the vendor's output than he or she would as a boss. On the other hand, customer and vendor do not submit to each other as deeply as subordinates do to bosses, because with multiple vendors and multiple customers they both have alternatives. Vendors also retain a base of independence from which to choose relationships and deals. This base of independence creates space for a level of innovation, integrity, and self-respect that is rare in traditional bureaucracy.

In this book we will describe a system of internal free markets that brings many of the benefits of the external free enterprise system to the relationships between the parts of a large organization. This "free intraprise" system is composed of a network of intrapreneurial teams or "intraprises." This system differs from traditional profit center systems in that it can work only if the customers are free to choose between alternative vendors. If internal vendors have a monopoly, as they do in a bureaucracy, then there is little feedback contained in their customers' decisions.

Like entrepreneurial teams organized in market networks, each intraprise is responsible for a whole little business, offering a product or service on the internal market. An intraprise may be a machine shop, like the one at Union Carbide's Texas City plant that discovered a less expensive way to repair pump seals. Soon they were selling pump seal repairs to other Union Carbide plants, which still retained all their previous choices of maintenance solutions. At the Taft, Louisiana, plant, the cost of using the intrapreneurs at Texas City was less than a quarter of what they had been paying an outside supplier.[2]

In our search for models of more open workplaces of the future, we looked to the effective networks of many smaller organizations, for instance, the many specialized high-tech firms in California's Silicon Valley, or the network of firms in Italy's Emilia Romagna region.

We noticed that all hugely complex products, like airplanes, automobiles, and space shuttles, are coordinated by a firm that relies on
decentralized networks of vendors that create the bulk of the value that
ends up in the final product or service.

We have seen entrepreneurial businesses linked in many partnerships and collaborations that outperform big, well-managed corporations. We have seen more important changes coming from small,
low-budget nonprofit experiments than from the most well-inten-
tioned government agencies. We know that idealistic bureaucratically administered third-world "development" projects often have
negative effects, while social miracles are put in motion by local small-
scale empowerment projects.

The Grameen Bank of Bangladesh, for example, makes hundreds
of thousands of small loans, averaging under a hundred dollars, to
help individuals, families, and community get stronger. They fund
"micro-enterprise" projects; the loans may pay for such things as a
street stall to sell things made in the home, a cow, or a wheel straight-
ener for a bicycle shop. Over 90 percent of the loans go to women.

Nonbureaucratic organizations, from the start-ups of Silicon Valley
to the Grameen Bank, often make an impact far beyond their size.
The combination of access to free markets, inalienable rights, and
democratic, grass-roots community action together are much more
empowering than socialist bureaucracies, as well as more egalitarian.

The rapidly growing numbers of worker-owned organizations,
especially those like Quad Graphics, Stone Construction Equipment
Corporation, or Springfield Remanufacturing, which combine worker ownership with substantial democracy and business education for
all, provide fascinating models. Ownership can motivate careful use
of organizational assets and provide a stronger base for freedom and
teamwork. The sense of independence and worth provided by ownership, even if the ownership is shared, can motivate higher commitment and participation from everyone than can socialistic bureaucracies. Yet the organizations we believe are most effective also bring
in more of the qualities of free market entrepreneurship than an equity position for employees.

Years ago many truly foresighted theorists began to predict that a
monumental change in workplaces was underway, a change away

from the civilization of uniformity and rote work imposed by the giant but simple machines of the early industrial era would accompany our move to a civilization of knowledge and customization. The changes are suddenly beginning to accelerate and take form. This book represents an early understanding of the emerging forms of organization appropriate for a world of knowledge work and customization. The tone of our offerings ranges from prediction, to firm proposal, to hopeful possibility.

In writing a book about what lies in the future, one faces a difficult issue of style. We are bound to be wrong in some particulars about the shape of the institutions that will eventually replace bureaucracy as the central tool for controlling and coordinating large organizations. Writing with the appropriate qualifiers would make the text end up a mess of "maybes," "probablys," and "our best guesses." To keep the book readable, we have opted for a more positive, even optimistic, style.

Judging from the title, this is a book of inclusive (if not grandiose) scope. Throughout the writing, our publisher Steve Piersanti continually urged us to be bold, to look at the big picture and not just stick to the areas of our existing expertise. Frequently, we found that following the trail of the essentials of organizational intelligence led us well beyond the knowledge we brought to this project. Following ideas to their logical conclusions often surprised us—finding the central importance for organizations of the future of democracy, networks, community, and internal market choice, for instance. We encountered many great thinkers along the way, people who know a great deal more about many of the topics in this book than we do, and we have more reading, interviews, and thinking to do. But that will have to wait for another book. Buckminster Fuller gave us courage when he said, "Dare to be naive." This book is our naive introduction to the world beyond bureaucracy.

Our hopes for this book are several. We hope to accelerate the transformation of organizations from bureaucracy to forms that develop everyone's talents and let people make a positive difference in the wider world through their workplaces. We will show examples of organizations large and small that have made progress toward postbureaucratic forms of organization that can provide models of new possibilities. We hope we can be of some help to people caught in turbulent changes within a bureaucratic organization. We believe that a clearer picture of why some principles of organization are dying and why others are gaining strength can help individuals choose where to place their bets and leverage their talents toward a better world. However, this is not a cookbook of remedies; it is a set of principles to guide those doing their own experiments to find out what will work in their situation.

This book is also a request for help and an invitation to collaboration. We will be publishing a newsletter and hosting an electronic conference on the issues raised by this book. We urge you to contribute to the newsletter or the conference. Let us know where we were helpful and where we were off base. Tell us about key issues or strategies we omitted. Most of all, send us stories of what worked and what did not. As explorers of freedom and community at work, you can add detail to the map of the land beyond bureaucracy.

We can be reached at :

175 North Main Street,
Branford, CT 06405 USA

Voice phone: (203) 488-4009

Internet: pandco@aol.com

America on Line: P and Co

*Network for Freedom and Community at Work
Bulletin Board System:* (203) 458-8523

> Gifford and Elizabeth Pinchot
> November 1993

Part I

The End of Bureaucracy

[The bureaucratic] organization is becoming less and less effective, ... it is hopelessly out of joint with contemporary realities, and ... new shapes, patterns, and models are emerging which promise drastic changes in the conduct of the corporation and in managerial practices in general. So within the next twenty-five to fifty years, we should all be witness to, and participate in, the end of bureaucracy and the rise of new social systems better able to cope with 20th [and 21st] century demands.

WARREN BENNIS

1

Organizations That Engage Everyone's Intelligence

Any company that's going to make it in the 1990s and beyond has got to find a way to engage the mind of every single employee. If you're not thinking all the time about making every person more valuable, you don't have a chance. What's the alternative? Wasted minds? Uninvolved people? A labor force that's angry or bored? That doesn't make sense!

JOHN F. WELCH, JR.

RADICAL CHANGES in the nature of work are revolutionizing what it is to be a human being in modern society. Every institution is changing as the relationships between employee and employer, woman and man, offspring and parent, student and teacher alter in deep and permanent ways in response to the need for all to contribute their intelligence, creativity, and responsibility to society. After decades of narrow focus, employees are being asked to consider the whole, to be innovative and care for customers, to work in teams, and to figure

3

out their own jobs and coordinate with others rather than just follow orders. Nearly all growing sectors of work require technical and human understanding, acute observation, creative problem solving, and skill in collaboration.

Bureaucracy as we know it, a structure defined by chains of dominance and submission, cannot survive these changes. It is leaving center stage and becoming just a bit player in the wings. Many huge companies that were successful over generations with tight bureaucratic patterns of organization and control have been driven into desperate fixes. For example, in 1992, General Motors, IBM, and Sears lost a total of $32.4 billion, which *Fortune* pointed out was more than four times what the Persian Gulf war cost U.S. taxpayers in 1990–91.[1] They had far to fall: Just two decades ago, these three giants were among the top six companies worldwide by stock valuation. They were masters of hierarchical coordination and expert in extracting obedience from massive groups of employees. Now they struggle to replace bureaucracy with structures and processes that reduce the role of the hierarchy and encourage more intelligent, collaborative self-management.

Bureaucracy is no more appropriate to sophisticated work today than serfdom was to the factory work of the early Industrial Revolution. As unskilled work disappears in advanced nations, most work is not rote repetition. Whether repairing a copier or calculating benefits in the human resources department, employees today continually use their education, experience, and native intelligence to make the decisions that guide their work. More and more, the only useful workers are "self-starters" who take responsibility for their area and the whole organization.

Serfdom "worked" for the landowners in agriculture, but it was too gross a form of control for the complexity and subtlety of industrial production. Similarly, bureaucracy worked for mass production of commodities but produces organizations too slow and inflexible to deal with today's pace of change. Bureaucracy is too simple-minded to deal with the multidimensional complexity caused by the diversity of customers, employees, partners, suppliers, and technologies. Bureaucracy fails to meet today's challenges because it discourages employees from using their native intelligence and sociability to run their own area of the organization.

In intelligent organizations employees put their heads together to milk opportunities, co-create products and services, find and solve problems. They "get in over their heads" and help each other emerge with stronger skills and a bit more wisdom. Employees run their areas like small businesses, serving their internal and external customers with care and working with others across the organization to make sure the whole system is going well. Everyone, not just the people at the top, is exercising his or her intelligence and responsibility at work. We see evidence of this all over the place.

The collapse in the early 1970s of the Rotterdam shipbuilding industry threatened the existence of many departments in Endenburg Electrotechniek, especially one that contracted electrical work for the local shipbuilders. Management came to the electrical department and told them what they had dreaded to hear: that they would probably need to shut down the department and reduce staff.

Deliberations focused on these painful changes until one electrician suggested an alternative: The department members could dress up in shirt and tie and solicit business for the other departments of the company. This way, they all began to see, business expansion in other departments would compensate for the lost business in their department. If they got business for other departments, they would soon be called in for the electrical work and be back in business themselves. Departmental staff developed a plan with a three-month time horizon, submitted it to management, and got the go-ahead. This tactic was completely successful, and board members who had been demanding staff cuts resigned.[2]

A self-managing team of workers in Digital Equipment Corporation's Enfield plant quickly handled a potential problem with a big customer at their daily production scheduling meeting.[3] They had just discovered that their customer's shipment would be arriving a day late, which might shut down production in the customer's just-in-time system. The large shipment of circuit boards that had been set out Monday afternoon for second-day delivery pickup was still on the dock Tuesday morning. Unbeknownst to the team, UPS had taken a Monday holiday that the plant did not celebrate. Now, instead of Wednesday, the customer would get the circuit boards Thursday. What should the team do? Go ahead and send it for

Thursday delivery? Send it the more expensive way by overnight courier? Call a manager to get a decision?

What the team did was send someone out of the meeting to call the customer and determine which parts of the order would be needed for Wednesday's production. Now what should they do? Unpack the boxes and repack them separately for rush and regular deliveries? Because this team of ordinary workers owned the whole process, they came up with a better solution. With the customer's cheerful approval, they created a duplicate order for the urgently needed boards, put it into the day's production schedule, and shipped it by overnight courier. The packed order sitting on the loading dock went out at the same time for second-day delivery. Because the same boards were reordered every few days as part of a just-in-time delivery, the duplicate boards were used within the week. The self-managing team handled the whole situation in a few minutes without any intervention by management.

Even when a company's formal structure remains bureaucratic and monopolistic, it is often becoming more possible for employees to choose how to do the work. Note, for example, this story reported in the *New York Times:*

> George Marchese and two co-workers needed less than 90 minutes the other day to cut down and remove a dead silver maple tree in front of Teresa Mele's house in Bensonhurst. Two men would return later to remove the stump and fill the hole with soil. Before this month, as many as seven workers might have done the same job....
>
> Mr. Marchese and his crew are part of a two-month test by the department to learn whether employees given new freedoms to set their own working conditions, like planning their routes and workloads, can improve performance and save the city money....
>
> Ms. Gotbaum, the Parks and Recreation Commissioner, was "absolutely blown apart" by the [positive] results.[4]

Regardless of the ultimate outcome of particular experiments, the principle has been established beyond doubt in innumerable instances: *Workers will be far more efficient if they have a hand in designing their own work than if work design is performed by management and handed down for compliance.* This fact flies in the face of bureaucracy's most basic tenet, that it is the job of management to design and coordinate workers' jobs.[5]

✳ HOW INTELLIGENT ORGANIZATIONS MEET TODAY'S CHALLENGES

A system that manages work from any distance by setting uniform procedures and issuing simple orders cannot deal with the fact that we no longer face a uniform or simple world. Increasingly often, uniform answers are not responsive to the diversity of inputs and outputs required. Resources are distributed all over the world's surface. Markets are segmented into smaller and smaller categories. As knowledge doubles and redoubles, technology divides into even more specialties, and each organization must master and integrate more of them. Global competition and the demands of customers, citizens, and the environment are driving change throughout all institutions. To handle this complexity and the rapidity with which many of these factors are changing, we need to create organizations capable of meeting demands for speed, multidimensionality, flexibility, creativity, and complex solutions. Here are the ways some organizations are using the intelligence of all their people to meet these challenges.

Collegial Freedom—Hewlett-Packard (Speed)

In the late 1970s and early 1980s, Hewlett-Packard set its sights on the computer business. Before that HP had been in the instrument business. Most of its instrument businesses were relatively small and only weakly interconnected. If, for example, an oscilloscope product line made an independent decision on how to serve its customers, the medical group was not deeply affected. Until it developed ambitions in computers, HP had been a confederation of highly independent business units sharing technology, a culture, and a great reputation.

In the instrument business mode, HP used the intelligence of nearly every engineer as a decision maker. Each little business had freedom, and all workers were close enough to those running the business to be heard and even to get a piece of the freedom for themselves. Entry into the computer business changed that easy freedom. Rather than opting early on to make components to someone else's standard, HP created its own computer architecture. That meant the company had to field a complete line of equipment: Everything HP made in computer systems had to hook up to everything else.

The necessary interconnections of the computer business created a dilemma: how to create the integration needed by the computer business while preserving the freedom and independence that had made Hewlett-Packard great? Not being an autocrat, John Young, who became CEO in 1977, opted for consensus management and set up councils to coordinate the various businesses and make sure everything worked together. A central R&D group designed all computer products, and a central marketing group made marketing decisions.[6]

The result of all this centralization was better integration in some cases but also slow decisions and broad-brush policies that often were not responsive to the specific needs of the business units. According to Willem Roelandts, an HP vice president, HP, which had been faster and more responsive than large competitors such as IBM and DEC, began to slow down and seek the "least common denominator" in committee decisions to settle differences between divisions.[7] The results were not good. For example, the long-awaited Spectrum workstation was not competitive with Sun's comparable products in either price or graphics. The PC business floundered.

Company founders William Hewlett and David Packard, long since retired from active management, decided something had to be done. They went into the field to find out what the troops thought was wrong and what they thought should be done about it. When they returned, working with the senior management team, they abolished a lot of committees and let the divisions make their own decisions again.

Divisions worked together. They formed teams to coordinate when this was needed, but at the same time they had freedom to move rapidly to meet their own customers' needs. Since then, results have been excellent. HP has come back with a highly competitive workstation, has created what may be the most talked about laptop in the industry, and has kept its dominant position in laser printers against a barrage of competition.

In 1992 the printer business produced 40 percent of HP's income.[8] This business is in many ways the model of an intelligent organization, and it owes its existence to an act of decentralization in the middle of the centralization era: the 1981 decision to make, in partnership with

Canon, a laser printer that would work with competitors' computers as well as HP's. This decision honored the old Hewlett-Packard intrapreneurial spirit over the prevailing view that printers were developed to sell computer systems, and thus should be designed to work only with HP computers.

Today after decentralization, HP as a company is light on staff, and the printer group is light in comparison with the rest of HP. For example, the ink-jet printers, a major part of HP's printer business, has nine thousand people across six sites. Rick Belluzzo "runs" that business out of a small leased office with four people—himself, an R&D manager, and two secretaries. This works because they have moved beyond bureaucracy—almost all tasks and responsibilities, including much of the coordination between teams running the five separate businesses within the ink-jet group, are delegated to the teams themselves. Each team has its own market focus and complete decision-making power and accountability. Within the ink-jet printer business there are teams for low-cost DeskJets, portable printers, network printers, large-format graphics printers, and consumable supplies.

How is a group with nine thousand employees and five separate businesses integrated when there is almost no staff to coordinate it? Art Lane, the group R&D manager, works with the teams to get technology shared and to encourage collaboration in designing a part (such as a common ink-jet printhead) where economies of scale suggest the teams should work together. He does not tell them what to do, and there are not enough people on Belluzzo's staff to tie things together. When a common problem arises, a team gets together from the different entities to handle it. Sometimes the impetus for collaboration comes from Belluzzo and his staff; sometimes the teams identify and solve problems among themselves. When there was a problem with the paper curling, people were not sure if the solution lay with redesigning the printer or reformulating the ink, so the team got experts from the consumable supplies area as well as from the various printer segments.

The distributed nature of the business got a real test when it was discovered that the CFCs (chlorofluorocarbons) used to clean circuit boards were contributing to the depletion of the ozone layer. Belluzzo summarized what happened:

When corporate environmental people decided that we had to stop using CFCs to make printed circuit boards, we all signed on. All the sites were asked to put together a plan to get out of CFCs. We shared resources to develop and test new ways of cleaning circuit boards and tracked our progress by the quarter. My conclusion is, it's hard to get things started from the center in a distributed organization, but once you do, small teams execute faster.[9]

Part of the secret to the printer division's success is illustrated by the way they do market testing. In the old days, market managers got frustrated trying to get R&D to build what customers wanted by describing customer needs in market research reports. Now R&D sits with the marketing people behind the glass watching the focus groups. Everyone has direct experience and a deeper appreciation of what customers want. There is less need for bosses to coordinate when the customer's voice is heard strongly by all.

Similarly, HP thrives on a "healthy paranoia about competition." Competitive tracking is the early warning system that allows them to make good decisions. They buy competitive products and do comparative testing with customers. They track each channel of distribution independently and begin reacting the moment anything changes in any one of them. Once, when HP was in its centralized phase, it took nineteen signatures to react to a competitor's moves by making a pricing change on a piece of software. Now the teams in each segment of the business react at once by changing their own prices. Close observation of the environment and a structure that allows quick reactions are essential elements of organizational intelligence.

Because very few orders are issued from above, it might seem as though this HP business group is composed of a bunch of independents who occasionally cooperate. In fact, they are highly interdependent and work as a team on a regular basis, even when this involves some sacrifices. For example, as the years go by, responsibility for generating profit shifts from one area to another within the business. Each takes its turn shouldering the burden of producing profit, so the whole ink-jet business is a reliable profit maker even though one segment may have to run thin margins or invest extra heavily in R&D for a year or two to fight off an aggressive competitor. Sharing of the load without worrying about who is getting ahead is a critical piece of the HP system for producing organizational intelligence. It comes with trust that everyone will be treated fairly and the knowledge that everyone knows what is going on. People in the printer division know one another because they do not move around the organization as people do in some companies (IBM, for example). Most of the managers have been around one another long enough to form a community in which the enemies are the competition, not other people in the HP printer business.

Sixty Thousand Products—3M (Multidimensionality)

The 3M Company manages sixty thousand products of astounding variety. They make sandpaper, surgical drapes, roofing granules, sticky tape, recording media, chemicals, dental supplies, insulation for clothing and sleeping bags, and electrical connectors and even sell services such as consulting and training on quality. Thirty percent of their sales are from products or services new in the last five years, and since 1973 the company has more than quintupled its sales on a steady trajectory of growth.

Successfully managing this diversity may not seem like much of an accomplishment, but most bureaucracies limit the effective use of employees' intelligence so that the organization can only be good at a few things at a time. To manage many businesses in many different markets with consistent innovation requires great organizational intelligence. The 3M Company is like a chess champion who can play fifty opponents at once and win most of the games. This ability to manage many things at once is increasingly relevant. In today's world, there are fewer and fewer opportunities to win by addressing large markets in an undifferentiated way.

The intelligence required of organizations today is not the genius of a few great strategists at the top. To do many things simultaneously and well requires an organization with breadth and depth of thinking power. It is not enough to have many smart people throughout the organization; many long-gone bureaucratic firms had enough smart people. To achieve organizational intelligence, the system must support large numbers of people in applying their intelligence in a free yet coordinated way.

Writing reports to people layers above in the bureaucracy who then make the decisions is an inefficient and ineffective way to use intelligence. Complex, multidimensional thinking, difficult to express in writing, is useless for influencing a hierarchy. Intuition looks flabby in a report. The experience of living with a customer or playing with an embryonic technology informs our own decisions but is difficult to explain to others, especially others in a superior position. Few in the hierarchy have the time or patience to explore the complex details of small and distant businesses. The businesses have no time to wait. People's intelligence can be used effectively only if they are trusted to act on what they observe and learn.

The 3M Company achieves organizational intelligence through a culture with powerful antibureaucratic elements. One element is lack of reverence for management—the old myths about 3M all concern innovators who defied management to champion an idea. People at 3M learn from these legends that it is good to overcome fear of another's superior rank and stand up for what you believe is right. The company is not without bureaucracy, but its strong tradition of greater respect for doers and innovators than for the hierarchy opens cracks for innovations to move through the system.

The division of 3M into about fifty autonomous business units is a structural means to achieve greater organizational intelligence. The management team of each business has substantial freedom and a tradition that encourages them to pass that freedom down to others in their domain.

In 1949, the founder of 3M's culture for innovation, Chairman William McKnight, summed up the philosophy that put 3M ahead of more bureaucratic competitors:

> As our business grows, it becomes increasingly necessary for those in managerial positions to delegate responsibility and to encourage [those] to whom responsibility is delegated to exercise their own initiative. This requires considerable tolerance. Those [people] to whom we delegate authority and responsibility, if they are good [people], are going to have ideas of their own and are going to want to do their jobs in their own way. It seems to me these are characteristics we want in [people] and [they] should be encouraged as long as their way conforms to

our business policies and our general pattern of operation. Mistakes will be made, but if the [person] is essentially right [himself or herself], I think the mistakes [he or she] makes are not so serious in the long run as the mistakes *management* makes if it is dictatorial and undertakes to tell [people] under its authority to whom responsibility is delegated exactly how they must do their job. If management is intolerant and destructively critical when mistakes are made I think it kills initiative, and it is essential that we have many with initiative if we are to continue to grow.[10]

The wealth of new products that 3M is famous for comes from a series of now "traditional" beliefs that empower people at lower levels to use their brains. Foremost among the beliefs about how to manage new product development is the idea that new products should be brought forward from within the divisions by a self-forming team that includes one person with a technical (R&D) background, one person with a marketing background, and one person with a manufacturing background. Managers sometimes "help" this self-forming process along by urging people to join a team, but in general the voluntary nature of the process is respected by avoiding orders. In this system, people with ideas take charge and move ahead by forging alliances with people from other functions, regardless of their position in the hierarchy. The first test of a new idea is the intrapreneur's ability to sell it to two other peers from the other two required functions. This puts all the initial screening of new ideas down at the level of ordinary knowledge workers and also encourages teamwork, thus achieving greater distribution of organizational intelligence.

Harnessing the entrepreneurial spirit within the organization (intrapreneuring) is critical to 3M's success in managing innovation. Intrapreneurial teams are empowered to take a product all the way from conception to commercialization and beyond—in theory, all the way to becoming the management team running a new division.

Made to Order—Wabash National (Flexibility)

The truck-trailer business has been tough. The industry produced 214,300 trailers in 1988 and only 140,500 in 1991. Between 1986 and 1991, Fruehauf's production declined 64 percent. Other major producers, like Strick and Great Dane, dropped 25 percent. In the same time period, upstart Wabash National grew 150 percent, taking its share of the market from 3.1 percent to 10.1 percent.

There are many secrets to Wabash's success, but they start with creating an organization that uses the heads and hearts of employees to change and respond faster. One of their truck-trailer customers, Russ Gerdin, president of Heartland Express, Inc., says that when he goes to other trailer manufacturers with a new idea, they tell him it cannot be done. "Wabash says, 'Let's see what we can do.' They let us talk to their engineers."[11] Then Wabash designs and produces a custom product in partnership with the customer.

Wabash makes special low-slung trailers for Disney to haul laundry through underground tunnels in their theme parks. Their trailers for Federal Express come with built-in rollers. Special deep-well trailers (with five patents) haul glass plate for Libbey Owens Ford. "We've built a manufacturing operation that can accept change constantly — because we have had to," says CEO Don Ehrlich. "On any given day at Wabash you can see 15 different types of trailers for 15 different customers coming off the production lines," remarks Charlie Ehrlich, head of manufacturing.[12]

Wabash, in a traditional industry, is producing a product with more customized intelligence per pound. The result is not only phenomenal growth in a declining industry but also trailers that on average get a 5-percent premium. They do this by producing exactly what customers want. "We want to get to the point where we're producing 100 percent proprietary products, and we're the sole source of supply in 100 percent of the cases."

Wholesale Change—Eastern Region of the U.S. Forest Service (Creativity)

In 1985, Max Peterson, chief of the U.S. Forest Service, challenged the service to "find ways of building on our traditional values and begin looking for new ideas."[13] Associate Chief Dale Robertson went to work cutting bureaucracy. He and his staff found that a stack of policies, regulations, and procedures seventeen feet tall was inhibiting innovation, so they simplified.

Then, looking for more wholesale change, Robertson sponsored four pilot studies that gave managers much greater freedom of operation. Four new ways of doing business were introduced:

Maximum autonomy allowed by law. Pilot project forests could change any regulation or process as long as the change was legal.

Lump sum budgets. At that time Congress gave the Forest Service its funding in about four hundred separate line items, each of which had to be spent or given back.[14] Lump sum budgeting let each pilot forest needing something not in their budget economize elsewhere and use those savings to buy it.

Failure versus learning. Each pilot forest was to try lots of new ideas, knowing not all would work.

Bottom-up change. Management's job was to create an empowering environment; ideas for operating changes were to come from the workforce.

The result, according to Karl H. Mettke, a management analyst in the Eastern Region of the Forest Service, was "a rush of new ideas," including flextime, workers choosing supervisors, and the elimination of unneeded paperwork.[15]

By 1987, two years into the pilot, there were substantial improvements in service to the public and an average of 18-percent increases in productivity. That was enough for Floyd J. (Butch) Marita, Regional Forester of the Eastern Region, and he requested and won "pilot" status for the whole Eastern Region, meaning that the whole region operated under the new liberating rules. According to Marita:

> The secret of PILOT in the Eastern Region is giving our people freedom...letting them go, letting them do the things they do best that meet the mission of the Forest Service. We trust our people and their judgment.[16]

The whole Eastern Region was introduced to new responsibilities and freedoms with Project Spirit, a program whose six letters stood for the powerful combination of a concern for results (Success, Productivity, Innovation) and a climate that empowers people to get those results (Risk, Intrapreneuring, Trust).

Instead of seeing creative workers as a problem, the division put their ideas to work. For example:

> Simplifying the process for paying vendors saved $500,000 per year.

Patrolling on mountain bikes gave far better coverage of trails. "Rangers on bicycles definitely have a friendlier feel to them than somebody driving up in a one-half-ton pickup truck," said Public Affairs Director Jim Carlyn.[17]

Rather than viewing the public as an obstacle to the plans of professionals who know best, Stu Kohi worked with an advisory board of disabled users to figure out how to make the forest more attractive to them.

The region implemented more than 90 percent of over twelve thousand employee suggestions.[18] "One of the greatest things we have changed is the thinking that workers get in the way," says Mettke.[19] According to Mettke, the overall transformation brought to the Eastern Region "the end of bureaucracy as we know it."

The end of bureaucracy includes moving from a functional staff structure to an integrated team concept in which people of all disciplines work together to manage the forest. This reorganization has happened a little differently in each forest because the plans for how to do it were designed by the people in those forests, not at regional headquarters. Even the Eastern Region's headquarters is now organized in five teams, one for each of the five key elements in the strategic plan.

From a management cost-cutting point of view, Project Spirit is a success: "The results have been astonishing. In a few short years, we have reduced our regional office budget by over $3,000,000 and eliminated over 50 positions. These resources have been redistributed to our national forests. At this time, our regional office budget remains the lowest regional office operating budget in the Forest Service."[20]

A key element of Project Spirit is "ecosystem management," a concern for the whole ecosystem as opposed to just the "tree farm." Our national forests are chartered for multiple uses, including timber production, recreation, wildlife habitat, and watershed management, but the Forest Service fell into a pattern of focusing primarily on timber production. The public's priorities are shifting. As population grows and ecological awareness increases, recreation and wildlife protection have become higher priorities. A bureaucratic Forest Service has had great difficulty in meeting a complex set of conflicting goals that includes preserving nonrenewable resources and also fulfilling congressional purposes such as using timber sales to balance our payments for Japanese autos.

In addition to work teams and project teams, the Eastern Region uses cross-functional teams to understand the complex effects of any plan on plants, insects, mammals, fish, birds, and people, instead of following the book or allowing the forester's viewpoint to dominate. Using the intelligence of teams, the Eastern Region is moving beyond single-use-dominated thinking to deal with whole systems. "'For example, when you create an opening in the forest for deer, what does that do to the other critters?' said Regional Forester Butch Marita. 'When you have a team of people making decisions like that, you know the answers almost immediately. You can move faster and save time and money.'"[21]

How much further can the Eastern Region go in managing our forests more intelligently? Congress continues to micro-manage, so Forest Service people may have good cause to say many of the remaining problems are not their fault. But that "victim" mentality is not prevalent in the Eastern Region, so there may be many more pleasant surprises to come.

Cost-Effective and Sustainable—
Pandole Brothers Farm (Complex Solutions)

We are increasingly confronted with complex dilemmas that do not permit simple or universal solutions, especially as a concern for ecology takes center stage. The segmented thinking of bureaucratic functions cannot deal with the rich interrelationships of the biological world.

Darren Moon, general manager of the five-thousand-acre Pandole Brothers Farm in Kern County, California, learned the benefits of ecological farming by devoting a thousand acres to organic fruits and vegetables. The results were so good the farm has applied many of the techniques of organic farming to the remaining four thousand acres of produce sold through normal channels. The style of pest management has changed from "prophylactic" spraying by the calendar to the careful observation of biological systems and judicious use of insecticides.

No single intervention solves the whole problem. Integrated pest management includes detailed soil tests, application of trace minerals as needed for plant health, release of predators for specific pests as they appear, changed tillage, rotations chosen with insect life cycles in mind, and, when needed, targeted applications of insecticide. Not only do workers monitor pest population trends, but they also check to see what the population of natural predators is doing and if the natural defenses of the plants are building fast enough to limit pest damage without need for spraying.

These new techniques have completely changed the organizational climate at the Pandole Brothers Farm. There is a new zest and commitment in the farm management—the new game of integrated pest management is more challenging and more fun. The field managers' cars are filled with books. They go to the field with handheld instruments to test soil moisture, mineral ratios, the total biological activity of the soil, and plant vitality. Field managers get to make important decisions and in the process learn something new every day.

The saving in pesticides exceeds $1 million a year. They use only one-tenth the pesticide they did when they sprayed by the book. Even more important, the Pandole Brothers are prepared for coming regulatory changes and a future that will be hard on those farmers who have not cultivated these new skills and the ability to integrate them.[22]

Ecology and other complex issues require a distributed organizational intelligence that is incompatible with the system of bureaucracy. In a bureaucracy, new issues to manage create new organizational entities whose approval is then required. Ways to say no proliferate. The kind of changes that survive an approval chain of fourteen signatures will not be the bold experiments or quick responses needed to simultaneously deal with environmental, social, political, and ethical concerns while still satisfying customers and other stakeholders.

✳ ADVANTAGES OF THE INTELLIGENT ORGANIZATION

Bureaucracy produces simple and shortsighted answers in an era when anticipating interconnections and dealing with long-term implications is—and will continue to be—a requirement for survival. Global change continues to accelerate, pushed by the spread of technology and communications and the impending arrival of another billion people. Employees— and ecosystems—are demanding more consideration, new forms of competition are appearing, customers expect new responsiveness, jobs are being eliminated, management's role is in question, and it turns out that everything *does* connect to everything else.

The organizations that are smart enough to deal with the complexity and fluidity of today's world have what computer people call a "mutable architecture," meaning the structure shifts to face the problems at hand. As the business opportunities and challenges change, people are changing their work processes, their connections, their relationship to technologies, even the values and directions embraced. At 3M new product teams form around ideas as they occur. A "15 percent rule" gives employees 15 percent of their time to check out ideas they think might turn out to be useful, so the early stages of a new project are guided by intrapreneurial discretion, not management evaluations. Intrapreneurs do not have to face an approval process until after they have recruited a team of coconspirators, developed the idea a bit, and refined it in response to the challenges raised by others representing many different viewpoints.

The self-managing teams of Digital's Enfield plant were also flexible. When a woman whose machine was a critical step in a process mentioned that she would have to take her child to the doctor that afternoon, another operator volunteered to take her place. He was able to do so because he, like most people in the plant, had been trained to operate many different machines and his main machine was more lightly scheduled that day. Without management's help, the organization changed its form to adjust to reality and keep running without missing a beat. Similarly, workers at Endenburg Electrotechniek altered the primary function of their department and thereby averted layoffs.

Bureaucracy is a system that achieves coordination by confining people so narrowly that there is no chance for most to use a broad range of talents. The intelligent organization, by contrast, is designed to tap the intelligence and the variety of talents in every member. As a result, it can:

♦ Deal with more issues at once, such as caring for one another, customers, the town, and the community

♦ Face many competitors simultaneously and deal more effectively with all of them

♦ Implement whole-systems thinking without robbing units of local flexibility

♦ Better identify core issues and address them rapidly

♦ Learn from experience how to do new things, not just what not to do, and better remember what was learned

♦ Rapidly apply what was learned in one place to others

♦ Integrate learning across the organization and use it creatively and flexibly

♦ Attend to all the details and supporting competencies that add up to cost-effective, superior performance

The Rise and Fall of Bureaucracy

The monster [of bureaucracy] thinks the common man is too dumb to
think for himself and that the monster must do his thinking for him.

DAKOTA FARMER, 1938

GIVEN THAT BUREAUCRACY is in such ill repute today, it is hard to
remember that it once was considered a great organizational innovation. By organizing the division of labor, by making management and
decision making a profession, and by providing an order and a set of
rules that allowed many different kinds of specialists to work in coordination toward a common end, bureaucracy greatly extended the
breadth and depth of intelligence that organizations could achieve.
Begun as a system of organizing government activities, it has spread
to big businesses and large organizations of all kinds.

Max Weber, who launched the systematic study of bureaucracy as
its role in Western society began to explode in the late nineteenth
century, saw bureaucracy as both the most efficient possible system
and a threat to the basic liberties he held dear. Weber predicted the triumph of bureaucracy because of its greater efficiency: "The purely

bureaucratic form of administrative organization, that is the monocratic variety of bureaucracy, is, as regards the precision, constancy, stringency and reliability of its operations, superior to all other forms of administrative organization."[1]

Weber would have been surprised (even frightened) by how accurate his prediction of bureaucracy's triumph has proven. During the last hundred years, the landscape of society has changed dramatically as large bureaucratic organizations replaced small family enterprises in retailing, manufacturing, and services. Many not-for-profits, from Blue Cross to the Audubon Society, have adopted the bureaucratic form. Even family entrepreneurship has taken a step toward bureaucracy with the shift from hosting a hometown diner to owning a franchise.

Bureaucracy created a system capable of effectively managing the massive investments, division of labor, and large-scale mechanized production of capitalism. Its organizational power drove the initial rapid growth of the steel, chemical, and automobile industries. Bureaucracy united AT&T as it established a peerless national communication network with rank on rank of managers structured by the Bell System Practices—a set of policy manuals that provided detailed and explicit instructions for every task. IBM added customer focus to bureaucracy and created an organization effective enough to give it forty years of preeminence in the new computer industry.

Despite all these successes, respect for bureaucracy is declining. As in so many other areas of life, what brought great success in the past has become the limitation of today. Suddenly everyone knows that bureaucracy is slowing us down and keeping our organizations internally focused and uncreative. It is time to question bureaucracy. What is the basis of its success? Why is it suddenly less useful than it was? What can we do about it? What are the alternatives to bureaucracy?

✳ WHAT BUREAUCRACY IS AND WHY IT CONQUERED ALL

Bureaucracy gained preeminence because it worked for many of the needs of the industrial age. It increased the effectiveness of hierarchy by reducing some of the worst abuses of power and by providing a rational way to manage tasks too complex for any one person to comprehend. Let us look more closely at why it worked so well. There is

consensus among social scientists that the six characteristics of bureaucracy, all part of Weber's original description, are roughly as follows:

A hierarchical chain of command

Specialization by function

Uniform policies covering rights and duties

Standardized procedures for each job

A career based on promotions for technical competence

Impersonal relations[2]

To this list we add an operating principle of bureaucracy suggested by
Fred Emery:

All coordination done from a level or more above the work being
coordinated[3]

A Hierarchical Chain of Command

The bureaucratic organization is structured as a pyramid with an
absolute boss on top who divides up the overall task of the organization and gives responsibility for each subtask to subbosses who divide
responsibility yet more finely and so on through an unbroken chain of
sub-subbosses that stretches down to every employee. In the 1980s,
huge organizations such as General Motors, Sears, IBM, and the
U.S. government had as many as twelve layers of management
between the CEO and the worker—too many, as it has turned out.

The establishment of a clear chain of command was a powerful
way to bring order to large groups in a common enterprise. The chain
of command resolved potential conflicts by granting clear responsibility, authority, and accountability for each potential decision. Each
boss and subboss in the chain of command was given an absolute
monopoly of power over a task or function and then held accountable for it. This greatly simplified the boss's task of making sure the
organization executed commands.

Limitations of Prebureaucratic Autocracy. Autocratic organizations without a clear chain of command run out of steam at about a hundred
persons. Many entrepreneurs fall into this trap by assuming the role
of a "craftsman entrepreneur," a person who maintains control of a

BUREAUCRACY

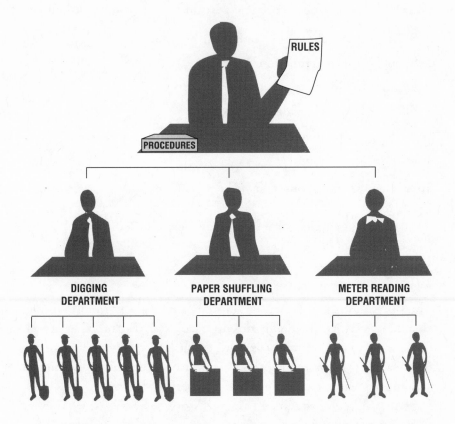

growing organization like a fine craftsman with many assistants. Rather than establish an effective chain of command, he or she tries to be everywhere making all decisions throughout the organization for a big group of helpers. The result is the classic growth curve of the craftsman entrepreneur: rocky start, smooth expansions, rocky leveling out as if bumping against a ceiling.

Such entrepreneurs might explain all the ups and downs of their business as changes in the market, but in fact they are suffering from the limitations of the prebureaucratic form of autocracy. To the extent the entrepreneur continues to be an absolute ruler, he or she cannot go beyond the scope of business that can be understood and managed by a single omnipresent manager. Some entrepreneurs caught in this craftsman role appoint subordinate managers, but by continually countermanding the orders of those managers, they fail to respect

THE CRAFTSMAN ENTREPRENEUR

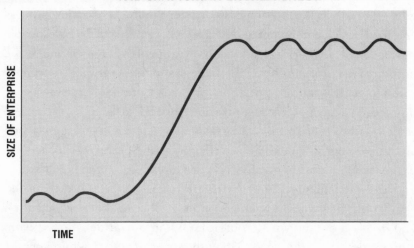

SIZE OF ENTERPRISE

TIME

the chain of command they establish and thus disempower their managers.

Delegation and Empowerment. Those entrepreneurs who succeed in expansion commonly introduce a chain-of-command structure, which by its nature delegates power and increases the thinking power of the organization by empowering more brains to take action. The business may grow when supervisors and middle managers are empowered in a limited but significant way to make decisions about their areas and to establish procedures and issue orders. Postbureaucratic entrepreneurships are growing just fine with decentralized teams and lateral networking taking the place of chain of command. Nonetheless, the innovations of bureaucracy, including the divestiture of some of an owner's power to a hierarchy beneath, served the goal of growth in earlier eras.

Specialization by Function

Bureaucracy achieves efficiency through specialization of labor. In fact, the organizational structure of a bureaucracy is created by dividing the overall task into a series of well-defined specialties or functions. Each function is given responsibility for a defined set of tasks and given the tools needed to accomplish that task. The boss gives orders and assigns tasks in such a way that all the parts add up to a coherent whole.

With specialization, different varieties of engineers study exactly why efficiency is lost in each of many steps in the production process and then design equipment and procedures to raise yields. Salespeople perfect their selling skills, and financial professionals manage the liquidity and profitability of the business with increasingly sophisticated tools. In general, specialization leads to more effective ways of doing each aspect of the organization's overall task.

Before the specialization of bureaucracy, each craftsperson learned all of blacksmithing or all of barrel making and performed all aspects of the job from start to finish. Craft production can often be satisfying and have artistic merit, but in the Industrial Revolution it worked against the mechanization and economies of scale that specialization and division of labor made possible. As organizations moved from craft production to division of labor, the strict hierarchy of bureaucracy provided the clout to set aside the traditions and concerns of craftsmen and to make each new innovation part of the rules and procedures of the organization.

Specialization can contribute to organizational intelligence by allowing people to concentrate on each little aspect of what the organization does. With many specialists, each good at his or her special area, the organization can bring great intellectual pressure and ingenuity to bear on each of the many different aspects of the business.

Uniform Written Rules and Policies

A bureaucracy is governed by uniform written rules and policies that in a corporation, profit or not-for-profit, are set by the board and the management. These rules define the rights and duties of employees and managers. The most basic rules concern who can give orders to whom.

In a bureaucracy, the boss is responsible for the actions of all the people under him or her and has the right to give them orders that they must dutifully obey. The employee's primary responsibility is not to do what is right or what needs to be done but only to follow exactly the orders of his or her immediate boss.

The written policies of a bureaucracy also guarantee employees regular wages as long as they are employed and, in some cases, even a pension for long-term service. These forms of compensation are quite different from those of the feudal systems, in which each level in the hierarchy, from serf on up to the local lord, often took a piece of the action, however paltry, in their domain.

Written rules concerning rights and duties partially offset some of the worst aspects of chains of command by reducing the potential power of any petty tyrants at the supervisory and middle management levels. Supervisors disciplining employees have more precisely defined powers, which both empower them to a degree and limit arbitrary behavior.

Standardized Procedures Defining Each Job

In a bureaucracy, fixed procedures govern how employees are to perform their tasks, sometimes to an astonishing degree. Frederick Taylor, an engineer who became known as the father of scientific management for his work in the early part of this century, recorded and then taught the exact motions of the most productive workers in a factory so that everyone else doing that task could make the same motions.[4] This reliance on established procedures is in stark contrast to the system of "make it up as you go along," characteristic of an entrepreneurial start-up or, at worst, the arbitrary personal whims of a feudal lord and his powerful minions.

Uniform rules and procedures written down and stored as official documents increased the intelligence expressed in organizations by instituting a crude "memory" of lessons learned. Written rules and procedures extended the power of the commands, standardizing the actions to be learned through frequent turnover of employees. Change could be accommodated if it could be written down and not bump into an existing rule. Standardized procedures could serve to make lessons learned in one part of the organization more broadly effective and to overcome irrational resistance to more effective ways of doing things.

The Professional Career

Success in the bureaucratic organization is defined as a lifetime career of advancing to higher levels in the chain of command. Rising in the ranks provides both power and symbols of status. Promotion is achieved through technical competence in one's specialty and efficiency in carrying out orders.

The professional career provides a "contract" between employee and organization: In its simplest form, a person devotes him- or herself to the organization in exchange for secure work and wages. The full-time professional manager was married to the organization for life. In return, the organization promised a stable or rising salary, a pension, lifetime employment, and a chance to rise in the hierarchy.

Before bureaucracy, favoritism and nepotism destroyed the efficiency of organizations more than they do today. Even today, there are many cultures in which a boss confronted with a choice between promoting an incompetent relative or another employee has no culturally acceptable alternative but to opt for the incompetent relative. In its ideal form, bureaucracy subordinates these family loyalties and other sympathies to the goals of the organization through a policy of promotion for measurable technical competence. In a government bureaucracy, in the civil service and the police and fire departments, for example, this policy is often manifest in exams that are prerequisites for moving to higher level positions. The promise of a good bureaucratic career allowed organizations to recruit, train, and retain highly skilled specialists.

The lure of rising in the hierarchy and the security of a professional career was an important element in bureaucracy's success, providing a strong motivation for long-term loyalty to the organization. Yet most will not make it in a bureaucracy, since the only success is moving upward. This carries the seeds of disappointment later in one's career when the pyramid has narrowed and only a few can move up to the next level.

Impersonal Relations

In a bureaucracy, relationships are from role to role rather than from person to person. The organizational structure and job description define what is expected of an individual in each role, and the holder of a particular role is expected to carry out its responsibilities in a rational and unemotional manner. Therefore, emotions are not to be displayed: The coolly analytical win, and the open and caring lose.

Impersonal relations helped move bureaucracy beyond nepotism and favoritism by preventing family feeling or friendship from getting in the way of enforcing rules and making tough decisions. It kept managers' sentiments from getting in the way as they wrenched work-ers away from the satisfactions of craft production and toward the bureaucratic routines and unthinking work of the assembly line.

All Coordination from a Level or More Above

In a bureaucracy, workers do not figure out how to coordinate their work with their peers. The boss divides up the work and defines each person's job so that added together those jobs produce the output that is the boss's responsibility to manage. The boss's boss then pro-vides coordination between units, and the units, therefore, do not need to coordinate with one another. All coordination must rise up and pass through the next higher boss.

Employees are not paid to think broadly; their job is to stay with-in the "boxes" defined by their job descriptions and the standardized procedures. Above all, they are forbidden to coordinate with their peers, who are either subordinates of the same boss or of another one elsewhere in the organization. To do so would rob the bosses of their authority.

Coordination from above worked well during the early Industrial Revolution when huge numbers of employees unskilled in the mechan-ical arts had to be quickly fitted to a job in the "satanic mills."[5] Turnover could be extraordinary. Near the turn of the century, Ford Motor Company's Highland Park, Michigan, plant had to hire fifty-four thousand workers a year just to keep thirteen thousand working.[6] With such rapid turnover, workers had little time to understand the whole and needed a simple and clearly defined assignment.

✳ WHY BUREAUCRACY NO LONGER WORKS

The fully developed bureaucratic mechanism compares with other organizations exactly as does the machine with non-mechanical modes of production. Precision, speed, unambiguity, knowledge of the files, continuity, discretion, unity, strict subordination, reduction of friction and of material and personal costs—these are raised to the optimum in the strictly bureaucratic administration.

MAX WEBER

The world no longer needs the machinelike organizations bureau-cracy produces. The challenges of our times call for lively, intelligent organizations. Bureaucracy was efficient for certain kinds of repetitive tasks that characterized the early Industrial Revolution. It no longer works so well, because its rules and procedures are often diametrically opposed to the principles needed for workers to take the next step toward greater organizational intelligence. These principles include more responsibility to define and direct one's own job, more responsibility to coordinate with others, and a shift in authority from one's boss to one's "customers."

■ THE CHANGING NATURE OF WORK

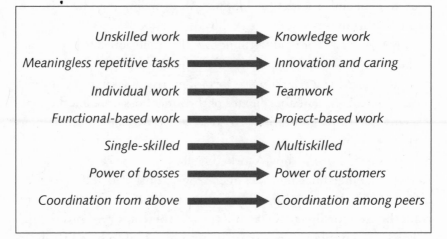

Unskilled work ➡	Knowledge work
Meaningless repetitive tasks ➡	Innovation and caring
Individual work ➡	Teamwork
Functional-based work ➡	Project-based work
Single-skilled ➡	Multiskilled
Power of bosses ➡	Power of customers
Coordination from above ➡	Coordination among peers

From Unskilled Work to Knowledge Work

Peter Drucker has been telling us for decades that more and more of work, both technical and nontechnical, is knowledge-based. We no longer need many unskilled assembly-line workers; most of the jobs in factories involve technical knowledge and training. What is more, few of the jobs in a manufacturing organization are in the factory. Most "manufacturing" jobs are in functions such as marketing, design, process engineering, technical analysis, accounting, and management, which require professional expertise and mastery of a large body of knowledge. This same trend toward more knowledge workers is present in service industries, not-for-profits, and government. Drucker estimates that one-third of all jobs are already filled by the highly paid and productive group he calls knowledge workers.[7]

The very nature of knowledge work, which involves information gathering, imagination, experiment, discovery, and integration of new knowledge with larger systems, means that bosses cannot order about knowledge workers like the ditch diggers or assembly-line bolt turners of yore. If knowledge workers are any good at all, they soon learn more about what they are doing on a specific project than their boss. Knowledge work inherently has a large component of self-direction and teamwork and is hampered by remote control from distant bosses. As we move beyond bureaucracy we will find ways to organize so that all work is knowledge work, bringing everyone's native intelligence and collaborative abilities to bear on constantly changing ways of achieving shared goals.

From Repetitive Tasks to Innovation and Caring

Since the passing of craft production, management has been responsible for organizing people to work efficiently at narrow, boring jobs. This has meant that the managerial role was as much to limit the intelligence and potential of employees as it was to elicit talent. Now the mindless repetitive jobs that bureaucracies were designed to manage are rapidly disappearing. Machines do more of the routine work, and the work that is left requires initiative and flexibility. As a result, the job of leaders is more nearly to bring out people's talents around a common vision.

What sort of work will be left as machines get smarter? What do people do so much better than machines that it will provide human work for the foreseeable future?

People are much better than machines at innovating, at seeing new possibilities within fluid and imperfectly defined systems and knowing what to do. Innovation in this sense includes the creative salesperson who sees what the customer really wants and bends the system to get it. It includes the member of a quality action team who makes an intuitive leap that exposes the real root cause of a problem to measurement and analysis. It also includes the intrapreneur who sees how to use company assets to generate more revenues and thus create more jobs.

Another apparently irreplaceable human talent is caring. As more work becomes service, caring about and for others becomes increasingly important. People do not generally sue doctors just because they make a mistake. They sue them because they make a mistake and relate to patients in a way that says they do not care. Good salespeople keep customers because the customers can sense that they genuinely care. Good intrapreneurs are able to break through barriers within the organization when others sense that they care more about the result than about personal success. Good leaders spread intrapreneurial zeal when it comes from inner values that all can get behind. Leaders elicit commitment when their people sense that they care about them, the group's success, and their mutual contributions.

The rules of bureaucracy forbid caring and, in particular, acting on the basis of the inner values one holds dear rather than out of strict obedience and loyalty to the boss. We find no examples of innovation where the intrapreneur did not break some bureaucratic rules. Most often the intrapreneurs and team members were carried away by a passion for an idea that aligned with deeper values—that promised at least in some small way a better world. We know few con artists who can long fool the alert into thinking they care when they do not.

Caring, like innovation, must come from the inside: We cannot order people to innovate or to care. We also cannot order people to use their intelligence; people engage their intelligence when they have reason to care, when they are part of something bigger than themselves and see that their wider interests are served by the work at hand. Bureaucracy is too autocratic and rule-driven to motivate and manage the intelligence that is brought to innovation and caring. Creativity and connecting with others require engaged relationships, personal responsibility, and flexible thinking and acting. Thus, as the rules of bureaucracy block both innovation and caring, they block the essence of modern work.

Education, Innovation, and Caring. The Tofflers pointed out in *The Third Wave* that universal public education had the purpose of teaching obedience, punctuality, and the ability to sit still a long time and do mindless, repetitive work.[8] In the early industrial era the ability to endure boredom was a key survival skill. Although education has improved a bit, bureaucracies have done little to prepare the average worker for the innovation, teamwork, and caring that constitute much of modern work.

For years corporations have used effective training in creativity and innovation (for a chosen few), but these lessons are generally remedial. They seek to restore what was destroyed by education. We need educational systems today that preserve "childlike" curiosity and give practice in teamwork, initiative, and collaborative big-picture responsibility.

Many of our current practices in education not only block innovation, they also blunt one's ability to care, to engage heart and mind in one's work. People who act on what they care about jump out of their seats. They fail to follow the lesson plan and ask too many questions. They help their fellow students rather than maximizing their own grades. Many schools are getting better at teaching children to care about one another and to treat one another with respect, but still follow the bureaucratic model in the way both teachers and students are treated—forced to measure up to defined procedures rather than pursue goals with creative innovations, evaluated on individual performance instead of teamwork and collaboration, taught compliance rather than participative self-management and democratic processes.

From Individual Work to Teamwork

Bureaucracy replaces the natural ability of humans to find ways to work together with the more sterile discipline of the chain of command. It is not rich and lively enough for today's fast-paced changes and challenges. Virtually every recent management innovation that works relies in part on the power of teams. A "Total Quality" program gives power to teams to examine processes and make them work better, a task that until recently belonged exclusively to managers. Because knowledge workers cannot produce much of value alone, their work takes them across organizational boundaries to search for integrated information. In reengineering, case teams replace isolated functions. In lean manufacturing, ordinary workers take responsibility for the whole and run for help whenever trouble shows up.

When three members of a thirty-two-person work team at Hoechst Celanese's Salisbury plant left the team, the remaining team members had authorization to replace them but decided not to do so.[9] As is so often the case, the people doing the work knew more than the bosses about where work and expense could be saved. Organizations become more intelligent when they find ways to bring the intelligence of every member into supporting the purpose and goals of the organization.

From Functional Work to Project Work

As knowledge workers shift from static jobs to solving a series of problems or seizing opportunities, they do so in work organized as projects. Each project in this complex world generally requires a cross-disciplinary team. These teams then learn together as the project evolves. Soon, their bosses in the functions they "report" to become too distant from the work to manage the decisions for the teams. As a consequence, control shifts from the functional organization of bureaucracy to project teams.

Specialization will continue to be a critical part of every complex organization. But because of the interconnection of issues in a complex world, more and more work will involve integrating the viewpoints and activities of specialists, and less and less will be performing tasks completely within those specialties. As a result, each employee will have to be both a specialist and a generalist.

The 1956 Pontiac was designed with a concave sculpted panel with many vertical ribs indented between the two taillights. The door to the gas cap was neatly hidden between two of the vertical ribs. Because the cracks at the edge of the gas door fell where the eye already expected a vertical line, the door did not break up the uniform sweep of the design.

The design worked aesthetically, but a senior manager reviewing it was afraid car owners would be unable to figure out where to find the gas cap. Rather than raising the concern with the designers and asking them to deal with it in a thoughtful way, he ordered the gas cap door chromed, ruining the whole sweep of the design with an anomalous chrome square.

Managers cannot bring out the intelligence of everyone in the organization if they pretend they can do better thinking in a few hours than a project team that has wrestled with the problem for months. Instead of issuing arbitrary orders, they need to raise concerns and trust the project team to find a way of handling them that integrates with all the other issues guiding the design. Paradoxically, as issues become more complex and specialties more differentiated, it becomes increasingly necessary for teams of diverse specialists to themselves integrate their work with the work of other teams. Management can never understand all the trade-offs and creative solutions that get the team where it is. Heavy-handed intervention leads to inconsistencies—or worse. In an intelligent organization, participation is widespread to help expose all the issues as early as possible. Individuals with multiple skills are brought together to cover more viewpoints in a team of manageable size, and the team does its work guided by feedback, not commands.

From Single-Skilled to Multiskilled

As Fred Emery has pointed out, no system can exist without redundancy to provide reserve capacity when something does not exactly follow the plan.[10] Bureaucracy gets its margin of safety from extra bodies. If extra work of one kind appears because customers ordered a different mix of products than expected, a bureaucracy has extra workers of that exact type waiting in the wings, or it falls short of meeting the orders. The same situation arises if someone is sick: Another "identical" worker needs to be waiting to do the job. This system of narrowly defined skills and extra bodies is expensive and inflexible.

In a typical multiskilling program, responsibility shifts to teams, and employees get raises for each new skill they acquire. At Lechmere, Inc., a twenty-seven-store retailer, cashiers at the Sarasota, Florida, outlet get pay raises by learning to sell products, and sporting goods staff get raises by learning to operate the forklift. With a multiskilled workforce, when bottlenecks appear, whether through absenteeism or a sudden rush of one kind of work, someone can step in and get things moving.[11]

Bureaucratic relationships between organized labor and management prevent multiskilling by adherence to numerous contractually defined job classifications. Unions today do well to negotiate for more training and education to make members more widely employable. Unionized companies as entrenched as National Steel and General Motors "have improved morale, speed, and efficiency by loosening job classifications and developing a broader more flexible workforce through cross-training employees."[12]

From the Power of Bosses to the Power of Customers

For an organization to be responsive, customers' wishes have to have a strong influence on the people doing the work. Relaying this sort of information through bosses is too slow—and besides, they may not be there to hear what customers want.

This sort of thinking applies to internal customers or "users" of a unit's output as much as to external customers. In a rapidly changing world, if internal customers cannot get what they need promptly and flexibly, the system will not be able to serve external clients promptly and flexibly. Freedom of choice between alternative suppliers gives users of internal services the power enjoyed by real customers—the power to say no to one and yes to another. Once internal customers have this power, the attention of those internal suppliers shifts from pleasing their bosses to winning customers. If they have customers, the boss can be pleased; without customers, they had better find new work.

From Coordination from Above to Coordination among Peers

Clearly, new systems of coordination and control are needed. In a bureaucratic system, employees are not responsible for coordinating their work with others at their level; that is their boss's job. They need not think about the big picture beyond doing their specialty well—to do so would be presumptuous. It is the job of senior management to figure out how it all fits together, so cross-functional concerns are referred up to a level of management that can resolve them. When coordination is the boss's job, cross-functional, or horizontal, communication with one's peers is frowned upon as either a waste of time or a usurpation of the boss's authority.

In postbureaucratic organizations, most of the coordination between functions and even businesses is done by teams. In 1988, John Hanley, vice president for product development at AT&T, needed to cut in half the product development time for cordless phones. The old product development system was a series of handoffs from R&D to Manufacturing to Marketing to Sales. Hanley formed teams that included people from each of these functions and gave the teams authority to make decisions about almost everything except their deadline: They would be finished in one year. Rather than wrestle with the bureaucracy, the teams worked together as intrapreneurial

■ REVOLUTIONARY CHANGE
IN THE STRUCTURE OF OUR RELATIONSHIPS

What Bureaucracy Is	Why It Once Triumphed	Why It Fails Now	What Replaces It
Hierarchical chain of command	Brought simple large-scale order Bosses brought order by dominating subordinates	Cannot handle complexity Domination not best way to get organization intelligence	Visions and values Teams (self-managing) Lateral coordination Informal networks Choice Free intraprise
Specialization Organization by function	Produced efficiency through division of labor Focused intelligence	Does not provide intensive cross-functional communication and continual peer-level coordination	Multiskilling specialists and intrapreneuring Organization in market-mediated networks
Uniform rules	Created a sense of fairness Clearly established power of bosses	Still need rules, but need different rules	Guaranteed rights Institutions of freedom and community
Standard procedures	Provided crude organizational memory Able to use unskilled workers Overcame old ways	Responds slowly to change Does not deal well with complexity Does not foster interconnection	Self-direction and self-management Force of the market and ethical community
A career of advancing up the ladder	Bought loyalty Furnished continuity of elite class of managers and professionals	Fewer managers needed and more educated workforce expects promotions; therefore, not enough room for advancement	A career of growing competence A growing network to get more done More pay for more capabilities
Impersonal relations	Reduced force of nepotism Helped leaders enforce tough discipline and make tough decisions	Information-intensive jobs require in-depth relationships	Strong whole-person relationships Options and alternatives Strong drive for results
Coordination from above	Provided direction for unskilled workers Furnished strong supervision required by rapid turnover in boring jobs	Educated employees are ready for self-management	Self-managing teams Lateral communications and collaboration

generalists. They did market research, decided how much each product should cost, what its features would be, what it should look like, and how it should work. The result: half the development time, better quality, lower cost.

Reality has become so complex and multidimensional that there is no way of dividing the organization into chains of command that will work for all aspects of the challenges faced. As a result, integration is achieved through peer-level cross-organizational communication rather than through the hierarchy. Huge volumes of cross-functional communication are needed because every important process crosses the boundaries of the organization. The general manager does not have time enough in the day just to relay communications; the process is not fast enough. Besides, as you may remember from the childhood game of "telephone," in which a verbal message is whispered from person to person down a long line of kids, communications relayed through too many humans get garbled. In the intelligent organization, communications whenever possible are direct, without intermediaries.

In the industrial era, the large-scale but stable means of production pushed us toward distant, formal, and unequal relationships at work. Today, our complex and intelligence-intensive tasks push us toward relationships that are close, open, honest, and more nearly equal. Because "organization" is about how we structure our relationships, these new realities will completely change our ideas about methods and patterns of organization.

The nature of work in modern high-tech workplaces calls on people in many positions in the organization to take responsibility for processes and services that intimately affect the customer and the wider community. Even in small service businesses and government agencies, the goods and services produced are knowledge- and information-intensive by virtue of the skills and intelligence of the people with their hands on the work processes. When a medical unit delivers life-saving help to patients, its members must intelligently apply hundreds of technical instruments, drugs, and procedures to a variety of unique customers—and learn anew as the knowledge and technology are continually updated. This is as true of the technicians as the physicians. What works in a society of knowledge workers will be completely different from what worked before.

3

Clues to
Bureaucracy's Successor

The two forces that we have always placed in opposition to one
another—freedom and order—turn out to be partners in generating
viable, well-ordered, autonomous systems.

MARGARET J. WHEATLEY

OUR SOCIETY HAS a peculiar monopolistic bias in organizational
design. In the design of the economies of nations we believe that freedom of choice produces efficiency and that monopoly leads to bureaucratic waste and suppression of liberty and innovation. Yet in the
design of organizations—firms, nonprofits, and government agencies—we too often believe that internal monopolies of power lead to
efficiency and that free choice and the associated plurality of providers
invite inefficiency. Following this unwarranted faith in monopoly, we
make staff groups sole-source providers of certain kinds of service. We
set up numerous oversight groups whose permission we must ask
before proceeding. We give groups organized around each function

monopolies over their disciplines. More generally, we give bosses a monopoly of power over the work lives of their subordinates.

In a bureaucracy, if someone needs a task done that falls within the domain of another function, he or she has no choice of who performs it. The resources are assigned or denied by the manager of that function, and, if that manager is not forthcoming, there is no recourse except going over his or her head — at best a risky business. Similarly, a business unit whose technology is applicable in the market of another business unit is often constrained not to compete. This happened years ago at 3M, when Gift Wrap and Fabric, a small division that made flat "nonwoven fabrics" for decorative ribbons, developed a product that fell within the domain of another group, Medical Products.[1] Nonwoven fabric is sheet material made like paper, but using synthetic fibers instead of wood pulp; for example, it is used in filament tape and the large untearable envelopes used by overnight delivery services.

Pat Carey and Walter Westberg, who worked in new products for the Gift Wrap and Fabric Division, had invented an economical way to mold nonwovens into three dimensional shapes. Looking for new applications, they decided to make a molded nonwoven face mask for surgeons that would fit better and filter better than the tied-on flat gauze pads that were customary. The team also tried to sell face masks for use by the people who work in grain elevators and other dusty environments. They were not having success in either market.

Dust masks were a territory open to the intrapreneurs for the Gift Wrap and Fabric Division, but the other market of interest, surgical masks, technically belonged to the Medical Products group operating out of the Retail Tape Division. The Medical Products group was also developing their own face mask for the operating room. It had a molded styrofoam outer rim to seal to the face and a round nonwoven filter in the front.

The intrapreneurs of Medical Products were concerned that Gift Wrap's one piece face masks would mess up the market for their own surgical face masks, which they believed were technically superior. They put pressure on the Gift Wrap and Fabric Division to stay out of the hospital market.

According to the rules of bureaucracy, the Medical Products people were within their rights—their group had a 3M-wide monopoly on
the medical marketplace. But Carey and his team were determined
to continue, believing both that their product gave the best combination of protection, comfort, and price and that surgical sales were
too good an opportunity to ignore. With typical intrapreneurial defiance, they continued trying to sell to physicians until they were ordered
to stop by the vice president and general manager of the Gift Wrap and
Fabric Division.

A direct order to cease and desist might have been the end of the
molded nonwovens technology, but at 3M in 1959, the rules of bureaucracy were sometimes treated as suggestions. The interlopers halted
activity until a local distributor of safety equipment who had been
trying to sell Gift Wrap's molded masks came to them with a situation
that demanded action: Rochester Methodist Hospital had a serious out-
break of staph infections and believed the carriers might be physicians. The distributor thought the molded masks might be perfect to
stop the epidemic. Molded masks were better than the flat gauze
masks then in use at Rochester Memorial in two ways. First, they
were technically a better filter than gauze—probably fine enough to
catch the fine droplets of saliva thought to be carrying the disease.
Second, they sealed better to the face, so particles of saliva would not
escape out the sides when surgeons and nurses talked.

Pat Carey, disobeying his vice president in the grand old tradition
of 3M intrapreneurs, gave the distributor permission to give the hospital masks to test. The tests were successful, but when the hospital
tried to order more masks they were not able to buy them because
Gift Wrap had been ordered not to sell to the medical market. The
hospital went to Burt Cross, a friend of the hospital and a member
of the 3M board, and asked for help. Cross cleared the way, and the
Gift Wrap intrapreneurs set up a small factory in the basement to
produce the Rochester Memorial order.

Since the Gift Wrap molded nonwoven mask was selling well in the
medical market, and theirs was not, Medical Products began selling
the Gift Wrap version instead of their own. Gift Wrap soon turned
over marketing of surgical masks to Medical Products, but continued to do manufacturing and development until the market was large

enough to support separate manufacturing and development in Medical Products.

By then the industrial market for the one piece molded masks had taken off. Molded industrial face masks eventually led to the sophisticated, high-performance respirators that are now the core of 3M's Occupational Health and Environmental Safety Division, one of 3M's fifty major operating units.

This story illustrates the difficulty bureaucracy has in dealing with the complex and interconnected nature of business reality. Bureaucracy demands that reality be divided into neat areas of responsibility, but customer needs and technological possibilities refuse to stay in those divisions, regardless of how cleverly the lines are drawn.

☀SYSTEMS FOR ORDER AND CONTROL

Bureaucratic organizational architecture is based on figuring out the most rational pattern for establishing monopolies. This seemingly sensible task is made difficult by the fact that there is no possible pattern of monopolies that will work at all if the situation faced by the firm is complex. For example, in the 3M story, the pattern that worked well for thinking about businesses based on big customer segments (such as separating the markets in medicine and industrial safety) created a wall blocking new ideas when the technology of one business crossed over into the market of another.

At 3M, great effort has been put into technology transfer between businesses with some very good results. Technology is transferred both formally and informally. The development of Post-it™ Notes is a case in point. Art Fry heard about an adhesive that just barely stuck to things from another 3M researcher on the golf course. He learned more about it when Spence Silver exhibited his curiosity at a seminar put on by the Technical Forum, an organization of all technical people in the company. The company has also created a number of other cross-organization channels that increase freedom of choice and thus increase the rate of innovation.

Monopoly limits intelligence by taking exclusive power in an area, thus inevitably reducing others' choices, freedom, and initiative. In the larger economy, choices among different options create pressures for efficiency and responsiveness. For example, the whole motion picture industry is organized in networks of subcontractors, not in big companies with many employees. Subcontractors in the network must be reliable and very good at what they do or else they do not last long in the business. The result is speed, flexibility, and low overhead, and one of the few industries in which the United States continues to excel in worldwide competition.[2]

What makes this pattern work is that choice instead of hierarchy is used as its basic system for order and control. The many artists — from actors to carpenters, cinematographers to makeup artists — who make up the complex temporary organizations that create a movie have greater freedom than they would as employees. They also have a powerful motivation to keep their skills honed and strong reason to create results that please the directors and others who choose whom to hire. Of course, this system can lead to insecurity and exploitation, and the motion picture industry is plagued by dubious ethics — pointing to the need for community standards and supports to balance freedom of choice. Still, the most talented, at least, can pass over projects they do not like or directors who mistreat them and continue to find work.

Choice allows producers and directors to use the talent most suited to the project at hand. It allows them to ask for the performance they want and expect — not grudging compliance, but a best effort of intelligence and heart. Everyone in the system lives on reputation. When a project goes well, all gain. If a relationship is difficult, the director and actor involved both damage their reputations.

Within companies, government agencies, and even nonprofits, there is still a philosophical bias against structural systems based on choice. The potential redundancies required for real choice in conducting an enterprise — for example, when there is more than one staff service provider or internal supplier to choose to do business with — are often considered inefficient and disruptive. The bureaucratic form of organization has promoted diametrically opposed beliefs about the value of free choice in the places we work and in the economies of nations.

When times get tough in bureaucratic organizations, the informal organization introduces more choice into the system. Operating groups in crisis seek help wherever it can be found. Productive relationships grow across boundaries, and a group from one division might be paid

■ HOW WE SEE SYSTEMS THAT INCLUDE CHOICE

	IN BUSINESS	IN NATIONS
NAME FOR CHOICE	*Redundancy* *Duplication*	*Liberty* *Choice* *Free Enterprise*
NAME FOR LACK OF CHOICE	*Clear definition of* *roles and authority*	*Monopoly* *Domination* *No rights*
COST OF CHOICE	*Duplication increases* *cost*	*Competition* *reduces cost*
PREFERRED SOURCE OF EFFICIENCY	*Static efficiency* *Economies of scale*	*Dynamic efficiency* *Innovation*

to provide services to another division. This, it seems for a moment, is the beginning of a more flexible and more intelligent organization.

Unfortunately (in our experience), the periods of open system choice are short-lived. Once the crisis passes, we hear the words of bureaucracy restoring itself: "We need a clear definition of roles here— who is responsible for this function?" "It's too expensive to have two groups doing the same thing. Let's combine them into one group." "With no one in charge, this thing is out of control." But the bureaucratic thinking that destroys network organization and reduces the choices that make it possible is based on faulty premises about what works.

Redundancy Versus Choice

Bureaucracy attempts to achieve efficiency by eliminating redundancy. However, all systems, including bureaucratic ones, have redundancy, and the type of redundancy typical of bureaucratic monopolies is more expensive and less functional than the redundancy in systems based on choice. The necessary redundancy in bureaucratic systems comes from having each monopolistic function staffed up for peak loads. Part of the capacity of each function is thus idle or engaged in make-work tasks much of the time.

As marketplace demand shifts the mix of what is needed, some functions in a bureaucracy will be overemployed and others underemployed. Thus the further we move from uniform mass production into customization and service, the more redundancy bureaucracy needs in order to deal with the variations of customer needs.

Intelligent organizations provide capacity for changing circumstances not by having extra people but by having people able to switch jobs as demand for different tasks shifts. Everyone takes charge of increasing his or her own productivity and readiness to face change. Teams serving customers who can choose to use them or not develop the flexibility to change what they provide in response to changing needs, which means each individual acquires a variety of skills and capabilities. Systems disciplined by competition between "redundant suppliers" respond flexibly and efficiently to change. Bureaucracies do not.

Fixed Roles Versus Flexible Networks

Bureaucracies hope to achieve responsiveness by "having someone in charge" who is able to make quick decisions. When systems get complex, the opposite occurs; bureaucracies are notorious for being unresponsive. People in intelligent organizations have the freedom and education to change their roles flexibly. As circumstances change they use different linkages in the network as needed. These changes in roles and linkages are the network structure of the intelligent organization constantly changing *itself* to adapt to the work to be done.

✳FROM MONOPOLY TO FREE MARKETS

All the nations with strong international positions in the production of high-technology products, fashion goods, or complex services use some variety of free market choices to engage the independent energies of many firms and many entrepreneurs. These free market systems create a regulated but self-organizing economy. An orderly network is created by the voluntary relationships formed between independent firms. Each firm chooses its connections with suppliers, customers, and partners. Collectively, the independent businesses in a free market nation achieve a level of integration, connection, and order that government-run economies cannot. Collectively, networks of firms deal with the complexity of the great variety of customers and their ever-shifting needs and wants: changes in weather, politics, and raw material supplies; rapidly evolving technology; and, to a growing degree, environmental challenges.

Consider, for example, the results of using a central bureaucracy to run all the major industrial, agricultural, and service enterprises of a national economy. Most of us were not surprised that the Soviet Union failed to reach the productivity levels of societies with a market economy. We knew about the shoddy goods, poor selection, and long lines to buy anything of value. But most of us were shocked as the Iron Curtain lifted to see that despite the avowed humanitarian goals of socialism, the Soviet Union's standards for health, safety, and environmental protection were appallingly low. Each passing month reveals new disasters created by the Soviet Union's massive bureaucratic industries. By contrast—and despite the U.S. history of world leadership in high-resource, and high-waste, growth—regulated private industry in the United States has done a better job of controlling pollution than the even more bureaucratic state enterprises. The record of government bureaucracies in managing their own pollution is appalling.

Perhaps, after considering the environmental record of our own government bureaucracies, we should have anticipated some of the problems we have found in the former Soviet Union. Our Department of Defense, unable to focus on its core mission and also deal effectively with other demands, dealt with the issue of pollution by getting Congress to excuse it from complying with environmental regulations. Now we have hell to pay at old nuclear weapons facilities such as the Hanford site in Washington state.

Managing the vast system of the Soviet Union effectively was so far beyond the scope of any hierarchy's intelligence that the central bureaucracy gave up on subtler issues like safety, the environment, and humane treatment of people to concentrate on what was most necessary and most threatening: the simpler commodities of survival and defense. Planning and administering the fulfillment of these few priorities proved to be more than two million very clever bureaucrats could handle. Many Soviet citizens saw the failures of their system to produce high-quality consumer goods or follow basic industrial safety standards as proof of the incompetence and selfishness at the top, but the problem was more one of system design than poor selection of leaders. No chain of command can effectively administer the economy of an industrial or information-age nation, regardless of the quality of its leaders.

Bureaucracy was designed to coordinate the masses toward a simple objective according to the wishes of the man (or less likely, the woman) on top. It worked for the armies of Napoleon and the organization of immigrant workers in the early American textile mills in Lowell, Massachusetts. Those who rose in the ranks did so by devotion to the power of the center, a focus that excluded concern for individuals outside the power structure and concern for the larger community or the environment. The power structure itself, inherently monopolistic, focused attention inward and upward on obedience to the center rather than outward for observing and serving the wider common good.

Bureaucracy is increasingly in trouble because it produces organizations unable to deal effectively with many conflicting priorities at once. Thus bureaucracies have difficulty when asked both to be productive and to care for the environment; both to be efficient in the short run and to care for future generations. This single failing makes bureaucracy inappropriate for an age in which we are running up against environmental limits.

Breaking Up Monopolies to Restore Market Effectiveness

The solution to the bureaucratic stagnation of the economic affairs of a totalitarian nation does not lie in training bureaucrats to be more empowering. It is a fundamental shift of power that changes how decisions are made. When the state-owned monopolies are broken up and subjected to competition and a regulated free market, power begins to shift from bureaucrats creating inefficiency by defending their turf to the customers asking vendors for what they really need. Decisions formerly made in central government ministries far from the action are now made more accurately, rapidly, and efficiently by buyers and sellers considering prices and quality in the marketplace. For example, the Italian garment industry, which comprises thousands of tiny independent vendors interlinked to create a productive, self-organizing part of the economy, clearly creates more stylish, better-fitting, and even more durable clothing than the monopolistic Soviet system ever did.

The free market system does not work well where monopolies exist. The same applies to monopolies *inside* large organizations. These inside monopolies include all sorts of normal "boss" prerogatives, such as the exclusive right to review someone else's performance, and the right to say what everyone below can and cannot do and, more confining yet, what they must do and how they must do it. It is also customary to grant exclusive control of a function in a given area, exclusive access to a certain group of customers, or exclusive rights to perform certain services, such as machining prototypes or making circuit boards for a business unit. All these monopolies prevent the system from interconnecting in any ways except those the organization designer specifically anticipated. No organizational designer is good enough to create an intelligent organization that way.

Organizations such as AT&T and Hewlett-Packard and Hoechst Celanese are supporting voluntary relationships among multiple internal as well as external suppliers and partners, giving us good models of more freedom of choice among options.[3] For example, AT&T PR Creative Services provides operating groups with another choice of internal supplier for public relations services. They can hire their own public relations people, contract with the main corporate public relations group, or hire the maverick PR Creative Services Group. Many do a combination of all three. One key contribution of PR Creative Services (whose motto is "What you want when you want it") was to make all the other internal suppliers of PR more aware of the importance of timeliness of service.

Just as individual workers and teams gain in productivity when empowered with choices among alternatives, business units become more productive when they can choose between internal and external suppliers of components and services. Normally, such choice is between a single internal supplier and various external suppliers. But, as we shall see, choice among various internal suppliers can also be highly beneficial. The internal suppliers sharpen up their offerings to remain viable, learn from one another's innovations, and increase the efficiency of the whole system.

The "free *intra*prise" system we will describe later in this book uses marketlike transactions between an organization's *internal* enterprises and functional groups to gain better service, efficiency, flexibility, or variety.

✳ORDER IN THE FREE MARKET

In a free market system, order arises despite the fact that no one is in charge in the sense of sitting at the top of a hierarchical chain of command. Unless we work for the federal government, we do not report through a chain of command that leads up to the president or prime minister. And yet, guided by market forces, we respond as though led by what Adam Smith called "an invisible hand" to do things that serve our customers and thus (with some critical, and growing, exceptions) the good of society. The "invisible hand" not only shapes the individual entrepreneur's actions, but, more important, it also shapes many independent units into well-ordered productive networks.

No strategic planner at an auto maker could possibly trace all the firms involved in adding value to what eventually becomes an automobile. Each of the auto manufacturer's suppliers has hundreds of its own suppliers who, in turn, each have hundreds of suppliers, and so forth. The chain reaches back until nearly every sizable firm in the world selling anything to other firms is probably involved. Fortunately, even though no one maps, controls, or understands fully the details of how it all fits together, this complex and exquisitely responsive system works. Such is the power of a self-organizing system: A detailed order more locally and globally appropriate than any a hierarchy could design comes from the actions of a large number of apparently independent entities that function in an open system of individual and group freedom.

A case in point are the jobs created by the chains of entrepreneurial companies spawned by Silicon Valley companies such as Hewlett-Packard, Apple, and Intel. These "parent" organizations have given birth to thousands of companies launched by former employees, creating through a "multiplier effect" many hundreds of thousands of jobs.[4]

✳SELF-ORGANIZING SYSTEMS

When we think of organizing, the idea of hierarchy leaps to mind, or a picture of an "organization chart" in the shape of a pyramid. Yet for most of us pondering the workplace, it is becoming obvious that there are many alternative forms of organization. The changes we are seeing as organizations move beyond bureaucracy are all moves from order imposed from above to an order generated from everywhere within the system—to self-organizing systems. A self-organizing system is a system made up of autonomous units that by virtue of their relationships with one another create a systemwide order. It happens without the need for an ordering authority outside the system or a point from which order emanates within the system.

In his book *The Self Organizing Universe,* Erich Jantsch describes an incredible range of highly organized human, biological, and physical systems, all of which are self-organizing. Consider the largest and most complex system we know, the universe. Matter and energy, following what appear to be a relatively small set of rules, such as conservation of energy and mass, gravitation, and the laws of thermodynamics, have over time organized themselves in a system of great complexity and spellbinding beauty and coevolved highly detailed and interactive structures, ranging in size from clusters of galaxies to atomic particles. In the words of systems scientist Jantsch, life itself is a self-organizing system that demonstrates "the optimistic principle of which we tend to despair in the human world: the more freedom in self-organization, the more order."[5]

Dynamic self-organizing systems are everywhere. Science, for example, has no overall boss; that rapidly growing body of knowledge is organized by the choices of many institutions and many scientists competing to be heard and believed. In the free enterprise system, the evolution of business enterprises is guided by customer choice, collaborative talent, the limiting rules of society, and the requirement of solvency. As customers, we choose among alternatives in products, vendors, and distribution systems. As workers, we choose among employers, including the possibility of self-employment. As vendors, with a bit of luck, we choose which customers to serve and what to offer them. All these choices create a complex web of productive relationships that outperforms any command economy.

The fact that none of the most complex systems is organized by chain of command is damaging to the basic assumption of bureaucracy—namely, that hierarchy and rigid control are necessary to create order. Just the reverse turns out to be true. As Peter Senge has pointed out, this is why centralized economies fail.[6] When we attempt to bring order with centralized controls, we destroy the many self-regulating systems that would otherwise correct system errors. When monopolies replace vibrant free choices, seen in cooperation and competition, we get stagnation and the crude order of broad-brush policies and commands. Only a context of freedom allows the exquisite responsiveness that comes from full use of everyone's intelligence in a constantly changing network structure that coevolves with its changing environment. Greater freedom in self-organizing systems leads to greater order, not less.

The free market, as we have seen, is not an isolated case of the superior performance of self-organizing systems over hierarchical controls in human affairs. Literature, art, science, and mathematics are self-organizing systems for developing and distributing information. They depend on free choices and free access to stay open for learning and development. In the end, no hierarchy determines what is good art or good science. No vote is taken; no majority rules. Each scientist, each reader, each art critic, each buyer decides for himself or herself.

If a few big monopolies have all the purchasing and funding power, the process of science or art will no longer serve truth, beauty, or society as well as it does, but instead will tend to serve the power structure. When governments or other centralized institutions step in to administer institutions that produce an information product, we get bad science, bad art, and even dubious truth, often serving the power needs of the hierarchy instead of offering the benefits of open information. When Stalin decided Darwin's theory of evolution did not fit communist ideology, Soviet biologists adopted the evolutionary theories of Lysenko (or pretended to) and lost self-respect and the respect of the worldwide biological community. Likewise, the government-approved paintings that were called socialist realism pleased the hierarchy more than they inspired the common Soviet worker. The same distortions of reality and self-serving designs may appear if the hierarchy attempts to control the truth and the development of collective intelligence inside a corporation or a government agency.

Government can shape a self-organizing system without destroying its capacity to create order. High fuel taxes lead to the production of more efficient cars and trucks and also shift the balance from trucks toward more fuel-efficient ways to move freight, such as trains, ships, and pipelines. Congestion-weighted road-use taxes can shift traffic away from rush hours and further encourage the use of public transportation or the construction of housing closer to work. Government funding of education builds a more capable populace and something closer to equal opportunity for all. Nations create rules within which entrepreneurs and corporations and nonprofits operate, but the governments of intelligent nations depend on those organizations to choose their own missions, forms of organization, partners, suppliers, and preferred customers. If government interferes too much, the vitality of the system may be lost.

As the world becomes more complex, we need to think in terms of self-organization not only for large systems, such as national economies, but also for organizations as small as business firms, nonprofits, and government agencies. Our metaphors and analogies will shift from bureaucracy's mechanistic systems to those of inherently self-organizing systems such as living organisms and whole societies.

Kay Hubbard, an advocate for human resource development at the Donnelly Corporation, a highly successful manufacturer of automotive parts, puts it this way: "We take a complex view and grow our systems. We don't take a static viewpoint on any subject. This company is an organism, not a mechanism."[7]

Once we begin seeing a company as an organism, different rules apply. The systems are "grown" rather than designed and implemented. The boss is no longer "in charge." He or she is part of the system, which is healthy or ill as a whole.

One reporter who interviewed many Donnelly employees observed, "The idea of a living organism shows up during conversations with employees. There is no party line filled with clichés. Instead employees offer lively and original conversations about the business now and in the future."[8] The employees are lively because they are part of an organism that is alive. They need to understand where the business is and where it is going because, to the degree that it is self-organizing, they are part of the guidance system.

As the complexity organizations manage goes beyond the capacity of bureaucracy to deal with, our challenge is to design and implement the conditions for effective self-organization. One basic condition is making sure that there are real options to choose among. If people do not have choices of whom to work with and how to work together, they cannot influence organizational design. If business units cannot choose among alternative vendors, they cannot self-organize in free intraprise networks.

Corporate bureaucracy is based on the assumption that ordinary people are not capable of looking out for their own self-interest, much less the interests of the business as a whole or of the larger society. Although people have shown their ability to organize themselves for the common good in countless small entrepreneurships, nonprofits, and social agencies, bureaucracies operate as if people were incapable of productive self-organization and collective self-management. Totalitarian governments, and to a lesser degree socialist governments, have operated on this same assumption, and it has been disproved by the comparatively greater success of more egalitarian democratic societies with freer market economies.

Bureaucracy produces an unambiguous and simple order easily understood from the top. It cannot produce both systemwide integration and detailed local adaptability because it uses too small a percentage of the brain power of the organization to design and implement the structure and processes. Organizational systems that open up the relationships between people to increased choice and collaboration achieve a more detailed and accurate order than any bureaucracy because they allow people more opportunity to self-organize, require more responsible self-management, and work to engage the intelligence of nearly every employee, supplier, and customer to collaboratively design ever-changing systems that create ever-increasing value.

✳FREEDOM OF CHOICE AND THE DISCIPLINE OF SURVIVAL

Our understanding of the self-organizing system of all life offers insight into the integration and efficiency that weave all this autonomy into a common order that focuses on serving customers and improving conditions for all. We know that evolution proceeds through two linked processes: the origin of new varieties (variation), and (natural) selection among those varieties. On the whole, those varieties having the best fit to their environment persist and multiply; the others perish. The outcome at any one time is an intricate web of life, organized into a coevolving system characterized by both competition and cooperation.

In self-organizing socioeconomic systems, our free choices—based on our values and goals and all we have learned—are the primary form of selection and thus the primary source of discipline. Meaningful selection requires options to choose among—different vendors, more than one style of painting, more than one candidate, more than one employer, more than one theory. In the marketplace of ideas that is science, scientists from diverse funding bases, each with a commitment to independence, choose which competing theories to believe and build upon. This produces far better science than a command from on high telling us what to believe.

In a free market, companies and intraprises that are less efficient in creating value for customers lose money and are eliminated. The libertarian can appreciate this sometimes cruel discipline as the necessary price of freedom from bureaucratic control by a government or corporate hierarchy. Without the discipline of marketplace choices, freedom can lead to confusion, chaos, selfishness, waste, and despair.

✳CHOICE IN THE CONTEXT OF COMMUNITY

There are many important choices that we must make together because they cannot be made alone. If 95 percent of us choose to live in a world that still has blue whales, far less than 5 percent of us can still hunt them to extinction. We cannot choose to live in an unpolluted world unless we all pollute less. We cannot choose individually to live in a society with low levels of violence, robbery, extortion, and fraud unless we decide as a society not to tolerate those behaviors and create communities and institutions to prevent them. We cannot individually choose to live in a society in which everyone is entitled to an education unless others consent to help fund educational opportunity for all. We cannot choose to work in an organization in which people share information freely unless others share information too.

Many of the most important choices—the choices that make life likely to be happy or sad—are not individual choices but group choices of the context within which individuals operate. These whole-systems choices must be made by the community as a whole. Individual freedom offers no guarantee that the system will be open to all, not just a chosen group. Marketplace freedom has produced unprecedented wealth, a profusion of goods, and also unprecedented environmental destruction and spiritual confusion. The fundamental challenge of our time is how to direct the wild productivity we have unleashed to more constructive ends without killing what is good about it.

Because our workplaces are the communities in which many of us live much of our productive lives—and because they indirectly affect the quality of life of us all—we must ask what is known about creating productive and worthwhile communities. This question is not new; it has been a principal concern of philosophers, sages, prophets, rulers, and religious and political groups since before recorded history. Now we have new evidence: Of the ten nations with the highest per capita income, the only ones that are not highly pluralistic are those whose primary source of wealth comes from oil. The pluralistic "advanced nations" are all committed to a measure of market freedom, democracy, and support for all members. The more information intensive economies become, the more essential to performance pluralism will be. There is growing consensus on a number of points such as the following:

Societies in which the power of all institutions of authority is limited and every member has inalienable rights outperform those with absolute rulers.

These rights obviously include free speech, the right to associate with others of one's own choosing, and some form of individual and small-group ownership of the means of support.

Societies with deep respect for truth, widespread information sharing, and education outperform societies that ignore truth, keep facts hidden, and educate only the elite.

Societies in which people treat one another according to some form of a golden rule perform better than uncaring societies whose members are inured to acts of cruelty against one another.

The precepts of every major religion support good treatment of fellow members of the society. Without this foundation, people sink into mutually destructive feuds.

All advanced societies provide a variety of safety nets to carry individuals and their families through disruptions.

More egalitarian and democratic societies, which extend the principle of choice to everyone, outperform less participative societies with greater differences in opportunity, access to power, and wealth (compare Korea and Hong Kong with Brazil and India).

Societies with a dream, with common goals and values, in which individual benefits and common benefits intersect, outperform societies whose dream has dimmed.

Some of these lessons, such as free speech and even internal market freedoms, translate easily to the task of building an effective community within a corporation, nonprofit, or government agency. But "community" is not something that can be lowered onto an organization from above. Community is something that by its very nature must be created by the people themselves. The most that can be done from above is to create a context in which people are more likely to create a community.

Community develops when people find the intersection of their self-interest and the common interest of the whole. Community is established when the bulk of the people take responsibility for working together to design and build a better system, a better environment for everyone. Community exists when high status is accorded to those who give the most to the whole group, not those who have succeeded in grasping the most for themselves. Community is thus rooted in something we might call democracy if the word had not been co-opted by the process of voting for representatives, which is but a tiny part of the kind of popular responsibility that builds community.

Democratic ideas and free market ideas have difficulty surviving in a bureaucratic climate because they run directly into the basic prejudices and rules that animate the bureaucratic system:

"Bosses do the coordination and workers do what they are told."

"We cannot give ordinary people choice, or they will make bad decisions."

"Someone has to be in charge."

But we cannot use the full intelligence of every member of the organization unless the people who are closest to every problem have the primary responsibility for finding the solutions and taking action. This means we must find systems that empower people with as much choice as possible concerning what they do and how they do it. Bureaucracy cannot orchestrate systems based on choice because the basic architecture of bureaucracy is defined by monopolies of power. Only systems based on relatively free internal markets and relatively free interchange with the outside world have the intellectual capacity to discipline and control so many activities, so many details, so many priorities, and so many challenges all going on at once.

Developing Widespread Business Judgment

In intelligent organizations many of the tasks and responsibilities formerly held by bureaucratic management are divested to those responsible for getting the work done. This way of doing things demands more of ordinary people, who, with a little training in group dynamics and problem solving (or a little practice with a trained facilitator), soon prove far more capable of mature judgment than dominating managers imagine.

The real key to developing good judgment is practice making decisions and living with the consequences. This requires a system that allows people to make mistakes together and to clean up the mess without recriminations from above. That many bureaucracies do not encourage this form of learning goes a long way toward explaining why so many of them end up with the ultimate organizational disaster—a strictly hierarchical system stalled by managers who have not been given the opportunity for hands-on learning of business judgment early in their careers.

Although freedom of choice is an essential part of the answer, the necessary learning will not occur within completely laissez-faire environments. Each person and each group have to understand the mission of the organization and what matters to customers and the world so they can contribute real value.[9] The environment that creates organizational intelligence includes a context rich in information, feedback, mentoring, and measuring. Small groups will learn to manage their many connections to others inside and outside the organization and to create among themselves a flexible and evolving network of intelligence. Teams of doers will learn to monitor and assess their own efficiency and finances. They will abide by and continue to develop specific rights and practices to keep the systems open, learning, and collaborating.

✳TWO INSEPARABLE ASPECTS

We have come to respect two inseparable aspects of the nature of intelligent organizations. First there is choice—requiring specific freedoms and rights. The great symbol for the beginning of the intelligent organization is the lever over the head of every assembly-line employee at Toyota that stops the line if something is wrong and calls for help to fix it. This great leap of faith in ordinary workers' intelligence and integrity is the beginning of a revolutionary shift: from trusting in the power of bosses to trusting in well-designed systems with built-in freedom and choices for all. Choice is the basis of people having freedom and taking responsibility for their shared enterprises. We can move beyond bureaucracy with distributed intelligence only if people have the freedom to be effective in partnership with their teammates and mentors and contribute as they see best. The more freedom we have, the more we rely on learning from and sharing others' expertise and working out detailed common goals and directions.

But freedom alone does not produce an effective system. Freedom without a community of common concern and rules of fair play degenerates into the worst aspects of human character: violence, exploitation, theft, and environmental destruction. These can be somewhat held in check by bureaucracy, but only at the cost of innovation, flexibility, organizational intelligence, customer service, personal growth for employees, and joyful work.

To combine the best of freedom and community, organizations will have to go well beyond what most nations have achieved. Community is breaking down, and our systems of self-organization as yet fail to cope with the fact that our current systems have greatly exceeded the long-term carrying capacity of the planet. This failure of community and all our institutions is a great opportunity, however. Organizations that find ways to build community, such as the Body Shop, which has converted the routine job of selling soap, shampoo, perfume, and cosmetics into a crusade to save the planet, have substantial competitive advantages. Anita Roddick's army of trained salespeople learn the virtues of every product and remain loyal, giving the Body Shop one of the lowest turnovers in the business.

For most organizations the move to organizational intelligence will be wrenching, no less a change than the old communist nations face today. Many traditions and habitual behaviors stand in the way. But once one organization begins the journey, its competitors must find a way to move ahead as well, or succumb. In a world in which freedom and meaningful community are hard to find, anyone who finds ways to build in a bit more of either reaps disproportionate benefits.

The Seven Essentials of Organizational Intelligence

Anyone can break something up into small pieces. The trick is to knit them back together again into a whole without compromising their autonomy.

DAVID NADLER

THE INTELLIGENT ORGANIZATION of the third millennium will be structured from many smaller interacting enterprises, more like a free nation than like a totalitarian state. Intelligent organizations will be pluralistic to the core, preferring conflict between competing points of view and the struggle of competing suppliers to painful and costly discoveries that management control at a distance does not have all the answers.

Citizens of the organization will have rights—free speech, the right to associate with others across boundaries and ranks. The power to make fundamental work decisions, such as what to do and with whom to do it, will continue to be divested by the hierarchy and gradually distributed to smaller, more flexible self-managing groups who are responsible for their own work processes and accountable for their results. The experience of everyone's being empowered and getting lots of feedback from their choices and their wider partnerships will make the work groups information-laden learning laboratories.

The newly emerging forms of organization will rely more on result-focused teams and less on hierarchy, more on shared vision and less on rules, more on choices and less on command. Employee groups will be organized around the time-honored entrepreneurial mission: to design ever-better ways to conduct their enterprises and create a stream of exchangeable value. These small internal enterprises can be relatively independent of the hierarchy because what they deliver is measurably valuable to the process of serving customers. Their means will be collaborative enterprise, in which members work together to serve their internal customers as well as look out for the interests of the business as a whole. Just as free enterprise and the power to act entrepreneurially enliven a national economy, internal free enterprise and the power to act intrapreneurially enliven an intelligent organization.

Architectures of intelligent organizations will be flexible, shifting to meet new challenges and responding to local situations. What will make them responsive is not the brilliance of organizational designers sitting at the top but the decisions of people in the middle and bottom of the organization who freely choose the connections needed to make their area work in coordination with what is going on elsewhere in the organization. Such flexible systems need new, more participative forms of discipline and control to sort out which connections and groups of connections are working and producing the most value and which are a waste of time. They also need guarantees that choice is widely distributed, so that all members can contribute their diverse talents and experience and develop and express their intelligence.

✳ NECESSARY CONDITIONS FOR ORGANIZATIONAL INTELLIGENCE

As much as possible, the method of coordination is changing from management control to direct responsibility and control by doers working in interconnected groups of peers. A dilemma results: On one hand, these doers need a high level of individual and group autonomy to foster personal engagement and initiative. On the other hand, they need a high level of interconnection within and outside the group to be responsive to the bigger picture. Bureaucratic organizations discourage both individual initiative and wider responsibility, even when attempting to empower.

Postbureaucratic organizations foster both the open choices of markets and the collaborative choices of community. Both market choice and community choice need structural processes and principles to keep the systems open and to ensure that individual needs and common needs will converge.

In writing this book, we struggled with deciding the relative importance of many factors supporting organizational intelligence, a task made more difficult by the fact that they all interconnect. We certainly understood firsthand from our marriage and family the paradox of simultaneous needs for freedom and connection, and the responsibility to express both in any relationship. For years we debated the subject of healthy organizations and covered flipcharts with pictures of what might constitute organizational intelligence; we tested the ideas with clients and reviewed the literature.

Seven necessary conditions for organizational intelligence emerged that appear to encompass most of the others. These conditions are interdependent in the sense that they do not necessarily work well separately. They span the inherent paradox of human organization — the advantages of high levels of freedom and rights, along with the benefits of strong community and sensible governance. Many of the

■ WHAT IT TAKES TO BUILD AN INTELLIGENT ORGANIZATION

FREEDOM OF CHOICE	RESPONSIBILITY FOR THE WHOLE
Widespread truth and rights	*Equality and diversity*
Freedom of enterprise	*Voluntary learning networks*
Liberated teams	*Democratic self-rule*
Limited corporate government	

best knowledge-based businesses are providing the conditions for lots of freedom and lots of interconnection.

The three conditions listed on the Freedom of Choice side of the chart foster an open systems environment for liberated individuals and groups. The three conditions on the Responsibility for the Whole side of the chart help create an environment in which freely taken individual and group choices work together wisely for the benefit of all. The seventh condition, and the base of this chart, is a system of organizational government in which the center's roles and powers are limited.

Each of the seven items receives at least a chapter's worth of attention later in the book. Here we give an overview of our basic ideas and how they interconnect.

✳ FREEDOM OF CHOICE

On the Freedom side of the chart, the three building blocks are conditions for developing responsible choices in members of an organization. We cannot make responsible choices if we do not know what is going on or if we do not each have the power to act, so we need widespread truth and rights. Freedom of enterprise releases the innovative energy of individuals and groups to challenge the status quo by preventing monopolies of power from squelching them. Intelligent organizations use internal market systems to bring forth the highest and best use of internal resources. Teams are the basic building block of organizational intelligence. If they are not liberated to develop and use their collective intelligence, no superstructure above them will avail.

Widespread Truth and Rights

To work, freedom requires well-informed people. We cannot expect individuals to use freedom effectively if they are kept in the dark. Intellect functions most effectively when it has good information to work with. The alternative is what computer scientists call "garbage in, garbage out." Bureaucratic organizations, not trusting the intelligence and goodwill of their employees, keep information from them. This creates a self-fulfilling prophecy: Employees denied information become indifferent to organizational success because they lack the information to make intelligent choices.

The intelligent organization is a rich bath of what former CEO and best-selling author Max DePree calls "lavish communications."[1] DePree established lavish communications by example—management provided everyone in his company with the relevant information about all aspects of the business. The management of intelligent organizations keeps employees up-to-date with reports on such subjects as

♦ Financial results in detail

♦ Current productivity measures

♦ Customers' needs and wishes

♦ Market share and news about the competition

♦ The strategies of the organization

♦ How those strategies relate to local priorities

♦ Quality statistics

♦ Customer satisfaction statistics

♦ New products and services in development

♦ Pollution, waste, and cost of energy use

But openness in management information is just the beginning. The flow from management must be augmented by torrents of peer-to-peer communication across all the boundaries of the organization.

The free flow of information needed to produce organizational intelligence will not take place if people in the hierarchy hold the power to block the acquisition or communication of knowledge. For this reason members of the organization must be protected by guarantees of their right to speak and write to others in the organization and to go about collecting the information they need to understand and contribute to the system. When people do not have the right to speak out and confer with whomever they choose, the system stops facing reality and makes terrible and expensive mistakes.

Freedom of Enterprise

Modern work cannot be done by rote. People need authority to make localized, decentralized choices in everyday work. In an intelligent organization, everyone uses his or her individual intelligence to find problems to address, to decide whose help is needed, to do work in

ways that make the most of everyone's talents, education, and experience. In some sense virtually all knowledge work consists of making
choices—what words to write next, where to find sources of information, which techniques to apply, whom to believe.

Without freedom of action, individuals cannot use the full power of
their intuition, their judgment, or their experience. Without freedom
to make choices and decisions together and the power to act on them,
teams are ineffective. Without guaranteed rights, teams find that the
bureaucracy and the bosses gradually take control over every aspect
of work life. Intelligent organizations thus protect every member's
freedom of enterprise by creating systems in which people who see
what needs to be done can find a way to get it done.

The choices ordinary people make, including which leaders to
follow, what projects to support, and what connections and relationships help them get their job done, create the architecture of the informal organizations within bureaucracy today. But these choices are
officially denied and often discouraged. The formal architecture of
all intelligent organizations of tomorrow will have these freedoms as
its foundation.

When there is choice along with high standards of performance
and relationship, responsibility and learning develop together. Self-
management within groups and communities provides continuous
feedback about the consequences of actions. If people can be in
touch with the consequences of their actions, they will learn and be
responsible.

Imagine within a large decentralized organization an internal marketplace for services and components. Imagine that each team may to
fulfill its production responsibility in a variety of ways—choosing to
buy inside or out, choosing how to serve internal and external customers—while focused on the ultimate customer, not the hierarchy.

The strength of this "free intraprise" system is that these "intraprises" obtain their legitimacy not from the corporate bureaucracy but
directly from their customers' willingness to pay. Power flows not
from the hierarchy but ultimately from the external customers of the
firm. The welfare of the customers and the organization as a whole, not
the welfare of the bosses, focuses the creation and delivery of value.

Free markets do not just happen, however; they are institutions that must be created. For example, the body of law needed to create a smooth-running free enterprise system is so large it requires years of study to gain a good working appreciation of it. It takes time for organizations to develop practices that make free intraprise as effective as it can be. Inside organizations, new accounting systems are needed for internal intraprises that buy and sell on an internal market. Markets do not produce useful guidance unless there are choices of vendors and customers. How can we break down the internal monopolies of bureaucracy into smaller independent suppliers? How can we provide inside the organization the meaningful equivalents of freedom to start a new enterprise? And how do we get everyone engaged in learning and collaborating to improve offerings and delivery? As our discussion proceeds, we will describe in some detail ways to bring the benefits of free markets and freedom of enterprise inside corporations, nonprofits, and government agencies.

Liberated Teams

The many revolutions currently going on in organizations, whether through the quality movement, cycle time, reengineering, high performance work systems, or organizational learning initiatives, all have this in common: At their core is a basic shift of day-to-day control and feedback systems from the hierarchy of command to collaboration within and among teams. Project teams, process analysis teams, intrapreneurial new product teams, quality action teams, market focus teams, and so on are used for many purposes and are succeeding where bureaucracy has failed.

Liberated teams are proving to be such a powerful force for integration and productivity that they form a basic building block of any intelligent organization. Teams serve as the autonomous unit of the system, as cells do in biological organisms and families do in free societies. Given the right context, internal teams can generate the passion, engagement, and developmental speed of an entrepreneurial venture. In addition, a team is something to belong to, a support group and a political unit with more standing, more clout, than the individuals in it.

As part of a team one can have more impact and get more done. Self-managing teams use the intelligence of every member to produce results that show, "All of us is more than any one of us." Intelligent organizations provide teams with the information, processes, and training they need to be primarily self-managing.

Peter Senge says that team learning is the bridge to organizational learning.[2] Teams provide opportunities for personal development, changing the comparative drudgery of work at the base of the hierarchy to the satisfactions of collaborative learning and achievement. The experience of making decisions and sharing responsibility for large pieces of a process gives honest feedback to the actors. Learning springs from the wealth of communication in the team's collaborations within itself, with other teams, with suppliers, and with customers. These knowledge-based collaborations, when embedded in shared mission and values and operating at a high level of responsibility and self-management, become the superior system of control. The organizational challenge of the decade is finding a practical pathway from entrenched bureaucratic control structures to an empowered confederation of teams.

✳ Responsibility for the Whole

The freedoms in the first column of our chart—truth and rights, empowered teams, and freedom of enterprise—liberate the power of the individual and of teams and focus attention on the customers. These freedoms can themselves transform bureaucracy, but the transformation will be neither balanced nor complete. Other complementary forces and institutions are needed for people to connect, collaborate, and give each other community support—especially to get complex and knowledge-intensive work done. Bureaucracies disconnect people. The connecting forces in the Responsibility for the Whole column are conditions for productive collaborative relationships between organizational members and others they work with and serve.

The power of the internal market must be balanced by the power of the organization as a community. A community cares about all members and supports them with education and a safety net. It has a vision or focus that guides members toward a common goal without compulsion, and it has shared values that define the boundaries of acceptable behavior. A community provides the central governance needed to deal with all the issues (from environmental pollution to the distribution of income) that free markets address poorly.

Equality and Diversity

Both equality and respect for people's right to express their individuality are core values in the community of difference. For liberated members of organizations to choose actions that enhance the whole, everyone must trust in the fairness of the system and be secure in a certain safety that is not derived from dependence on those in power. Fear interferes with intelligence and prevents letting go of the old and welcoming improvements. Bias and favoritism discourage initiative and innovation. To use the intelligence of all members of the organization we must strive toward equality for all.

Societies that effectively guarantee rights, promote truth, and work toward equality outperform totalitarian ones in which the few live vastly different lives than the many downtrodden. Equality does not mean that all people are the same or will be paid the same. The external market will not allow us to pay all people the same; if we try, people with scarce talents will leave for better opportunities.

But in a deeper sense, no matter what we pay, people's lives are equally important. Equality begins conceptually with the idea that all people are of equal value: Everyone is treated with respect regardless of artificialities of rank. Gradually ranks will dissolve to enable more productive distinctions among people, such as differences in training, skills, experience, viewpoints and approaches, and ways of adding value.

Equality grows beyond mere justice with attention to maintaining equal opportunity. Years ago DuPont lost Bill Gore (who left to found the highly successful Gore Associates) because back then it had an educational caste system. Gore reported that despite his success in new products, he realized as a young man that he could not go much further at DuPont until he acquired a Ph.D.[3] These sorts of inequalities are unnecessary and a way to waste talent and destroy loyalty.

Equality is well served by continuing education, a commitment to help every employee who stays with the organization become all he or she can be by funding and making time for learning. Though on-the-job learning remains critical, the further we go into the information age, the larger percentage of our time must be devoted to more general study and research. For example, Hazel Henderson, consultant to organizations worldwide and author of *Paradigms in Progress*:

Life Beyond Economics, among other books, says she now has to spend fully half of her time learning and keeping up with new developments in the world, leaving the other half for writing and consulting.[4] An organization that provides time and funding for study creates more nearly equal opportunity and avoids a future full of employees with obsolete knowledge.

The quality of relationships a company has with its customers may be the primary competitive advantage available in most industries. The way employees treat customers is a mirror of how employees are treated in the organization. Thus the quality of relationships between members of the organization is a strategic issue that determines the very fabric of the organization.

In a bureaucracy, the pattern of relationships between people is defined as who is dominant over whom. It is straightforward but not harmless: Dominance and submission bring out the worst in people.

The quality of relationships in a formal hierarchy is limited by fear, flattery, and power politics. Bureaucratic organizations are as intelligent as they are today because most of their thinking is done in the informal network, where relationships are more nearly voluntary and as a result far better. Great leaps in organizational intelligence can be made by legitimizing and protecting the informal network—and that brings us back full circle to the essential rights, such as freedom of association and privacy.

Diversity can flourish in an open system in ways it cannot in one that is closed. The more innovation required of a system, the more diversity can be its ally. Creativity is the combination of things in ways they have not been combined before. The more different the inputs—achieved by bringing together people with contrasting backgrounds, viewpoints, and personalities—the more likely we are to get breakthrough outputs.

Voluntary Learning Networks

To have a flexible and responsive organization, intelligence must be distributed throughout, with all individual minds interacting to create a continuous and current knowledge that can be rapidly disseminated and applied. The organizational form that accomplishes all this interconnection is a continually changing network of connections. No management could design a network of this complexity; it has to be created on the fly by the choices of people seeking the connections they need to get their work done.

To achieve this, the power to decide and act must be distributed. The best organizations promote the emergence of informal organizations and encourage new cross-functional working alliances to serve customers. They create conditions that enable the dismantling and reemergence of new groupings, processes, and structures as new needs emerge. These new alliances develop across all traditional boundaries within the organization and between people within the organization and outside it.

The network organization substitutes for hierarchical simplicity an amorphous and fluctuating complexity of relationships. In a sense it is these changing relationships that create the information and output serving the organization's mission.

We think of individuals and teams as analogous to nerve cells. To form a brain, the nerve cells must be whole and healthy, and they must be freely interconnected—so they can constantly send and receive information from other nerve cells and receive nourishment and oxygen from the system they serve and help coordinate. The connections change as the system learns. To form an intelligent organization, the individuals and teams must be whole and healthy, well supplied with information and resources, and able to connect and disconnect as they learn.

A complex organization needs more subtle and shifting connections than any single person or committee could design. There is growing proof that freedom of individuals and groups to choose their economic alliances and processes—as in a well-ordered free market structure (that is, one that contains law and justice and appropriate limits)—produces the most prosperity and often the most intelligent use of resources. Why? Most simply, the choice of market partners and vendors creates network organizations with links appropriate to each task. Market-mediated networks are far more flexible and responsive than bureaucratic monoliths.

All the systems of building the networks needed to create the organizational brain have this in common: They are self-organizing systems based on voluntary connections. Perhaps this should not surprise us, because the brain is also self-organizing. There is no master plan for the ten thousand or so connections each nerve cell in the brain makes to other nerve cells. Rather, each cell grows according to its own nature, which includes responding to what the other cells around it are doing. The result is a complex and intelligent network. Given a good environment, we have that same capacity between people. Given a mission, markets, and customers to guide them, groups acting according to their own nature will link together to form complex networks of contractors and subcontractors that achieve the mission and deliver good value to the final customers.

Democratic Self-Rule

Though the intelligent organization is full of enterprising individuals and teams, and its network of buyers and sellers provides much of the needed integration between teams, there is still a need to decide on the larger context for individual and group initiative. This context includes overall mission, goals, methods of communication, internal laws or policies, internal regulations, rights, and more generally the balance between responsibility factors and freedom factors. Participative democracy is the preferred means for establishing this context.

The lessons of democracy most needed now in corporations and government agencies are lost if the word *democracy* is defined to mean representative democracy. If the bureaucracy still makes all the decisions, getting to vote for which bureaucratic administration will run our lives does not free us enough to produce high levels of organizational intelligence. We already have that system of democratically established bureaucracy in our governments, and though it prevents the worst tyrannies, bureaucracies still flourish. By analogy, having worker representation on corporate boards may help, but certainly it has not by itself transformed the relationship of worker to organization.

The benefits of democracy owe as much to the rights that limit the power of the government bureaucracy as they do to the election of representatives. Rights that expand what we can do in our own lives, rights like free speech, freedom of association, and even the rights that establish our right to change jobs, move to a new city, own our own houses, or form our own businesses, do as much to keep the government bureaucracy off our backs as our right to vote for a new administration. The democracy most urgently needed to form intelligent organizations is a fully participative means of self-management.[5]

Democratic self-rule begins at the local level and then extends by giving everyone a voice in how the whole system works. Establishing local collaborative self-management means finding systems that allow teams to coordinate and control their own work, including ways to link up with other teams to gather information, obtain resources and services, and integrate work across organizational divides. Democratic self-management of the larger picture means finding ways to give everyone a voice in shaping and implementing the mission of the organization and in creating the context that guides, supports, and limits local freedoms. Ideally, all members of the organization feel they have contributed to aligning the activities of the organization with fulfillment of its mission.

Limited Corporate Government

No society of any size exists without a government. No organization can exist without an analogous "government," generally at both the central and local levels. The question is what kind of a government to have.

Government can be expensive both in dollars and in the ways it can sap the vitality of the self-organizing systems of the governed. Governments limit freedoms and so are naturally in tension with the rights and freedoms that create the vitality of the system.

The central governments of intelligent organizations are limited, because the role of the center is neither to run the intraprises that together deliver the organization's mission nor to supervise the teams and intraprises. Rather, the role of the center is to create the conditions that empower others to build effective intraprises.

The functions of the government of a medium-sized intelligent organization include

◆ Making necessary laws and rules of operation

◆ Supervising the score keeping (for example, setting and enforcing accounting standards)

◆ Seeing that effective systems are in place to ensure the quality that external customers expect

◆ Providing regulations or incentives to ensure environmental sensitivity and compliance

- ◆ Setting standards (such as communication standards)
- ◆ Creating a safety net
- ◆ Operating a justice system
- ◆ Supporting the common defense when a part of the system is attacked
- ◆ Making common investment in infrastructure, technology, or distribution
- ◆ Setting up common logistics systems
- ◆ Sharing funding of education

✳ ORGANIZATIONAL FREEDOM AND COMMUNITY

Many of these ideas are probably familiar. We see free markets and democracy at work in nations. Freedom of choice and the force of community are seen in many informal organizations, nonprofits, and community-based change organizations; many small and large entrepreneurial business organizations; and even in well-protected pockets of freedom within mature bureaucracies. Yet in most organizations today, freedom and community are not available consistently. They are the gift of particular managers and leaders rather than elements integrated into the structure and processes of the organization. In the future, freedom and community will be as basic as bureaucracy and hierarchy have been to organizations of the twentieth century.

Part II

Creating Freedom of Choice in Organizations

I asked myself what mattered more to me than anything else, besides peace, and replied: freedom. I spelled it out further: freedom of conscience and opinion. Freedom from want and fear. Democracy cannot exist without bread and with a secret police. Or without pluralism and with a claim to monopoly. I would add that wishing to ordain happiness by decree means stifling freedom. Through no merit of my own, I was born into the tradition of the labor movement and the intellectual world of European Social Democracy. I have seen their weaknesses, particularly in Germany, as well as their greatness. Readiness to suffer overcame the determination to struggle. Totalitarian communism has shown itself to be the wrong road, claiming many victims, a road paved with economic and social failure. Civil liberties and social justice always have to be weighed against each other. A social state is free only if it avoids the danger of proliferating bureaucracy, does not allow itself to be constricted by planning, and emphasizes its commitment to individual responsibility.

WILLY BRANDT

Widespread Truth and Rights

In old-fashioned mass-production plants, managers jealously guard
information about conditions in the plant, thinking this knowledge
is the key to their power. In a lean plant, such as Takaoka, all
information—daily production targets, cars produced so far that day,
equipment breakdowns, personnel shortages, overtime requirements,
and so forth—are displayed on "andon" boards (lighted electronic
displays) that are visible from every work station. Every time anything
goes wrong anywhere in the plant, any employee who knows how to
help runs to lend a hand.

JAMES P. WOMACK, DANIEL T. JONES, AND DANIEL ROOS

THE SIMPLEST WAY to integrate everyone's intelligence into the guidance system of the organization is to present lots of information about
what is going on for all involved to see. Rapid dissemination of truth-
ful information gives people the opportunity to organize and manage
themselves in a way that corresponds to constantly changing realities. Will Schutz said of his decades of organizational work, "What I
discovered was that perhaps 80 to 90 percent of the organizational

problems dissolve if there is an atmosphere of truth. Truth is management's grand simplifier."[1]

In a bureaucracy, loyalty to the bosses and the status quo can be a higher virtue than honesty and the free exchange of information. An organization steps beyond bureaucracy by encouraging everyone to "face reality as it is, not as it was or as you wish it were," as General Electric's CEO, Jack Welch, put it in one of his six rules of effective organization.[2] Facing reality depends on full information and full participation—many people putting their partial truths together, listening to every discordant voice, and willing to follow truth wherever it may lead.[3] Searching for truth so that people may steer a complex organization is the most basic manifestation of organizational intelligence, and it depends on everyone's freedom of speech, inquiry, and initiative.

Face Reality, Communicate Candidly

Welch's first commandment is, "Face reality, even when doing so is uncomfortable, and communicate candidly, even when doing so may sting." The result is a rough, "hockey player" style of meeting in which everyone gets right to the point and says what he or she means. The legend is that people who habitually hedge their message or say only what they think the boss wants to hear are fired.[4]

It wasn't always so at GE. In the late 1970s, when we moved to a neighborhood near the GE headquarters, we began to hear jokes claiming to mimic the way executives spoke—the words coming out very slowly with long pauses between phrases. It was as if there were fourteen different internal censors time-sharing the brain and every phrase had to be checked to make sure it was correct and violated no rules before it could be uttered.

Then Jack Welch came with a charter from the outgoing CEO, Reg Jones, and the board to make GE a faster-moving, more entrepreneurial concern. As new programs for reducing bureaucracy moved through the massive corporation in the mid-1980s, Welch found that many managers were blocking the changes, demanding more work from fewer people without including them in the planning and decisions. Many of the lower-level people were more aware than their managers of the needed changes but were unable to speak up, and the rest had no chance to envision the new goals. In 1988, Welch said, "We've got to force leaders who aren't walking the talk to face up to their people."[5] To get rid of bureaucracy, Welch rigged the system so that the fears that caused some executives to obscure the truth were replaced with some justified concern about getting caught not telling the truth. Now candor is considered the core of the productivity revolution.

Since 1989, outspoken truth has been practiced in the safety of the "Work-Out" procedures. Work-Out is a forum where three things can happen: Participants can get a mental workout, they can take unnecessary work out of their jobs, and they can work out problems together. Initially the Work-Outs were three-day sessions begun with a talk by the boss. He or she typically roughs out an agenda to eliminate unnecessary meetings, forms, approvals, and other scut work. Then the boss leaves, and the group breaks into five or six teams, each to tackle part of the agenda and prepare a presentation to be made to the boss on the final day.

The first sessions are really about building trust. Says Welch, "You have to go through the administrative part of it. If you jump right into complicated issues, no one speaks up, because those ideas are more dangerous."[6]

On the third day, the boss takes a place at the front of the room. Often the boss's boss and other senior executives come to watch. One by one, team members rise to make their proposals. By the rules of the game, the boss can make only three responses: agree on the spot, say no, or ask for more information, in which case he or she must charter a team to get it by an agreed-upon date. The session gives workers a safe way to taste empowerment. The same goes for the bosses: Even if *their* bosses are in the room, they are forced to make their own decisions. Their bosses cannot overrule them later without jeopardizing the whole process.

Work-Outs are now enrolling customers and suppliers as well as colleagues. Occasionally Work-Out teams form themselves, springing up in response to a problem or opportunity rather than a formal charter.[7]

The truth—including rigorous disclosure of practices and results—opens the door to intelligent decisions, including decisions that do not support the status quo. Truth telling is not necessarily incompatible with bureaucracy, but in the political struggle to rise through the hierarchy, truth and openness are often early victims. Employees who voice hard truths are too often seen as disloyal, because the truth may call the boss's work performance into question or be seen as a threat to the reputation of the group.

One of our clients put it this way, "I've sat through too many meetings in which we all agreed on what seemed to me a foolish plan. Not choosing that 'hill to die on,' I kept quiet, only to learn later that half the other people in the room didn't believe in it either. We all went along with what we thought the boss wanted to hear. This fearful clamming up goes a long way to explaining why we were not more competitive."

Bureaucratic systems can train us in the art of denying reality to please the hierarchy or prevent exposure of errors. When this happens the system careens out of control, literally no longer in touch with reality.

Years before the moon landing, Abraham Maslow was at a dinner where the discussion revolved around who would get to the moon first. "Don't worry," Maslow said. "The Russians will not get there for twenty years."

With the triumph of *Sputnik* so recent, everyone wondered how he could count the Russians out with such certainty. With prodding, he went on. Maslow described a countdown he had witnessed at Cape Canaveral. Twenty-four hours before the scheduled launch he listened to the countdown.

"General Electric!"

"All systems go!"

"Rockwell!"

"All systems go!"

And so it went until one of the many vendors had a glitch.

"Consolidated Hydraulics!"[8]

"We have a problem."

Then the countdown paused while the people involved, and anyone else who could help, worked out the bugs.

Maslow explained that though the Soviets could succeed with a brute task like building rockets with the huge throw weight and orbital velocity to launch a *Sputnik,* the task of landing on the moon and returning safely was too complex for their bureaucratic systems. In the Soviet system, Maslow suggested, the person buried in some functional hierarchy who suspected a glitch would be likely to cover it up rather than disgrace his boss and destroy his career. Maybe he could fix the problem in time, or maybe the blame would fall elsewhere if the fault caused a major problem. In the Soviet Union it was more dangerous to tell the truth.[9]

Our early space program was full of feisty iconoclasts of a type unlikely to rise in a mature bureaucracy. The program depended on the goodwill and competence of a myriad of companies, large and small, working together creatively and in extraordinary coordination. As Maslow predicted, no system created by a hierarchy of bureaucrats has yet succeeded in landing on the moon. It was accomplished by dedicated people working in networks of trusted collaborators, all doing what they did best. The collaborations crossed boundaries of business and government, and linked groups of subcontractors from organizations that might also have directly competing products. Since then, more time and a larger budget have allowed bureaucracy to creep into NASA, resulting in less for more—for example, the disastrous suppression of concerns about the *Challenger's* seals.

Dominance, Submission and the Truth

Perhaps the reason a network of subcontractors is more effective than hierarchy at managing complexity has to do in part with the relative status of the players. All the independent firms making up a network are, in fact, formal equals. This is why "Consolidated Hydraulics" could admit they needed to have a hold on the launch countdown— their status as an independent firm was high enough that they could afford to be honest. The truly submissive will say whatever the boss wants to hear.

The built-in dominance and submission of the hierarchical system reduces truth: Seniors often do not feel they owe subordinates the full truth, and subordinates rarely dare tell seniors the whole truth. Even when the truth is told, neither feels obliged to believe it. Flawed projects continue long past the point when anyone intimately connected with them still believes they can succeed. No one wants to tell the bosses that the project he or she begged them to back is no longer any good. In complex projects many small untruths and withheld truths add up to major delays and cost overruns or even disaster. Truths are easier to face up to and voice in a climate of openness, trust, and confidence, a climate devoid of recrimination. The more equal the relationships, the more possible it is for truth to flow.

Openness, Truth, and Confidence

Mike Harper became CEO of ConAgra in 1974 when it was a struggling grain and poultry processing company. He articulated the way he thought his company should be run to achieve healthy earnings growth. As a result, a dollar invested in ConAgra stock in 1974 was worth $170 in 1993.[10] Here is part of the secret in a bit of the ConAgra Philosophy titled "Openness, Trust, and Confidence":

> We will create an environment in which people can be extremely open with each other, founded on trust in each other and confidence in each other. Trust and confidence are built on openness. We must visibly and consciously reward openness. Priming the pump may be an extremely important tactic, and every officer and every manager in the company must undertake an individual responsibility for priming the pump of openness.
>
> They must take the risk of trusting. They must take the risk of having confidence in their subordinates, peers and superiors.
>
> Truth, openness and confidence are reflected in such things as:
>
> Admitting uncertainty and seeking help
>
> Admitting problems and seeking help
>
> Expressing positive or negative feelings
>
> Being direct and straightforward about personal relationships; inviting critique and feedback
>
> Asking for, and giving, support
>
> Feeling free to offer ideas and suggestions
>
> Feeling free to challenge traditional ways of doing things
>
> Feeling free to confront issues and people directly and openly[11]

Allowing criticism of how a company does business can be painful or seem dangerous. Bureaucracies, like dysfunctional families, tend to make wholesale antitruth rules. Suppressing information and communication makes things seem stupidly simple at times, bafflingly abstruse at others. Part of the reality we sometimes deny in a bureaucratic setting is that all members of a system do deserve to be told all the relevant truths and to be given all the information needed to function well.

Widespread Dissemination of All Business Information

Max DePree, author of *Leadership Is an Art* and legendary former CEO of Herman Miller Furniture, treats employees to "lavish communications"—to far more information than they could possibly need.[12] Surprises result: People find more ways to use information constructively than the leaders dispensing it would ever have guessed.

Good self-management depends utterly on access to information. It would be foolish to expect people to exercise good business judgment about how to use their time and other resources at their disposal if they do not understand what is going on. People in intelligent organizations share all relevant information widely; it is every member's right to see the books and be supported in understanding what is going on.

Detailed Measurements, Feedback, Benchmarking

Truth is not always kind. Though truth sets us free, it also kills old habits, beliefs, and patterns. Defining the important truths about the system's performance that can be measured over time serves to focus the system on results, not power. Facts replace the opinions of those in power as the key to "reality."

Respect for truth is the basis of useful measurement. We have to ask, What do we think this measurement means? Does the way we got these data support that meaning, or have we begun the tempting process of learning to cheat the intention of the measurement? If the system is to respond rapidly and accurately, truth cannot be sacrificed to convenience, politics, or traditions.

Measurements become a tyranny if we take measured performance as a complete picture of reality. We cannot measure the future or the contribution of projects that have not yet born fruit. Overreliance on measurement sacrifices the future. Meaningful measurements used to improve the system (not to establish blame) are a powerful discipline. The measurements everyone needs to see concern both overall system performance and the details of more local systems and processes. When there is open discussion of measurements throughout the organization, everyone can share responsibility for getting results.

Measurements and Responsibility. The quality movement has taught us that we have to find out what customers want, measure if we are producing it reliably, and fix whatever is getting in the way of ever better performance. Measurements posted where all can see them can in themselves be a powerful discipline and meaningful incentive.

The Rogan Corporation, a small plastics manufacturer, established a gain-sharing program in 1983 as a hard-headed attempt to keep the company solvent. Rogan had just made a huge investment in expensive technology deemed essential to staying in business. Employee incentives were introduced to encourage everyone to increase productivity and efficiency. To do so, employees needed a wealth of new business information.

> For a gain-sharing plan to succeed, employees must see a link between their performance and their pay. Accordingly, Rogan has institutionalized regular publication of the company's production and financial results. The company posts every day's shipping totals on the factory walls. It is the weekly gain-sharing report, though, that Rogan uses to focus everyone's attention on the production improvements and efficiency. Every Friday Rogan or one of the four other members of his steering committee... reviews the report with every department and shift. The committee members know that it is crucial that each of the 65 workers in the program understands his or her own potential to affect the bottom line. And people have learned — as evidenced by the variety of ways employees have taken it upon themselves to make improvements on the shop floor. They have contributed more than 300 ideas for making production more efficient.... Rogan considers the program a triumph.[13]

Responsibility for End Results. We quote another section from the ConAgra Philosophy, "Responsibility for End Results," which aims to spread the benefits of feedback throughout the organization:

> With the freedom to act comes responsibility for end results. No one should feel that he or she is expected to have a perfect batting average. We recognize that people in responsible positions often face tough decisions. But we will be measured on the basis of end results, and that holds true not only for operating management, but for staff as well. People throughout the company should feel that it's desirable that their contributions can be measured. This is the way that they, in turn, can build self-confidence and demonstrate their worth to the company. It is also a way that each of us can learn to improve. If our results are measured, and they don't come up to what we think they should be, then each of us will have the opportunity to improve them. We want a results-oriented culture. We are dealing with very real things, and we want the pride that comes from achievement of objectives.[14]

Truths are easier to face up to, voice, and act upon when responsibility for measurement and correction is shared more equitably. Timothy Firnstahl, CEO of a restaurant chain in Seattle, abolished the majority of his central office functions and turned over most of the responsibility for each restaurant to the local restaurant staff—including paying their own bills and doing their own information gathering. "In the marketplace," he says, "information's role is to stimulate action. You might even say that knowledge not acted upon is worthless.... [Thus] information's most important feature is believability." In the decentralized restaurants that pay most of their own bills, the information necessary to figure out how to make the payroll from the restaurant's receipts is all generated and analyzed by the people in the restaurant. "Because we create all our information from scratch, we believe it," Firnstahl says.[15]

Empowerment, as opposed to dependency, is based on access to accurate and full information. In a business this is grounded in financial information that guides everyone's actions. Firnstahl elaborates on his abolition of centralized functions:

Among other things, I was eager to do away with the masking effect of home office accounting. Shipping off invoices to corporate for processing blurs their significance. They come back in effect sanitized, devoid of the emotional content that might otherwise spur line managers to higher efficiency.

The better approach, I decided, would be to do as much accounting as possible at the local level. It would give restaurant managers a far better grasp of how their revenue dollars were used. Analyzing and approving bills in-house would dramatize the fact that all management decisions incur expense.

Moreover, I wanted to put the fear of restaurant-death into my managers. Nothing is so wrenching as not having enough money to pay bills. A CEO can talk himself blue in the face about controlling costs, but a confrontation with insufficient cash to meet expenses is truly memorable. Now unit management would begin to see and feel the tenuous life thread of cash flow.[16]

Benchmarking. One way to face reality faster and get more honest feedback is for organizations to measure their results and practices against other companies. This benchmarking can force the organization to face the need to change. If done properly it does not just make "fast followers" but can be used to get ahead. Generally, to use benchmarking to get ahead of others in an industry one has to benchmark people in other industries. Toyota's famous Kanban (Just-in-Time) system came in part from studying distribution in American supermarkets.

The Multidimensional Nature of Truth

There is a danger that when an organization finally gets committed to truth it will define it too narrowly. Some kinds of truth are easy to measure, but that does not mean the kinds of truth that are harder to measure are less important. Production figures are hard numbers; customer satisfaction can be given a number, but the thing being measured is a feeling, not a number, and so never precisely measured. Nonetheless, the truth about how customers feel is equally important to production numbers.

Absolute truth is not given to human beings; what we get is partial truths. When the blind men all felt the elephant, each described the truth of his own perceptions, but the beast they described was very different. The one holding the tail had a different truth than the one feeling the side. The one with the trunk perceived a different reality than the one feeling the ear.

The truth perceived by someone at headquarters may be quite different from the truth perceived by someone in the field. The truth of a technical person may be different from the truth of a marketer. One is not right and the other wrong; the intelligent organization helps them integrate all their truths to make good decisions.

Experiencing Customer Truth

According to marketing guru Mike Lanning, several Japanese citizens were arrested recently in the parking lot of a mall while taking video pictures of people putting things in the trunks of their cars. What were they up to? The authorities' suspicions were aroused. It turned out they were innocent; they were Honda engineers getting a detailed understanding of how their American customers used trunks so they could do a better job of designing them.

The engineers were not going back to the office with a written report, nor were they relying on a survey of what customers like about trunks. Instead, they gathered more detailed information—actual videotape of hundreds of customers using trunks. With this information they were in a position to know far more accurately how each design change would affect their customers for better or worse.

Detroit's early experience with market research was not good. The Edsel design was assisted by an unprecedented amount of market research yet was also an unprecedented flop. The problem was that, in typical bureaucratic fashion, the research was done by one group and the design by another.

In the early 1980s Ford needed a design of breakthrough quality and turned once again to customers to guide the design of what became the Taurus. This time, however, the design was created by an integrated cross-functional design team, and the designers themselves were among those watching and talking directly with consumers. They discovered that little things previously assumed to be insignificant made a big difference in how drivers felt about a car. Some of the commentary on existing Ford designs was painful, but they listened and acted—and the Taurus became the best-selling car in America. Now that U.S. auto companies are significantly more open to taking in information, they are earning back customer confidence and market share.

Saturn's president, Skip Le Fauve, when asked to comment on rave reviews from worldwide automobile publications and consumer guides, responded, "Care about customers is really where it starts." Saturn went out and asked people who were driving Japanese imports what had attracted them to these cars in the first place, and why they kept going back. Saturn listened to what consumers said, put together a prototype based on their suggestions, and asked if it was what the consumers meant. When they said, "No, not quite," Saturn adjusted it. It took four or five iterations to finally get what they have got today: what their customers said they wanted. According to Le Fauve, the goal at Saturn is "to move beyond customer satisfaction to customer enthusiasm."[17] You can only get there by facing the truth in all its messy detail.

☀ RIGHTS FOR ALL

To level off the pyramids of corporate hierarchy and make the most of a flatter structure requires tools that cut far deeper than head-count reductions in management. For nations, these tools include the rights of free speech, free assembly, free enterprise, joint and private ownership, democratic decision making, and, of increasing importance, ongoing and empowering education. People are beginning to realize the importance of a similar set of rights for the members of large commercial organizations, which may be larger and wealthier than many nation-states. When some high-tech firms use one-third or fewer managers per unit of output as their competitors, they are not just tightening their belts; they are moving toward a fundamentally different power structure. To replace management overhead, they rely on local processes through which workers direct and control their own operations and "develop" their prime assets: themselves and their colleagues. The experience of team responsibility, backed up with lavish education and training, can help prepare everyone for the greater freedoms and rights of an intelligent organization.

■ IDEAS FOR A BILL OF RIGHTS FOR AN INTELLIGENT ORGANIZATION

Freedom of speech

Freedom of the press and E-mail

Right to inquiry

Open books

Right to privacy

Right to free association and continuity of relationship

Right to make and keep promises

Right to participate in democratic decision making

Right to develop one's knowledge and competence

Rights of individual and team ownership

Right to justice for all[18]

Governments and bureaucracies have a tendency to arrogate to themselves ever more power over the people within their domains. Something goes wrong, and bureaucracies create new rules and new departments to make sure it never happens again. Over time these rules and their enforcers build power to the point of oppression. Free nations use written guarantees of citizens' rights and justice systems to enforce them in order to keep the system open and free. Denying rights like freedom of speech and association, though compatible with the rigidly defined structure of a bureaucracy, is incompatible with the fluid networks of the intelligent organization.

Creating a system open to a free flow of information and ideas is not primarily a technical challenge; it is a political one. For example, in bureaucracies it is traditional to make access to information an issue of rank and position. Information is seen as power, and it is often hoarded rather than distributed. Only strong intention to keep a system open can overcome the very human desire to create barriers to the free flow of information.

Freedom of Speech

Freedom of speech is a right so basic we all would abhor a nation without it. Yet in many business and government organizations we visit, the culture of the organization does not support the right of any employee to talk with any other employee.

Societies lacking freedom of speech and press fall into layers of tyranny, with each layer using the tyranny they experience from above as an excuse to pass it on to those below. Business organizations may lack the power of totalitarian governments to imprison or kill, but managers do have the power to silence dissent, cutting off the intelligence of diverse viewpoints.

Freedom to Disagree and Challenge. Suppressing freedom of speech was so important to some that GM spent around $750 million to buy out and silence Ross Perot. The typical outplacement contract also includes an agreement not to criticize the firm you are leaving, though the payment in exchange is generally less. Most employees do not have to be paid not to criticize the chairman; they know better.

We have seen suppression of truth by fear of authority in everything from the savings and loan fiasco to the failure of the *Challenger* seals. Again, we quote a section from "The ConAgra Philosophy":

> An important quality of any organization is its ability to self-correct itself. Thus, the norm that "it's okay to openly disagree with the boss" is legitimate. A culture that allows for diversity, disagreement and dissent permits the possibility for self-correction and also sets the seeds for developing improved people and idea generation and testing. Such a culture sets the seeds for much more commitment in the organization.
>
> It has been said, "You can't really mean yes unless you can say no." Thus, if we want to encourage an organization to become committed to its tasks, we need to encourage the freedom to disagree. If one is always coerced to agree, then one becomes a compliant individual rather than a creative, challenging one.
>
> We recognize that sometimes individuals may feel uncomfortable either being disagreed with or playing the challenging role, so we need to encourage the quiet ones.[19]

One acquaintance of ours we will call Bill spoke out against the way the layoffs were being done at a major chemical company where he had worked for thirty years. Although he was perhaps less polite than he could have been, in most ways he was quite obedient to bureaucratic protocol. Bill never took his concerns above his boss's head, nor did he feed information to his boss's "enemies." But he would not stop talking about the layoff, even after his boss told him not to bring up the issue again.

After telling him to be quiet without result, his boss got angry and asked him to resign from the company. Bill said no. It would have been hard to fire him after thirty years of notably excellent work and appraisals that were never less than "in the top 10 percent." His boss busted him down two levels and asked again if he would resign. When the answer was still no, he busted him down to bench chemist, a long fall from the rank just below director. Bill was a stubborn man, and even with his pay cut, he would not quit. It finally cost the company $300,000 to get rid of a brilliant and honest man with a divergent opinion.

Bill's company is a good company, more honest and more caring than most. But even in good bureaucracies his story is not unusual. In another, nastier case an employee who would not shut up was silenced in a way that ruined a promising career. Managers who were threatened by what she was saying sent the finance department back through five years of her expense accounts and found three innocent and insignificant errors in arithmetic. Using this as "evidence," they publicly fired the truth teller for "ethical problems."

Unless freedom of speech is a right, many bureaucrats will use their power to silence uncomfortable opinions and disturbing truths. This sort of intimidation is one of the deep secrets of bureaucracy, but fear of telling the truth is still incompatible with organizational intelligence.

Many companies, including many innovative high-tech firms, work hard to make freedom of speech a basic right of every employee. They will not tolerate managers who use their power to shut people up. In 1982 the Dana Corporation published their now famous "Talk Back to the Boss" ad in *Business Week* in a bold and successful attempt to get through to their employees that free speech was expected and preventing free speech was not acceptable.[20]

The exchange of information is no longer a minor adjunct of what we do at work; it is central to an increasing percentage of jobs. No system should give those with more authority the power to silence the people below them. Human beings have their limitations, and they display their worst side when they can dominate others without listening to them. Too much power is dizzying, and the tendency to believe one's own press is almost irresistible.

In an age of information overload, access to truth is as much sorting out what truths are most relevant as it is making sure you have heard everything. Bureaucratic chains of command filter what comes to people in high places because more is sent toward the top than top officers can possibly receive. The problem is, the information received is filtered not only for relevance but also for protection of all the people who edit and pass on messages. The result is a distorted and often flaccid picture of reality.

Many Ways to Reveal Truth. In Japan, despite great respect for hierarchy, businesspeople are often better at revealing the truth. Ritualized humility allows one to hint at what one believes without implying the other is wrong. If that fails, there is always the extra license that comes after hours over drinks. What makes this all work is attention to creating relationships that are at once respectful and at the same time capable of signaling the truth.

In addition, many Japanese firms have policies that reduce the fear of a single boss's overwhelming power. Some of the best firms, for instance, pay every employee a salary that for the first fifteen years or so is based only on seniority and education. This practice reduces the power of immediate supervisors to intimidate employees by threatening to withhold salary increases and promotions and makes honest speech more likely.

It is surprising that the Japanese, with the great emphasis they put on not offending or causing the boss to lose face, should have a culture in which more truth can filter up from the bottom. Paradoxically, because respect for hierarchy is so ingrained in their culture, their organizations had to evolve acceptable ways of expressing difficult truths to bosses without giving offense, or they would never have been able to compete in the world market. Their collective skill at moving business information rapidly is an example of the fact that those who have the worst problem are often the first to solve it.

Freedom of the Press and E-Mail

If freedom of speech and access to the truth are radical ideas in many organizations, freedom of the press is more so. Can groups of employees publish a magazine that satirizes or even politely questions the actions or styles of senior management, or would that be disrespectful and bad for morale? Can they write about corporate strategy or debate a corporate policy, or would that be presumptuous or even a security risk?

A free press punctures some of the puffery and privilege that often accumulate around power. As with *glasnost* (openness), Gorbachev's greatest internal success, the great organizations of the third millennium will suffer the outrages and indignities of an internal free press and emerge stronger for it.

A free press on computer networks is now changing the U.S. Forest Service. According to Karl Mettke, Eastern Region management analyst, "Networking in the Forest Service has probably done more damage to bureaucracy and the tradition of control-oriented culture than anything else." The Eastern Region has a distributed information processing system—everyone has access to computers and can communicate anywhere in the United States. In their efforts to unravel bureaucracy, the Eastern Region created the Dreamers' Network, with the purpose of sparking creativity, opening doors to new thinking and risk taking, and providing an opportunity to share creative and intuitive experiences. Within eighteen months of its inception, the network incorporated three thousand subscribers in the Forest Service, a cascading "mailing list" to the national forests, and fifty or sixty people outside the Forest Service (who receive hard copies). The newsletter "Creativity Fringes" is published on the network as a way to share information and philosophy.[21]

Right to Inquiry

Although broadcasting honest, detailed, and timely information to all employees is a first step toward fulfilling the right to know, knowing general information is not enough to allow workers to do their jobs. The emerging class of knowledge workers not only have their own specialized skills, they also continually gather new information and seek out experts in other fields. Because an ever larger portion of the workforce is involved in this sort of work, the rights of inquiry are increasingly essential to efficiency and organizational intelligence.

The right of inquiry is the right to take the initiative to cross boundaries of the organization to gather information. This means the organization must trust people to poke around, to initiate research, to ask questions without always being asked why they need to know.

Right to Open Books

Jack Stack, the legendary hero of the Springfield Remanufacturing revival and author of *The Great Game of Business,* says that you cannot get employees to act like owners unless they can see the financial results of their work.[22] Springfield Remanufacturing, unprofitable and about to close, was a division of International Harvester that rebuilt engines. The management team of Springfield Remanufacturing offered to buy it rather than see the plant shut down.

A highly leveraged buyout of a money-losing business requires a very rapid fix. There was not time for management themselves to figure it all out. To get everyone involved in saving the company, they set up an employee stock ownership program and a bonus plan for company performance.

What changed people's behavior was not just having shares in the company but being treated as owners. Because management shared all financial reports with every employee and gave them basic courses in finance, everyone knew exactly what the numbers meant in terms of bonus, and more important, job security. As a result, everyone was working toward the same goal — survival.

Springfield Remanufacturing held classes to teach every employee to read both the balance sheet and the income statement. The income statement showed how fast they were losing money; the balance sheet measured how long they could go on losing money at that rate before their creditors shut them down.

Every employee learned not only what would have to happen to save all their jobs but also how his or her job could contribute to making the company viable and getting it into a state in which the bonus plan could begin paying.

In their desperation, management had made a very simple but important discovery: To get employees to play the game of business, you have to show them the score. They also discovered they had to bare the books on a weekly basis, because once every month was not frequent enough to keep people focused on survival.

Information about what is going on with the business spreads rapidly at Springfield Remanufacturing because employees are very interested in it. At first they were interested because the survival of the company — and thus their jobs — was in immediate danger. As the company became more secure, they remained interested because they are owners and share in success and failure. Employee ownership can help spread truth, particularly when the organization is small enough so everyone feels he or she can make a difference.

Today Springfield Remanufacturing is thriving: 1993 financials show $74 million in revenues, up 13 percent from 1992, with profits of $1.5 million.[23] None of this would have been possible without open books.

Right to Privacy

Never show fools unfinished work.

R. BUCKMINSTER FULLER

Paradoxically, in addition to giving ordinary employees the right to ask questions, we must also give each person and team the right to keep their early work hidden. Bold new ideas cannot stand the light of immediate publicity and attack. Smart innovators share them only with a few friends in the early stages.

Just as many tropical fish will not reproduce unless there are plants in the tank so that they (and their offspring) have somewhere to hide, innovation does not take place if overscrutinized by official systems. Perhaps this is why so many important Silicon Valley conversations take place off the premises in coffee shops and cafés.

In the 1920s, 3M developed a system for advancing unpopular ideas, a system that allowed some privacy, time, and space to make mistakes and helped overcome people's hesitancy at finding new ways to do things. Dick Drew, the inventor and founder of 3M's entire sticky tape business, was as a young man working on the development of masking tape. After being told to stop working on it by a succession of managers all the way up to the chairman himself, he continued on, but kept a low profile. When the fruits of Drew's defiance began earning the company significant revenues, the chairman at the time, William L. McKnight, made sure that the "courage of one's convictions" became a central value of the 3M culture. In McKnight's reign, people could not get beyond a certain point at 3M without demonstrating the courage to stand up to authority. Top management was composed of executives who had demonstrated this courage and appreciated it in others. Managers boasted to one another about how their employees had pulled off some innovation right under their noses without them ever finding out. One-upping the boss was considered commendable, and so was letting your people get away with it.

Letting people hide ideas in the experimental stages serves two purposes. First, it makes it much safer to do experiments because stupid little mistakes can be hidden and will never see the light of day. Of course, it would be better still if people did not have to hide to avoid fear of ridicule, but in the real world a private space for quick and dirty experiments speeds up innovation. Second, it creates much higher quality information for others to review, because they only see the ideas that have passed the early experimental stage. A working prototype may communicate more useful information in thirty seconds than the results of a design feasibility study can provide in a three-hour review.

Computers and Privacy. Computers have contributed greatly to the potential of the intelligent organization, but in the matter of privacy they often have a negative effect. For example, it is harder to hide secret projects in R&D when computers demand an accounting and project number for every person hour. It is harder to have candid conversations if corporate staffers can pull up old E-mail files to check what was said.

Should free speech and the right to privacy normally afforded by private verbal communication be built into E-mail systems? Should employees be allowed to store and exchange encrypted messages? Should the government be allowed to limit our ability to encrypt? The candor required for organizational intelligence may well require the ability to control who is listening.

Right of Free Association and Continuity of Relationships

Many businesses are beginning to grant within the company the rights and freedoms we now consider normal for citizens in their relation to the state. Consider the right of free association, the freedom to choose relationships. An organization structured on free choices of how and with whom to do business can be seen in the management principles of Bill Gore: "We have no difficulty finding the leaders: they have people following them."[24] This principle gives associates the right to choose their own leaders and blurs the hierarchy enough so that everyone can take a leadership role concerning those issues each knows and cares most about.

Bill Gore made the right of association the center of his philosophy at Gore Associates, a rapidly growing purveyor of products from high-tech electrical insulation and Gore-Tex® fabric to reverse osmosis filters and artificial aortas. He called his organizational philosophy "The Lattice Organization," meaning that anyone can talk directly to anyone else in the organization without having to check with intermediaries. Informal cross-boundary relationships give organizations much of their intelligence and ability to integrate diverse viewpoints, but too often bosses view these informal contacts as dangerous. At Gore Associates the formal system for running the company is much more like the informal network of more hierarchical companies.

Many habitual beliefs can act as barriers to free association. When bosses are promoted, are they allowed to keep in touch with their old protégés who stayed behind, or is that interfering with the new manager's turf? Are teams allowed to recruit the members they wish? Can successful teams go on working together if their partnership has clicked?

Guaranteed rights such as free speech and choice of associates give each member of the organization the right to choose the inputs they need to construct an accurate picture of reality. The right of teams to stay together preserves the value of learning to think and decide together Much of the organization is embodied in the relationships chosen, developed, and preserved.

Authoritarian governments have traditionally kept people down by preventing them from getting together to oppose the government. Dictators have long used the method of divide and conquer; they win by getting those who might oppose them to fight among themselves rather than associating and generating mutual support. In a free society we cherish the right to meet with whomever we wish.

Right to Make and Keep Promises

There is no easier way to deprive people of their sense of dignity and their ability to be effective than denying them the essential ingredients of integrity. One of the cornerstones of integrity is a person's word. Of people of integrity, of the citizens who are welcomed in every society, we say, "Their word is their bond." At the core of bureaucracy's ability to depersonalize and infantilize the employee are the rules that keep ordinary employees from making and keeping promises to anyone but their boss.

As organizations become more effective, they take promises made to customers seriously, regardless of who made them. Yet promises made by one employee to another may not be considered very important. If a promise is made that the project will be done in three months, that promise can be lightly set aside by a boss ordering that more time be spent on something else. What this does to worker relationships generally is not given much weight. Yet if a person cannot give his or her word and make it stick, deep relationships are difficult to form, trust disappears, and, in the end, commitments, even those to customers, become impossible to keep.

Gore Associates has realized the importance of the commitments employees make to each other. Gore has a system in which employees have great freedom to find their own place in the company. The formal organization is surprisingly absent. What forms of discipline take up the slack? "At the core," said Bill Gore, "is this: an associate keeps his or her commitments. If you don't like your job, you are free to seek another, but before leaving complete your commitments to your teammates."[25]

This principle of fulfilling commitments is probably the sine qua non of freedom. In the intelligent organization it means that employees would be responsible, not just to their bosses, but to their peers.

A Safe Base. Truth is often suppressed in bureaucracies because people are afraid to tell the truth. If they displease their bosses they will not get a good raise or promotion; they may even be fired. The safest thing to do is to keep quiet. Independent entrepreneurs with a large number of customers have a safer base for telling the truth. Not having a boss, they can say what they please as long as it does not offend a whole class of customers. As a result they tend to be more outspoken. Perhaps this is why Jefferson believed a nation of small farmers rather than employees was the essential base of individual independence needed to form an effective democracy.

Later in this book, in chapters 7 and 8, we will discuss ways to create the safe bases inside an organization that will give employees the security to speak out. The key is to let groups of employees act and feel like small entrepreneurial teams, producing what their customers want to pay for, not pleasing someone in the chain of command. We will show ways to accomplish this by giving teams something like ownership of what they create, ownership in the sense that bosses cannot take a successful enterprise away from the people who made it succeed.

Rules about free speech alone cannot give employees the security needed to create an open flow of information. As long as one person has too much power over another, the forces suppressing free speech can be at once pervasive and subtle. We cannot legislate against the raised eyebrow or the frown, nor can we discover the real reason why one employee received an excellent appraisal and another was rated unsatisfactory. As long as the chain of command is the fundamental method of control, truth will always be compromised.

Right to Participate in Democratic Decision Making

In advanced nations, the right to be ruled by a democratic process rather than a totalitarian ruler is among the most cherished of all rights. Democratic decision making has broad application inside organizations. The democracy that governs decisions within self-managing teams is a basic building block of the intelligent organization. If democracy means any system that increases the rule of the people over their own lives, then anything that increases choice in the system increases the level of democracy. Finally we are seeing more and more democratic input into designing the collective context — the policies, infrastructure, and "laws of the system." The more the organization uses the intelligence of every member, the more democratic it is.

This challenging subject is treated at greater length in the chapters of Part III.

Right to Develop One's Knowledge and Competence

Although the universal right to an education is not one of the rights in the original Bill of Rights of the United Nations, the right to an education has become the norm in advanced nations. In the information age, to lack an education is to be disempowered.

Intelligent organizations cannot afford for their members to become obsolete through lack of continuing education. Members cannot afford the risk of losing their ability to add value. As part of the strategy for productivity, as part of the social safety net, and as an inalienable right, each member of an intelligent organization has a right to have and a duty to pursue continuing education.

The more broadly educated the people in an organization are, the more kinds of truth they can share. This is why firms like Motorola make a strategic goal of bringing everyone up to the seventh-grade level. Only if everyone can read is it easy to distribute information widely. Unless everyone can understand numbers, statistical process control involving everyone is not possible.

Educational goals go well beyond basic literacy and math to include a growing repertoire of work skills. Workplace education in the intelligent organization encompasses specific technical skills, team building, innovation, business formation, and financial realities. Communication skills are basic, derived from lots of experiences with openness, as in GE's Work-Out processes. Free speech is as much a skill and habit as a right.

For rights to be exercised responsibly, everyone needs education in interpersonal skills and collaborative work processes and decision making. Education for democratic self-management includes training and experience in establishing values and co-creating vision, which then shape the day-to-day work.

The new management education being created to support skills in participative self-management is truly revolutionary. We hope the more involved and empowering style of educating inside corporations will spread to education outside work in order to prepare everyone for the responsibilities that underlie true freedom.

Right to Equal Justice for All

One area of truth that matters deeply to people is the truth that lies behind administering justice. The right to due process plays a big role in democracies because hiding the truth in issues of justice opens the door to great abuse by those in power.

A number of companies are creating justice systems that are independent of other forms of administrative power. This separation of powers is a critical part of what makes democracy work and is equally applicable for the justice systems that help ensure the basic rights within an organization. Rights mean little if they are administered in a closed system by those in power. The function of central governance in organizations, discussed in chapter 15, includes ensuring rights and justice for all, and in doing so limits all the acts of governance from inappropriate power and influence.

✸FREE TO KNOW, FREE TO ACT

Obviously the free movement of information throughout the organization increases organizational intelligence. The better the quality of information, the deeper the level of truth. The more honesty and wisdom are embedded in the information, the more it contributes to organizational intelligence. But information alone does not cause an organization to act intelligently. For widespread sharing of information to lead to higher levels of organizational intelligence, people must be free to act once they know what needs doing. That freedom begins with a letting go at the center and the assumption of responsibility throughout the organization.

6

Freedom of Enterprise Inside Organizations

I was wrestling with decentralization because at heart I'm a decentralizer. But...it became increasingly clear to me that the real issue of effectiveness, of winning in the marketplace, was finding ways to make the company work horizontally.

LOUIS V. GERSTNER

ONE MAJOR STEP toward organizational intelligence is the decentralization of power: moving to the periphery decisions that were once part of the center's monopoly of power. In Hewlett-Packard, Hallmark, Motorola, AT&T, Microsoft, and other organizations, many of the traditional tasks of the center are being moved to divisions, departments, units, and teams. Decentralization of power is easiest to do when the organization can be divided into business units that can afford to be quite independent—almost as if each were a separate company with its own customers.

Decentralization does not replace bureaucracy with some other form of coordination and control. Instead, it generally creates a somewhat better form of bureaucracy. Though this often enough provides a substantial competitive advantage, it falls short of the dream of creating an organization based on teams all of whose members are empowered. The smaller, almost stand-alone businesses formed by decentralization still tend to have too many people to function as a single team. In many big organizations the new business units are themselves divided up with a version of the more traditional chains of command.

Decentralization into smaller business units allows more integration between functions like marketing and R&D to take place, but there is a price to be paid: Integration between businesses may decline as they are separated into smaller units, calling for more bureaucratic coordination from above. To the extent bureaucracy dominates the decentralized groups, they lose the advantages of entrepreneurial self-management.

The next step beyond classic decentralization takes organizations not to a better decentralized kind of bureaucracy but instead to ending reliance on the chain of command as the fundamental instrument of integration and control. The new systems of control are decentralized in a different sense: They rely on establishing the conditions under which the self-determined choices of smaller units create an order and a pattern of integration more effective than any that could be designed or administered from above.

Surprisingly, in a world in which government agencies often copy innovations in corporate management, the pioneering work in large-scale self-organizing business systems has been done, not by corporations, but by governments dealing with how to manage a whole economy. As we pointed out in chapter 3, people faced complexities in dealing with one another on the scale of nations that were beyond the capacity of bureaucracy centuries, even millennia, ago. Nations began to experiment with self-organizing economic systems long before individual firms needed to.

As countries evolve more complex and productive economic systems to deal with higher levels of complexity and productivity, they pass through stages of organizational structure similar in many ways to the stages corporations, nonprofits, and even government agencies follow as they grow larger and more complex. The stage of simple monarchy, in which a single ruler has absolute dominion over the subjects, is analogous to that of a business with a single all-powerful owner/entrepreneur. Progress toward greater whole-system intelligence for either a business or a nation comes with increasing freedom and autonomy for the units within it, especially when this freedom is combined with voluntary rather than imposed connections to other parts of the system.

✳ SIMPLE MONARCHY

In the simple monarchy one mind is fully empowered: the ruler's, or in the monarchical business, the owner's. Everyone else is placed in a subordinate position with limited scope for independent action or whole-system thinking. In the following figure we see an organization with a single empowered person. Everyone else, at the behest of the monarch, is performing a function such as collecting taxes, enforcing royal decrees, and defeating royal enemies.

In this form of organization, subjects or employees have few rights. The monarch can have subjects' heads cut off, or the entrepreneur can fire employees at will—which means people must do whatever pleases the monarch.

The intelligence of monarchy is extended through functional organization. The monarch or the entrepreneur delegates functions to key subordinates. Rulers used ministers to supervise functions like tax collection, the army, the navy, the sheriff's department, and so on. Similarly, as we have seen, entrepreneurs may delegate functions like manufacturing, sales, finance, and perhaps R&D. In a simple monarchy with delegation by function, all issues that involve more than one function are still decided by the ruler or CEO. This setup limits the number and complexity of cross-functional issues the organization can handle.

SIMPLE MONARCHY

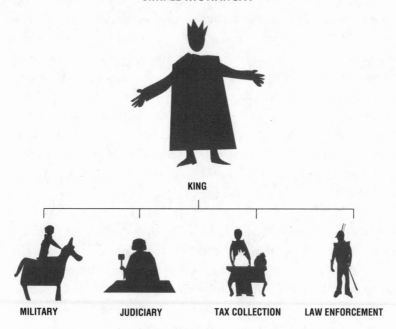

FUNCTIONAL ORGANIZATION

❋ DECENTRALIZATION AND EMPIRE

As monarchs conquered more territory, their domains became large, diverse, and complex, so that a system with one person making all important cross-functional decisions created a major bottleneck. Successful sovereigns then moved from simple monarchy to empire.

Political Empires

An emperor ruled over a number of countries, each with its own king or queen subordinated to the emperor. The result could be both a greater number of places for integrating whole-country issues and some ability to handle greater diversity effectively. Giving power to subordinate rulers allowed emperors to exercise better control over newly conquered countries that spoke a different language, were too far from the emperor's home castle for day-to-day supervision, or were too small a part of the whole to get a large share of the emperor's attention.

The emperor received taxes at all times and troops in time of war, but the local monarch was still free in most circumstances to use his or her brain effectively in all the day-to-day issues of running a small country. The people got quicker decisions and more effective justice and administration than they would have if the more distant emperor had ruled directly.

Because empires empowered more brains to function effectively within a single organization, they were able to manage a greater breadth of cultures and countries and thus to control more land. In a simpler, agricultural era when having more land led directly to more surplus grain and thence to more troops and thus greater military effectiveness, empire was so effective that the bulk of the world was conquered by one empire or another.

Corporate Empires

By the 1920s, organizations such as DuPont and General Motors began to reach a level of size, diversity of enterprise, and complexity similar to that which earlier required sovereigns to shift from simple monarchy to the decentralization of empire (see following illustration).

When the recession of 1920–21 created stress, both DuPont and General Motors shifted to a multidivisional decentralized structure,

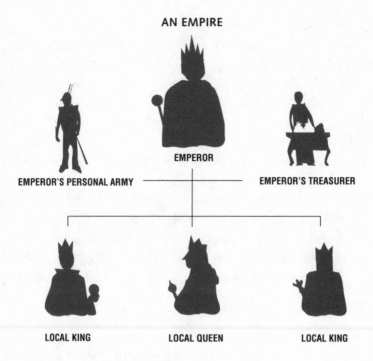

AN EMPIRE

EMPEROR'S PERSONAL ARMY

EMPEROR

EMPEROR'S TREASURER

LOCAL KING

LOCAL QUEEN

LOCAL KING

DECENTRALIZED CORPORATION

OTHER STAFF

CEO

FINANCE STAFF

GENERAL MANAGER
OF CHEMICALS

GENERAL MANAGER
OF PLASTICS

GENERAL MANAGER
OF FIBERS

which took them a big step toward resolving the problems that occur when bureaucracies become huge. It was not a coincidence that they both changed at the same time. The Du Pont family owned a sizable block of General Motors stock, and the chairman of GM at the time was Pierre Du Pont. Alfred Sloan organized General Motors into separate car divisions for every pocketbook, beginning with Chevrolet for the working man, moving up through rising income brackets with Pontiac, Buick, and Oldsmobile, and ending with Cadillac for the plutocrat. Decentralization allowed General Motors to focus more intensely on the desires and needs of each different type of customer.[1] Meanwhile, at DuPont, decentralization into businesses was so successful that by the end of the decade others, like Union Carbide and Allied Chemical, had copied it.

Rather than treating the organization as one gigantic business, they broke their companies into a number of separate businesses, each organized much as it would have been had it been a stand-alone company. Each division (DuPont called them departments) was run by a general manager who had nearly all functions, including sales, manufacturing, and R&D, reporting to him. Finance remained under the control of headquarters.

Decentralization into independent business units created organizations with several times the capacity to manage complexity, but it did so without calling into question the basic rules of bureaucracy. With more general managers in the system, each with an autonomous and functionally complete business team, the decentralized system had a greater integration capacity: It brought a detailed cross-functional intelligence to more products and more varieties of customers. This increase in organizational thinking power is analogous to the greater processing power computer systems can attain through parallel processing and decentralized architectures. Everything does not get jammed up at the top.

Decentralization into many divisions was a powerful cure for the unresponsiveness of large functional monopolies and the overspecialization to which large bureaucratic organizations are prone. In smaller business units, people in the functions were closer to one another, closer to the general manager, and closer to the customer.

Decentralization Is Not Enough

Why, given the many successes one could list, is decentralization not a complete answer for achieving organizational intelligence?

Decentralization is not enough to produce the intelligent organization because decentralization only empowers the little kings and queens, the baronesses, earls, and duchesses. It does little to change the lot of either the serfs or the common workers. Dividing into smaller and smaller autonomous business units according to the rules of bureaucracy runs into problems of dis-integration long before the bulk of the people in the organization are empowered. If we want to empower the ordinary knowledge workers who create most of the value added by a corporation, we need a system for pushing autonomy deeper into the ranks of the ordinary people than divisionalization can ever go.

If we try to keep empowering more people by continually decentralizing into ever-smaller divisions, the units will become far too small to achieve economies of scale. They will find they need to share more resources between divisions to achieve efficiency. They will need to share more information between divisions to keep up on technology and marketplace events. They will find that many divisions routinely call on the same customers and that more coordination is needed.

Decentralization into ever smaller stand-alone business units cannot be continued indefinitely, because autonomy without interconnection is not always appropriate. For example, how finely can an airline that serves many cities be divided before that process becomes absurd? Should it make each route a stand-alone division of the company with its own planes, advertising programs, and flight crews? Should it further divide each route into separate businesses by class of service, such as first-class, business, coach, and special fares? It is clear that if we use a bureaucratic system of organization, continuing to divide into stand-alone business units reaches the point of absurdity long before every business unit is small enough for everyone in it to feel empowered.

When divisionalization goes too far for efficiency but not far enough for empowerment, the bureaucratic system of coordination creates a genuine dilemma: If the organization moves back toward centralized, functional control or consolidates into larger business units, the ability to coordinate among functions is reduced, and system response time slows down. If the organization goes to smaller business units, coordination across the units becomes the limiting factor. This dilemma can be mastered only by abandoning most of the basic precepts of bureaucracy.

Matrix Organization. Some organizations attempt to solve this problem by patching a matrix organization onto an otherwise bureaucratic system. They find that matrix organization is incompatible with the rules of bureaucracy. As the number of people with authority over an area increases, so does the power to say no. When many people can say no, nobody can say yes. At best they can say, "I don't object." Soon the system acquires so much "no power" and retains so little "yes power" that nearly all experiments and challenging adaptations are stopped.

The secret is creating a "matrix of yes" rather than a "matrix of no." A matrix of yes is created when for every input and every kind of permission there is more than one place to go. The free enterprise system is such a matrix of yes. If you need money, there is more than one venture capitalist to get it from. If you need a marketing manager or a supplier of custom welding or carbon fiber screws, there are many options. Free *intra*prise, the internal equivalent of free enterprise, also creates a matrix of yes with its redundant suppliers.

✳ FREEDOM OF ENTERPRISE

The Industrial Revolution brought a level of complexity to nations that the information age has brought to virtually every mid-sized or larger organization. The key to creating the Industrial Revolution was not greater empire or division into smaller kingdoms within the empire; these things only empowered more barons. The next step that allowed the Industrial Revolution to occur was a shift of power from the feudal hierarchy to the inventors and entrepreneurs of common birth.

James Watt and Eli Whitney were not aristocrats, nor could they have created and marketed steam engines and cotton gins as the loyal retainers of a great lord. The large-scale intelligence-in-action needed for the Industrial Revolution required freedom for, and control of resources by, commoners. This freedom for commoners in the economic sphere did not come from creating a better version of feudalism but from a shift in focus from feudal hierarchy to free enterprise. This did not happen all at once in every area of enterprise. For a considerable period two economies coexisted in Europe: a feudal one in agriculture and a marketplace-driven one in industry and trade.

Nations that placed the greatest reliance on free markets, particularly England, industrialized first. The shift to a market economy was not just more decentralization in the hierarchical mold, it was a shift from hierarchy to the network of voluntary transactions governed by the marketplace.

The role of the king or queen changed. The monarch no longer administered the economy by dividing it into pieces and appointing an aristocrat to rule each of them. Rather, he or she stood above the fray, not taking sides or deciding whom to promote. The merchant entrepreneurs were self-appointed. The government taxed the merchants and provided justice and a place to resolve disagreements. The government provided walls and soldiers to protect the marketplace but did not protect merchants from internal competitors.

As large organizations enter the information age, a similar transition is taking place in the way they are structured. A business enters the information age when the interconnections needed overwhelm any conceivable bureaucratic structure. Knowledge workers create this situation, because to use their brains effectively they have to cross boundaries and freely collaborate. However the organization is divided, huge volumes of collaboration are needed across the divisions.

Because the rules of bureaucracy require coordination from above, strict specialization, and reliance on the chain of command, cross-boundary communications must all go up the chain of command to a common boss and then down again. Huge bottlenecks begin to restrict needed communication. For this reason, many large companies that stick to the basic rules of bureaucracy keep reorganizing over and over again, hoping someday to find the holy grail, the perfect organization. But the problem is in bureaucracy itself: There is no way to break the organization up into autonomous businesses so as to both empower enough minds and retain enough interconnection between businesses.

Teams and projects, increasingly divorced from the hierarchy, do more and more of the work of the organization. New entities that make their living between the divisions spring up. Divisionalization will not be enough to empower them; they require the freedom of an internal marketplace economy.

At Yale University, the growth of geographic information systems (GIS) has created interesting opportunities for collaboration between departments. GIS allows researchers to manipulate maps, each representing a specific type of information, in layers. By overlaying the maps with very different sorts of information, patterns common to both layers may emerge. Various departments at Yale could benefit from using GIS maps, but the maps, the systems to manipulate them, and the staff to operate these systems are all expensive. To solve these problems, Yale set up the Center for Earth Observation with joint funding from a variety of departments, including Geology, Anthropology, and Forestry.

Art Gleason, the center's one employee, operates the system to assist professors in their research. When we talked, Art was working on understanding an epidemic in Venezuela. The epidemiologists had charted rapid growth of a disease over a ten-year period. Why was it becoming so prevalent? They suspected it was carried by rodents that appear in great numbers only after an area is deforested. By overlaying maps of vegetation patterns and disease patterns, and comparing variances over a nine-year period from 1979 to 1988, a correlation emerged that supported their hypothesis. The result: answers to help fight the disease. With these sorts of successes, the Center for Earth Observation will soon pay for itself. Professors in each department are finding interesting new avenues of research that lead to new sources of funding.

As successes in interdepartmental cooperation grow, we will discover that in a systems thinking age, the bulk of opportunities lie not within single departments but in the interaction between departments. Organization by department underexploits anything that falls between, so new intraprises like the Center for Earth Observation that serve and connect multiple departments are becoming the norm. They do not fit the hierarchy and so they form a new class of intrapreneurial employee like Art Gleason, who is only twenty-one years old and currently far lower in status than a departmental professor. Ultimately, as collaborations become even more critical, intrapreneurial employees who operate between departments will be seen as important to the progress of science.

✳ FREE INTRAPRISE

The alternative to a national economy run by the government bureaucracy is not a system run by a better bureaucracy; it is a national economy largely guided by the self-organizing systems we call the free market. In the world of knowledge work, we need self-organization not only for large systems such as national economies but also for organizations as small as business firms, not-for-profits, and government agencies. The alternative to corporate bureaucracy is not merely training managers to behave in an empowering way within a bureaucratic structure; it is developing a system of freedoms and institutions analogous to free enterprise, a system of organization we call free *intra*prise.

Free intraprise empowers ordinary employees to start a "business" (or intraprise) within the organization if they can find the customers and capital to do so. The Center for Earth Observation is such a "business." The story that follows concerns a small staff group within AT&T's corporate public relations division that builds relationships with internal clients at AT&T to give those clients more choice. As part of the reengineering of AT&T corporate employee communications in the late 1980s, Jerry Santos planted the seed that developed into AT&T's in-house PR agency, AT&T PR Creative Services. Starting with a nucleus of several people dedicated to face-to-face communication, he expanded the group's charter to tackle all forms of PR communications.

Santos recruited Steve Aaronson, formerly a speechwriter in AT&T's sizable PR organization, to help the group evolve into a full-service PR agency. Salaries were paid out of corporate funding, and the group told other PR teams that they were available to lend a hand on important projects involving PR planning, speech writing, news media relations, and production of brochures and other publications. In the first year the group handled over a dozen projects, such as helping communicate a massive corporate restructuring, and planning a major press conference to introduce the AT&T Universal Card.

But something was seriously wrong. Word of the group's talents spread, and client requests steadily grew. But the more demand rose, the more overworked and underfunded the group became.

At the same time, the small PR teams dedicated to each of the company's twenty-odd business units were unhappy with the group's seemingly "elitist" approach. Clients often requested help beyond the group's capacity. Aaronson decided which projects they could and could not handle based on which requests he thought were most critical to the company. The group would then support those selected critical projects, at no charge to the client organization. Services were "free" to the users—so demand continued to skyrocket.

Finally, Santos and Aaronson worked with the group to establish a true PR agency model, based on hourly rates and client billings. The group, now called AT&T PR Creative Services, adopted time sheets, created a system that would render monthly bills to clients, and devised a set of rates and business practices similar to those used by many PR agencies.

The group's customers are generally other PR groups in AT&T who have a big project and a tight deadline. They are PR teams that support a business unit, AT&T's corporate PR group supporting corporate projects, and some non-PR clients from other AT&T divisions. None is required to use AT&T PR Creative Services.

Creative Services wondered if people would use their services now that they had to pay, but that turned out not to be a problem. Clients liked the can-do attitude of the hungry intrapreneurial team, and there was plenty of urgent work to be done.

Though the group got the best advice it could find, it underestimated the overheads it would be charged by the corporate offices. The rates the group set covered expenses only if the staff billed upwards of fifty hours a week, leaving no time for vacations, training, staff meetings, paperwork, or lunch. Because they were afraid to say no to customers, there were a lot of late nights. In the beginning the pace was exciting, but over time it wore thin. (We mention this underestimation of overhead because it has happened in virtually every example we know of a staff group's going from a cost center to supporting itself by direct billing, and we hope this warning will save others some grief.)

Because their rates were set below the value of their services, the group continued to get demand in excess of what they could do, but they were afraid that if they raised their rates they would lose their clientele. Finally, on a planning retreat, they faced the facts. They were good, and they could get the business, but the group was approaching burnout. With some trepidation they raised their rates for 1993 an average of 20 percent. To their great relief, they still had plenty of work.

An unexpected side benefit of raising their prices was that the nature of the work they were asked to do gradually shifted. With their new rates in effect, clients began giving the more routine kinds of overflow work to outside firms that could hire younger people and operate with lower overheads than any AT&T group. For that type of work, outsiders were less expensive and more than adequate. Increasingly, AT&T PR Creative Services people found themselves involved in more interesting work that stretched their capabilities and used their years of experience. They were involved in planning as well as executing the work.

The shift in AT&T PR Creative Services' mix of projects demonstrates how a free internal market provides honest feedback and allocates resources to their highest and best use. No other way of signaling the kind of work the group was capable of doing would have worked as smoothly. They can still do "What the clients want when they want it"; it is just that the clients increasingly want to use them to their full capacities. In the days when they allocated their services bureaucratically, Aaronson accepted projects based on what he thought each job was worth to AT&T. Now the people buying the service make that decision, voting with their dollars. The result is better decisions because the users of service have more information about what matters to their businesses than Aaronson did.

Begun with five people in 1988, AT&T PR Creative Services now numbers more than thirty regular staff, plus about the same number of freelance writers and other professionals. The group has grown mainly because it addresses the competitive realities of its client organizations—realities that include a bias toward staff downsizing and precise cost control. Santos views AT&T PR Creative Services as "a postbureaucratic PR organization that emphasizes competitiveness."

purpose of group

"The reason PR Creative Services exists is to be fast and flexible, to fill all the unanticipated needs," Aaronson said. "The group responds literally within hours when there's a crisis or urgent need — such as a new business entry, an acquisition announcement, or a Baldrige Award win. Responding to the need to win business, our motto became 'Giving customers what they want when they want it.'"

feedback

Every year, the group asks clients to rate its work on the requirements most important to them, such as producing results consistent with objectives, speedy turnaround, knowledge of the client's business, and cost competitiveness with freelancers or external agencies. In the five most important requirements, clients rate AT&T PR Creative Services 4.5 on a scale of 1 to 5.

Says Santos, "Our customer ratings and growth prove that an internal 'intraprise' can be fully competitive with the best the outside has to offer. AT&T people were always good. The key to our performance and customer focus is that we have been living in a competitive environment for several years. As a result we now take very good care of each and every customer."

PR agencies generally use gross billings as a rough measure of size and success. In 1993, AT&T's PR Creative Services group had gross billings of over $15 million, ranking it approximately among the country's top twenty PR agencies. Marilyn Laurie, AT&T senior vice president of public relations, sees the group as possibly the "wave of the future" for AT&T's sizable PR organization:

> The group started as a small-scale experiment to add a quick, flexible, and focused project capability to our organization — and it has enabled us to handle projects that are critical to our business. But more than that, it's shown us many of the operating principles for running a successful internal PR agency. Despite unrelenting cost-cutting throughout our business, Creative Services has kept a healthy balance sheet and has grown to meet demand. Based on its success, we're now building a time-tracking system for AT&T's whole PR organization. We're applying the lessons we learned through Creative Services to the way we manage and evaluate work throughout AT&T public relations.

Without choice, inefficiency and fat creep into the system. The place to find out if an innovation is possible or a service valuable is not with charts and graphs at corporate meetings. The best way to prove that greater productivity or better service is possible is to show it by letting an intraprise provide it.

When employees create an intraprise, the form of discipline changes from dependence on the hierarchy to interdependence with customers and suppliers. Customers, not bureaucrats, are the basic disciplinarians of the free enterprise and intraprise systems alike. Rather than having a bureaucrat decide, free choices by buyers and sellers throughout the system determine what is efficient, what is desirable, what works best, and what creates the most value. Because there are many different potential customers, the result of that pluralistic discipline is greater freedom at work than bureaucratic systems ever provide. One no longer rises or falls on the opinion of one other individual.

Often without viewing it as a systemic change, and sometimes by accident, corporations driven by strong need or opportunity are allowing choice to create a freer internal marketplace. This happened at DuPont after Scott R. Shultz, manager of the Information Services group at one of DuPont's plants, was asked to look into a new technology for accelerating software development called computer aided software engineering, or CASE.

After investigating, Shultz was so impressed with the CASE technology that he sold management of what was then called the Fibers Department on a new group to apply the technology inside their department. The Fibers Department, which made fibers for textiles, carpets, and industrial uses like tire cords, was one of DuPont's largest and most profitable. It also prided itself on leading the corporation into new information services technologies. Shultz's new group within Fibers was called Information Engineering Associates (IEA). They made a name for themselves in projects such as building a database to track the qualities of every bobbin of fiber as it moved through the Kevlar® plant in Richmond and a system for a fibers plant in Canada that tracked how each process was maintained.

IEA was not the originator of the CASE system they were using, but over time they became very skilled at using the tools to create custom databases faster, less expensively, and more reliably than any competitor writing programs one line of code at a time.

Part of the reason for their success is a methodology they called the time box. Rather than taking a year and developing the "perfect" system, they gave themselves a time box of about sixty days. They then designed the project so they could deliver working software that would do the job the client wanted done well enough to "gather the low-hanging fruit." Once the client had experience using that software, they would design another time box to take the software to the next level of sophistication, and so on until the information systems were aligned with the customer's needs.

The old system — getting the specifications for the "perfect" system, then delivering it a year or more later — encounters problems because the users' needs always seem to change over the year. In a sixty-day development cycle, one is shooting for a more nearly fixed target. CASE tools allowed them to create higher quality software not only because it was more reliable but, perhaps even more important, because its shorter development cycle allowed them to meet the customers' real needs faster and with greater ownership by the users.

As IEA became better at using CASE tools and the time box, their reputation spread, and soon other groups within DuPont asked IEA to write programs for them. A customer of DuPont's Medical Products Department, which makes clinical blood analyzers, had a major problem. In the beginning of the era of AIDS, the New York blood bank needed a highly reliable method of keeping track of every pint of blood, and they needed it yesterday. They asked IEA for help and got the database needed in short order. This success let Medical Products deliver a service that far exceeded a major customer's expectations by rapidly meeting their real needs.

IEA created a groundwater database to track the water quality found in the test wells around DuPont's Savannah River site. Suddenly IEA found themselves going from being a staff organization supplying software engineering to groups in their own Fibers Department to being an "intraprise" with clients all over DuPont.

IEA made many of the traditional mistakes of staff services groups "going intrapreneurial" — in particular, underestimating their overhead and marketing time so they had to overwork to break even until they raised their rates. They faced the classic problem of how to receive money for their work from other departments when the accounting system was set up to treat them as a cost center, not a revenue generator.

Blessed with support from corporate finance and their own "can-do" attitude, they quickly developed systems for billing customers in other departments. Because no provision for staff profit centers existed, they became a "negative cost center," meaning that they used the cost center accounting forms but ended up with their profit showing as a negative in the overall cost category.

In general the quality of their work overshadowed their problems. The revenue the group generated provided an accurate picture of their contribution to their internal customers because those customers had at least three other choices of where to buy software: their own departmental information systems groups, the corporate information services function, and a variety of outside vendors.

Encouraged by their mentors to test their competitive mettle in the marketplace outside DuPont, IEA established an external sales force. Soon they had projects such as creating a parts inventory system for Navistar, which at the time was making money primarily by selling parts for its International Harvester brand trucks and tractors. They also created a system for the banking industry.

By 1988, IEA was generating enough revenue to employ 120 people. The internally focused free intraprise of IEA provided the efficiency of a single group serving many departments and at the same time increased rather than decreased choice for the users in every department. They provided cost-effective software development for a number of departments and drove the rapid spread of a new and useful technology throughout the company. Soon, the people at corporate information services were also using these same tools effectively. It is very doubtful if this technology would have spread as fast had DuPont allowed only one source of information services technology in the company.

From Centralized Staff Services to Free-Market Insourcing

A debate rages back and forth between proponents of the efficiency of centralized service and those who believe that decentralization of functions will create greater responsiveness to divisional needs. But these two solutions are merely alternative flavors of bureaucracy and miss the larger point. Whether centralized or lodged in the divisions, proponents of both centralization and decentralization imagine services that have a monopoly over the customers they serve. Neither proposes to use the discipline of choice; they merely argue over who should be in charge of the monopoly. Effective solutions to the dilemma of whether or not to decentralize will come when the terms of the debate change from centralization versus decentralization to monopoly versus multiple options.

Centralized Staff Services. When staff services are placed at corporate headquarters level, users deep in the organization experience what looks to them like a distant monopoly. If they do not like the service, there is nothing they can do about it except complain—which is unlikely to improve the service in the long run. Seeing the drawbacks of dealing with a monopoly, general managers of divisions seek to get more responsive staff services by bringing the functions within their own domain.

CENTRALIZED STAFF SERVICES

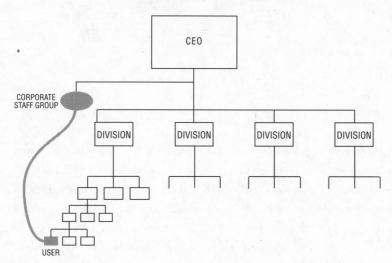

Decentralized Staff Services. Moving staff services from the headquarters to the division level does not change users' experience appreciably, however. The divisional staff service can still look like a distant monopoly. To be sure, users have to work their way up one less level to reach someone who can influence the staff group. But if they are actually several levels down, the difference may be academic. It is impossible either way.

The change to a division-level staff fails to give significantly more satisfaction to humble users because it addresses the wrong problem. Again, in determining the quality of services, the key organizational issue is not centralization versus decentralization but monopoly versus choice.

STAFF SERVICE MOVED TO DIVISIONS

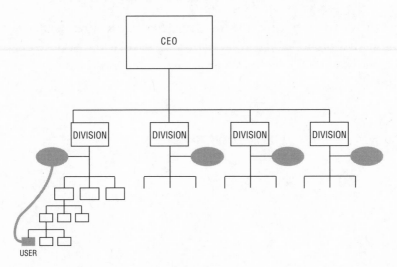

Competing Headquarters Staff Providers. Introducing choice between two headquarters staff providers changes circumstances dramatically. A user deep in the organization chooses between two headquarters staff suppliers. Competing staff units want her business, so they each treat her like a customer. She gets good service because the old corporate staff has been divided in two. The two staff providers may still be in a reporting relationship to headquarters, but the real power influencing their destiny stems from the choices made by people like our user.

Because both these groups charge for their services rather than allocating costs, they are very interested in getting her business. She has not only choice but the power of the customer to demand what she needs. In the end, their managers will ask whether they have enough business to cover their costs or not. This is the fundamental discipline of the free intraprise system. The free choices made by all the different units define the productive relationships that are the structure of the organization.

FREE MARKET INSOURCING

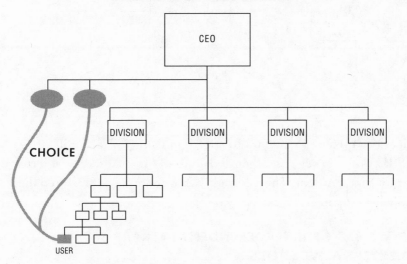

Multiple Sources of Staff Services. The most effective free-market system of insourcing will incorporate choice among services originating from both headquarters and various other locations. In most cases, choice arises within bureaucratic organizations not by design but by accident. Users of headquarters staff services may have some choice of which staff professional to use, and this can provide useful feedback on the performance of those professionals. In the case of DuPont's IEA group, users of software development temporarily had their choice among IEA, their own divisional information services, and a headquarters-level information services group.

This new choice in DuPont occurred by accident rather than design, however, and it was short-lived. Once the corporate information

CHOICE AMONG MULTIPLE PROVIDERS

services organization came up to speed on using CASE tools, they asked IEA to stop serving other divisions and focus on serving customers outside DuPont. This allowed IEA to continue but restored the monopolistic logic of bureaucracy.

✳ NETWORKS OF INTERDEPENDENT INTRAPRISES AND EXTERNAL VENDORS

The overall pattern of an intelligent organization is a network of interdependent intraprises and external vendors. Some intraprises focus on serving external customers directly. In our first book, *Intrapreneuring,* we focused on these external intraprises as a way to generate new sources of revenue. Now that we are looking at the bigger picture, we distinguish these externally focused intraprises from the equally important intraprises that serve internal customers.

Internal businesses created to serve internal customers can do so more efficiently than bureaucratic departments ever could. In fact, it is a combination of both kinds of intraprises that promises to solve the problem of how to create a highly integrated organization out of lots of small, highly autonomous cells. Large businesses can consist of relatively small externally focused intraprises served by a network of internal intraprises and external vendors.

Small in Size but Large in Effect

Because people do their best work in teams with two to twenty-five members, the great majority of intraprises in a mature intelligent organization will turn out to be partnerships of this size.[2] The internal marketplace will reward small, highly focused intraprises that provide, at world-class standards, services much needed by the organization. Tasks larger than such a group can tackle alone will generally be accomplished, not by bringing more people into the intraprise, but by subcontracting parts of the work to other intraprises.

The fact that an intraprise is small does not mean that it has a small effect. If it did only the marketing strategy and big-picture product planning, an intrapreneurial team of less than twenty-five might manage a several-billion-dollar personal computer business by subcontracting sales, distribution, R&D, and production to other intraprises. Consider the following scenario:

A new model of personal computer would be created by an alliance of intrapreneurial teams, each performing its own specialty. Under the direction of the intraprise responsible for the PC business, market research intraprises would work with hardware, manufacturing process, and firmware[3] intraprises to help define the next generation of personal computer. The manufacturing process team put together by the main PC business intraprise would choose and begin working with several manufacturing site intraprises to make sure the designs were manufacturable within a reasonable capital budget and that adequate manufacturing capacity would be available by roll-out time.

The circuit boards might be made by one intraprise and power supplies either bought on the outside or supplied by another intraprise. The assembly would be done in two plants that each had several "operator" intraprises composed of liberated factory workers who would bid in teams to operate and manage a process or even a whole production line. These primary "operating intraprises" might then subcontract some of maintenance and use independent bookkeeping and robotics programming intraprises.

A large sales intraprise (breaking the rule of twenty-five) would take the product global, though it would subcontract to many national and regional sales rep organizations in distant parts of the world.

INTERNAL NETWORK OF THE PC BUSINESS

CUSTOMERS

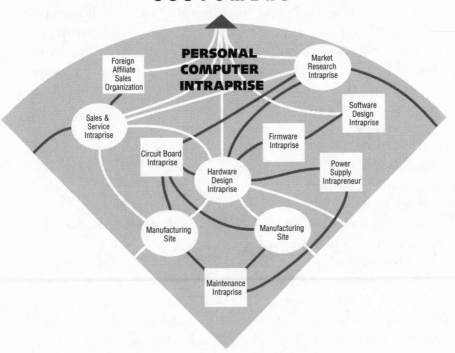

Many of these internal intraprises might have long-term partnerships and even profit sharing with the PC business intraprise. Others would have contracts based on performance. Even more important in motivating every internal intraprise to provide excellent service would be the effect of their performance on their long-term reputation. Can-do problem solvers and teams with a history of being part of breakthroughs in efficiency and quality would get the most critical and high-paying contracts.

Although the team managing the whole PC business might choose to deal with only a limited number of vendors internally and externally, hundreds more intraprises might be involved as second- and third-tier suppliers. Some intraprises might be as small as one person, a single software engineer, for example, essentially an internal freelancer who moves from project to project without need for a permanent boss.

As a result of the free-intraprise network of many small teams, very few members of the organization are buried as faceless cogs in a giant machine. Nearly everyone is involved in the game of business, working hard to make sure the output of their team, their small-scale intraprise, continues to contribute what its customers want cost-effectively. This pattern of subcontracting and resubcontracting creates the networks of human-scale teams that are the future of effective organization.

The complexity of networks is frightening to those trained in bureaucratic patterns of organization. If we drew a real network it would not fit in this book and would reveal this truth: The connections in a self-organizing network are too complex for anyone to understand in total. That is why to get everything as interconnected as it needs to be, we must abandon structures designed from above.

The organization as a whole, of course, is more than just the PC business and the intraprises serving it. Let us say this company also has three other main lines of business: workstations, industrial controls, and communications equipment. Each of these three market areas is run by an externally focused intraprise that also uses services such as sales and service, circuit board fabrication, hardware and software design, final assembly and testing, and so forth. The illustration on the next page shows how the four business units share the internal resources in hardware design (two providers), manufacturing (two plants), and market research (one provider).

The network organization has the advantage that one can achieve business focus, responsiveness, and, at the same time, reasonable economies of scale. In all cases except market research, the external intraprises have a choice among internal vendors, which goes a long way toward ensuring responsiveness. At the same time, in none of the three functions is the number of separate organizations as large as it would have been had they been organized in the traditional divisional model with each of the four lines of business having a complete functional organization. Technology moves easily between the divisions, as does market knowledge.

The intraprises that serve internal customers also have greater freedom and control of their own destinies than they would in either a functional organization or a traditional divisionalized one. They can bias their business toward serving the intraprises they enjoy working for. They can network with one another to form stronger teams.

PC DATA SYSTEMS

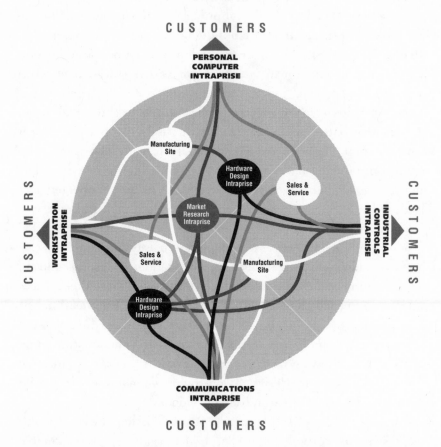

Each of the internally focused intraprises is not just a single-function service organization. It is also a business with its own tiny marketing and sales function, its own finance and bookkeeping, its own strategic and educational planning, and its own R&D devoted to creating and getting ready for new services it will offer in the future.

Of course, these rudimentary functions do not create full-time jobs; they are done part-time by the people who also provide whatever specialties the intraprise sells. They do, however, give everyone in the intraprise a visceral sense of how a business works and experience in helping to run it.

It is in small businesses like these intraprises that people learn how all the parts of a business fit together. America's Cup skippers do not learn their craft as deckhands on a big boat; they learn to sail with their hands on the tiller of a dinghy that responds almost instantly to every change of wind and helm. Similarly, the free-intraprise network organization is constantly giving its members the experience they need to develop good business judgment.

Whether internally or externally focused, each intraprise is a whole business, selling and delivering its service and surviving only because it creates more value than it consumes. The bulk of the value created by this organization is provided by a flexible network of internal vendors, each of which serves several line enterprises.

Relationships of Productive Interdependence and Freedom

Free intraprise defines a new relationship between organizations and their working members. Members are not dependent on the organization; rather, from a safe base of independence, each member or team chooses those relationships that create productive interdependence. Bureaucracy in all its many variations inherently produces patterns of dominance and submission. Free intraprise relationships have the more equal balance of power seen in peer-level relationships of partnership, teamwork, and the network of buyers and sellers. In a bureaucracy there is fierce political competition for a diminishing number of places as one rises in the hierarchy. In free intraprise there is a more constructive kind of competition: seeing who can serve customers best.

The free intraprise system is free because the system is flexible and filled with choice for everyone involved. Individuals and teams can choose what to contribute and how to structure their work as long as they deliver enough value to customers to cover their costs. Each individual is free to form an intraprise of his or her own or to join in one or more intraprises with others. All those choices create the structure of the system and then change it when it is not working—as though an "invisible hand" were guiding everyone to provide value for customers.

Although there is considerable room for personal preference and even idiosyncrasy in the free intraprise system, all of these choices are ultimately aligned to the external customers' needs and wants. Intraprises serving external customers subcontract to intraprises that give them a good deal on what they need to serve those external customers better. Only those intraprises whose work adds value to the external customer well in excess of their costs will long survive. For all its freedom, free intraprise produces a powerful customer focus no bureaucracy can begin to match.

■ RELATIONSHIP OF MEMBERS TO THE ORGANIZATION

	Bureaucracy	Free Intraprise
Source of authority	Assigned a reporting relationship	Customers that value what one offers
Responsibility	To follow orders	To produce end results
Action	Determined by chain of command	Chosen together with team, customers, and selected suppliers
Support	None—peers have little power to protect one in tough times	Part of a team, an intraprise that is a small community in its own right and thus protects its members
Development	Arrested by subservience	Allowed full freedoms and responsibilities of adulthood
Dependence	Emotionally dependent on the boss whose decisions determine one's fate	Self-supporting and interdependent with customers and suppliers

Rights and Institutions for Establishing an Internal Free Market

Everywhere there was the same sequence of events, the same creative evolution: fortress-towns, monastery-towns, administrative towns, towns at the crossroads of trade routes or on the shores of rivers and seas. This parallel development proves that the market economy, the same everywhere with only minor variations, was the necessary, spontaneously developing and in fact normal base of any society over a certain size. Once a critical threshold had been reached, the proliferation of trading, of markets and merchants, occurred of its own accord.

FERNAND BRAUDEL

WITH THE BURGEONING COMPLEXITY of the modern economy, the critical threshold has been reached inside many larger organizations, and internal markets are beginning to appear. Free enterprise has a long history of dealing effectively with great complexity. By comparison, the experiments with free intraprise in firms and other organizations are just beginning.

An organization wishing to establish an efficient internal marketplace has to pay close attention to creating the conditions that will allow it to function effectively. In this chapter we describe a number of the basic rights and institutions that are needed to support an effective full-blown free intraprise system. In particular, we will discuss the right of ownership, the right to form intraprises, payments and budgets, and the right to make and honor commitments.

Although something close to these rights and institutions are all familiar to us in our lives as citizens of free market nations, when applied inside a corporation, nonprofit, or government agency, they still seem radical because they strike so deeply at the heart of bureaucracy. It may therefore be difficult to imagine the existing management of most mature organizations, including perhaps your own, adopting them. We ask you to suspend disbelief long enough to focus on what is necessary rather than merely what is politically possible. When there is a gap between the two, bet that in the short run organizations will do what is politically possible, but in the long run those that survive will find a way to do what is necessary. The path of transformation will be very different in different companies, but the thousands of years of experience civilization has had with variants of marketplace economics give us strong clues to what is needed to make free market systems work, and thus where the process of change is headed.

✳ THE RIGHT TO FORM INTRAPRISES

An effective market depends on competition. Rules that prevent would-be competitors from entering the fray bias the system toward dominance by the few. That is why freedom of enterprise, the right of any citizen to form an enterprise, is a central part of the institution we call the free market. Starting a legitimate business is very difficult for an ordinary worker in North Korea, still difficult in much of Europe, somewhat easier in the United States, and easier still in Hong Kong.

In the summer of 1983, Hernando de Soto, with his Institute for Liberty and Democracy of Lima, Peru, ran a simple experiment. De Soto's team went through all the procedures an ordinary Peruvian citizen would have to go through to legally establish a small garment factory. Four university students, under the supervision of a lawyer, filled out all the papers necessary and called on all the bureaucratic agencies needed to get the approvals the law required. When absolutely necessary, they paid bribes. Keeping careful time sheets, they estimated that it would take a citizen of modest means 289 days of dealing with the bureaucracy to legally establish a garment factory.[1] They created a list of all the necessary steps to obtain approvals and discovered the list was thirty meters long.[2] Clearly, owning a legal business was beyond the means of ordinary people, even those possessing entrepreneurial zeal. In Peru, the right to operate a legal business is a right that applies only to the oligarchy, members of the small number of wealthy families who own and control much of the nation. Making it difficult for ordinary citizens to start a business (along with strong restrictions on imports) protects the oligarchy from competition and, therefore, from any need to run their businesses efficiently.

De Soto sent his team of lawyers to Miami to do the paperwork necessary to set up the same business there. They did the paperwork in a matter of hours and within a few days were chartered and ready to go.

Hernando de Soto is the author of *The Other Path*, a breakthrough book on the economics of the informal economy.[3] Why did he consider the barriers governments create to forming a business important? His reasons go beyond exposing the injustice of empowering the few and disempowering the many. Those nations where it is easier for entrepreneurs to operate are generally either growing rapidly more affluent or are already rich. With the exception of those blessed with abundant oil, nations where starting a business is impossible for ordinary citizens are generally poor.

In *The Other Path*, de Soto shows why this pattern occurs: Members of the oligarchy generally operate very hierarchical organizations, so productivity by those on the bottom is poor and wages are low. When the poor attempt to improve their lot by starting their own businesses, they are pushed into a shadowy underground economy. Operating illegally imposes many costs and keeps the informal entrepreneurs poor and their operations inefficient. Operating beyond the law, they have little access to capital, must not advertise or even be very visible, cannot seek the court's help to adjudicate disputes, and so forth. Although the network of informal entrepreneurs in Peru has produced

50 percent of the housing in Lima and 95 percent of the public transportation, including both informal bus lines and informal taxis, it is still far less efficient than it could be if allowed to operate legally. Keeping the entrepreneurs down in a nation, or the intrapreneurs down in an organization, reduces productivity and impoverishes members.

If the basic right that creates a free enterprise system is the right to form an entrepreneurial enterprise within the nation, the basic right that creates the free intraprise system is the right of an employee or group of employees to form an intraprise within the organization.

An intraprise is a business still legally owned by the larger organization but operated and controlled internally by one or more employees of the organization. An intraprise may serve internal or external customers or both.

The right to form intraprises liberates the energy and intelligence of the ordinary employee. A team of people who believe they can do something better than it is currently being done are free to try to sell their idea in the form of a product or service.

The right to form an intraprise is the right of intrapreneurial individuals and teams, without leaving their employment in the larger organization, to leave their jobs working for the bureaucratic chain of command and instead create an intraprise of their own, which then pays their salaries. This right is not absolute, of course. It is limited by considerations such as the following:

Having enough customers and business to pay salaries, overhead, and other expenses

Giving reasonable notice and finishing up their commitments to their old jobs

Having adequate "capital" to see them through the start-up phase (we will explain where this comes from in the next chapter)

Not violating the laws and policies of the organization (or the external government)

In a free intraprise system, would-be intrapreneurs do not have to sell their ideas to their chain of command. Bureaucrats can be champions of the competing old way and are liable to resist the new ideas that may make their skills, systems, and capital equipment obsolete.

Instead, in a free intraprise system, the intrapreneurs must sell their ideas to the customers who will benefit from them. This shift from the power of the chain of command to the power of a network of customers is the power shift that ends the dominance of bureaucracy and makes the higher levels of organizational intelligence possible.

In order to defend the turf granted to each member of their "ruling class," bureaucracies generally make it difficult or nearly impossible for employees to form intraprises. For example, they argue that allowing an intraprise to compete with a bureaucratic function introduces redundancy and waste. When two or more staff groups find themselves in competition and therefore acting more like intraprises, they are often combined. When an externally focused new business intraprise begins to succeed, it is often taken from its founders and given to a group of "more experienced" managers. Making intraprise formation difficult places an economic drag on the system and favors the established units over the newcomers, with the predictable effect of reducing innovation, decreasing efficiency, and increasing the distance between the elite and ordinary employees.

As long as entrance to a market is highly regulated, you get a privileged oligopoly, not free enterprise. This pattern dominated most of Latin America for much of this century and has caused great poverty.

Within bureaucratic organizations the barriers to free intraprise are generally strong and more absolute than the barriers to free enterprise in the state-controlled economies of Latin America. By restricting the freedom, creativity, and productivity of ordinary employees, barriers to an internal free market constitute part of the cause of the wave of downsizing and suffering in many corporations, nonprofits, and government agencies. There is not enough creativity and entrepreneurial drive in the chain of command to create new ways of creating value for the organization's customers. By making more use of internal markets to liberate the intelligence and energy of every employee, the organization can find the creativity to serve customers more effectively and attract added revenues.

Forming Intraprises with Internal Customers

The issues surrounding the right to form intraprises are simplest when those intraprises serve other parts of the organization rather than directly serving its external customers. There are few, if any, good reasons to prevent internal intraprises from forming to provide better or more cost-effective services to the rest of the organization. If those businesses with external customers are well run, they will buy only services that allow them to be more effective. As a result, only those intraprises that deserve to survive will do so. No senior management group need make this decision for them and their customers.

Existing internal monopoly suppliers (that is, bureaucratic functions) that would rather not face intrapreneurial competition will argue that senior management should prevent the formation of competing intraprises because a single vendor will be larger and therefore more efficient. They are referring to what economists call economies of scale—for example, a larger factory can afford more automation and therefore produce more cheaply. In the real world, sometimes larger units are more productive, and sometimes they are not. But granting monopolies rarely increases long run efficiency or effectiveness.

How is senior management to decide in a specific case whether economies of scale or the virtues of competition and intrapreneurial energy are more important? The beauty of free markets is that they do not have to. The internal marketplace will give a better answer than any study or any bureaucratic decision. If smaller groups are less efficient and provide no compensating advantages, the internal market will rule against them and for the larger, more efficient supplier. If intrapreneurial units survive, it is because their customers believe they provide a better deal.

Regulation of Internal Intraprises

In certain cases some regulation of internal intraprises will be necessary to keep them from pandering to their internal customers. For example, imagine that there are competing intraprises each willing to certify that a plant meets corporate standards for emissions and safety. Some corporate oversight or licensing is needed to be sure the desire to land the certification business does not lead them to be too compliant with their customers' desire to be certified without making necessary but expensive process modifications.

There is good reason to oversee and even regulate the activities of internal intraprises but little reason to merge or reorganize them against their will. If two intraprises would be more effective merged, that is for them to decide. The danger of allowing a central organization to force mergers is illustrated by the demise of the British motorcycle industry. When BSA got in trouble, the government "saved" it by forcing a merger with the far healthier Triumph. When it was apparent that the merger was sinking Triumph rather than saving the old BSA, they forced a merger of the dying duo with the quite healthy but smaller Norton. The result: the demise of all major British motorcycle manufacturers.

Free intraprise organizations do not favor rules that prevent a willing intraprise and a willing internal customer from doing business. Again and again we have seen corporate staff groups move in on internal intraprises and claim exclusive rights to their customers. "We are responsible for providing these services to the divisions," they say, thereby reestablishing a monopoly and putting the intraprise out of business. This happened, for example, when DuPont's Information Engineering Associates (IEA), which began by serving internal customers, was asked to give up that business and focus exclusively on external sales. Free intraprise organizations rarely permit headquarters staff groups to reassert their monopolies.

Forming Intraprises with External Customers

The control issues surrounding the right to form an intraprise are more complex if that intraprise will sell directly to the organization's customers than if it serves only other parts of the organization. The primary issue requiring more centralized attention is how to prevent the profusion of creativity inside the organization from creating confusion and indecision in customers. Sometimes it is better to offer customers one integrated solution rather than a host of pieces for the customer to choose among. Too many new products can confuse customers, as some believe Apple's burst of new products in 1993 may have. Simplifying the offerings may in some cases mean stepping on the toes of intraprises whose external initiatives would add confusion to the market.

This concern for customers' convenience should not be confused with the "sticking to the knitting" argument that is popular today. AT&T's core business is not public relations services, but if AT&T PR Creative Services serves external as well as internal customers, this does not introduce confusion into the telephone marketplace, nor should it draw senior management's time from more important issues. In a bureaucracy it is very important to stick to the knitting because the organization's capacity for thinking is limited. In an intelligent organization a greater diversity of enterprise is possible without taking away from the main thrust.

Even though bureaucratic systems often restrict external venturing when it would be better to let it run free, this is still a complex issue. There are a number of legitimate concerns:

How does the organization maintain its focus?

What forces other than price bend intraprises toward serving in a way that adds greatest value to the whole?

If intraprises enter and leave businesses frequently, will the market cease to trust the corporation's commitment to being around to support and upgrade what it sells?

If an existing business division has achieved a monopoly in a given area of business by applying a proprietary technology, does it make sense to let a new intraprise using the same proprietary technology compete and drive down the price?

In what ways can the organization allow freedom and still create a simple, fully integrated offering to customers?

A brute force solution to these concerns is to require "permits" for all intraprises *selling directly* to external customers. This system is similar to the old Soviet system requiring "export permits" for any sale outside the Soviet Union.

Giving a corporate group the right to issue all export licenses will relieve worries and prevent troubles while the organization is learning to use free intraprise through the growth of intraprises that serve internal customers. One hopes that the permitting body will not be in the pocket of the existing businesses but simply concerned with finding good resolutions to the tension between providing an attractive and somewhat integrated face to customers while at the same time giving adequate channels to the organization's creative energies. If so, this system of permitting will be far more effective than just letting existing business units have monopolies over their customers.

One way to organize the process of limiting externally focused intraprises is to have several larger "trading companies" or "distribution organizations" within a company that each represent many smaller intraprises with products or services to sell outside. By agreeing to represent a smaller intraprise, the trading company or distribution organization is making the judgment that the smaller intraprise's offering is suitable. This system creates a small number of organizations selling directly to customers, keeps confusion under control, and still gives innovative intraprises more than one route to the external market.

Distribution organizations would in some cases be more than sales groups. In a computer company, for example, they might also be systems integrators, figuring out ways to combine the diverse capabilities of an intelligent organization into a coherent, easily grasped solution to the customer's problem. Even in product companies, they would provide services as well as products.

The appropriate level of freedom to compete with other operating groups and intraprises in the external marketplace varies greatly from industry to industry. Some companies, like 3M and Procter and Gamble, allow their units to compete fiercely in the external marketplace. People at 3M say, "We would rather have one of us eat the lunch of an existing 3M business than wait until some other company eats it for us"; 3M makes continuous product innovation a first priority and therefore allows divisions to compete. Procter and Gamble offers Tide no protection from its other detergent brands; the company gets the best results letting the brands fight for market share. In the process, external competitors lose more than P&G.

In the computer business, the issues are not as clear. For years Digital did very well by insisting that nearly all their computers conform to the VAX architecture. The incredible compatibility from desktop VAX machines to huge top-of-the-line networks of "minis" was very attractive to customers. To achieve it, Digital had to suppress the urge to build computers based on newer, more modern architectures. For years this strategy paid off. Then came a period when new architectures were needed even at the cost of some incompatibility, and Digital found itself behind in technologies such as RISC. Would it have been better to be just a bit more liberal with "export permits" and funding for other architectures? Could Digital have supported

VAX with one mainline distribution group and had another for divergent ideas that might someday become important? Would they then have been ready, or would this have diluted VAX energy too much? These are tough issues with no general answers. Only those close to the action know the answers.

In the intelligent organization, there is a bias toward the right to test ideas in the marketplace because that is the route to learning about new markets and new technologies, but this right is not as nearly absolute as the right to form an intraprise whose customers are internal.

✳ RIGHT OF OWNERSHIP

Boris Yeltsin was racing down Broad Street beaming after we visited the New York Stock Exchange in February 1989. "What do you like most about it?" we asked.

"The technology," he replied.

Later, at lunch with part of the entourage of Soviet economists, we discussed how the stock exchange worked. They wanted a Soviet stock exchange right away. "Where should we begin?"

"With private ownership of businesses," we replied, but there was as yet little enthusiasm for that.

In totalitarian states all property belongs to the state. Citizens may use things, but they can be taken away at any time by those above them in the chain of command. In a Communist state—or a corporate bureaucracy—to protest this power would be dangerous and futile.

It is customary in some quarters of our country to make fun of the framers of the U.S. Constitution because it devotes so much space to protecting the rights of private property. But with the terrible exception of slavery, the guarantees of private property rights were and are liberating.

In seeking liberty from excessive government power, property rights are one of the most sought-after of economic rights. Once we move beyond tribal-sized societies, if citizens cannot have property, then for all practical purposes everything belongs not to the people but to the bureaucracy that manages that property. As long as the government owns everything, we are little more than slaves. It does not help to say we all own it collectively, because in truth a few at the top will conspire to control everything.

In the days of absolute monarchs, it was customary for those in high places to take whatever they wanted from those below. The introduction of property rights that could not be infringed without due process of law created a great bulwark protecting the ordinary citizen from the state, which is to say, from those who run the state.

One way to make people "owners" is to give each employee a share in the ownership of the whole. This can be very helpful, particularly in organizations small enough so a single employee or single small team can feel that doing their part well will have a significant impact on the performance of the whole. The successful companies that combine employee ownership with other kinds of employee participation in decision making are becoming too numerous to ignore. Something synergistic happens when employees both own a piece of the action and have increased responsibility for the success of the company as a whole. There are phenomenal successes, like the rescue and growth of Springfield Remanufacturing, which began as a leveraged management buy out of a failing business and rapidly proceeded to shared ownership, information, and decisions with employees. Back from the grave, Springfield Remanufacturing's stock has gone from ten cents a share in 1983, when the debt to equity ratio was ninety to one and the ESOP (employee stock ownership plan) was formed, to $18 a share in 1991.[4] In huge organizations some of the motivational power of employee ownership of the whole organization is lost; what is needed, then, is some more localized and specific form of ownership.

We have long known that private property can be a more effective system for taking care of resources than bureaucratic control. People take better care of the houses they own than the houses they rent, no matter how efficient the landlord may be. In many jobs, employees literally own the small tools they use. Auto mechanics' tools are not the property of the car dealership; they buy them with their own money and bring them to work. Not even the manager can "borrow" them, because they belong to the mechanic, and the result is they do not get lost or abused.

Private ownership works well for tools, sometimes even large ones, but it is less obvious how to apply it to something like a business unit or a brand name. In many cases, private ownership in the legal sense may be more than the organization wishes to grant. The organization may want to give people effective control of an asset without taking the asset off its books and outside its legal control. Because "ownership" represents the right to control and dispose of something, ownership often exists informally. For example, it is becoming traditional for employees to take their personal computer and the software on their hard drives with them when moving to a new office at the same company. Though legally still owned by the organization, the computer "belongs" to the employee in some real sense as long as he or she remains an employee. This informal ownership is the beginning of what we call "intra-ownership" — a kind of ownership that has power only inside the organization. The rights granted by intra-ownership are not as broad as the rights to own property in the outside world. For example, the rights to "intra-property" do not survive if the employee leaves the company. Intra-property rights give the employee the right to use the personal computer within and for the company, but not necessarily to use it in an after-work business for private gain.

Informal intra-ownership works well for personal computers. For things of greater value and more political significance, informal intra-ownership guarantees little. If a team's intraprise becomes successful, what keeps powerful bureaucrats from reorganizing and taking it away from the team? If we mean them to "own" it, we need a formal intra-ownership that can be set aside only with due process.

The rules that establish the institution of intra-ownership include the following:

Intra-property may be owned by individuals or intraprises.

The intra-owner controls the asset until he or she transfers ownership to another individual or intraprise or leaves the organization. In the case of leaving, intra-ownership may revert to the corporation or may be left to someone else.

Intra-property in the eyes of the outside world is still property of the larger organization.

The intra-owner can use the intra-property for any legitimate purpose of the organization but not to break the law or to defy policy.

The intra-owner may or may not be constrained from using the intra-property for personal pleasure or personal gain (for example, using an intra-owned personal computer to moonlight).

How far do rights of intra-ownership go? What can the owner not do with property that still in the eyes of the larger world belongs to the organization? Each organization will have to work out rules for different kinds of intra-property.

Registering Intra-ownership. Governments issue deeds for property and titles for vehicles to reduce confusion about who owns them. Both to reduce confusion and to cut through the bureaucratic habit of owning everything, intelligent organizations create the equivalent of a "town hall" where intra-property can be registered and disputes settled.

Joint Ownership of Intraprises

The institutions that create the free enterprise system include not only individual but shared forms of ownership, including partnerships and joint stock corporations. Joint operation of an intraprise is often the perfect vehicle for a team. As work becomes complex, the peer relationships required for good communication and teamwork do not always allow for one to be the owner and the others to be hired hands. The right to join together in a common intraprise with shared ownership is a basic necessity of information-age efficiency.

✳ A MECHANISM OF EXCHANGE (INTRA-MONEY)

Perhaps the most liberating of economic institutions after the idea of private property is the institution of money. One cannot fully appreciate what a liberating influence the existence of an agreed-upon medium of exchange is until one sees what people have to do in societies with an ineffective medium of exchange.

In 1990 we went to a family and organizational system conference in the Soviet Union. Our conference host's plans were upset when the conference facility canceled our reservations one month before the event. In the business mores of the period and place, they really could not be blamed, because another customer had offered hard currency for the facility for the same time as our reservation. With the ruble being of questionable value, no one could expect promises to stand against the irresistible force of hard currency.

Our ferociously determined and hardworking hosts combed the countryside for another facility. The best they could come up with was a rather nice Communist Youth League Pioneers Camp (think Boy Scouts). Communism was pretty much out of favor by then, and the camp was empty. It seemed perfect, but they could not accommodate us because, though they had rooms, they had no beds.

"Ah," said our hosts, never easily discouraged, "what if we could obtain the beds; would you be able to provide space for our conference? Then, after we left, you could keep the beds and rent the rooms to other guests." "Yes, of course, then we would be back in business," said the potential innkeepers.

Our conference organizers at the time had plenty of rubles, so they combed the Soviet Union for beds. This almost impossible job was given to the group's foremost "scrounge," Sasha. Finally Sasha found a warehouse where there were plenty of beds. They wanted ten thousand rubles for them, and our hosts had far more in the bank. Unfortunately, the money our hosts had was in the form of "symbolic money" instead of "real money."

At first when we heard this, we thought that "symbolic money" was a disparaging term for the ruble, but it turned out their symbolic rubles were in a form worth even less than a big pile of ten-ruble notes: They were on deposit in a bank. To withdraw them was not merely a matter of writing a check; they would have to prove to the bank manager, a government official, that the rubles were going to be used for a socially correct purpose.

Our friends were active in politics, as all good businesspeople must be when government plays an active role in business. Sasha went to their friend, the mayor of the district, and told a sad story: "If this family systems conference does not happen, we will not learn the techniques to counsel families through the tough years ahead. Families will break up, children will be crying, and teenagers will turn to crime," said Sasha with tears in his eyes. "The Soviet psychologists desperately need to know these Western techniques to strengthen families and develop new kinds of organization. They will build a model social services program for your district, which can be a model of social services throughout the Soviet Union."

The mayor understood the urgency and wrote a strong letter assuring the bank that the purpose for the funds was of the highest social good. He warned of the dire consequences that would result if perestroika destroyed the old Communist safety net before our friends could help the Soviet Union design and deploy a social services net to catch those who had difficulty adapting to the new conditions. He urged the bank in the strongest terms to allow our friends to withdraw the money to buy the beds on which this whole venture depended.

The bank manager reviewed the proposal, but because the bank reported to a Soviet ministry, not the district, he felt no obligation to obey the mayor. He declared the reasons were not good enough. The bank would not release the funds.

After a moment of gloom, the conference organizers regained their entrepreneurial zeal. They just could not give up, having already spent months planning the conference, then locating the beds. The beds were sitting there, but for how long? One of the organizers knew someone who knew the bank manager's secretary. Polite inquiries were made, and it turned out the manager was soon to go away on vacation. As soon as he left, Sasha resubmitted the request to the assistant director of the bank, who, he said, "was a woman and therefore understood the importance of children's happiness." She released ten thousand rubles. We enjoyed the conference and the beds. It is a lot of work to do business with a medium of exchange that passes through a bureaucratic approval process.

Though this story is strange to Western ears, are there not parallels in the lot of many intrapreneurs in bureaucratic organizations? When they receive a "check" from their customers, it is generally not even deposited in their account but disappears into the general fund of the corporation or government. To get any of it back, they must, like Sasha, prove that the purpose for the expenditure is worthy.

Many problems arise from the lack of a proper mechanism for financial exchange between different parts of an organization. When intrapreneurs deliver services to another part of the organization, the accounting system often cannot handle the payment. Meetings are held; bureaucrats argue about the price. After a while people say, "It's not worth it. It's easier to deal with outsiders."

When a medium of exchange is missing, opportunities between divisions do not get exploited. Though a certain number of these things can be done in the informal organization, the difficulty of transactions between business units makes organizing into the more flexible and efficient network of free intraprise services virtually impossible. The result of discouraging free financial exchanges is a strong architectural bias toward vertically integrated business units that "own" all the capabilities needed to produce their product or deliver their service. This bias, an inevitable result of not having an efficient medium of exchange, destroys the efficiency and flexibility possible in a free intraprise network.

Intra-money

The most powerful solution for speeding and simplifying internal transactions is to create an effective internal medium of exchange. In essence, units of the organization need to be able to write checks to one another without bureaucratic review. We call this institution "intra-money." If, for example, I need some electron microscope pictures to analyze a product I am about to introduce, I get help from an electron micrographer in another part of the organization with whom I have had no previous exchange. I ask for several hours of work and offer intra-money as payment. The electron micrographer can add that intra-money to the account in which she is saving for an upgrade of her instrument (which the bureaucracy does not seem to want to fund), she can save it for repair services when the microscope goes down, or she can use the intra-money to buy a training course she wants. The added freedom that intra-money provides gives her a good reason to stay late and do my pictures.

Intra-money is a frontal attack on the power of the bureaucracy, just as money in the end became a frontal attack on the unlimited power of the king. It gives strength to the cross-boundary collaborations that are needed to take advantage of the size and diversity of large organizations. It develops intrapreneurs ready for a larger role. It makes freestanding intrapreneurial service providers possible. Without some low-friction medium of exchange for internal transactions, there can be no free intraprise worthy of the name.

✳ RIGHT TO MAKE AND HONOR COMMITMENTS

Many exchanges involve more than an instantaneous trade; they involve the making and keeping of longer-term commitments. In a bureaucracy, no one other than the officers or the board generally has the formal right to make a binding promise to another employee. All promises made about such things as who will work on a project or what resources will be available can be set aside by those above in the chain of command. This greatly increases the cost of doing business.

Typically, effective managers get around the fact that they are not empowered to make contracts by making informal promises that they then strive mightily to keep. But it is not always easy to do this when the system does not value the integrity of its members enough to allow them to keep their commitments. For example, the vice president of operations for a regional U.S. railroad offered his engineering officers a deal. Because there were cycles in the availability of capital to maintain the plant and equipment, the managers feared there might be a capital freeze just when they needed to replace track or rolling stock. As a result, they routinely replaced equipment well before the end of its useful life.

"Don't put in for major repairs to the plant years before they are needed" he begged. "Instead, put them off until the year when they actually should be done, and I will personally guarantee that they will be approved that year."

Several of the officers reporting to him made great savings for several years. Finally they came to the end of the safe lifetime of sections of rail. But at that time there was a corporate capital spending freeze in effect. Although he shook the system with all the power he had, the vice president could not get their requests approved. The result was a number of derailments. No one involved escaped with their sense of integrity intact. The vice president is gone. Nor would those managers ever save money for the corporation with the same spirit. They went back to padding their requests and playing the wasting game that goes on in every bureaucratic budgeting process.

The ability to make and keep promises is essential for self-esteem and a sense of responsible adulthood. It is also essential for building effective organizations. In an effective internal free market system, intraprises form contracts with people and with other intraprises. They are

able to make long-term agreements, and, as long as the intraprise is solvent and physically able to keep those agreements, the hierarchy lacks
the authority to set them aside.

✳ A SYSTEM OF JUSTICE

A system in which contracts can be made requires a system of justice to adjudicate disputes. One major drawback of informal systems
for creating agreements is that the informal organization generally
has only rudimentary methods of delivering justice. For an extreme
example, consider the informal organizations needed to circumvent the
government bureaucracy in Lima, Peru.[5] In Lima, 95 percent of public transportation is provided by informal bus lines and gypsy cabs.
Suppose a passenger in an informal cab fails to pay. What options
does the driver have? He cannot go to the police. If he reported the
incident, the police would confiscate his "illegal" cab. He can forget it,
but if that happens too often, he cannot make a living. Because no
justice system supports the gypsy cab driver, too often the dispute is
settled with violence and even murder. People not willing to use threats
are at a disadvantage, and more important, most of the subtler or
longer-term kinds of agreements are never made. The society without
justice becomes not only mean but also shortsighted. How vividly
this reminds us of bureaucracy, where all too often justice is primitive.

As in our life outside the organization, the justice system of the
organization deals with two sorts of legal actions, disagreements
between individuals and intraprises and situations in which an individual or intraprise has broken the organization's rules. In the case of
"civil" disagreements, the justice system of an intelligent organization favors mediation, with right of appeal to a court. In a case of
breaking the organization's rules, intelligent organizations have their
own courts where those accused of breaking internal law may be
tried. As "everyone is equal before the law," an independent judicia-
ry inside an organization becomes a vital tool for making sure the
powerful do not ignore the rights of ordinary members. To some, having and enforcing laws seems contrary to the intrapreneurial spirit. It
is not. Boundaries of acceptable behavior are an essential agreement
of any society, organization, or team.

The quality of an organization's system of justice can provide a significant competitive advantage. A high-quality system of justice is

swift, inexpensive, and fair. It encourages productive activities and discourages a litigious frame of mind. It provides great latitude for innovation and new ideas and at the same time moves swiftly to stamp out destructive behavior.

In our lives as citizens of nations, we have become inured to inefficient justice and bad law. Our legal system is held hostage to numerous special interest groups. Work on better internal legal systems for intelligent organizations creates a fresh playing field for political philosophers and pragmatic leaders to collaborate with the members of the organization to develop better answers. Perhaps after simpler systems are tested in corporations, nonprofits, and government agencies, we will have models for faster and more collaborative ways to resolve disagreements and administer justice in nation-states.

■ GUIDELINES FOR ESTABLISHING A FREE INTRAPRISE SYSTEM

1. *Establish quick and easy systems for setting up intraprises, at least for those serving internal customers.*
2. *Establish institutions for defining and registering joint ownership of an intraprise.*
3. *Create the rights of intra-property, and empower the justice system to make sure no one ignores them.*
4. *Create an accounting and control system that allows every business unit and intraprise to function as if it had a bank account in which intraprises can deposit receipts and "write checks" against the balance.*
5. *Create a system for registering agreements and contracts. Make sure everyone treats promises, their own and those of others, with great respect.*
6. *Create a fast and efficient internal justice system with fair courts and judges to which disputes can be taken.*
7. *Create an effective process for rapidly establishing a body of internal "commercial law." Use the larger society's commercial law as a starting point, but seek simpler and faster procedures.*
8. *Promote worker ownership of the whole organization to increase cross-system cooperation.*

8

Corporate Financial Systems for Free Intraprise

When Europe came to life again in the eleventh century, the market economy and monetary sophistication were "scandalous" novelties. Civilization, standing for ancient tradition, was by definition hostile to innovation. So it said no to the market, no to profit-making, no to capital. At best, it was suspicious and reticent. Then as the years passed, the demands and pressures of everyday life became more urgent. European civilization was caught in a permanent conflict that was pulling it apart. So with a bad grace, it allowed change to force the gates. And the experience was not peculiar to the West.

FERNAND BRAUDEL

THE FINANCIAL SYSTEMS that support a vigorous free intraprise system are viewed with great suspicion by many who currently control power in bureaucratic institutions. When things are more or less under control, they say no to the internal market, no to letting intraprises keep any of their profits, no to any accumulation of capital other than at the center under their own direct control. As in the change to market systems in whole societies, the move to build internal market institutions in organizations is happening now only where it is necessary.

Organizations battered by more entrepreneurial or postbureaucratic competition, suffering from repetitive downsizing, and seeing no other way to restore pride and profitability will experiment with broader application of free intraprise. So will smaller organizations needing a distinctive advantage to keep up with larger, better-financed competitors, and younger organizations wishing to avoid growing up to be bureaucratic and slow. To become free intraprise organizations, they will have to reinvent their internal financial systems.

✳ HOW INVESTORS GET PAID IN A FREE INTRAPRISE CORPORATION

When a business unit in a conventionally decentralized corporation takes in money, the funds go directly into the corporate account. Headquarters then gives funds back to the business units in the form of separate budgets for both expenses and capital expenditures. Because headquarters generally gives the divisions back less than it took, the remainder is available to pay dividends, debt service, and corporate overhead and to make investments.

An intraprise with the rights and freedoms of an intelligent organization operates by different rules than a business unit in a bureaucracy. With certain exceptions, an intraprise with market freedoms "owns" its receipts and is authorized to spend them as if they were an approved budget. This puts the intraprise on much the same footing as an independent enterprise that deposits receipts in the bank and is "authorized" to write checks as long as its bank balance is positive.

This freedom, though necessary to escape the bonds of bureaucracy, raises serious questions: How does an organization made up of liberated intraprises gather the funds it needs to pay debt service, headquarters overhead, and dividends? How do we know that intraprises will not spend all their receipts, leaving nothing for these other essential activities and obligations?

The basic answer to these questions is simple: Headquarters levies "taxes" on the intraprises to get the funds it needs.

Taxes

Governments, national, state, and local, get the funds they need by collecting taxes from individuals and organizations. The headquarters of a firm organized as a free intraprise network taxes intraprises to get the funds it needs for overhead, debt service, dividends, and investment.

The idea of headquarters taxes is not new. The headquarters of a bureaucratic organization gathers its expenses and allocates them as overhead to the operations it supervises. This overhead allocation is in effect a "tax" by headquarters on the various operations. In our proposed model of an intelligent organization, these taxes are sufficient to cover not only overhead expenses such as salaries for headquarters staff and the safety net but also dividends, debt service, and corporate investment. This system, under which headquarters takes its tax on an intraprise but otherwise grants the intraprise the right to spend its revenues as it sees fit, is currently more prevalent in not-for-profits than in large for-profit corporations. In a university, for example, a scientist who wins a grant pays the university an overhead percentage but keeps the remainder to do with as he or she pleases. The granting agency may determine how it is spent, but for the most part the university does not.

As mentioned earlier, this system is quite different from, and more empowering than, the way most multidivisional for-profit corporations allocate funds. Generally all funds are collected at the center, which then owns them. The enterprises within the corporation prepare budgets asking for funds, and the corporation decides how much money each division will get and, to a greater or lesser degree, how they will spend it. In this bureaucratic system, the center has far more power over enterprises, but this power does not bring with it greater certainty of making a good profit — or even of making ends meet.

The bureaucratic system of centralized budgeting does not encourage frugality. In practice each division submits the largest budget they think they can get away with, knowing it will be cut. Experienced managers use great creativity to hide "fat" in their budgets. Some of the fat is designed to be found and cut because that gives people at headquarters the feeling they have done their job. Other deeply hidden fat is there as emergency reserves to be used as needed for unanticipated difficulties. The problem is, whether difficulties arise or not, any remaining fat must be spent, or the ruse is exposed. No such games need to be played in a system of free intraprise with fixed tax rates. Attention shifts from negotiating budgets and plans with more senior managers to satisfying customers and managing costs.

There are a number of types of taxes, each with strengths and weaknesses. Taxes on profit have the drawback that many intraprises may choose not to report profit but instead raise compensation to absorb any surplus. Thus the corporation needs a tax that takes the money "off the top." Taxes of this kind include sales taxes, value-added taxes, and pollution taxes.

With off-the-top taxes, intraprises will pay the taxes before calculating profit and loss and thus adjust their operations and compensation to leave a portion for corporate headquarters. Paradoxically the result of this combination of freedom and off-the-top taxes is that headquarters receives a flow of funds for its purposes that is far steadier than it was under the old bureaucratic system.

Fluctuations in demand are more of a problem to the intraprises than to an off-the-top tax collector. In order to balance their own books, intraprises tighten and loosen their belts as circumstances change, for example, by raising and lowering compensation and work load. Except in dire emergencies, headquarters gets its cut first.

All taxes distort the workings of the market, favoring some outcomes over others. It is for this reason that we recommend value-added taxes over a sales tax on all intraprise transactions, internal and external. A sales tax on all intraprises discourages the network structure. A bureaucratic business unit generally "owns" all the internal entities that make major contributions to its product or service and thus has no internal transactions and so pays sales tax only once. With a "sales tax" on internal transactions, a network pays tax on each transfer between nodes. Thus, for each external sale, a system with multiple tiers of internal suppliers will pay several times as much as an equivalent operation run in the bureaucratic fashion. A better solution in this case is a tax only on external sales or a value-added tax. A value-added tax allows each intraprise to deduct what it buys, either externally or from other intraprises. A tax on external sales is particularly hard on virtual organizations, trades, and distributors, which generally work on thinner margins. A value-added tax is more balanced and is also good because all intraprises pay it. Thus all may feel they are customers of the headquarters organizations.

One form of tax that produces a desirable distortion is a pollution tax. Taxes on profit, value added, or revenue all cause a distortion in that they discourage things we want more of. Pollution taxes focus tax avoidance energy on doing away with something truly unwanted. They can thus simplify the task of bringing the organization into compliance with environmental regulations and raise the revenue needed by headquarters at the same time.

At first glance, it may seem that taxes on the pollution intraprises create would generate trivial amounts of revenue. But for many organizations, pollution taxes could cover all of a modest headquarters overhead. Consider internal taxes not just on toxic waste, but on paper, energy use, noise, parking, and commuter congestion, and all use of nonrenewable resources.

Strategies for Lowering the Headquarters Tax Rate. When headquarters imposes a heavy tax burden on intraprises, they become more expensive than their outside competitors. Headquarters can lower the taxes it needs by keeping its operations very lean. The best way to do that is to view headquarters overhead activities as billable services whenever possible. They can then be spun out of the government headquarters as several independent intraprises, competing to serve the intraprises that want their services.

Among the largest items in the remaining budget of many lean headquarters organizations will be debt service and dividends. Much or all of the funds needed for these two items can be raised by charging intraprises interest on the capital they have "borrowed" from headquarters.[1] Other major items in overhead are payroll-related expenses, such as health care, pension benefits, training, and a safety net. Intelligent organizations develop fair systems for charging intraprises for payroll-related expenses. With these sorts of strategies, the remaining "headquarters overhead" taxes can be kept low.

✳ CAPITAL

NEW HAVEN, May 13, 1992. Working part time at a community center, Sandra Rosado saved $4,900 to go to college and escape the web of welfare that all her family had known since they moved here 12 years ago.

But her thrift and industry have led to a bureaucratic nightmare for Miss Rosado and her family. First state officials, who discovered her savings account, told her mother to spend the money so the family could remain eligible for the Aid to Families with Dependent Children program. Then Federal authorities ordered the mother to repay $9,342 in benefits she received while her daughter's money was in the bank.

The case, which had been in and out of state courts as Mrs. Mercado challenged the order, highlights what critics across the political spectrum say is a major flaw in American social policy—the rule that limits a welfare family's assets. Will Marshall, president of the Progressive Policy Institute, a Washington research institute, said, "We have got to get rid of these perverse policies that penalize poor people when they exercise personal initiative and responsibility."[2]

It is hard to view this story without outrage at the state and federal bureaucracies. But similar stupidities of system are so common in the life of the manager in a bureaucratic enterprise that they pass unnoticed. If you spend your budget, you get approximately the same budget again next year. If you save and underspend your budget, you generally get your next year's budget cut by the amount you saved. This nearly universal bureaucratic practice has the same effect on managers as the welfare system has on Sandra Rosado's peers. They soon give up saving.

Capital, like money, is seen by social critics as an institution favoring the powerful. However, widespread ability to save and build for the future is the key to a wider distribution of power. In a totalitarian state all capital belongs to the state. In a bureaucracy all capital belongs to the organization. No one can save. No one can accumulate the fruits of past frugality or success and retain the right to spend them when they choose to pursue new dreams.

We badger managers in bureaucratic systems when their actions seem shortsighted. What else should we expect? We have removed the ability to invest in the future by the way we budget. By contrast, an entrepreneur knows to the dollar how much capital she has. If she sacrifices in the short term for long-term gain, she knows how fast she is running out of capital and about how long she can hang on until she must have positive cash flow or else. If she wins the gamble, she gets to keep the winnings.

How different is the lot of her spouse if he is working in a corporation. If he manages his responsibilities at work to focus on the long term with some sacrifice of short-term profits, he has no idea whether his corporate masters will transfer him or shut down the projects in which he has invested time and resources. If he is transferred to another job, the history of reduced earnings on his watch remains part of his record; the future gains he has invested in accrue to the new manager who replaces him. The new manager then "proves" himself better than his predecessor by harvesting the fruits of the farsighted manager's plantings.

Even if the corporate manager remains in place and succeeds, he only has another "Attaboy." He still must beg his masters for the funds to try again. Unlike the entrepreneur, regardless of his successes, the employee accumulates no fund of capital he can spend to pursue corporate objectives as he sees fit. This man does not need more courage; he needs the institution called intracapital.

We originally created the idea of intracapital as a reward system. Let us suppose a team does something wonderful for the organization and we wish to reward its members. Perhaps they created $50 million in new profits or got five thousand people off welfare and into productive jobs. If we give them a bonus of $1 million, all their co-workers will be envious. Suddenly rich team members may quit their jobs and either retire or start a business of their own. The Silicon Valley is full of engineers and programmers who retired young after cashing in stock options. If instead we give them $1 million to spend on behalf of the organization, they are rewarded by being empowered to act freely within the organization. This gives them a good reason to stay and benefits their co-workers.

We call this form of reward by empowerment intracapital. It is a special kind of budget that does not go away until it is spent—the opposite of a bureaucratic budget. A bureaucratic budget is renewed each year if it is spent and goes away to the degree that funds are saved. Intracapital is like a bank account: used up when spent, but if unspent there next year. This system, needless to say, leads to more careful spending than the bureaucratic budget, which is notoriously wasteful.

Intracapital is the reward that works twice. Not only is it an effective reward, but it puts funds in the hands of the most pragmatically creative people in the organization — the proven innovators.

In an intelligent organization intracapital is not generally a gift from management to those they would reward; it is created when an intraprise saves or invests some of its profit for future use by the intraprise. When an intrapreneurial team accumulates intracapital, it has an alternative source of funding. The team can use its own intracapital for its new projects.

Intracapital is another face of the institution we call intra-money. When we use the word *intracapital*, we are thinking of intra-money's role as a means of storing value over extended periods of time. Intracapital is thus the tool that allows and encourages ordinary members of an organization to defer gratification and manage for the long run.

The Intracapital Bank

A sensible first step in creating the institutions of intra-money and intracapital is the establishment of a headquarters-sponsored intracapital bank. In the beginning it is the place where intraprises (and individuals) may keep their intra-money and the bank on which they write intra-money checks. Any individual or intraprise with intra-money in an account can write a check on the intracapital bank to any other individual or intraprise. This creates a low-friction medium of exchange for internal transactions. Having all internal transactions on the bank's computer makes calculating intraprise profitability quick and easy.

The intracapital bank is also the institution that converts intra-money into checks for paying outside vendors. It provides for an accurate record of all external spending by intraprises. In theory intraprises should be able to buy what they need with the intra-money they have in their accounts. In practice there may be some inspection of large external payments of "real" money before a company check is cut.

Intracapitalism As Empowerment

The institution of free enterprise would be far more limited if entrepreneurs' only source of capital were the government or their own savings. Entrepreneurs capitalize their projects with other people's money. Similarly, an effective free intraprise system needs effective institutions for intracapitalization—a way for successful intrapreneurs to capitalize their projects and their intraprises by getting other successful intrapreneurs to invest in them.

As pools of intracapital increase, intrapreneurial teams will have more options for funding. They may have intracapital savings both individually and in an intraprise account that they can draw down and invest. They can seek funding from "headquarters" if their idea is "strategic" for the organization as a whole. If headquarters has established a "small intraprise" program, young intraprises can go there. Finally, they can seek "venture intracapital" from other intrapreneurs who have accumulated more intracapital than their own needs currently require. This may include would-be suppliers and customers of the start-up intraprise who have a vested interest in seeing it succeed.

As a free enterprise system matures, a class of mentor/venture intracapitalists will emerge who, rather than running intraprises, concentrate on finding, funding, and nurturing other people's intraprises. The ones that survive in the venture intracapital game will need good business judgment. They are not given intra-money to invest because they are well-connected politically at headquarters; they have intra-money either because they are successful intrapreneurs with intracapital of their own or because they are trusted by other successful intrapreneurs as intra-money managers.

As the body of intracapital in the system grows through successful intraprises, the sources of funds in the organization become increasingly pluralistic. What emerges is intracapitalism—a network of investors operating in many different forms. "Private" intracapital banks will arise in competition with the central intracapital bank, which may eventually take on a role much like the central bank of a nation.

We believe that though many of the forms of capitalism will eventually appear in a free intraprise organization, the dominance of money power that makes capitalism repugnant to many people will be greatly lessened. Why? Because as we enter the information age the power of talent is growing relative to the power of money. Because as social and environmental issues become more pressing, the need for community, with its more humanistic, egalitarian, and multigenerational bias, is slowly gaining on the lure of solo success.

Free intraprise is not really free as long as the bureaucracy controls access to all the capital within the organization. That situation is analogous to one in which all capital is dispensed by the government of a nation. We would not call such a system free enterprise. The institution that liberates the free intraprise system from bureaucratic control of capital is the institution of intracapital. Just as the institution of capital is necessary to a free enterprise system of any complexity, intracapital is necessary to a free intraprise system of any complexity.

✳ HOW OWNERS GET PAID (A SIMPLE CALCULATION)

Let us consider a highly simplified example of how owners get paid.

Assume that through taxes and use-of-capital charges the headquarters collects 10 percent of the overall organization's revenue above and beyond what is needed to service debt. A separate tax on payroll funds payroll-related expenses including the safety net. Two percent is used to pay for the small headquarters staff and their associated expenses, leaving 8 percent. Of that remaining 8 percent headquarters "profit," 4 percent is paid in taxes, 2 percent is paid as dividends, and 2 percent is retained for the headquarters investment fund and general liquidity. Each year these 2 percents add to the cushion at headquarters or to the funds available for headquarters to invest. If some of the 2 percents retained in earlier years have been invested in successful intraprises, they will in time bring returns that add to the capital fund at headquarters.

While the headquarters group is accumulating net worth under its direct control, the rest of the organization is building additional locally controlled net worth. Each intraprise that earns intracapital adds to the retained earnings and net worth of the organization above and beyond the 2 percent retained each year by headquarters. Of course the corporation will have to pay tax to the national government on intraprise profits, so the intraprises will reimburse headquarters.

The intrapreneurial individuals and teams who have significant amounts of intracapital have been selected by the marketplace for their overall business acumen. They will probably, on average, invest intracapital funds with a higher rate of return than a corporate capital committee would. But even if they lost 100 percent of the intracapital they created each year, the corporation in this example would still report an 8 percent pretax return on sales. The investors get paid from a tax that comes off the top before intraprise profits are calculated, so if the system as a whole grows and prospers, they will do well.

✳ COMPENSATION OF INTRAPRISE MEMBERS

In a free intraprise corporation there are two kinds of employees: those who work for the corporate hierarchy—the equivalent of government employees—and those who work for intraprises, the equivalent of people employed in the private and nonprofit sectors. The compensation of the employees reporting directly to the headquarters "government" can continue according to systems much like those used today, though even these must be updated to reflect the preponderance, in the middle salary ranks, of high-level professionals and experts rather than managers. The compensation of intraprise members can rest largely on the ability of the intraprise to earn the money needed to pay them. Members of the intraprise have to find some agreeable way to divide up the money the intraprise makes, but the total pot for compensation is limited by what others are willing to pay for the intraprise's products and services.

There are huge motivational advantages to allowing intraprises to improve the lot of their members by finding ways to better serve their customers. In a flattening organization, bureaucracy's inability to find a way to motivate other than through promotion is one source of its undoing.

Earlier, in an age of expanding middle management, growing bureaucracies could offer all hard workers excellent prospects of promotion up the management ladder. In the era of downsizing and lean management structures, promotions are far and few between. The system requires ways for people to progress without promotion up the chain of command. Free intraprise allows people to better themselves in the absence of a hierarchy. In principle it allows everyone to do well if everyone takes responsibility for his or her own growth and ends up being highly productive.

In most cases, competition will keep free intraprise salaries from getting out of hand, but there is always the possibility of finding a sustainable competitive advantage that makes certain intraprises unreasonably rich. This need not worry the stockholders, who, as we saw in the section on stockholder compensation, will probably get theirs off the top, but it may trouble others in the firm. Too great a differential of compensation can tear at the fabric of the community, and some way must be found to limit the tendency of the rich to get richer and the poor poorer.

In the early stages of creating a free intraprise system, organizations will be reluctant to let compensation for members of an intraprise be set by the intraprise, even if that compensation is limited by the intraprise's income and cash flow. Keeping some corporate control of intraprise salaries will ease the tensions between those operating in the free intraprise system and those still reporting through the corporate chain of command. Fortunately, putting some restraints on the salaries in intraprises will not prevent the free intraprise system from functioning as long as several features are in place:

> Intraprises are allowed to have true team rewards in which success benefits all team members in some proportional way.

> Intraprises are not forced to rank members of the intraprise against one another.

> Intraprise members are allowed to buy into the reward game by risking their own intracapital or taking some of their salary as shares in the reward pool for the whole team.[3]

✳ STAGES OF FREE INTRAPRISE

Early-Stage Free Intraprise

A corporation is responsible not only to customers and the people in the organization but also to its stockholders. Let us assume the stockholders still put in place the top management team. Then in a practical sense, the top management team and their subordinates are "the corporation."

If the level of trust in free intraprise is moderate, the safest way to begin may be to confine free intraprise to internal intraprises. Businesses with external customers would still be "owned" by the bureaucracy, and the managers of those externally focused businesses would still be appointed by the corporate management. If the corporate management reports to the board of directors elected by the stockholders, this plan should give enough conventional control of all monies coming into the corporation.

Having efficient free intraprise units provide the corporation's conventionally managed, externally focused business units with more cost-effective services changes little that stockholders need concern themselves with, except that it increases the profitability and effectiveness of those businesses. From the investors' point of view, no threatening loss of control or loss of ability to collect profits would occur as internal intraprises competed to better serve their "nationalized" business units.

Other than creating the policies and mechanisms of a free intraprise system for them to operate in, and insisting on a few standards of operation, the free intraprise economy could be almost ignored at corporate headquarters. Getting good value from intraprises would be the business unit managers' responsibility, needing little more corporate oversight than if they purchased their services from an outside vendor.

Middle-Stage Free Intraprise

As the voluntary free intraprise sector expands, the next step is to begin pushing staff units from monopoly into the competitive arena. This is done first by having them bill for all activities and giving their internal customers choice. At the same time this is happening, the middle stage begins opening the doors to externally focused intraprises. These can be start-ups or pieces of the bureaucratically owned business units that ask for the right to split off and become freestanding intraprises.

During the middle stage, many new intraprises serving external customers will arise. For example, John Fischer and a team of intrapreneurs converted part of Digital Equipment's service function into a group of intraprises called Operations Management Services.

They stopped thinking of providing services as merely a means to support product sales of Digital's hardware. Instead, they saw it as a business in itself, in which, for a fee, they provided full information management services to their customers. Rather than focusing on just servicing Digital's products, they provided service on whole systems, including equipment from many of Digital's direct competitors. When systems problems arose, they did not blame the competitors; they made the competitors' equipment work. Operations Management Services grew dramatically in a period when much of the rest of Digital Equipment was downsizing.

Mature Free Intraprise

No one can yet envision a mature free intraprise system. Perhaps there will be adequate intracapital and free intraprise experience to convert nearly all the value-adding entities of an organization to intraprises with employee intra-ownership. Perhaps headquarters still will be a major intra-owner of many of the larger intraprises. Time will tell.

＊RISKS IN THE FREE INTRAPRISE SYSTEM

Any good financial person considering the implementation of any new system, including free intraprise, will try to imagine ways in which the system might under certain circumstances produce bad results. Let us consider a few "paranoid fantasies" and see how a free intraprise system might deal with them.

Net Losses in the Intraprise Sector

If the intraprises on average lose money, the "profits" gathered by headquarters could be offset by losses in the intraprises. This could happen during a downturn in the business cycle.

In general intraprises are better equipped than the average bureaucracy to weather downturns in revenue without losses. Given flexible compensation, intraprises will tend to reduce compensation in hard times rather than accumulating huge losses. At the same time, intraprises with good savings may choose to draw on their intracapital resources rather than lay off members of the team or cancel long-term development projects that will be needed in the next upturn. By doing so they benefit stockholders in the long run, but they could push the organization into temporary losses headquarters could not control.

Intraprise losses funded by drawing down intracapital savings cannot be sustained indefinitely. As intracapital dwindles, intraprises will cut their costs to match revenue. To maintain solvency in the face of temporary losses by the intraprises, organizations should ideally maintain their financial ratios so that they could, if necessary, borrow an amount equal to the total of all intracapital savings.[4]

In general, because taxes paid to headquarters and flexible compensation will go far to stabilize profitability, the ability of intraprises to draw down their intracapital will not make free intraprise organizations more vulnerable to downturns than bureaucratic ones.[5]

A Run on the Intracapital Bank

Any bank has problems if all its depositors withdraw their funds at once. The intracapital bank has fewer problems than most in that intraprises cannot easily convert intracapital deposits to paper money. To withdraw funds they have to buy something worthwhile. Therefore net negative savings are likely to occur, as discussed earlier, only if there is a big downturn and all the intraprises are losing money and drawing their savings to stay alive, or if there is a sudden burst of growth and all the intraprises are financing rapid growth. To deal with these issues, the central intracapital bank can

Maintain adequate liquid reserves like any other bank

Raise the internal interest rates during a liquidity crisis to encourage savings and discourage borrowing

Put emergency tariffs on goods purchased from the outside to keep cash inside the organization

Ask headquarters to curb its capital investment programs

Ask everyone to put off major capital spending programs unless absolutely necessary

Borrow more money from the outside

These remedies will produce a better response than the typical across-the-board cuts that bureaucracies adopt when stressed. Across-the-board cutbacks produce great waste when implemented indiscriminately. Financial force fields such as tariffs and changes in interest rates permit the spending with the highest return to continue but encourage delay in all cases in which the cost of delay is not disproportionate. Using financial force fields, the organization brings the intelligence of every intraprise into play for making the necessary trade-offs. By contrast, using a centralized system to act rapidly in a complex system guarantees that many foolish and costly mistakes will be made.

Headquarters Hit with Tax Bill for Unexpected Intraprise Profits

If the intraprises make profits, the corporation will pay taxes on them in addition to the taxes due on the monies that are gathered but not expensed by headquarters. Where will headquarters get the funds to pay these taxes on intraprise profits? In a well-run intelligent organization, the intraprises are responsible for all tax liabilities they generate and make payments in good time. The accounting intraprise they hire makes sure they pay them to the headquarters tax fund on time to avoid corporate penalties for lateness. Having to account for and pay their share of government taxes is no more a burden on intraprises than what is faced by their external competitors, who also pay taxes. Furthermore, it makes them responsible for the tax consequences of their actions.

In general, as we have seen in these examples, free intraprise systems are more robust and able to deal with stress than hierarchical ones. This should not surprise us, because we see a similar pattern in free enterprise versus totalitarian regimes.

9

Outsourcing and Insourcing

When an American buys a Pontiac Le Mans from General Motors, he or she engages in an international transaction. Of the $20,000 paid to GM for the car, about $6,000 goes to South Korea for labor and assembly; $3,500 to Japan for advanced components such as engines and electronics; $1,500 to West Germany for styling and design engineering; $800 to Taiwan and Singapore for small components; $500 to Britain for marketing; and $100 to Barbados or Ireland for data processing. The rest—less than $8,000—goes to strategists in Detroit, lawyers and bankers in New York, lobbyists in Washington, insurance and health-care workers all over the country, and GM shareholders—most of whom live in the U.S., but an increasing number of whom are foreign nationals.

ROBERT REICH

PRODUCTIVE SYSTEMS are in fact not single companies but networks of companies in which almost every connection has been chosen from alternatives. Boeing, for example, makes few of the things that go into an airliner from scratch. They do not make aluminum, nuts and bolts, glass, tires, or fabrics; they buy them. They also buy complex components, such as hydraulics, electronics, and jet engines. If Boeing tried to design and make all the components that went into an airplane, starting with mining the ores and drilling for oil, their attention would be scattered, and planes would be a great deal less capable and less reliable than they are today.

The network of vendors that supplies Boeing absorbs a lot of the complexity of building an airplane. For example, most of the responsibility for engine reliability and performance is shifted onto part of that network, thereby leaving Boeing free to think deeply about the integration of many good parts into an effective and safe whole airplane.

Delegating big chunks of the complexity of a business to trusted suppliers creates a supporting network outside the control of the organization's bureaucracy. Outsourcing is the norm in many fast-moving industries such as personal computers or fashion. Nike, for example, outsources 100 percent of its athletic shoe manufacturing to "production partners" and concentrates on research, design, marketing, and sales.[1] Apple Computer learned early that it could move faster by outsourcing major components such as circuit boards, industrial design, and application software while focusing on creating an operating system with a unique look and feel. Of the $500 it cost to build the original Apple II, $350 was in components purchased from the outside.[2]

Outsourcing is not limited to products. Commodore Computers had a good reputation for cost-effective hardware but a poor reputation for service. Then it outsourced customer service response to Federal Express. Together they set up a technically trained special unit called Commodore Express in Memphis, the Federal Express hub. Commodore Express handles 88 percent of all customer problems on the phone. If a machine needs physical repair, Federal Express picks it up and drops off a loaner or replacement. Federal Express even does the repairs. Positive response on Commodore's customer surveys tripled in the first year of Commodore Express.[3] This turnaround in customer perception shows that the right long-term partnerships in service activities can provide a major strategic advantage.

In *Intelligent Enterprise,* Professor James Brian Quinn recommends outsourcing the bulk of the activities currently performed by an organization that are not contributing to what is or could be a core competence. He advises companies to examine everything they are doing to see what could be done better by an external firm. First, he suggests we consider each "nonproduction" activity within the organization as a service that could be either produced internally or bought externally. Next the organization should ask if it is or could be the best in the world at delivering that service. Then the organization should choose to perform only those services in which it can be the best in the world, focusing particularly on those in which being best matters the most (the core competencies). Everything else, Quinn believes, should be outsourced to firms that can do the tasks better or more cost-effectively.

Quinn predicts that, if done honestly, this process will result in massive outsourcing because "virtually all staff and value chain activities are activities that an outside entity—by concentrating specialists and technologies in the area—can perform better than all but a few companies for whom that activity is but one of many."[4]

The Dangers of Outsourcing

IBM discovered the strategic dangers of outsourcing when it hired Microsoft to develop the operating system and Intel to produce the central processing unit (CPU) chip for its new personal computer. Here is what happened:

In 1980, Frank Cary, IBM's chairman, could no longer contain his belief that personal computing was essential to IBM's future. He gave Bill Lowe one year and his strong personal support to produce a personal computer for IBM. Within a few months Lowe was transferred, and the job fell to Don Estridge, who gathered a team of productive mavericks from all over IBM in Boca Raton, Florida, far from headquarters.

To design, build, and launch a new computer in one year, the team had to break a lot of rules—including the one that said everything significant had to be done internally. IBM's own plants and services, including even the sacrosanct quality control, were treated as if they were outside vendors. The inside functions could bid, but the team was free to accept the offer with the best mix of timing, cost, and quality. IBM's bureaucratically bound internal suppliers could not meet the deadlines. More entrepreneurial competitors could, and

IBM hired Microsoft and Intel, among others, to produce key components for the new personal computer. The IBM PC was built almost entirely with parts from outside suppliers.

The initial success of this outsourcing strategy was stupendous. The PC came to market on time in the fall of 1981. In its first four months, sales were $40 million. In the third full year of business, revenues were $4 billion. The PC intraprise had grown faster than any entrepreneurial start-up company in history.

In 1984, the IBM PC was a perfect illustration of how effective outsourcing can use the virtues of free markets to cut through bureaucracy. By the end of the decade, however, the story was an equally powerful example of the dangers of excessive outsourcing. By then IBM had discovered that the core competencies they had counted on, such as computer systems design, systems integration, and marketing muscle, gave IBM surprisingly little clout in the PC business. Microsoft, with the operating system, and Intel, with the CPU, held the cards, and both were selling their wares to the clone makers.

While IBM, without a reliable proprietary advantage, struggles against clone makers, Intel and Microsoft are in the catbird seat. Microsoft, which had $24 million in sales in 1982, just after the IBM PC came to market with Microsoft's operating system, made a profit of $700 million in 1992.[5] Intel made $1.1 billion. Intel and Microsoft's combined market value according to *Fortune* had risen to $48 billion, surpassing IBM's market value, $30 billion.[6]

If IBM had supplied the operating system and CPU chip for the IBM PC, they would not be battered by clones today; they would be profitably supplying the clone makers with proprietary chips and software. When the PC was born, IBM had world-class capabilities in both operating systems and the design and manufacture of chips. They turned outside for strategically critical components, not because they lacked the capabilities to produce them, but because those capabilities were tied up by bureaucratic limitations.

When Louis V. Gerstner, Jr., was brought in to save IBM he observed, "I have never seen a company that is so introspective, caught up in its own underwear, so preoccupied with internal processes.... People in this company tell me it's easier doing business with people outside the company than inside. I would call that an indictment."[7] Gerstner is right that this is an indictment but not so much of IBM as of all bureaucracies. We have heard the same thing over and over again from our clients in many different organizations. In general, what middle managers say is,

> It is much harder for us to do business with another division of our own company than to deal with an outsider. Vendors have to do what we want or we find someone else. With our own divisions, if we ask for something that they don't want to provide, we end up in a political battle that escalates to the highest levels and threatens all of our careers. It is easier just to put up with mediocrity, or go to the trouble of setting up relations with an outsider.[8]

Quinn and others, like Charles Handy and Tom Peters, spotted the trend to outsourcing in its early stages and are right in seeing huge potential. No organization can be the best at everything. But at the same time no organization can afford not to use its talents by letting bureaucratic barriers get in the way.

Though we believe outsourcing can be extremely valuable, we are concerned that part of the drive toward outsourcing comes from the low levels of efficiency, service, and innovation provided by internal functions and staff groups in bureaucracies. There is a risk that too much outsourcing can weaken the long-range core competencies of an organization. Often we need to find a way to do things effectively inside, not just give up on doing them.

One of the major advantages of outsourcing is that it takes functions out from under the chain of command and puts them into the dynamic networks of free enterprise. This advantage can be achieved inside the organization by opening up the internal system to free intraprise. Liberated internal suppliers can often provide greater value than their external competitors, because they have freer access to all the knowledge and technology throughout the organization. An organization with effective internal sources of supply has many more strategic options than those possessed by bureaucracies that have been forced to turn outside by the inefficiency of their internal monopolies.

Core Competence

In their 1990 *Harvard Business Review* article "The Core Competence of the Corporation," C. K. Prahalad and Gary Hamel think in terms of the capabilities a company has or can build that lead to competitive advantage. They call a broadly useful capability like miniaturization for Sony or small motors and transmissions for Honda a "core competence" and suggest that the strategy of the company focus on no more than five or six of these competencies.[9]

Charles Handy, in *The Age of Unreason,* jokingly refers to one reorganization scenario that suggested outsourcing everything except the CEO and his car phone.[10] For a while it looked as if Drexel Burnham Lambert had a one-man core competence in Michael Milken.

But most core competencies are not in the minds of a few brilliant people. According to Prahalad and Hamel, a core competence appropriate to a large organization is not just one skill but the blending of many skills and thus the work of many people and many parts of the organization. "A core competence should be difficult for competitors to imitate. And it *will* be difficult to imitate if it is a complex harmonization of individual technologies and production skills. A rival might acquire some of the technologies that comprise the core competence, but it will find it more difficult to duplicate the more or less comprehensive pattern of internal coordination and learning."[11]

Given that a core competence comes from harmonizing a complex array of developing technologies and production skills, the ability of the organization to work together across boundaries is critical. Outsourcing cannot solve this problem, because the essence of a core competence is that it is what the organization itself possesses. It is the reason others with competencies of their own continue to join in partnerships. But the ability to work across boundaries is bureaucracy's core weakness.

According to Prahalad and Hamel, one characteristic of a core competence is that it can be applied across many different markets. Years ago 3M hit upon a core competence and a way to manage it. Richard P. Carleton, longtime 3M technical leader, put it this way: "If you get an idea and the idea is basically new, if you can coat it on 3M equipment in an efficient way to meet a demonstrable need, then you've probably got something worthwhile."[12]

The company was committed to a core competence and an intrapreneurial way of exploiting it across many different markets. An intrapreneur whose idea aligned with the core competence of applying coatings and adhesives had a good chance of seeing his or her project blessed even if it took the company into new products and new markets. The result was that 3M perfected a set of skills that it applied over and over again in innovative ways. Though no 3M business was huge, the sum of all businesses using the same core competence became large indeed.

The Components of Competence

A broad organizational competence, as we have seen, is created by developing and integrating smaller competencies. A critical fact, pointed out by Professor Quinn is that most activities consist of delivering a service, even in a manufacturing firm.[13] The more we break down processes into their component parts, the more it becomes obvious that all or nearly all human activities that add value can be seen as services. Quinn points out that most of the value added in manufacturing comes from services such as accounting, research, promotion, logistics, design, sales, and distribution. Even on the shop floor, where people maintain machinery, weld parts, and test circuits, they are performing tasks that on the outside are sold as services.

Quinn teaches that once an organization sees its activities as services, the ones not part of a core competence can be turned over to the logic of the marketplace to find the best and most cost-effective way to get them accomplished.[14] This logic unlocks a powerful tool not only for getting better cost-effectiveness in nonstrategic tasks, but also for more effectively pursuing the components of core competencies and their integration.

All of the strategists talking about core competencies discuss the importance of developing best-in-the-world competencies, each of which supports a number of business units. Yet these centralized strategies have the potential of increasing the weight of bureaucracy and decreasing the power of people close to the action to make decisions based on the opportunities they see. This creates a genuine dilemma: how to create strategies for core competencies that cross several business units without returning to a system of centralized planning and control. One way out of this dilemma is to "hollow out" the business units by moving many of the components of core competence into intraprises that serve several "front-line" business units.

If for nearly every component capability of a core competence there are several intraprises able to deliver it, those intraprises will be in competition to raise the standards of excellence. The units will continually seek internal partners with other capabilities so they may win business together from the many strategic business units who apply that core competence to a set of products or a set of customers.

The core competencies themselves will be embodied not in bureaucratically controlled monopoly suppliers to the business units or bureaucratic functions within the business units, but in service units dedicated to making the core competencies produce marketplace results for their customers. The organization supplying a competence to a front-line business unit will be a flexible network made up mostly of small teams with a very tight focus and the determination to be the best.

Steering Toward Core Competencies

Let's say that "the center" of the organization has identified a strategic core competence to develop. Given the freedom inherent in the free intraprise system of organizing productive networks, how can the center influence the system to focus on producing more of that capability?

Several ways of doing this are possible without destroying the greatest strength of free intraprise, its ability to self-organize:

Forbid or tax the outsourcing of services or components that embody the core competence.

Subsidize those intraprises that deliver the core competence.

Provide low-cost loans and start-up capital to intraprises in the core competence area.

Break up internal monopolies in areas of core competence so internal competition keeps each component skill honed.

Encourage business units to allow groups of their employees with critical skills to sell those skills to other business units.

✸ THE INTELLIGENCE OF MARKET SYSTEMS

Free enterprise, free intraprise, outsourcing, and insourcing all share a common strength: to make business decisions they rely on the detailed local intelligence of market systems rather than the blunt centralized intelligence of bureaucratic systems. The marketplace tests ideas of great complexity and, with great efficiency of thought, finds good answers. Unlike a marketplace, bureaucratic systems of allocation not only fail to apply detailed intelligence to decisions about things that are small in relation to the organization as a whole, but their process of thinking about the things they do address is inefficient.

This characteristic became particularly clear during a visit to the Soviet Union when we saw how the Soviet ministries were struggling to make good decisions for the whole Soviet economy. One issue we learned about centered on whether it made sense to use titanium to make the runners for children's sleds. Many things had to be considered. In 1990 there were no competitively determined prices for titanium in the Soviet economy. In order to know its value, the administrator in Moscow had to know how titanium was produced and what went into each step, all the way back to the mine. Then, to make a rational decision about whether sled runners should get the available titanium, the administrator at the center had to compare the use of titanium in sled runners to all other possible uses and weigh the value of titanium in each other use. Because doing this analysis in detail is impossible, crazy decisions such as building ordinary sled runners and milking equipment out of titanium were common.[15]

In a free market economy these decisions are both decentralized and simplified. When the buyer in a free market decides whether or not to use titanium, the price summarizes the necessary information about what it costs to make and what its value is in all the other competing uses. Looking at that one price, the manufacturer of sleds would decide whether to use titanium or not. Though our bureaucracies know the prices of commodities, we often see very odd allocations of bureaucratically provided services: Lawyers are used for tasks clerks could perform. Tasks are performed for reasons no one can remember.

Insourcing, like outsourcing, takes decisions a bureaucracy would bungle and turns them over to the cutting intelligence of marketplace choice. The price tells buyers and sellers nearly all they need to know about various suppliers' costs or the value their customers currently place on their products and services. This precise feedback motivates both customers and suppliers to act on the highly condensed information about whole-system supply and demand contained in a free market price. They are motivated to act in ways that are generally in the direction of the best interests of the overall efficiency of the system. If titanium were worth more in some other use, buyers would bid up the price until the highest-value users got what they needed. If the costs of producing titanium were much lower than the price buyers were willing to pay, titanium producers would gear up to supply more.

Insourcing and outsourcing alike have both the strengths and the weaknesses of free markets. They fail by themselves to make good decisions about the environment, the distribution of income, the human spirit, or what we leave to future generations, but despite these limitations (which must be addressed by other institutions), what they do is remarkable. They take the great complexity of the world we live in and the tasks organizations understand and create a framework to address them with detailed and decentralized intelligence. In this, insourcing and outsourcing are equal, and both are necessary to organizational intelligence; neither alone is enough to ensure that all aspects of community survival are addressed.

Assembling Complex Projects

The bigger and more complex a project, the greater the probability that it is the work of a network of vendors coordinated by one or more systems integrators. Subcontracting is superior to bureaucracy for handling complex tasks because, done well, subcontracting provides a more efficient way to break up complex tasks into clear commitments and responsibilities. Because subcontractors have long-term reputations, and because the deliverables, timing, and prices are subject to negotiated contracts, larger projects can be chunked into pieces and still fit together without exceeding the human mind's capacity to encompass what it needs to know about the whole.

The project leader purchasing most inputs from known vendors faces less politics and can afford to know less about the subcontractor's business than a boss need know about a subunit she supervises. If the project manager trusts the subcontractor, all she need comprehend is the deliverable, the quality, the delivery date, the reliability, and the price—not how the product or service is being produced. The project manager is free to address those few coordination and planning issues that must come together at the center of the project.

The subcontractors are free to converse and make sure they integrate what they are doing.

The subcontractor has more freedom than an employee or a bureaucratic work unit to choose how to create the deliverable and exert greater efforts to deliver it to specification and on time. In a bureaucracy the senior manager often spends time listening to excuses and adjudicating disputes about whose fault it was. Subcontractors are more likely to stay up late to make sure there are no failures and thus nothing to dispute. Integration by a network of freely chosen subcontractors has proved to be inherently faster, more accurate, and capable of carrying more useful information than the disciplines of hierarchy.

By outsourcing, firms move an area of that value-creation process from bureaucratic control to marketplace control, thereby increasing the intelligence of their system. This same advantage can also be achieved internally by introducing internal choice and thus free intraprise insourcing.

Free intraprise insourcing works because it replaces hierarchical coordination with the disciplines of the market. Almost all the transactions are voluntary choices among alternatives, and are conducted within the relative equality of a customer-vendor relationship. This changes the relative status of the players. All the independent firms making up a network are formal equals, which leads to more openness and truth.

In the moonshot described in Chapter 5, "Consolidated Hydraulics" could admit it had a problem and needed to hold up the launch: The company's status was high enough that its people could afford to be honest. Consolidated was not one individual in a hierarchy but a whole organization with a lengthy history of success to back it up and a highly valuable reputation for honesty to maintain. Not so for its Russian counterparts, who were individuals in a bureaucracy and thus more vulnerable. The truly submissive will say whatever the boss wants to hear. The dominance and submission that form the backbone of the bureaucratic system bring out fear, cunning politics, feigned stupidity, and irresponsibility. The free market, especially in a world in which buyer and seller know they will meet again, brings out responsibility and more adult behavior.

✳ CHOOSING BETWEEN OUTSOURCING AND INSOURCING

To move beyond bureaucracy, large organizations will generally use a combination of insourcing and outsourcing. Sometimes the decision of which option to use will be obvious: One clearly provides better quality or price. In other cases the organization may wish to favor one or the other for long-term strategic reasons not fully reflected in the current marketplace offerings and prices.

Economies of Scale Versus Economies of Intimacy, Integration, and Scope

Apple and Compaq cannot afford to go into the CPU chip manufacturing business, so they leave CPU design and manufacturing to companies such as Motorola and Intel that provide the same chips to many different computer manufacturers. When a size and scale of operations larger than an internally focused intraprise could reasonably attain is required for cost-effective operations, outsourcing is almost inevitable.

Sometimes information technology enters an area where large size has been a great advantage and gives the small organization the tools to compete effectively. Tasks that not long ago required a mainframe, such as financial analysis or searching large databases, can now be done with a personal computer. External vendors of legal databases such as Lexis and Nexis provide even the smallest law intraprise with research resources comparable to those of a large external law firm.

■ COMPARATIVE ADVANTAGES OF OUTSOURCING AND INSOURCING

Outsourcing	Insourcing
Economies of scale	Economies of intimacy, integration, and scope
Lower fixed costs	Intraprise profits
Outside knowledge brought in	Trade secrets kept inside
Easy-to-shed capacity	Development of a loyal and flexible competence
Focus on core competencies	Capacity for growing new competencies

Changing technology is also creating situations of overwhelming advantage to the larger provider. For products such as standard software packages, the development cost is so high and the marginal cost of an additional unit so low that only a few large competitors can survive. Intraprises offering software development to internal customers will generally survive only if they provide powerful company-specific benefits such as the ability to customize with knowledge of how the company does business or a greater ability to keep trade secrets.

Lower Fixed Costs Versus Intraprise Profits

When activities are outsourced, fixed overhead is permanently eliminated. If those services were inefficient or unable to change with the times, this helps the organization to cut costs. On the other hand, the external suppliers are making a profit that could be made by an equally effective internal intraprise. If an internal intraprise can do the job as efficiently and well as a profitable external intraprise, insourcing that activity improves the bottom line.

In many endeavors, economies of scale are not as important as knowing and caring about customers. This is particularly true of many services, ranging from software customization to clerical support.

As outside consultants, we spend time getting to know things an internal consulting intraprise would already know. Given that they are disciplined by a free internal market, internal service providers have a substantial advantage in "economies of scope," meaning they can apply the same knowledge of the company to many different business units. Whereas outsiders can focus on a narrower specialty to achieve efficiency, internal vendors can apply their knowledge of the company's procedures, technologies, customers, and culture again and again over a broader range of projects. As they move from customer to customer internally, they also provide an integrating function by connecting different parts of the company that should work together.

Outside Knowledge Brought In Versus Trade Secrets Kept Inside

External vendors have an inherent advantage in experiencing a wider variety of clients and thus potentially being more up-to-date on the state of the art in the outside world. Intraprises partially overcome this disadvantage in worldly experience through "gatekeepers" who keep active contacts in the outside world through memberships in associations, external meetings, and judicious use of their own external subcontractors and external coaches.[16]

Outside vendors who also work with competitors not only bring information in, they also take it out. If they help one company design a state-of-the-art plant, they take what they have learned to their next job, which may be for a competitor. This creates an interesting dilemma for outsiders. If they never use what they learned at one company to benefit another, they may have little experience available to sell. On the other hand, if they teach what they learn in one company to others, trade secrets are rapidly lost.

An internal intraprise has an easier time with trade secrets. They are generally free to apply everything they have learned on one internal job to the next because it is all within the same company.

In areas where an organization is behind its competitors or wants to release what it knows, external vendors are often the best choice. When an organization has a secret competitive advantage, great care must be taken in revealing it to outsiders. Insourcing is prudent for all core competencies and all activities that require knowing a broadly useful trade secret.

Easy-to-Shed Capacity Versus Developing Loyal and Flexible Competence

When it is time to shed capacity, it is far easier to cut back use of an external vendor than to lay off employees. For this reason many companies prefer outsourcing when doing something new that may not be continued or when handling temporary peaks in work.

In the pressure to get drugs to market faster, most pharmaceutical firms use external contract research firms to perform some of the research required by the Federal Drug Administration. For example, Miles, Inc., spends 20–25 percent of its clinical research budget on contract labs. "We don't want to staff up for peak demands," says Lawrence Posner, senior vice president for medical affairs. With total clinical research on new drugs running about $8 billion a year, the contract clinical research portion accounts for about $1 billion in annual sales and is growing at 15 percent a year.[17]

In the case of contract research, important secrets about upcoming new drugs are exposed to contractors, but the danger of their leaking to competitors is small. Contract research firms are not in the business of providing advice on new product strategy. Because their services are limited to testing drugs and producing paperwork for the FDA, their most important learning is about how to do tests and how to write reports. They can apply that learning to the next client without releasing any confidential information about their clients' product strategies.

Under other circumstances, however, the issue of loyalty may be critical. In *The Prince* Machiavelli compared different methods of conducting war.[18] He considered three types of army, one made up of your own people, which he called native troops, one made up of mercenaries, and one made up of a composite of the two. History, he observed, supported the use of native troops whenever possible. Native troops are more loyal; it may be dangerous to rely on mercenaries.

IBM, as we saw earlier, discovered the dangers of "using mercenaries" when Intel and Microsoft grabbed the richest segment of the personal computer market they were hired to help launch. Schwinn discovered the dangers of contracting out manufacturing and relying on distribution and brand name when Giant Manufacturing of Taiwan, which supplied frames to Schwinn, used the manufacturing capacity, knowledge, and reputation acquired working for Schwinn to enter the U.S. market with their own line of bicycles.[19]

An internal intraprise is less likely to betray its internal customers. Furthermore, if one intraprise grows at the expense of another, the consequences for the whole organization are far less serious.

In choosing what to outsource and what to insource, organizations need to consider that they must retain a robust set of internal competencies that will put them in position to seize new opportunities and weather changes. Organizations that put all their eggs in one basket by relying on just a few core competencies and outsourcing everything else can afford no mistakes or unexpected changes in the competencies that create market dominance.

Focus on Core Competencies Versus Capacity for Growing New Competencies

Outsourcing permits companies to do what it takes to be the best in a comparatively limited range of key endeavors. The opportunities for confusion are minimized because the organization's intelligence can be focused on a set of core competencies and not be distracted by less critical activities. But there are risks in such specialization.

According to the theory of core competencies, strategists and other leaders identify what internal capabilities could provide a sustainable strategic advantage. The ones they choose become the core competencies of the organization, and everything else is a candidate for outsourcing. This methodology depends on being able to identify years in advance which competencies will provide strategic control of key markets and which will be commodities. Taking the time to review old strategy documents reveals the difficulty of this task. In one such review, our client found a strong negative correlation between the new businesses that were declared strategic and worthy of extra investment in a strategic review done fifteen years earlier and those that had in fact become important successes. Though the big losers had generally been blessed by the strategic review, most of the eventual big winners had survived official disapproval and limited funding in their early stages.

Strategy is based on best guesses, so the best strategies are robust, meaning that they will work out pretty well in a wide variety of potential futures. In rapidly changing businesses with significant innovation, the keys to success keep changing. Technologies of secondary importance suddenly move to center stage. Outsourcing can be dangerous if things do not turn out exactly as foreseen.

For larger firms, it is far safer to eliminate the effects of bureaucracy within the firm so internal suppliers of components and services can be genuinely competitive with outsiders. In the early 1980s when the PC was being developed, IBM had world-class operating system people and was the largest chip manufacturer in the world. But these departments could not provide world-class service to the intrapreneurial personal computer team because they were bureaucratically organized. If IBM had had quick moving, cost-effective intrapreneurial suppliers of operating systems and CPU chips in 1980, they would own the PC market today and be worrying about antitrust charges rather than profitability and market share.

With changes coming ever faster, no strategist can be smart enough to predict exactly where the future lies. Successfully dealing with change depends on constant experiment and exploration. In a free intraprise organization, different intraprises explore and experiment with developing many different capabilities. Although management at the center of the organization may decide to assist the development of what they see as strategic competencies, they need not decide if the intraprises can afford to develop competence in areas they have not designated. That can be left to the working of the free intraprise system, which will give significant resources only to those who provide value.

Having many intraprises, an intelligent organization can cost-effectively focus on, and keep up in, more areas of competence than any bureaucracy could manage effectively. Even if the planners guess wrong, intraprises acting in their own interests will develop strategies for developing competence in emerging technologies and for gaining access to emerging markets. They will do this at a reasonable cost or not at all. Though internal providers in a bureaucratic organization may hold other parts of the organization hostage to their experiments, internally focused intraprises in an intelligent organization cannot do so.

Humane Reasons for Insourcing

What should companies do if they discover that 55 percent of their employees are performing service tasks in a manner or at a cost that is substantially inferior to a best-in-the-world standard? Many mature bureaucracies are discovering themselves in predicaments like this. Outsourcing is easy for a Nike or an Apple Computer because they outsourced nearly everything from the start. It is more difficult for a company that would have to lay off 55 percent of its workforce.

Given the effect of massive downsizings on morale, not to mention the pervasive social consequences of major job loss, the most humane solution is to try to find a way to bring internal service providers up to par with the external competition before allowing wholesale outsourcing. There is no way to achieve excellence in so many areas if they are managed and rewarded bureaucratically. Their chances of becoming world class are much better if they have experience as intraprises competing with other internal vendors first.

✳ THE TRANSFORMATION OF A BELEAGUERED LAW DEPARTMENT

The law department had come to represent some of the worst traits of bureaucracy.[20] Users from the operating departments saw Law as complacent, slow, expensive, and risk-averse. Users were given no choice as to which lawyers to use. Because they paid a fixed allocated cost regardless of how much legal service they used, they made requests for legal assistance just to "cover their asses" whenever there was even a remote chance that trouble might arise later. They had no concern about cost and no real idea of what the services they used cost the company. As a result, the volume of requests far exceeded the supply of lawyers. There were lengthy queues and delays, providing a classic example of what happens when those who specify the work and those who pay for it are different.

Knowing from experience that they could never catch up with the excessive demand, the lawyers became inured to their clients' cries of urgency and settled into a comfortable pace. Rather than focusing on reducing the requests for service to the truly significant or increasing the system's efficiency and throughput, they responded to pressure for faster turnaround with rules and procedures that isolated them from the "emotional" appeals of their clients.

When critically urgent issues failed to get attention, the clients got so upset they appealed to the senior management to intervene and get the law department to give their projects higher priority. Senior management found themselves spending time lobbying the legal department to give priority to their people's urgent issues. As more of the legal traffic was expedited by intervention from above, routine traffic became slower, and expedited traffic became routine. The department was in a continuing state of emergency and costly delays used up large amounts of management time.

Benchmarking

When Maurice Le Clerc became head of the law department, he vowed to provide better service; he was determined they would no longer be the butt of company jokes. Most of his staff and even his clients accepted the situation as inevitable, but his goal was to build a law department able to compete with the best outside firms in service, cost, and quality of work.

He knew that getting the department ready to compete would take years. In many cases their customers went to outside firms even though they had to pay for these services and the department's services were available to them at no incremental cost. Maurice was determined to build a department that could compete on an equal footing and win. Only then would they get respect.

His first effort was to benchmark the legal department against several good private law firms. The private law firms cost a bit more per hour, but in general appeared to be about 30 percent more efficient. More important to many clients, they were customer-focused and timely. Though the benchmarking study created a pressure for change, even becoming 30 percent more efficient would do little to reduce the backlogs. Many in the law department saw the backlog as proof that they were understaffed, but in a time of downsizing increasing the size of the department was out of the question. Maurice saw the problem differently. He recognized that the people who were making requests for service were totally insulated from the costs. The first step was to make them aware of what internal legal services cost.

Pricing

The resistance in the company to making customers pay out of their own budgets for the internal legal services they were using was too strong for a frontal attack. As a first step Maurice settled for sending out dummy bills so at least users knew what their requests were costing. Even this small step toward eventual free intraprise generated shock waves. People had no idea their requests were costing so much. "Your overheads are outrageous," they complained. "Your people are too slow." Several lawyers in the department were terrified by the strength of the reaction. "If we show them our costs and they don't like them, they will insist on being able to spend the money on outside firms, and many of us may soon be looking for work." Maurice reassured them that by the time they had to compete in level competition with the outside firms the department would be ready.

Maurice had the ear of the chairman, who was very interested in the experiment, so after six months of dummy billing they took the next step. In the next budget cycle, 80 percent of the law department's former budget went to the customer departments according to their historical usage patterns. They could now use this money to buy the legal services they wanted. The remaining 20 percent was allocated to serving the needs of corporate headquarters.

Maurice knew the department was not yet ready to compete with outside firms, so he kept in place the procedures that made it difficult to use outside firms. The biggest difference was that the clients now asked for estimates before submitting requests for service. Because service now came out of their department's budget, many users had to get approval from their bosses to buy legal services. There was far more discussion of what was needed and how much it would cost before work began.

Not surprisingly, many things that had been routine before turned out to be unnecessary. Trivial repetitive tasks were turned over to clerks with boilerplate contracts. "Cover your ass" requests for opinions declined 70 percent. The result was to bring the backlog down from about eight weeks on many simple transactions to less than two. Lawyers began to appreciate delivering value for the dollar as clients prioritized their requests. But although the worst backlogs and gross misallocation of legal time were largely handled by charging for the service, complaints continued to pour in — clients still felt the service was not competitive with the outside. Another benchmarking study backed them up.

Competition

Maurice knew that if he allowed operating departments to use outside law firms, the result would be wholesale defections by clients to outside firms. This would cost many of his friends their jobs, lead to unacceptable overstaffing, or both. Even if he ignored the human implications, the outplacement costs alone were unforgivable. Taking the department into battle with outside firms before it was ready would not achieve his objective of building "a world-class law department within the company that can stand up to the best outside competition and win." On a more private note, it would probably put his performance so seriously in question that he would not be around to finish the experiment. Instead of giving clients the freedom to outsource legal services before the inside services were competitive, he decided on a gentler form of competition — a free intraprise solution.

Maurice divided the law department arbitrarily into three units, each of which had the right to bid for any client business it wished. At first people argued that three competing internal "law firms" would require additional staff. This turned out not to be true.

"Implicitly," Maurice argued, "you are claiming monopoly is more efficient than competition because competition requires redundancy. Our common experience does not bear out this belief. Competition drives out the fat in the system far more efficiently than bureaucracy."

"But you will have to have three of every specialty," they cried. "I don't see why," said Maurice. "Private law firms specialize. If there isn't enough work in a specialty to support two specialists, one will emerge as the best, and market forces will drive the others into new fields where there is work. On the other hand, it may turn out that in many cases we end up with lawyers with slightly broader specialties and practices. This corporation was able to field a relatively effective law department when it was only a third of its present size, and so the corporation can probably field several law groups without disastrous loss in the economies of scale."

The immediate effect of Maurice's free intraprise "big bang" was that almost overnight most of the lawyers became customer-focused. At first there was surprisingly little change in who worked with whom. The clients had personal relationships with lawyers and continued to work with them. Backlogs continued, and nearly all the lawyers had work.

As time passed the forces for adjustment increased. Customer focus and the presence of choice drove the system toward greater efficiency and less unnecessary work. Increasingly, some lawyers found themselves with unbillable time. Their plight was made more annoying by the fact that others were turning work away. Management spent much of its time counseling the less popular lawyers. The Client Relationship Skills Course suddenly became very popular, but among a significant minority deep dissatisfaction with the new system remained. One veteran summed it up, "If I had wanted the stress of competition, I would have taken a job in a private firm and earned a fat living as a partner. I came here for security and a comfortable pace."

Several of the less busy lawyers then began a whispering campaign. They approached the controller saying that customer-focused law departments were inherently dangerous and wrong. "To be sure," they argued, "there will be a beneficial shift away from the excessively risk-averse attitudes of the past. We have learned that we were spending too great a part of our energies considering all the reasons why a project might create exposure to liability. We needed to focus more energy on finding ways to do new things with a minimum of legal exposure. Now that we have learned these lessons, we can fix them in the context of the old system. It is enough to put factors like 'creativity in finding ways to get what the business needs done with an acceptable level of risk' into our performance appraisals. We don't need customer choice."

Phil Calamari, one of the most effective "conservative wing" lawyers, spoke out at the monthly headquarters legal staff meeting. "We don't need free intraprise to give us courage, we have courage. But that courage must not blind us to a real danger, the danger that some of us, driven by the urge to increase our billings, will bend over too far to help clients pursue ideas that are inherently full of legal risk. In this new free choice system the corporation is increasingly at risk."

News of the speech spread like wildfire. A day later the chairman came to Maurice, worried. "One of the major purposes of the law department is to keep me out of jail," he said. "Are you sure we have this thing under control?"

Maurice told the chairman that he was pretty comfortable with the current level of risk, but he could not rule out the possibility that in time, as habits changed, there might be a few excessively aggressive lawyers who put client satisfaction ahead of the security of the corporation. "We still have plenty of time before they begin breaking through what has been a strongly conservative legal culture," he said, "but I will get right to work designing a system that will prevent problems from arising later."

Maurice brought together a team of both lawyers and clients and asked Phyllis Warych, an inside facilitator from the quality department, to lead the group in a creative session with the objective of "finding ways to maintain the benefits of free intraprise without subjecting lawyers to the temptation to put the corporation at undue risk."

The session hit pay dirt by using an analogy process. Phyllis asked the group to consider what keeps accounting firms in line. "For example," she said, "the client has obsolete inventory carried on the books at full value. What force fields in our national system of enterprise encourage the accountant to insist on writing down the value of the inventory rather than continuing to carry an overvalued asset?"

Hands shot up. "Professional pride." "Professional associations." "The big accounting firms are kept in line by the SEC." "No, it's the IRS." "Who supervises them depends on whether it's a small firm trying to hide profits or a public one trying to fake them." The ideas poured out.

"In what ways could we use something like the relationship of accountants and regulators to control the risks hungry lawyers might expose us to?" Phyllis asked. Fears of ugly bureaucracies sprung up like dandelions in a spring lawn, but Phyllis kept asking for positive building even on negative ideas.

Gradually the idea popped up for an oversight body to certify each of the independent "law firms." In the end they created a tiny corporate legal inspection team with the power to discipline lawyers who failed to look after the safety of the corporation and its officers. Not surprisingly, the inspection teams found that old habits die hard; in the bureaucratic system there had been little pressure to help clients get results and great pressure for risk avoidance. Even in a free intraprise situation, most of the lawyers were still overcautious.

Opening the System

To encourage more effective internal competition and innovation, Maurice encouraged lawyers to "quit" the three major "law firms" he had created and form smaller "law firms" of their own. A number of smaller specialty groups formed, along with general practitioners who handled all of a business unit's legal problems and used the specialist firms as resources. Successful law intraprises were allowed to raise their billing rates and then their salaries to absorb some of their "profits." The lawyers in the less successful intraprises lowered their billing rates (and then worked longer hours or took lower pay to make ends meet). The less successful lawyers also sought employment with one of the growing legal intraprises that had excess work. The result was often a reshuffling of status. Older lawyers without clients found themselves at the bottom of the intraprises they joined to get work, while younger lawyers with excess business found themselves in positions of power.

After one year of internal competition, it became apparent that a game of musical chairs was beginning. The demand for legal services had dropped to the point where the department appeared to be 20-percent overstaffed, and it was increasingly clear who the winners and the losers would be. Those who could not maintain their billings to cover compensation and overhead were to be let go after accumulating a certain deficit, which depended on their years of service. But the cruelty of the inevitable musical chairs that was developing worried Maurice. It certainly did not encourage Maurice to open the system to more competition from the outside, so he decided to try the reverse, let lawyers market their services externally.

The results were mixed. Several lawyers became very good at selling their services outside, and some of the best were so encouraged by this that they left to join private law firms where they were paid better for doing the same work. Some specialists were able to cover a portion of slack time and still deal very effectively with their specialty internally when needed. The big successes were in a couple of strong specialty areas such as leases and rights-of-way, where the company name provided a marketing advantage. In these areas the company was legitimately stronger than outside competition. But in the end, Maurice had to let 10 percent of the old department go through an early retirement program.

After two years, the system was benchmarked again against the outside and declared ready in over half of the specialties to face outside competition. At this point Maurice opened the system to outside competition, giving the clients the right to go outside if they preferred. To cushion the transition he insisted on a 15-percent overhead charge on all outside contracts. This was positioned as an inspection fee to make sure the outsiders did not succumb to excess client pleasing, but it was in fact primarily thought of as a tariff to encourage continued use of inside resources whenever the decision was a close one.

✳ CREATING NETWORKS OF SUBCONTRACTORS INTERNALLY

Free intraprise is a system for bringing the discipline of marketplace choice into the relationships between some of the internal parts of a corporation or agency. It works only if there are enough options to choose among. Free intraprise differs from most traditional "profit center" systems, which meet with mixed results. In free intraprise, customers have choices between alternative vendors inside and sometimes also outside the company. In most failed profit center systems, the "customers" did not have choice, and so there was no free market to provide honest feedback on performance. The "profit center" system assigned arbitrary transfer prices to all transactions, then calculated how well each group was doing. Internal suppliers could infuriate their internal customers with slow delivery or inflexibility and improve their profit-center bottom line at the expense of the corporation as a whole. Their captive internal customers had little recourse but to complain. When the customers have choices, even just choices among internal vendors, those selfish behaviors soon cease.

To create an effective free intraprise system, we must make sure internal customers have free choice among alternatives and that an honest system empowers intrapreneurs to keep and spend, without bureaucratic interference, what they earn for the purposes of the intraprise.

Insourcing with choice (which is to say, free intraprise for internal suppliers) provides many of the benefits of outsourcing plus several of its own:

♦ More potential profit centers are retained within the company.

♦ Sufficient entrepreneurial spirit is left inside the firm to allow it to interface effectively with entrepreneurial firms outside.

♦ Trade secrets are kept in-house.

♦ Core competencies are managed with entrepreneurial energy.

♦ Useful secondary competencies are maintained that might later become significant sources of opportunity, competitive advantage, and profit.

♦ Fewer people need to be fired in order to set the system up.

10

Liberated Teams

If you really believe in quality, when you cut through everything, it's empowering your people, and it's empowering your people that leads to teams.

JAIME HOUGHTON, CEO CORNING

IT IS RUMORED in football circles that the offensive line of the New York Jets became tired of hearing Joe Namath tell the press about how *he* had won games with spectacular plays. So for a few plays the offensive line slacked off and let a number of linebackers and defensive linemen through. Suddenly Joe was no longer a hero, he was lying on the ground taking losses. By himself he could not do anything. After that, "Broadway" Joe never forgot that football is a team effort and that every success belongs to the whole team.

By teams we mean small or medium-sized groups of people who work closely together to produce a common product. Teams differ from a work group that meets to divide up the work but then does the work individually; real teams create things and learn together.

The growing prevalence of teams with autonomy to manage their area of work is the beginning of the conversion of bureaucracies to free intraprise networks. To function as whole businesses, intraprises may include a number of teams. Each of the intraprise teams will work with other teams inside and outside the organization. They may be further integrated by having overlapping memberships, as well as sharing wider company goals and rewards.

The autonomy required for high-performance teams is generally not sustainable in a bureaucracy. Only a system in which teams are responsible for their own production can permanently support the widespread use of autonomous teams. We believe a system of free intraprise provides the best basis yet found for a stable confederation of high-performance teams.

In the conversion to postbureaucratic organizations, teams form the basic unit of empowerment, small enough for efficient high involvement and large enough for the collective strength and the synergy generated by diverse talents. Within teams people can take wide responsibility for one another, for the organization, and for the quality of their products and services. Behind the success of such innovations as total quality, project management, high-performance work teams, time-based competition, reengineering, intrapreneurship, and a host of others is a shift in the location of power and decision making from individuals in bureaucratic management functions to more independent teams, both formal and informal.

These changes have been gradually unraveling bureaucracies. The power invested in the chain of command is challenged when employees make decisions in cross-disciplinary teams. The belief in the efficiency of specialization is undermined when multiskilling makes job assignments flexible. With good teamwork, the focus shifts from individual performance and individual careers to the success of the team as a whole. Rather than dealing with one another from their formal roles, employees in teams deal with one another as fellow humans sharing a common interest in exceeding customers' expectations.

✳ THE ROLE OF TEAMS

Teams have been successful in accomplishing objectives that range from giving suggestions for work improvement to running an area of work as an independent business. The many team-based innovations in ways to improve the quality and quantity of work in large organizations that have gained popularity in the last decades demonstrate "the inherent good sense of employee involvement—of just about any kind."[1] According to a 1987 study by Ed Lawler and others of the Fortune 1000, a wide range of benefits motivate an organization to shift to high-involvement organization: improving productivity and quality, motivation and morale; cost reduction and fast adaptability; developing individual and collaborative skills and the ability to initiate change.[2]

Yet the concept of "involvement" does not fully capture the role of teams in a free intraprise network organization. The many varieties of work improvements are about systems and processes that almost always involve other people, few or many, and naturally lead to a higher level of teamwork. There is a big problem when involving everyone does not include giving small groups autonomy to self-manage as business units. Without radical decentralization into human-sized units such as teams and small divisions, the processes of involvement in day-to-day decisions are either lumbering or worthless, as the history of Hewlett-Packard illustrates. Recall from Chapter 1 that in the mid-1980s HP management hoped to increase involvement while centralizing control but ended up with "flocks of committees" producing "least common denominator" decisions. The organization's processes of change, innovation, and improvement ground to a halt. When the founders intervened and decentralization followed, things became faster, more flexible, and more effectively participative again.[3]

A 1993 government commission led by John Dunlop found that teams have been established for generations in some large U.S. organizations. For instance, Filene's of Boston, a big retailer, used teams for aspects of self-management beginning in 1898.[4] Yet the bureaucratic paradigm gained strength over the decades in most large organizations, to be threatened only in the last half century. Quality control "circles" in the 1960s in Japan were self-directed study groups at the workshop level. Workers trained themselves in quality control concepts and techniques by collectively studying the only magazine on the subject. In later years, when the basics of quality were understood by most workers, many of the quality control circles focused on collaborative problem solving and idea generation.[5] Reports of their experience set off the beginnings of a team revolution in many companies worldwide.

The sudden burgeoning of teams and team solutions is in part a product of the complexity of our world, which demands radically more effective means of integrating what bureaucracy has split apart. Project teams integrate across functions. Quality teams follow cause-and-effect diagrams across the boundaries of the organization to find root causes of unwanted variation. Intrapreneurial teams, or intraprises, bring together all the people needed to make a new idea into a small business, in which everyone assumes a share of the responsibility for the implementation of the whole venture.

In reengineering, processes that were broken up as a series of steps between many functions may be redesigned so each piece of business can be handled from start to finish by a single small group called a "case team." If more processing volume is needed, more case teams are created. Instead of dividing the job into sequential tasks, a single team manages each transaction or customer like a miniproject from start to finish. The result is closer customer contact, no dropping of balls between specialties, radically faster cycle time, and lower cost. This principle is the exact opposite of the second principle of bureaucracy, namely, organization by division into specialties.

Teams in companies can gradually evolve beyond problem solving concerning the day-to-day operations and processes and take on self-management responsibility. In the late 1980s, in a furniture manufacturing facility of Steelcase, Inc., the eight hundred production workers were divided into teams of eight to ten and given problem-solving training. By the end of 1991, over $2 million had been saved as a result of improvements devised and implemented by the teams.[6] Many of the teams demanded more responsibility and were given more authority and support for self-governance in processes like budgeting and planning. According to one of the team facilitators/trainers, Tom Hyde, "Some teams have turned their departments into their own little businesses, and become involved in budgeting and planning." His fellow facilitator/trainer Tim Pipe adds, "Teams are becoming more and more involved. We'd like to see them become completely self-sufficient, making their own business decisions, planning their own futures. Some are very, very close."[7] In a free intraprise system, teams naturally evolve into small businesses, because an intraprise is a business with responsibility for its own output, quality, marketing, and solvency. As in a lean and flexible entrepreneurship, people in intrapreneurial teams can develop whole-business judgment. They succeed in finding and serving customers within the discipline of limited resources, high standards, and alignment of their work with the wider organizational mission.

✳ WHAT IT TAKES TO MAKE TEAMS WORK

The pervasive influence on our lives of bureaucracy, with its emphasis on individual effort, specialization, and hierarchy, has made it necessary to rediscover the foundations of the teamwork activities that once dominated human lives. Reams have been written on the attributes of effective teams; here we characterize those we consider basic to building an intelligent organization:

- ♦ A focus on survival
- ♦ Continuity of relationship
- ♦ Inspiring common purposes
- ♦ Measurable goals and deadlines
- ♦ Agreement on how and when
- ♦ A common fate
- ♦ Competent and committed team members
- ♦ Good communication, quick feedback, open information
- ♦ Network integration with other teams, intraprises, and enterprises

A Focus on Survival

Every team needs an outside source of authority to help focus its common work on results. In an outdoor survival situation, nature is the authority. Nature provides terrain, weather, possible sources of food and water. The team knows without debate that its job is to keep everyone alive until they reach safety.

For entrepreneurial and intrapreneurial teams, the marketplace provides a similar survival test. There are customers to be won, processes to run reliably and economically, financial reserves to maintain, and suppliers to be coaxed into superior performance. The entrepreneurial team knows that its job is to meet all those challenges in concert so they add up to business success.

Bureaucracy dulls the "natural" challenges an entrepreneurial team faces and, in particular, everyone's responsibility for seeing that all the individual responsibilities add up to success for the business as a whole. When responsibility is seen to reside at a distance, it is possible to say, when the whole project has failed, "I did my job, what more could they want?"

In a big bureaucracy, the customer is often a distant abstraction, but the chain of command is a real and compelling source of authority that can force people to seek the regard of the boss rather than satisfy the recipients of their work. Add the fears of downsizing and an accurate perception of powerlessness, and teamwork and customer focus falter.

Judith Bardwick, an advocate for increased responsibility and accountability at all levels of the workplace, talks about the transition from individual dependency on the hierarchy to team responsibility: "When people are scared and clinging to safety, there's no commitment to the whole. You don't get teamwork. As a result, organizational citizenship drops out. People stop helping others, they don't put in more time than is strictly required, and they won't share information."[8]

Under conditions of fear-based hierarchical authority, risky behavior—whether telling the truth or doing something new—is discouraged. Teams, by contrast, provide safety from the power structure to take risks and do new things.

All innovation and improvement involve risks of not succeeding. Risk is easier to assume when responsibility rests with the collaborative intelligence of a results-oriented team. It is easier to assume when the standard of success is winning customers and making ends meet than when it rests on the arbitrary judgment of bureaucratic seniors. Where teams are organized within a network of intraprises, their survival depends on customers won and lost, giving honest performance feedback that can promote responsibility.

Anxiety and a false sense of entitlement regardless of results have a lot in common: Both arise from a lack of personal control and a lack of support from colleagues and community. The resemblance of a bureaucracy to a disempowering welfare state suggests that real economic safety in the future will not come from dependency on a large organization but from belonging to small autonomous and accountable groups that are open to marketplace feedback.

Bardwick, a professor of psychiatry who applies her understanding of people to the hard-nosed reality of the workplace, says, "When people are not held accountable for performance levels, they don't perform."[9] Individual accountability is best ensured through the judgments of customers and enforced by the financial realities of the marketplace and the mutual commitments of teammates. Achieving wide accountability when individuals are supervised and assessed is a daunting task that has overwhelmed the ability of managers and supported the tendency of bureaucracy to dissipate accountability. Bloated bureaucracies have reduced accountability at every level, not only disempowering the workers but also pulling stunts such as seen in the savings and loan debacle in the late 1980s. By guaranteeing bank accounts, the FDIC relieved the savings and loan managers of responsibility for the growth of investment. Depositors cared less about safety, so the system veered off into higher interest rates and risky investments.

To survive, institutions everywhere are being forced through transformations that will be painful for many people as expectations change and jobs disappear. Bardwick describes the big change in GM from her particular perspective:

> You need a level of fear to provide the motivation to change. General Motors, the world's largest corporate bureaucracy, is beginning to change its traditional adversarial relations with at least some of its workers and to emphasize cooperation instead. Where once workers were required to shut up and follow orders, now they're being asked to think. A team of hourly and salaried employees managed to cut the number of parts in the rear doors of Cadillacs and Oldsmobiles from fifty-two to thirty. That reduced the number of stamping dies from ninety-three to thirty-eight, and the number of presses from ninety-three to ten. The company is saving $52 million a year.

What made the workers want to change? Did they have a deep inner desire to be empowered? Hardly. The change is the result of fear. All 310,000 plant workers knew that 40,000 GM workers had been laid off.[10]

We believe that most GM people do have a deep desire to be empowered, once given the wake-up call. The new focus on survival calls for new ways of working together that hand to everyone more control of their work lives. Change is always fearsome, maybe because it seems hard to control the unknown ahead. But as people learn in survival situations, team members can discover among themselves, in their diversity and common focus, new reserves of courage and ingenuity that vastly improve the chances of survival.

Continuity of Relationship

We trained hard...but it seemed that every time we were beginning to form up into teams, we would be reorganized. I was to learn later in life that we tend to meet any situation by reorganizing; and a wonderful method it can be for creating the illusion of progress while producing confusion, inefficiency, and demoralization.

PETRONIUS

In workplaces dominated by bureaucracy, the capricious power of the hierarchy to break apart successful teams is always a danger, so that team building rarely gets beyond the early stages. The networks of relationships that make organizations intelligent are difficult to maintain if people are moved out of positions just when they begin to know how to work together. In one big company, an intrapreneurial team we had trained as a start-up had just completed launching a successful new business. They enjoyed working together, and perhaps more important, they had learned to make the most of one another's talents and the least of one another's faults. The team wanted to continue growing their enterprise or work together on another project (they had several good ones in mind). But the powers that be gave their old project to a newly created team and reassigned them separately to new teams. They were alternately angry and depressed when they called us. "Don't they realize we have created something of value in this team itself?" they cried. Of course, the answer was no. Their bureaucratic bosses did not see that the team itself was of value because they conceived that such value as existed in human resources lay in the individuals, not in the relationships between them.

Though it is in the nature of bureaucracies to change the pattern of the chain of command to solve problems, progressive bureaucracies can occasionally create temporary pockets of continuity for intrapreneurial teams. The East Rochester Skunkworks, a small intrapreneurial new-product team at Xerox survived productively for over seventeen years. The team of twelve produced the concept models for a stream of new products and technical innovations, including the 2600 and 8200 copiers and the "yard bird" 2510 copier that handles sheets thirty-six inches wide and of any length. The copier, with upgrades, has sold over 100,000 units and also evolved into a successful thirty-six-inch-wide laser printer. With the help of those the team members called "the real heroes"—people in mainline manufacturing and engineering organizations who converted these prototypes into manufacturable designs—the team created products that brought billions of dollars of sales to Xerox. This was an excellent return on a small group of about a dozen professionals with a dedicated model shop.

During this time they learned one another's strengths and weaknesses and developed a highly creative and productive mode of working. As Xerox Chairman Kearns put it, "In many instances the [East Rochester Skunkworks] team really saved the day."[11]

Yet the team's survival and ability to operate freely were rarely secure. The team survived repeated bureaucratic attacks and foot dragging only because of high-level sponsors and extraordinary team efforts.

Despite their continuing success, in the spring of 1990 the East Rochester Skunkworks was disbanded. Insiders say the reason given was that in the highly focused organizational environment at Xerox today, there is simply no place to put mavericks. Virtually all the people who had "saved the day" and brought the company billions were put on the "surplus list" and/or forced into retirement.[12]

Bureaucracy does not create an environment stable enough to keep highly innovative groups functioning for decades at increasing levels of cooperation and shared expertise. Isolated in many ways from the bureaucracy, skunkworks are a great way to get innovation to happen. But, in the end, the organizational immune system generally triumphs. As one former skunkworks member puts it, "For those of you considering joining a skunkworks, reflect on where you last saw a skunk—dead by the side of the road."[13]

Free intraprise creates a far more secure base for team continuity. The group does not depend for its survival on a sponsor who may be transferred or take early retirement at any time. No one can arbitrarily reassign members as they do in bureaucracies. A member of an intrapreneurial team may remain on the team as long as the team wants him or her and the intraprise has the funds to pay his or her salary. Under free intraprise the team can accumulate intracapital from good times to see it through bad ones.

Team continuity does more than just allow more effective teams to build. It also leads ordinary teams and the individuals in them to take a longer-term view. With the present and immediate future secure, they can place attention on the factors that promote longevity—giving value to customers, mindful of *their* long-term interests as well. If the team is committed to the long haul, they have time to avoid problems before they occur and to prepare their offerings for the future. They will protect their futures by continually learning new skills.

Inspiring Common Purposes

Effective teams have a shared purpose that energizes everyone and gives them adequate reason to abandon self-aggrandizement, self-protection, and destructive internal politics. In Carl Larson and Frank LaFasto's review of seventy-five successful and unsuccessful teams, all successful teams had a "clear and elevating goal."[14] The most common feature of failed teams was that their goal somehow got subordinated to another agenda, generally set at a distance with no obvious benefit to the team's accomplishments or the organization as a whole.

Teams are less successful when the goal is not inspiring enough to raise people above selfishness and personal agendas; the team environment is not collaborative and so brings out selfish and defensive behavior; external organizational issues become more important than the goal; or the team is not accountable for real work with real results—

lacking, for instance, the natural discipline (clear bottom line) provided by direct sales to internal and external customers.

As Katzenbach and Smith point out in "The Discipline of Teams," the purpose that unites a team is different from the overall purpose of the organization.[15] Although management may give a team a charter, effective teams spend time understanding and shaping that purpose. This necessary reinvention of purpose occurs when the purpose grows and changes so that it better fits reality and resonates with the values of each team member.

It was fascinating to walk down a hallway in the Sisters of Providence Hospital in Anchorage, Alaska, because beside every doorway hung the mission of the team that worked in the room behind that door. Each team had figured out what service they performed and found a way of stating it that inspired even the casual passerby. It was hard not to stop and enter each room to meet the people who did such important work.

How can we create an environment in which inspiring team purposes are likely to develop?

Make the overall purpose of the organization clear and inspiring. By doing this an organization tells employees they are trusted to understand how their area relates to the organization's purpose and to use that purpose rather than detailed orders to guide their creativity and everyday behavior. Most people are not inspired by making more money for stockholders or filling hospital beds. They need to see how the organization makes people happy, prevents suffering, or makes the world a better place.

The mission of the Sisters of Providence Hospitals is stated as follows: "Paramount are the needs of the total person, the sacredness of life, and the services to the poor and elderly. Thus, it is Providence's responsibility to serve in whatever ways and means the people and the times require, consistent with the values of the Sisters of Providence." Although the hospital did well by standard business measures like occupancy, one never felt they were there to fill beds.

For AT&T, the mission of providing "universal service" kept the phones working all the time, sent repair people up the pole in storms, and extended service in rural areas despite the cost. It also provided a good argument for the higher rates needed to serve all and an implicit goal of making telecommunications something everyone used routinely. They succeeded.

Let teams define their own purposes. To a degree, team freedom can be accomplished by good leadership within a bureaucracy. Good leaders give teams time and latitude to make their assigned mission their own. But freedom to choose and define one's own purpose is accomplished more fully inside a free intraprise system in which teams are free to form around any work that needs to be done.

Give individuals choice of what teams to join. If members are recruited, not assigned, the people who end up in a team will tend to be those attracted to its specific purpose. Bureaucracies in which managers allocate staff find it very difficult to create the flexibility to accommodate much self-selection, especially after downsizing. People end up being assigned based on availability, skill, and project priority. Giving much priority to personal desire and enthusiasm is, in a bureaucracy, the exception rather than the rule.

Multiskilling is the first step toward increasing the flexibility needed for meaningful self-selection. Job posting helps get people where they want to be. Still more choice comes from a free intraprise system in which teams and their members engage in a process of mutual selection constrained by only two requirements: A team's responsibility for its financial solvency must be maintained (one cannot hire a major-league star on a farm-team budget), and each person must fulfill commitments to one team or intraprise before leaving to join another.

It might seem that this freedom would leave some necessary tasks undone. It is more likely that things fall between the cracks in a large bureaucratic system. In market systems, for better or for worse, when a customer has money to spend, someone shows up to do the work. To fill in the gaps in free market systems, small team intraprises become flexible in what they can do. As a result there are more teams able to do any specific job. Because they are ruled by the market, not bureaucratic rules, they will work longer hours now, if the price and job are attractive, in order to earn more vacation when the job is done.

Measurable Goals and Deadlines

Without a deadline, baby, I wouldn't do nothing.

DUKE ELLINGTON

Any realistic deadline is a spur to action, but the goals a team selects for itself are more effective in bringing out teamwork than goals dropped down from above without consultation. The best goals relate to real events, not arbitrary numbers — for example, to have the prototype ready for demonstration at the annual trade show or to deliver the customer's critical order on time.

Teams embedded in a free intraprise organization automatically create numerous goals and deadlines in the promises they voluntarily make to customers while pursuing business. If the team decides together to bid a job with a certain deadline, set of specifications, and price, they will work together as a team to meet the challenge. Deadlines are less realistic — and missing them more justifiable — in a bureaucracy where deadlines are set and tasks assigned from above without full team buy-in.

Working together on concrete goals helps build an egalitarian team, Katzenbach and Smith explain:

> As Outward Bound and other team-building programs illustrate, specific objectives have a leveling effect conducive to team behavior. When a small group of people challenge themselves to get over a wall or reduce cycle time by 50%, their respective titles, perks, and other stripes fade into the background. The teams that succeed evaluate what and how each individual can best contribute to the team's goal and, more important, do so in terms of the performance objective itself rather than a person's status or personality.[16]

Agreement on How and When

It is not enough to agree on the destination, there needs to be a common understanding of the pathway to be taken: "Team members must agree on who will do particular jobs, how schedules will be set and adhered to, what skills need to be developed, how continuing membership in the team is to be earned, and how the group will make and modify decisions."[17]

Effective teams have their own culture, their own standards of excellence. They agree on what kinds of quality—quality of output and quality of relationships with outsiders and insiders— the team holds to. They take breaches of standards seriously and work together to make sure these are not repeated. Members contribute leadership to each other in being tough about standards, not on each other.[18]

Bureaucracies block the formation of a team's own culture by subverting agreements on how the job is to be done. In an organization with strong functional control, a project team member may agree to accomplish a task in a week, only to have his or her boss assign a rush job with a higher priority. Each rush priority delays something else, causing a chain reaction of delays. If the task that gets bumped down in priority was on the team's critical path, not only is the schedule sabotaged, but the team becomes divided and angry.

If commitments are not very nearly sacred, the whole system spins out of control in a series of cascading delays, each of which is solved by creating yet greater delays elsewhere. Soon none of the teams has much sense of control over its own destiny, so people just follow orders as best they can, regret that they cannot keep their promises, and go home on time.

In a free intraprise network, a team's most precious asset is its reputation. Maintaining a reputation can require turning down business the team could accomplish only by breaking commitments to other customers. These details of integrity often seem unimportant to the chain of command but are an important basis for customer appreciation and loyalty.

A Common Fate

Sharing a common fate is a good reason to put aside selfishness and work for the good of the whole. Sailors learn in a storm that they are all in the same boat. If the vessel floats, their chances of survival are good. If it sinks, they all drown together—rich and poor, officers and deckhands. That is why taking a ship through a storm turns a crew into a team.

In an effective team, everyone shares a common fate. If a commitment is made, all share responsibility for it. If things go well, all win; if things go poorly, all lose. Bureaucratic reward systems work directly against this aspect of teamwork. It is all too common to saddle a team leader with a forced ranking system, meaning he *must* grade his people on a curve with some system like 10 percent excellent, 25 percent good, 25 percent satisfactory, 30 percent fair, and 10 percent unacceptable. If the team did a great job together, who gets the fair and the unacceptable grades? Some who are rated "satisfactory" after a peak experience in teamwork will lose faith in themselves and the system. Some will try to grab more credit next time.

Forced ranking solves a bureaucratic problem that does not occur in a free intraprise system, namely, the tendency of salaries to creep upward when bosses rate all their people good and excellent. In a free intraprise system, total team compensation depends on the team's ability to generate revenue, to sell themselves to customers who have a choice. Human Resources is not stuck being the "bad guy," because the market does it automatically.

For ten years in our consulting practice, we have been helping create team reward systems that put all the members of a team in the same boat; everyone's bonus goes up and down with changes in output and efficiency. The formulas vary with the situation, but the evidence seems clear: Team-based rewards greatly increase the focus on team results and work to produce better overall performance for the organization. A profitable intraprise gives everyone a bonus. An insolvent intraprise asks all to sacrifice.

From a bureaucratic perspective, team rewards are unnatural and unfair. What if the team fails but one member did his job well? This, of course, is exactly what we hope to prevent with team rewards. We want "doing one's job well" to mean getting the team to produce the result.

Free intraprise greatly simplifies the job of designing team rewards. In a bureaucracy there is wide variation in how accurately success can be measured. An isolated new-business development team operating in a skunk works can measure itself against its business plan. It can measure ROI, cash flow, and a host of other factors, and get a reward system as fair as the one entrepreneurs face in the free market. But how do you measure the success of a unit within a bureaucratically organized law department? There is no market feedback; the customers are captive. Soon we are back to bosses rating subordinates against one another and the loss of teamwork.

Good Communication, Quick Feedback, Open Information

Teams are no better than the information they run on. Thomas Drabek, an authority on disaster, tells this story about the tragic consequences of inadequate communications:

> I can recall the frustration in the sheriff's voice as he told of standing at the edge of a very dangerous river where flooding was occurring. He said he would never forget his sense of helplessness at seeing a woman in a tree being battered by the water while hanging onto a limb. Above were two helicopters — one from a state agency, the other from a military agency — and he (the sheriff) was standing there with his radio in his cruiser, but he was on a frequency that could only connect with his office.
>
> He called his office on his radio and tried to tell them where this woman was. The helicopters were going up and down the river and actually rescuing people out of trees. This woman, however, was underneath a bunch of limbs, and could not be seen from above. The helicopters were above him, and the woman was in front of him in the middle of the river, but there was no way he could talk to the pilot. The helicopter finally went by. The woman let go and was drowned. The next day, the sheriff went out and bought CB radios for himself and the pilots.[19]

In this case communication was too slow and indirect to provide the rapid feedback needed for good teamwork. Teams need good communication and rapid feedback. Rapid feedback replaces much of the need for supervision — everyone can see what needs to be done.

Network Integration with Other Teams, Intraprises, and Enterprises

The powerful interconnections that take place when a group works effectively to create a joint output are what make a team a team. Each team member also has contacts in many other teams and in many cases is also a core member of other teams.

Building an effective network for a team raises a dilemma: On one hand, a team needs to create cohesiveness — a sense of team identity, which means to some degree a feeling of "us" within the team and "them" outside it. High-performance teams have a strong sense of identity and their own special common cause that is different from (but contributes to) the overall mission of the organization. For this to happen, do connections within the team need to be stronger or more frequent than connections to the outside?

Bureaucracy keeps teams isolated, focused on their task as assigned from above. There may be good reasons for this pattern as well as reasons why it does not always work. Sadly, high levels of interconnection with the outside sometimes disperse the energies and slow the decision speed of a high-performance team. On the other hand, teams can become too isolated, too focused on their own internal connections and not sufficiently hooked up to and responsive to people and events outside the team.

The function of the boundaries around teams is similar to the membrane that surrounds a cell. If cellular membranes were fully permeable, the cell could not develop its own internal chemistry and would die. If instead its membrane were impermeable, the cell could not take in food or get rid of wastes. In fact, the membrane around a cell is semipermeable—screening out some things, passing others through, and actively pumping in what it needs and pumping out what it needs to get rid of. Effective teams can reflect the abilities of this marvelous membrane by screening out and trashing information overload, selecting inputs to pass on, and actively seeking the information and counsel they need to flourish. In a network structure, teams define and control their own membrane. In a bureaucracy, others far from the action try to dictate who gets what information and who works with whom.

In intelligent organizations, teams and their members reach out through voluntary collaboration with others to create a more integrated organization that uses more of each person's intelligence and makes wider use of the information and skills contained in both the organization and the outside world.

✳ EFFECTIVE COORDINATION BETWEEN TEAMS

There is a rich literature and an emerging consensus on how to build effective teams. Less is known about the structures and methods of governance appropriate for coordinating an organization built from liberated teams. How are we to coordinate within a single organization many different teams with missions that inevitably enter into one another's territories and bring one another issues to address? For example, in a chemical company a new-process design team will struggle to understand and address the concerns of an environmental emissions team, the several product intraprises whose products will be made in the plant, the several market segment teams affected, one or more safety teams, and so forth. All these viewpoints must work together from the beginning as different intraprises contribute to an overall design syndicate. To take another example, the management team of a German subsidiary must work with the teams having global responsibility for each worldwide product and each global market segment, and so on in dimensions from finance to human resources. No matter how the organization is divided, whether in a bureaucracy or in an intelligent organization, the divisions are at best inconvenient. At worst in a bureaucracy they become walls.

No hierarchy of command can sort out issues as complex as those raised by large numbers of teams whose missions interpenetrate. That complexity drives us to create a self-organizing system that guides the formation and direction of teams around common purposes without always telling them what to do. The system will allow individuals to come together in teams of their own choosing, to measure the value they create together, and to survive as teams only if the value they create justifies their costs and overheads.

We believe that free intraprise is a big part of the answer, especially for larger organizations. In a free intraprise network of teams, the survival of intraprises depends on their interdependencies with the other teams and intraprises in the wider organization. In an organization such as 3M, each of the frequent new products gets much of its success from participation in the wider organization, and that will be true in all intraprise organizations that are taking advantage of the benefits of being big. The common focus is frequently renewed when members of many teams and intraprises share democratic processes to inspire and clarify common purposes and principles.

Market systems, both free intraprise within organizations and free enterprise between, give the best results in wide-system integration and efficiency but do not provide the full answer to a thriving network organization. Markets do not necessarily encourage people to co-evolve a focus on the future, to promote and engage all the abilities of the people who work there, to share information and expertise, to contribute to society and to the welfare of people. Markets are poor at other wide-system issues, such as pollution, distribution of income, and equality of opportunity. Markets by themselves are poor at maximizing both freedom and cooperation, although much better than bureaucracies have tended to be. In the next section of this book we turn our attention to the processes in the workplace of supportive community, network interactions, democratic self-management, and limited government. Applied within organizations based on freedom and rights, these familiar social forces help integrate the efforts of people toward common causes. The challenge is for all to optimize their contributions to the work and to one another while never losing touch with wider-system responsibility.

Part III

Ensuring Responsibility for the Whole

We are tempted to assume that because totalitarianism appears to have collapsed in the former Soviet Union, freedom is automatically the wave of the future in Russia, Eastern Europe, and the world. But eliminating domination by authoritarian rule is only the beginning of freedom. The more difficult phase is creating the public motivations and attitudes that inspire a people to rise above personal and parochial interests and to be responsible for a larger common good. Every generation must create the self-restraint and the inner spiritual essence that give freedom its vitality and dynamism if freedom is to prosper under changing conditions. At the core, freedom is a political manifestation of a psychological or spiritual condition. Freedom is the product of a people's capacity to go to the core of their souls and to evoke constantly new and ennobling patterns of meaning and significance.

WILLIAM VAN DUSEN WISHARD

11

Community in the Workplace

The quest for a communal reality assumes the shape of a massive salvage operation, reaching out into many unlikely directions. I think this is the greatest adventure of our age.

THEODORE ROSZAK

FREE INTRAPRISE is no more a panacea for all that ails companies and government agencies than free enterprise is for nations. Marketlike freedoms inside companies can open up all kinds of possibilities for people to exchange yet can fail to help them find a common focus. Internal market arrangements by themselves do not necessarily serve the wider interests of employees, customers, owners, or nations. For instance, many actions a team might take could have consequences hidden for years. In his book *The Fifth Discipline*, Peter Senge warns about organizational "learning disabilities," such as the limited ability of human beings to react to the threats from slow gradual processes (from which most environmental and social catastrophes emerge).[1]

The effects of this kind of short-sightedness in both corporate and government bureaucracies is one of the most notorious characteristics driving the changes to more intelligent organizations. Developing new conditions for increased freedom and responsibility within organizations can set the stage for addressing the demands of the future, but internal markets have no more magic than national markets to guide intraprises and organizations toward long-term and wide-system responsibility.

Governments and large private organizations have traditionally looked to those on top to provide the direction needed to approach the future with wisdom, but this expectation is also proving to be unfulfilled. People have to create a future for themselves by sharing leadership and community because neither bureaucracies nor markets will.

Community serves as the vessel of vision, values, and mutually beneficial connections that guide the work of individuals and teams and shape market interactions. The ideal community combines freedom of choice and responsibility for the whole—everyone's relationships are full of choice and also collaborative, educational, vision sharing and value driven. We agree with Warren Bennis that the challenges of the future will require leadership more than ever, although we have tried to limit the scope of this book to innovations in organizational structure.

For the organization to develop widespread intelligence and long-range responsibility, the role of current leadership will be to develop leadership in all their people, to fulfill the joint aims of greater choice and stronger community. Kazimierz Gozdz, a community-building facilitator, says,

> Leadership in community is more than a person. It takes strong leadership to move people to get into the process of community. But once the state is achieved, the community becomes a community of leaders. Everyone knows that he or she has a contribution to make to the group. When the time, situation, or need is right, anyone can take up the staff of leadership. Even though there may be a hierarchy in place, when individuals hold to the process of community, that hierarchy becomes an efficiency rather than a power system. It allows everyone to know their responsibilities. It is the responsibility of the leader at the top of such an organization to be a facilitator, not a dictator. As one

such leader said in an organization that had developed a community, 'I just stand back and let everyone do their jobs.'[2]

The challenge in intelligent organizations is to establish strong and
effective community so that everyone contributes leadership. Leaders
in free intraprise networks will adjust the forces shaping internal and
external markets in order to keep the organization in touch with both
current realities and desirable futures. Market feedback distributed
throughout an organization composed of intrapreneurial teams will
sharpen the leadership skills of everyone.

Market economies have made enormous contributions to human
welfare; they have an unparalleled ability to create affluence, in part
from the remarkable combination of freedom and cooperation found
in networks of entrepreneurial suppliers. But nothing in the market
gets people to take responsibility for the qualities of the system as a
whole. That is the role of the people themselves through community
processes and leadership that develops and rejuvenates community.

In our nations and the communities within them, we struggle to
balance free enterprise with human and planetary needs. As we move
freedom of intraprise inside organizations such as businesses, government agencies, and nonprofits, we will need to consciously ensure
the health of egalitarian community that must underlie lively networks of productive people.

The weaknesses of market-dominated interactions are underlined
by critics such as Andrew Bard Schmookler, who says in *The Illusion
of Choice* that any economic system is prone to "biases and distortions"
that carry us "to a destination chosen by that system and not by us."[3]
These biases bring us ways of living that are a property of the system and not always what we really want out of life, nor what we want
for future generations.

Markets exist in a web of culture, tradition, regulations, and countless cooperative arrangements that serve to humanize them. In *The
Seven Cultures of Capitalism*, Charles Hampden-Turner and Alfons
Trompenaars describe the cultural differences in national economies
that provide competitive advantages. Among other insights, their
studies show that "collectivist values, the need to serve the group, is
a necessary, although not sufficient, condition for economic development."[4] Within organizations—often smaller, more focused and more

interconnected than nations—the success of systems of free intraprise depends even more on community collaboration and mutual service.

As Hampden-Turner and Trompenaars point out, the more superficial market relationships of exchange and competition can limit information exchanges and learning. In close community relationships with common goals and mutual responsibilities, people are very skilled at processing complex information. Hampden-Turner and Trompenaars summarize with an argument they credit to Robert Axelrod in *The Evolution of Cooperation:*

> The development of capitalism is really a function of evolving cooperation which spreads outward, pushing competition to its own boundaries. In early capitalism, individuals vied with individuals to serve customers. Early in this century competition was largely between companies, within which employees were expected to cooperate. The area of legitimized cooperation was spreading. By late century, wealth was not created within individual companies so much as among networks of cooperating companies, known as clusters or value-added chains....
>
> The calculus is that you will learn more quickly and more accurately among friends than among contestants, although contestants still represent benchmarks you aim to surpass.[5]

Although market freedoms by themselves do not create community co-responsibility, we find it interesting that friendly units in networks operating in the supposedly competitive marketplace evolve higher levels of cooperation than the units within supposedly cooperative bureaucracies. Centralized bureaucracies (both public and private) cannot produce the level of cooperation needed for collaborative intelligence. They are less effective at nurturing human development than open social networks can be. The government, and even most business bureaucracies, grew up to promote aspects of human welfare—defense and safety, feeding the poor, educating the masses, making an affordable car. But bureaucracies so segment responsibilities that humanity becomes a departmental rather than universal responsibility.

Not surprisingly, building community in an organization can pay. Herman Miller, Inc., has consistently paid attention to values that build community and at the same time has grown in sales from $2 million in 1950 to $50 million in 1976 to $865 million in 1990.[6]

Max DePree, the chairman, believes leaders owe their workers "a rational environment [that] values trust and human dignity and provides the opportunity for personal development and self-fulfillment."[7] We hear community in DePree's words because he sees workers as whole human beings. Unlike bureaucracy, community starts by recognizing the equal value of each human being. This does not mean we have to pay everyone the same to create community, but it does mean caring about their lives, their growth, their competencies, and their happiness as inherent values not just for what they do for motivation and the bottom line.

Herman Miller supports community in many ways. Everyone is part of the profit-sharing plan. The company shares all its numbers, problems, and concerns with every employee. "Videotapes of monthly officers' and directors' meetings reviewing all the business operations are shown to all employees at work-team meetings. Seemingly everyone in the company—from factory floor worker to the very top—talks about values and has intimate knowledge of the successes and problems of the corporation."[8]

Listen to DePree again as he talks about giving employees "space so that we can both give and receive such beautiful things as ideas, openness, dignity, joy, healing and inclusion."[9] Principles celebrating the value of each diverse individual may have been inspired by the death of the millwright in the factory DePree's father, D. J. DePree, founded.[10] When the elder DePree visited the millwright's family after his death, the millwright's widow read several astoundingly beautiful poems. Afterwards DePree asked her who had written them. "My husband," she replied. DePree suddenly realized that though he had worked with this man for years, there was a part of him he never knew: "Was he a poet who did millwright's work, or was he a millwright who wrote poetry?"[11] DePree told the story to his son Max, who was never again able to take people below them in the chain of command for granted.

We are learning that to the extent the control is taken out of the hands of the people, at least law-abiding ones, their self-interest and collective interests are more poorly served. Control at a distance, whether by government or by corporations, tends to be an amoral control that has limited attention for the quality of life of the local people or their long-term future. To limit the negative impacts of both markets and bureaucratic power within markets, we can only rely on people power—on people in enterprises and people within the functions of community collaborating toward healthy, productive societies. Public and private organizations stay on track only when they are guided by strong communities made up of people with the opportunity and motivation to make sure they serve the longer-range and wider common interests.

✳ WAYS MARKET FREEDOMS CAN WORK AGAINST THE COMMON GOOD

Without the balance of community responsibility, markets often produce results nobody would choose. When whole forests die of pollution and lakes lose their fish to acid rain, nobody has chosen these environmental disasters. When advertising and inequities create desires so intense that adolescents assault people for a pair of running shoes, nobody intended to drive them to violence. When families break up in the tension of joblessness, nobody decided to design a society with such stress that families would be destroyed. These events are unwanted side effects of the market system. Side effects of a free market that may work against strong bonds of community, whether inside or among organizations, include the following:

The rich get richer. Economies of scale and the advantages of using information over and over again gives a great advantage to the established and the large. Markets are not necessarily democratic: Power is based more on "one dollar, one vote" than "one person, one vote."[12]

Racial, social, and gender biases are magnified. Those who come to the market with advantages like money, connections, and education have more freedom than those without. As leaders in powerful institutions favor people that look and sound like themselves, one group moves ahead, and the others drop behind. The positive feedback of wealth and established position then takes over and magnifies the differences.

Consumption and production can be overvalued. It is clear that, at least in their early stages, market economies tend to focus people on the materialistic life. Things and services that can be bought and sold become the focus of attention; the enjoyment of what is God-given and free seems to drift away. Rising consumption comes to be seen as a good in itself—people can feel more responsibility to consume the market's offerings than to produce value. An internal market system needs a sense of community to balance the money-making focus with concerns such as employee health, family life, and the genuine interests of customers.

The present is given far more weight than the future. According to the rules of capitalism, the present value of trees that will be standing seventy-five years from now is discounted so that they essentially count for nothing. Even though we love wide black walnut boards, and old standing trees, according to the marketplace we cannot afford to grow the trees because they take so long to mature that the accumulated interest on the cost of not cutting them will eat up their future value. Our great-grandchildren will not thank us for such a value system. Many earlier cultures took pride in handing a world to their children in at least as good shape as the one they inherited. Markets have no such bias, so if we decide to accept such responsibility we must impose it.

Externalities are ignored. Economists use the term *externalities* to refer to all the effects of producing and selling something that are not taken into account by the marketplace. Externalities are assumed to be external to the business exchange between producer and seller. For instance, in a manufacturing operation, the cost of pollution is considered external to the transaction, whereas raw materials are paid for directly by the manufacturer and thus paid by the customer in the end. The cost of pollution or the loss of nonrenewable resources is borne by the society as a whole and not charged to the consumer, unless indirectly by government taxes or fines. In general, markets make inaccurate decisions wherever substantial externalities are involved. Biasing the system to attend to externalities is a responsibility to be shared between the community and the government of the organization.

Hampden-Turner and Trompenaars argue that traditional economic theory includes as "externalities" the core social values of humanitarianism, social conscience, equality, and environmental concerns. Externalities, they say, is "a polite term for what are widely seen as values subversive to the economic struggle, to the leanness and meanness necessary for survival."[13]

In moving to a free intraprise system of choice, everyone will have to take a share of the responsibility for alleviating the external effects of open market systems and to bring these issues into the very core of organizational concerns.

Some of the economic growth produced by free markets is of questionable social benefit. In the example of the movie industry, studies pour in suggesting a relationship between media violence and public violence. Market forces, it appears, encourage some producers to increase the violence in their films. Hampden-Turner and Trompenaars ridicule this form of market development. "Your culture will 'develop' from making such movies as *Public Enemy*, in which eight people died violently, to *Robocop* (32), *Rambo II* (62), and *Rambo III* (106). This is progress of a kind, and commercially profitable, but not development."[16]

Instead, we need cultures for capitalism that make strong value judgments about purposes and directions; otherwise, "a culture will simply pander to its own excess, selling more and more addictive drugs like alcohol, tobacco, violent movies, and cocaine, because wealth and, hence, 'achievement,' is attainable thereby."[15] Bureaucracies diminish responsibility by pulling it up the hierarchy, to a level where people have no time to think about local solutions to the complex dilemmas of our time. By imposing simple solutions and number-based management, bureaucracies often fail to be responsible to the many "stakeholders" whose interests, at least in the short run, appear external to the growth and profitability of the business.

✸ SYSTEMS TO ENGENDER RESPONSIBILITY FOR THE WHOLE

If our productive work communities rely increasingly on market freedoms and replace bureaucracy with responsibility gained through the lateral connections of the internal market, the burden of direction and integration will fall more on local community processes. Community responsibility tends to develop naturally in certain contexts, which we believe contain lots of freedom, empowerment, and practice in collaborative self-management. Systems that increase responsibility in the workplace incorporate many ways of collaboratively expressing freedom of choice:

♦ Legitimization of informal network alliances

♦ Shared responsibility for quality

♦ Intra-ownership and owning a piece of the whole

♦ Processes of democratic self-management

♦ Reengineering

♦ Intrapreneurship

♦ Autonomous work teams

♦ Evolution of shared vision and values

♦ Rewards for group success

♦ Widespread information and education about the bigger picture

♦ Continual training in work skills

♦ Measurement of results and full information for all

♦ A sense of safety, security, and wider-system membership

♦ Free internal markets

Ideally, in an organization it is easy to combine both freedom of choice and the mutuality of community: Everyone drives his or her own destiny, everyone contributes to the organization's intelligence, everyone shares responsibility, and everyone wins. In fact, reality is not that simple, and the two-sided nature of human existence—that we are at once individuals and in relationship, that we must be both autonomous and collaborative to achieve anything of value—is just as true in the workplace.

✳ CONFRONTING HARD CHOICES

If everyone's freedom of choice is to be extended through workplace community, we face the hard choices posed by the need to separate issues of common good and individual freedom and prosperity. The goal is to find contexts that maximize both community and freedom— the good of the whole and the good of individuals and small groups. The new organizational designs will encourage equal measures of freedom and cooperation, equal doses of market discipline and community collaboration. Anyone ignoring one side of this paradox will in the end be burned by it; both the individual and the common good must be pursued.

■ PARADOXES OF COMMUNAL CHOICE

Freedom	Cooperation
Choice of whom to work with and how	Long-term partnerships and stable networks
Individual freedom of choice and individual responsibility	Responsibility shared through collaboration and community
View of everyone as unique, all contributions different	View of everyone as of equal value
Diversity of individual contributions and rewards	Collaborative contributions and rewards
Freedom, empowerment, status earned by merit	Democracy/equality along with widely distributed leadership
More horizontal organization of equality with diversity	Great commonalities born of continuous education, "lavish communications," propagation of shared values and goals
Individual and team freedom and individual responsibility	Consensual self-management of the whole
Honoring of diversity, of people, and of ways to do things	Strong integrating focus, widely shared values
Focus on individual and small-group initiative and decision making	Continuous training and sermonizing about core values
Abhorrence of all bureaucratic defense of the status quo	Loyalty to the organization and group values and goals
Free speech and full information distribution	Manners of cooperation and privacy needed for innovation
Recognition of value of each individual, not wasting intelligence	Full responsibility of everyone for adding value to the collective efforts or leaving
Freedom to innovate, take risks, and self-direct	Security of principles and job continuity
No support of unworkable programs and products	No fear-based management
Fast-paced change and development, speed and flexibility	Long time-frame thinking
Demands of expanding markets for more egalitarian resource use	Sustainability of resource use

A list like the one above contains challenges to every member's self-discipline, demands everyone's motivation and engagement, draws on skills of collaboration and conflict resolution, and calls on internal "civic responsibility" from every member. The organizational structures—such as rights, laws, governance, and traditions—must be trustworthy to give people hope of achieving a convergence of their private self-interest and the interests of the larger whole. These objectives will not be achieved unless everyone deliberately pulls together toward them, certain that their own efforts will be matched by others. Courage, generosity, flexibility, and toughness in facing reality are the kinds of virtues needed for the responsibilities of freedom. In very intelligent organizations, everyone shares responsibility for the wider welfare of whole organizations, whole nations, and the whole planet.

We believe people have the collaborative capacity to make choices that align individual interests with those of the larger whole and also maintain the bottom line of survival and profit. Community and markets together form a delicate balance that is maintained through many small actions ultimately guided by an image of the future. Edward B. Lindaman, who directed planning for the Apollo moon shot, and Ronald Lippett wrote, in *Choosing the Future You Prefer,* "On the way to the moon the Apollo astronauts made tiny 'mid-course corrections' that enabled them to land at an exact predetermined spot. The corrections were small, but because the moon was far away they made a big difference. It is like that with us. Some of the changes we make in society, in our lives, and in our organizations seem insignificant, but over the years they can have major impact."[16]

✳ RESPONSIBLE COLLABORATIVE COMMUNITY

Community is not about entitlement but about building strong relationships that help people achieve mutual responsibility—and maximize their own self-interests in balance with maximizing the interests of others. Often the individual benefits from the communal activities, as when neighborhoods are safe, people are well educated, or the air is clean enough for all to breathe. Yet what about the conflicts? What about when the employees need more money, the neighborhood needs more jobs, the company needs satisfied stockholders? This is the kind of difficult balance we all struggle with. Reality is full of dilemmas, trade-offs, and challenges to find mutually beneficial solutions. Community can involve all the stakeholders in processes of conflict resolution and designing new solutions with wider benefits.

Community is not about government intervention—government bureaucracies are as threatening to freedom and community as private bureaucracies. We take some clues from David Osborne and Ted Gaebler, who have studied innovative community-based ways of providing nonbureaucratic government-type services that can serve as models for transforming both private and public bureaucracies. In *Reinventing Government,* they argue that the empowerment of local communities to handle many of their own problems (and seize opportunities) provides far better solutions than institutions and service providers tied to distant bureaucracies. Communities that solve problems for themselves instill confidence and new expertise in their members. We would like to apply Osborne and Gaebler's insights to the communities within and between workplaces.

Osborne and Gaebler cite the work of John McKnight, who chronicled a number of examples of nonbureaucratic community organizations outperforming other ways of benefiting citizens. After working for decades as a community organizer, McKnight came to believe that voluntary associations (such as neighborhood groups and nonprofits) strengthen community. Unfortunately, communities have been weakened to the extent that service functions have been pulled out of the hands of the people and into the hands of professionals and bureaucracies.[17]

Osborne and Gaebler summarize a number of reasons for the superior performance of nonbureaucratic community organizations that serve their members through local participative processes. For each benefit of community control they list, we follow with the parallel benefit of community control within the workplace.[18]

"Communities have more commitment to their members than service delivery systems have to their clients." Networks of intraprises have greater commitment to their members than bureaucratic staff service providers have to the groups they police and serve.

"Communities understand their problems better than service professionals." Those who do the work are proving they can provide greater workplace improvements and efficiencies because they understand their own work much better than management could.

"Professionals and bureaucracies deliver services; communities solve problems." Distant monopoly staffs create work for themselves; networks of intraprises solve problems to eliminate work.

"Institutions and professionals offer 'service'; communities offer care." Managers justify their existence by adding value from their superior position. Collaboration and participative self-management are ways of caring, people giving each other power and support so everyone can do his or her best work. This caring for one another spills over to caring for the customers as well.

"Communities are more flexible and creative than large service providers." Networks of intraprises are more adaptive and innovative than bureaucratic staffs.

"Communities are cheaper than service professionals." As more administrative functions, such as scheduling work, managing inventory, and handling budget detail, are turned over to local work groups, costs drop.

"Communities enforce standards of behavior more effectively than bureaucracies or service professionals." People tend to hold each other accountable for implementing actions they jointly planned or decided on themselves.

"Communities focus on capacities; service systems focus on deficiencies." Intrapreneurs and empowered work groups focus on what they can do; bureaucratic staffs focus on what might go wrong.

✳ EXTENDING FREEDOM TO MAKE COMMUNITY POSSIBLE

Small work communities are built on the quality of local relationships, beginning with the simple things. For instance, in a mutually supportive work group, we care about the other members of our group and reach out to help them when they are in need. We honor long-term relationships and do not turn our backs on a vendor or a teammate just because he or she had a bad day. We take responsibility as a group for seeing that everyone has access to the education he or she needs to stay creative and productive. We learn about other people's work and can share work with them. With awareness of our economic interdependence, we trade and exchange and buy from and sell to one another with the goal of mutual benefit. These mutual generosities go on every day all over the world.

Bureaucracy interferes with the mutual supportiveness of work-place communities. People cannot honor the give-and-take of collab-orative relationships or act out of genuine caring; basing anything on personal relationships violates one of the basic rules of bureaucracy.

The desire to contribute to the community, share with friends and neighbors, and be seen as bringing good fortune to all is more deeply rooted in the human psyche than the profit motive. Measured on the time scale over which instincts evolve, money is a very recent inven-tion. Contributing to the tribe has been with us a lot longer. Teams and organizations that build a strong community tap a deep source of motivation for organizational focus and success.

The Commitment of Employees, Customers, and Suppliers

Many employers are complaining about a decline in employee loyalty and commitment to the organization, and a recent study proves that there is substance in their concerns. The "National Study of the Changing Workforce" released in September 1993 by the Families and Work Institute in New York shows a mood of declining loyalty and changing priorities. "Companies that fail to factor in quality-of-employee-life issues when imposing total quality management or "re-engineering" or any other of the competitiveness-enhancing, productivity-improving schemes now popular may gain little but a view of the receding backs of their best people leaving for friendlier premises."[19]

The community of work that employees seek is not merely one that pays well or has good benefits. In the list of twenty possible reasons for leaving a job, salary and benefits both ranked in the bottom half. The top items were "'open communication,' 'effect on personal/fam-ily time,' and 'nature of work.'"[20] People are telling their employers that they want to be talked with as full members of the community; that they want consideration as whole people, not just as sources of pro-ductivity; and that they want meaningful work.

The flexibility and autonomy that employees want requires an orga-nization built from self-managing teams within caring communities. It is easier for managers to run things if everyone shows up at the same time and never takes time off to care for a sick child or to give a child's interests first priority. However, self-managing teams have repeatedly demonstrated that when the people doing the work are managing themselves, they are more than willing to figure out how to keep production humming when some members of the team have personal priorities that take them away from work. Giving each other that gift of flexibility is part of what bonds a community at work together.

Employees are demanding that their work give meaning to their lives, which creates a new business priority. Beyond making money, community at work is serving some larger social purpose. Companies like the Body Shop (lotions and shampoos) or Ben and Jerry's (ice cream) have converted ordinary businesses into social crusades. Their businesses support larger causes such as peace, preserving the lives of indigenous peoples in the rain forest, and aiding victims of torture. For example, they buy nuts and oils directly from indigenous peoples at prices that allow those people to continue living closer to their aboriginal lifestyles than would otherwise be possible. The employees of these companies become part of a community at work they do not want to leave.

Employees are not the only ones attracted by an honest concern for the larger issues. Increasingly, customers also care. The Body Shop has grown from £73 million in revenues in 1989 to £168 million in 1993. Ben and Jerry's has grown from $4 million in revenues in 1984 to $32 million in 1993.

In the best companies, the community of the organization is not an isolated system; it extends to include suppliers, customers, and the world. Apple Computer, with the help of Guy Kawasaki's evangelical marketing, succeeded in convincing many software developers that generating software for the Macintosh was part of the crusade against bureaucracy and conformity in computer systems. As a result, the Macintosh got the software it needed to be a credible platform far sooner than it otherwise would have. At the same time, the Mac's outlaw image did not make the corporate information systems folks a part of the community, so the Macintosh failed to penetrate the corporate marketplace, where, particularly before Windows, it could have greatly speeded up computer literacy and thus office productivity. Creating community always requires hard choices and the creative handling of dilemmas. Proper management of inclusion and the feelings of membership in a worthwhile community is a strategic issue.

✳ FACING THE ENVIRONMENTAL CHALLENGE AS COMMUNITY

We are at the end of the era of an industrial growth heedless of environmental and social consequences. The pressures for environmental responsibility are growing. Global warming and the ozone hole are deadly serious issues. The rate of species extinction is rising exponentially, and there is no end in sight. People are beginning to realize that the current course is not sustainable.

What business organizations have been doing is not good enough for the years ahead, despite the wonderful products and services available to those of us who can buy them. Industrial civilization as we know it is out of control, careening toward environmental limits without any sense of how it might restrain itself in time. One possibility is that we will do nothing until our systems collapse in disease, war, and famine. Another is that our organizations will prepare themselves to meet the challenges of an ever more environmentally demanding world. To do so they must become intelligent organizations, made efficient in dealing with great complexity by free intraprise and guided to the right objectives by the power of full information and a strong sense of commitment to wider communities.

The challenge business faces is not just how to bring the desired products or services to customers at a price they are willing to pay but also to focus on the wider needs of all the stakeholders—customers, employees, investors, collaborators, neighbors— present and future. Governments too are under an enormous challenge to convert their many toxic practices to sustainable ones. The Department of Defense, for instance, has had an abominable environmental record. Estimates of the cost of cleaning up the cold war's nuclear weapons facilities now exceed $200 billion, and the estimates keep growing with time.[21] How did this happen? The government excused itself and its contractors from the regulations it imposed on everyone else. But now that too is changing. After decades of irresponsibility, the Department of Defense is being strongly influenced by internal teams who are finding innovative ways to monitor and reduce environmental hazards.[22]

Proponents of freedom (ourselves included) have reason to pause for thought when considering the future. To be sure, freer systems, and especially free enterprise systems, have created in many nations an affluence for a fortunate majority undreamed of in earlier eras. But we also know the party is nearly over. If we go on in the current pattern of growth in population, energy use, and pollution—perhaps not in our lifetimes, but soon on the time scale of civilizations—we will inevitably hit the wall of environmental limits.

How can organizations, already burdened with pressures to reduce costs, increase quality, improve service, and innovate faster to keep their customers, also take on the burden of sensitivity to a number of ethical and whole-system concerns? The organizational intelligence to address all these issues simultaneously will not come from the chain of command. In a bureaucracy managers generally find it expedient to give long-term ethical dilemmas second priority while focusing on achieving the "numbers" on which their unit is measured.

Environmental and other larger social issues will only occasionally and in limited circumstances yield to broad-brush solutions. As we saw in the story of the Pandole Brothers Farm (Chapter 1), better environmental practices require close observation and adaptation to local conditions rather than brute- force solutions that work regardless of where one is. The center plays a key role in creating the rules and conditions that favor local care and local creativity, and the center can spread news of lessons learned in one place in hopes others will find in them something they can apply. But the center cannot mandate the solutions; the brute-force universal solutions that work best under central control are a big part of what got us in trouble in the first place.

✳ SHARED RESPONSIBILITY FOR PRODUCTIVE FREEDOM

Freedom and democratic self-management remain the foundation of hope, not only in nations but also inside the institutions where people spend their daily lives. Choice is the basis of community *if* relationships are both egalitarian and collaborative and *if* there are participative ways for everyone to share responsibility.

For those who work in organizations with internal market choice, how can community—rather than bureaucracy—help ensure decisions beneficial to all in the local workplace? More difficult, how can people participate in responsibility for the effects of the local workplace on the wider community? How do we adjust the system when the activities of many enterprises may conflict with ethical long-range choices? How can workplace communities contribute to wider-system responsibility?

The extra productivity that comes from being aligned with a supportive community with a shared vision is not an increase of 10 or 20 percent. The extra productivity for people involved in knowledge work and innovation, which is highly sensitive to the quality of relationships in one's network, is several hundred percent. This extra productivity gives organizations with strong internal communities the energy and resources they need to serve the larger community as well. As an additional bonus, organizations with a strong community have the potential for involving everyone in shaping the organization's movement into the future and coming to terms as a group with what is truly needed by society. With so many active minds observing the environment, such organizations are far less likely to be blindsided by unexpected changes or government regulations. They are ahead of the curve rather than behind.

Communities are not necessarily egalitarian, committed to diversity, or democratic, although the ones that begin to express the intelligence of all their members are. The community that helps coordinate the intelligence of all toward common ends gets its strength from freedom, choice, diversity, and equality. As organizational relationships in network organizations move from domination to partnership, there is a shift from a focus on individuals and their relative power to a focus on getting the job done together.

12

Equality and Diversity

There is almost no troubled situation that cannot be improved by rearranging it to distribute power more equally.

VIRGINIA SATIR

THE COMMUNITIES THAT SUPPORT organizational intelligence have two opposing qualities. First, they are built on an egalitarian spirit that treats everyone as being of equal value. To the degree that everyone is treated as a high-potential member of the community rather than a faceless cog in a machine, everyone can bring his or her full intelligence and talent to bear on the organization's challenges, large and small, local and global. At the same time, each person's unique individuality is developed in the communities of intelligent organizations. Individuals who collaborate see each situation from many different angles, generate creativity, and learn from one another. When combined in a community that can hold the tensions that differences imply, diversity will generate the broad organizational intelligence demanded by today's complex world.

❋ DIVERSITY AND THE COMMUNITY OF DIFFERENCES

One brittle way to achieve a sense of community is to build the community only on similarities—to build a community of people all presumed to share the same characteristics and viewpoints.[1] At the extreme consider Hitler and his Aryan race. Hitler brought "pure" Germans together by focusing hatred and persecution on others who by rights should have been considered part of Germany and part of the human race.

By diminishing the worth and power of those different from the chosen insiders, narrowly defined communities can achieve a dubious clarity of identity and provide meaning to the lives of those in the privileged group who are starved for attachment, status, order, and belonging. In workplaces, the class systems of hierarchical "levels" can provide a certain sense of belonging, but a class system also separates people and provides little of the warmth and resilience of communities that draw strength from the inclusion of all members.

Narrow communities are ultimately ineffective for two reasons: First, they lack the diversity of talent and ways of thinking that are necessary to solve many cross-disciplinary and cross-cultural problems; and second, their narrow definition of how members should think, act, and feel limits the personal growth and thus the capabilities of all their members. In a time when organizations, whether by choice, law, or globalization, have come to include people of many different heritages, learning to create an organizational community that spans diversity is a core capability.

Building a Community of Differences

A public agency in Oregon was sued for employment discrimination, and although its lawyers won the case, it was at a cost of $100,000. The news was out: Every agency had better be prepared to show how it had tried to fight discrimination.

The Bureau of Maintenance in Portland approached consultant Sharif Abdullah to provide cultural diversity training for management. Abdullah, who describes himself as a catalyst and facilitator, is more conventionally described as a lawyer, faculty member, and founder of the Forum for Community Transformation.

Abdullah was not drawn to the assignment. He suspected they wanted to hire him not so much to get managers to refrain from prejudicial actions as to provide damage control if they were ever sued. If they were only preparing to defend the agency by using him to demonstrate that they had been diligent in diversity training, it was not an appealing job.

An African American who aspires to be the "Indiana Jones of cultural transformation," Abdullah accepted the assignment mainly because at that time he felt he could use the work. When he met his first class of students, his attitude changed. These were not the kind of managers he was used to training—they wore orange jumpsuits to keep from being run down by crazy drivers, and they had calluses on their hands. Right away Abdullah knew that he, like his students, would be learning from diversity.

Some of Abdullah's typical training methods did not work. When Abdullah talked about the privileges automatically granted by being white or being an adult male, he met resistance from many who did not see themselves as privileged. As one worker put it, "If there are three crabs at the bottom of the barrel all pinned down by the weight of those above, does it make sense to talk about which one is more privileged?"

Things worked much better when Abdullah asked them to talk about themselves. They went around the circle, each person answering three questions:

How did you form your first impressions about race?

Who helped shape those early attitudes, and what did they say?

Was it a positive or negative experience?

One man who was born and raised in Montana had never seen a black person up close until he came to work maintaining the public streets. He told the story of his father, whom he still loved and admired despite his father's prejudice against black people. He recalled that when Martin Luther King was shot his father so approved that he said, "I hope the killer comes by here so we can feed him dinner and put him up for the night."

The man went on to say that he had learned from his own experience that his father's prejudices were wrong, but that he still heard his father's voice when he was with black people. Suddenly, against the rules of the exercise (which required everyone to hear whatever was said without comment), a black man began speaking. "John, I have always liked you," he said. "But now I like you more because I know how hard it is for you to like me."

Silence hung in the air, but the atmosphere was not uncomfortable. Later, as twenty-five people walked out of the room, there were smiles. They could talk about their true feelings and be accepted.

When people move from relationships defined by formal roles to touching one another as people, community begins. When the experience is made more, not less, magical by everyone's differences, that is the beginning of the development potential in a community of differences.

As the course was repeated through the department, barriers continued to fall. The county extended it to all six hundred department employees. Right after the Rodney King beating, one man was moved to tears. As he started crying in front of everyone, Abdullah's cofacilitator moved in to comfort him. Abdullah hated to stop his partner in an act of compassion, but he wanted to let it be okay for people to express real feelings in front of one another and not need fixing. At first some appeared uncomfortable watching grown men cry, and they stared at the ceiling to save their peers embarrassment. But as the bonds of community became deeper, crying became ordinary. Soon it was just, "Pass the Kleenex, and let's keep going."

After the first round of training, Equal Employment Opportunity Commission filings dropped from about three or four per month to none for two years. This record came in part from a decline in prejudicial behavior, but also from a change in ways of handling difficult situations after they occurred. Says Abdullah, "When something occurred, the person who was offended would not think 'Look what that white man is doing to me,' but 'That's Bob over there, and we can work this out.'"

After the compulsory two-part course, Abdullah offered a third voluntary module for "culture shapers," volunteers who wanted to work on changing the culture of the organization over the long haul. They worked on new ways of dealing with potentially inflammatory situations as they developed, as the following story illustrates:

Sharon, a black woman, was standing beside the county pickup and smoking while she waited for her assigned partner for the day, a white man, to join her so they could drive to the work site. When Ray arrived, she said cheerily, "How are you doing today?" His response was to say, "None of your damn business," as he brushed her aside, knocking the cigarette out of her hand, and drove off in the truck without her.

In a charged situation it would be easy to see this behavior as not only abusive but also motivated by gender and racial bias. Sharon had learned in the culture shaper course that the first thing to do in an incident of this kind was not to assume it was motivated by bias. Although she was angry and hurt, she went to several of her culture shaper peers and asked for help. Several of them were white men who felt that it would be easier for them to talk to Ray about what had happened. It turned out that Ray was just back from an appointment with his doctor, who had told him that he had life-threatening health problems. The question "How are you doing today?" cut through his last shred of self-control, so he lashed out and escaped as best he could.

Would he have behaved the same if Sharon had been a white man? Sharon's feeling about this question was, "Who cares?" A member of her community had a problem far greater than smashed cigarettes. Her feelings went out to him, and she rallied the community to give him support.

The true community of differences may or may not be free from prejudice. The important thing is that the bonds holding people together are stronger than the forces pushing them apart. What the county road workers had done was to build bonds of community strong enough to absorb strong doses of bad feeling and turn them into a further opportunity to reaffirm their commitment to one another as human beings. As one member said, "The relationships we had before moving toward community were unproductive. It was like having a third of the workforce staying at home. Now we're friends and we save each other work."[2] As the training sessions were closing, the workers issued a "Declaration of Interdependence," which Abdullah calls "an amazing document," because the drafters a short time before had been highly resistant to the elements of a workplace community.[3]

The Workers' Declaration of Interdependence

We the People...

who work together at the City of Portland, Bureau of Maintenance, sharing our skills, abilities and labor in service to our community, do hereby declare and pledge our interdependence.

DECLARATION OF COMPASSION

Equality begins here, with me.

I will treat all of my co-workers the way I want to be treated. I will actively practice compassion with everyone, including those who are not like me. I will seek, first, to understand, then to be understood.

DECLARATION OF DIVERSITY

We work as one.

Our diversity serves our community. We learn from each other. We support, and are supported by, each other. Our strength and power comes from our differences. I will respect each person's right to be different from me, whether or not I understand or like the difference. I will not discriminate against my co-workers because their beliefs and/or behaviors are different than mine.

DECLARATION OF CHANGE

Change begins with me.

I will respect each individual and support his or her growth. I will take responsibility for the shaping of the Bureau of Maintenance Culture.

I will take a stand.

I will make a conscious effort to encourage positive, constructive growth in my work place. I will support an environment which is free of hostility. I will make a conscious effort to intervene in behavior that I find inappropriate by supporting open communication and by establishing common goals and common ground.

DECLARATION OF ESTEEM

We are the best.

We all strive to be the best we can be. I will work to raise my own self-esteem and the esteem of others. I am proud of the contributions that all of us make to our work place and to our city. My co-workers and I are the Bureau's most valuable assets in serving our community.

I realize I will not always be able to live up to this Declaration of Interdependence; none of us is perfect. However, all of us, working together, can help make this a better community, now and in the future.

Beyond Legal Definitions of Diversity

The challenge is to build corporate communities supportive of many kinds of diversity, not just race, gender, and sexual preference, age and ethnicity, but also supportive of different ways of thinking and seeing the world. A true community comprising individuals of different specialties, cultures, types of intelligence, emotional experiences, genders, professions, cultures, and races can deal with most situations in more creative ways than a homogeneous one can.[4]

The importance of variety is made particularly obvious by what it takes to run good creative problem-solving sessions. The power of such a "brainstorming" session is primarily determined by the diversity of its participants. For example, to solve a run-of-the-mill "impossible" technical design problem, it might be adequate to gather scientists and engineers from a variety of relevant disciplines. But if a problem is truly difficult, we have found it necessary to include additional people such as science fiction writers, modern dancers, customers, bug watchers, and tugboat captains. We would probably do better still if we routinely included children in these sessions.

The greater the diversity, the greater the probability of breakthrough solutions. For example, to help with the task of designing coal-face mining machinery, a group assembled for a creative session included mining engineers and experts on designing farm machinery to get into the corners of fields. Also included was an entomologist who had studied the biomechanical structure of digging insects. With pictures of insect "digging tools" in their minds, the group unleashed a barrage of creative ideas.

In many large corporations, building a community of diverse individuals means extending it beyond the usual narrow groups, such as just marketing people or just R&D types. Even an entire plant or business unit may be too narrow for all the issues at hand. Different work specialties and backgrounds can contribute to a collective creativity for addressing the bigger issues of the future; people with different rhythms and styles stretch and inspire each other. In the culture of the average software firm, a certain tolerance for unique, somewhat eccentric personal styles seems routine. Perhaps it is necessary for the collaborative creativity, intelligence, and flexibility of the information industry. As we move toward knowledge work in which contributions depend on thinking for oneself, more businesses will support personal diversity, as long as the mavericks can collaborate fruitfully with their teammates and are good at their work. The challenge in a multidimensional organization is to create a generous sense of community that embraces everyone in one's profession or function, everyone on one's project teams, everyone in the business units one serves, and everyone in the surrounding communities.

In a community of differences, people are welcomed for their uniqueness as well as for their similarities. If everyone approaches his or her work from a similar perspective and always does everything the same way, the organization will learn almost nothing. As one of our professor friends put it, "My university is desperately trying to increase cultural diversity without any effort to increase intellectual diversity. They seek out people of various cultural backgrounds, all of whom think the same." Another friend says of her workplace, "We are always trying to find people who will fit in. Instead we should look for people who stretch our ways of thinking." Diversity keeps the system dynamic and experimental. It also encourages people to bring more of themselves to work.

Not everyone considers diversity in the workforce beneficial, however. According to the *Economist*, "Japanese businessmen have long been convinced that the cultural and racial uniformity of their work force has been the key to their remarkable success." By contrast, Americans have long held that immigrants give the U.S. economy waves of entrepreneurial energy and that diversity increases the creativity and entrepreneurial spirit of organizations. On the middle ground, European managers accept diversity as inevitable and pragmatically search for people who work smoothly with all nationalities.[5]

As globalization proceeds, there will be no alternative to diversity. Global organizations must be effective in many languages and many cultures. Diversity can provide a clear advantage as people learn to relate across barriers of different approaches, beliefs, customs, and languages.

Those of us who work together will be better able to appreciate one another's diverse qualities if we can learn the rudiments of one another's cultures. Lots of contact, lots of open communication with different kinds of people, is the easiest way to learn the potential advantages of collaborating with others. In organizations with the good fortune to have great diversity of any kind, letting members of teams stay together so people have time to get to know one another may be particularly important.

But diversity fails to enliven an organization if any particular group dominates. It fails if position, status, learning opportunities, and rewards are rigged to flow to the dominant people and groups.

Maintaining the Dominant Status Quo with Bureaucracy

Bureaucracies have tended to reduce the status and freedom of those who perform the tasks by taking the control and coordination of those tasks to the next level of the hierarchy. In large bureaucracies most managerial work is given to members of dominant groups, while much of the hands-on work is done by those people who do not have access to the managerial "union cards" of higher education, proper gender, and class. In addition, Merrelyn Emery points out, bureaucratic structures established a process of "de-skilling," reducing the potential of those on the bottom of the pyramid. Because control of the work is removed, learning and development are inhibited. Bureaucracy at its worst, Emery says, maintains the current power structure and its inequities by denying people "the opportunity to learn how the system works and therefore an opportunity to change it." The bureaucratic hierarchy of personal dominance serves to "further dispossess the already weak, powerless, and underskilled." The strong, cooperative lateral links that could strengthen everyone's standing and control in the organization are inhibited by bureaucratic competition and forbidden by the chains of command that maintain inequality.[6]

✱ BUILDING AN EGALITARIAN COMMUNITY

Great inequality is the enemy of community. Inequality creates envy that can overwhelm the binding force of common interest and make achieving the status of the fortunate more important than contributing to the success of the whole. In many huge organizations we find people struggling over rank and position while the whole ship goes down. One step toward the kind of cooperation necessary for organizational intelligence is to reduce the tensions caused by differences in status.

Most bureaucratic organizations will need to move a long way in the direction of equality of power and compensation to bring out the intelligence and talent of every employee. Of course, most organizations cannot pay everyone the same wage, and differences in power and influence are inevitable. What organizations can do is strive to create systems that allow everyone dignity, respect as whole human beings, and a voice in the processes and decisions that affect them—giant steps away from relationships of dominance and submission and toward equality. Skip Le Fauve, president of Saturn Corporation, says that the key to Saturn's having a productive and highly committed group of people is this:

> We treat people with dignity and respect. You've got to believe they all came to you genuinely wanting to do a good job. We believe that, basically, all people are good. If they are turned off, somebody turned them off somewhere down the line. Now, obviously, there are some people you can't reach, but for the most part, people really want to do a good job. They want to care about what they are doing, and they want to have pride in what they do.[7]

As Le Fauve suggests, respect comes from recognition of a common humanity and the assumption that everyone who signed on is willing to contribute to a community of common purposes.

Education and Training in an Egalitarian Community

Some of the inequalities found in twentieth-century organizations come from differences created by rank in the chain of command. Others come from genuine differences in people's current ability to add value to the system. The first can be dealt with by changing the structure of bureaucracy, the latter primarily through training and development. Effective training and development help give everyone in an organization the capabilities they need to move toward being equal to the more productive members of the organization. A strong commitment to educating every member of the organization is natural for an organization that cares about its members. It is also good business.

In 1992, Motorola spent 3.6 percent of its payroll cost on training employees. The company does not consider the $120 million wasted;

in fact, Motorola believes that within three years it gets back thirty dollars in productivity gains for every dollar spent on education. Productivity gains from 1987 to 1993 have saved the company $3.3 billion.[8]

Solectron, a high-tech assembler founded in 1977, has grown rapidly to $407 million in sales. The average employee gets ninety-five hours of training a year on company time. Says chairman Winston Chen, "Technology changes so fast that we estimate 20 percent of an engineer's knowledge becomes obsolete every year. Training is an obligation we owe to our employees." Such thinking won Solectron an enviable record of quality and growth and a 1991 Baldrige Award.[9]

At an even more basic level, companies are beginning to make the literacy of every employee a goal. William Wiggenhorn, president of Motorola University, gave this trend a major push when he wrote in *Harvard Business Review* that bringing every Motorola employee up to the seventh-grade level was one of Motorola's basic business strategies.[10] That this objective was necessary in one of the world's premier technology companies reveals the failures of our educational systems to provide basic academic skills. That it is being undertaken seriously is part of Motorola's commitment to every employee's future, and thus the future of the whole work community. As we progress further beyond hierarchy toward teamwork and widespread participation in decision making, more companies will eradicate the bias toward investing in education for management only and will pour on training for everyone.

Important as it is, training is not the only or even the primary way of improving employees' capabilities. Equally important is what happens during work. Periods of apprenticeship to different masters is a kind of training all but forgotten in the United States but one that works well for many kinds of learning. Making decisions in self-managing teams and then staying around to face the consequences may be the best way to acquire business judgment.

The focus on the development of individuals in large organizations is relatively new—when large organizations of employees began to spring up more than a century ago, they were not designed to benefit those employees.[11] Now that relationship is changing. Human beings are not very productive when treated as mere tools for productivity.

In his classic 1961 book *Excellence: Can We Be Equal and Excellent Too?*, John W. Gardner said,

> "What we are suggesting is that every institution in our society should contribute to the fulfillment of the individual. Every institution must, of course, have its own purposes and preoccupations, but over and above everything else that it does, it should be prepared to answer this question posed by society: 'What is the institution doing to foster the development of the individuals within it?'"[12]

In the decades since, organizations have been slowly coming to terms with the business necessity (not just the nicety) of developing all their individuals. As we turn away from authoritarian controls and rely on the collaborative intelligence emanating from teamwork and open-system freedoms, we demand more from each individual. For that to work, organizations have to be places in which people grow in understanding and responsibility.

A bureaucratic system based on chains of command guarantees massive inequality. Whenever someone says, explicitly or implicitly, "You must do this or else," inequality is reinforced.

✳ BEYOND DOMINANCE AND SUBMISSION

Too much of what goes on in bureaucratic organizations is a struggle for dominance or a retreat to submission. Successful managers can rise because they are feared and make others around them compliant and silent. Others ride behind their success, borrowing their power to intimidate others of still lower ranks. In fear, one's energy is sapped, one's vision is truncated, and one's options for trying something new appear more limited.

Many other types of relationship are possible: the friendship of equals, the close partnership of peers working together, and the mutually beneficial exchange of vendor and customer. The entrepreneur is guided by the market to serve customers without needing to be subordinate to them. None of these relationships is based on dominance and submission. Dominance and submission do not support organizational intelligence, because they do not bring out cooperative creativity, learning, or good communication of any kind.

Great imbalances of power isolate the powerful from feedback and honest information. The submissive person in a relationship "packages" all communications to fit the boss's preferences and preconceptions. At the same time, dominance tends to lead a "superior" to undervalue what subordinates say. Thus the dominant person ends up believing his or her own self-serving version of reality, and no one dares to correct it.

In a relationship of dominance and submission, those in the submissive role have a much better idea of what is going on than their masters, but this knowledge does not necessarily lead to productive behavior. To force people into submission one must break their spirits, much as a horse is "broken." Submission destroys initiative, creativity, self-esteem, and judgment and increases dependency and apathy. People come to understand that uncomfortable observations and creative ideas are not valued. The system dictates that the ideas are worth less, not because the boss's ideas are better, but because according to rank the people who have the ideas are human beings of lesser value. At some level, conscious or unconscious, they become angry, secretly hostile, or apathetic.

The pattern of dominance and submission that is formally built into the structure of bureaucracy affects not only the relationship between boss and subordinate but all the lateral relationships and relationships with customers and suppliers as well. Relationships with peers are always colored by what the boss will think. Customers often receive the same treatment from employees that employees get from management. In short, the human responses to both domination and submission provide a poor foundation for building effective organizations. Market systems allow greater possibility of equality, despite the limitations we emphasized in the last chapter. Neither customer nor supplier need be dominant if both have a choice. Although in a given situation one or the other may be more dependent, at least formally they are peers. In a market-based network of interpersonal transactions, power flows from diverse sources, such as the customer who chooses what to buy, the informal leader whom people choose to follow, the critic who tells the truth, the visionary who helps shape meaning, the salesperson who is intimate with the needs of customers, or the inventor who sees new possibilities. In robust systems, power is distributed, and many voices have a say.

Reasons for Hope

We believe that the hooks exist in the human character to link people many times more productively and more responsibly than they are in most of today's bureaucracies. We believe the pessimistic view is only a half-truth. Our job as leaders and members of any organization or community is to create an environment that brings out the best, not the worst, of what it is to be human.

When faced with compelling external challenges, as in times of war, many organizations achieve productivity that would ordinarily be considered miraculous. Even in peacetime, people in high-performance work teams, egalitarian new ventures, idealistic service, or nonprofit work often get extraordinary amounts of highly innovative work accomplished and have fun to boot.

Everyone who studies high-performance teams notices the egalitarian relationships that make them work. There may be an appointed leader, but the leader pitches in and does real work just like everyone else. Good peer-level relationships create the basis for trust, cooperation, and information exchange. Relationships of genuine friendship and caring permit members to work through conflict and differences to implement better ways to achieve common goals.

As the challenges organizations face become more complex, the distant, role-based relationships among people favored by bureaucracy are simply not enough. For example, what will it take to build an economy based on truly sustainable systems of production and service? What kind of relationships to co-workers, customers, and future generations will produce the level of community needed to motivate such a difficult change? Perhaps Kahlil Gibran was on the track of the guidance system needed by a society heading for environmental disaster when he said in *The Prophet,* "Work is love made visible."[13] This may seem a strange prescription, but it becomes less so when a senior systems scientist comes to the same conclusion. Donella Meadows, one of the original authors of *The Limits to Growth,* writes in *Beyond the Limits* that the elements of a "sustainable revolution" go beyond new technologies and better policy and include "visioning, networking, truth-telling, learning, and...loving."[14]

One is not allowed in the modern culture to speak about love, except in the most romantic or trivial sense of the word. Anyone who calls upon the capacity of people to practice brotherly and sisterly love is more likely to be ridiculed than to be taken seriously. The deepest difference between optimists and pessimists is their position in the debate about whether human beings are able to operate collectively from a basis of love. In a society that systematically develops in people their individualism, their competitiveness, and their cynicism, the pessimists are the vast majority.

That pessimism is the single greatest problem of the current social system, we think, and the deepest cause of unsustainability. A culture that cannot believe in, discuss, and develop the best human qualities is one that suffers from a tragic distortion of information. "How good a society does human nature permit?" asked the psychologist Abraham Maslow. "How good a human nature does society permit?"[15]

The intelligent organization depends on systems that allow and even encourage the best human instincts to emerge in everyone. A well-administered bureaucracy offers a certain security in controlling the baser human impulses with a more orderly form of dominance and submission. Yet the price in loss of human potential is too high; the organizations of the future will need everyone's best instincts and intelligence applied toward building a better world.

✳ MANAGING STATUS IN AN EGALITARIAN SYSTEM

People are social animals, with at least a history of interdependence that leads most of us to care deeply about what others think of us. Unfortunately for the fans of the egalitarian, concern for one's status generally incorporates a relative measurement: Am I higher or lower status than each person in my environment? The urge to raise one's status can motivate people to try harder and to do what the community considers worthwhile; yet within a context of dominance and insecurity, status needs can also be divisive, destroy initiative, and limit most people's contributions.

Bureaucracy both creates and destroys a large amount of status. It features lofty roles at the top of the pyramid replete with corporate jets, staff, and consultants to flatter the strongest need for symbols of power. On the other hand, it disempowers almost everyone else in the system and denies most employees the dignity, security, and self-determination that is part of the birthright of a free adult in many "less advanced" societies.[16]

In a bureaucracy, some people get excited over parking spaces, square footage of office space, the number of windows, minor differences in salary, and company cars. Others have enough self-respect to rise above petty status concerns but still care deeply about their position in the organization, especially when the freedom to get something done and the ability to do it right depend on possessing status.

Relationships between people involve almost continual implicit messages about relative status. These are conveyed by channels such as body language, word connotation, and tone of voice.[17] When people meet they are consciously or unconsciously sizing each other up. If humans are biologically ordained to communicate, care about, and pursue higher status, how then can we create egalitarian organizations? Does this go against human nature?

We almost certainly cannot create organizations in which everyone feels equal all the time, and in all probability we will never cure the majority of people of their drive for status. What we can do is create ways of handling status that are far less damaging to organizational intelligence than the ways it is handled in bureaucracy.

An intelligent organization can manage status better in three ways:

Make status more fluid so everybody gets a turn at attaining higher status as his or her skill and knowledge move to center stage.

Increase the total amount of status available in the system so the great majority can feel that they are in fact pretty high-status people.

See that the behaviors that lead to higher status are beneficial to the organization rather than divisive, destructive, or of benefit only in the short term.

Make Status More Fluid

The first step away from an organizational system based on dominance and submission is to move from a "pecking order" status system to a "territorial" status system. In a pecking order, every individual has a rank either above or below every other member of the flock, pack, or tribe. In a territorial status system, each individual or group is dominant over other members of the species when within the boundaries of its own territory. The basic rule is, "I am dominant on my home turf, and you are dominant on yours." Fights take place only at (or near) the boundaries. This gives every individual a chance to experience both dominance and submission in relation to others.

The "territory" in territorial status systems may be geographic, such as one's home or sales territory, or it may be metaphoric, such as an area of scientific expertise. Self-organizing human systems (such as the free enterprise system or the informal organization) tend to depend more heavily on the territorial status system. Such a system allows human beings to carry out dignified and fulfilling transactions with others and, equally important, creates far more productive organizations.

The hierarchical organizations in which most people still work are a structured hybrid of pecking orders and territories. The vertical dimension of these organizations, that is to say, the chain of command, resembles a pecking order. Your boss is, at least in theory, always dominant over you during work hours, as is his boss over him, and her boss over her, and so forth up to the chief. However, this pecking order only defines one's relationship with those above and below in the chain of command. Most other members of the organization report through different chains of command; thus they are neither superiors nor subordinates. When they are from different chains of command, the relationship between most members of a modern organization is more like a territorial status system than a pecking order. Marketing may defer to R&D on a highly technical point but demand a dominant voice on advertising strategy. Underwriting may defer to Actuarial on assessing broad categories of risk but not on how a specific risk should be fitted to those categories. The dominance of different functions depends on whose intellectual turf is most relevant to the decision.

The more fluid it is, the more helpful a territorial system of status can be for removing the difficulties of a bureaucratic system. If people own issues and are completely dominant within the area of their expertise, they will get little useful help from outsiders and greatly limit their potential for creativity. If instead they go out of their way, like gracious hosts, to grant others visiting their domain the right to make important contributions, more cross-fertilization will take place. If everyone treats issues as interdisciplinary and thus gives everyone present a chance to speak, the intelligence of the whole group will be tapped.

A fluid territorial system gives people a status that fluctuates. They have something important to say; the group turns to give them full attention. Others have something to say, and they in turn listen with respect. No one is the hero all the time. In the end, territories may look a little like a Mandelbrot set—a map in which each person can find a bit of his or her "color" to stand on deep within another's domain.[18]

Human beings have the predispositions needed to form both pecking orders and territorial patterns. Intelligent organizations by culture and structure discourage pecking orders and support territorial needs without encouraging the "turfiness" and parochial perspective that is the greatest weakness of territoriality.

Increase the Availability of High Status

People who believe they have high status perform better, particularly if the work requires more than a modicum of self-direction, as most jobs do. At first glance total status seems limited by the fact that everyone cannot be higher than everyone else, so it seems that the best job that can be done is to fairly apportion this limited resource. A closer look shows that the total amount of status available within any system is highly variable and can be greatly increased by making more ways for more people to win.

Research suggests that about 85 percent of American males believe they are better-than-average athletes. This could be self-delusion, but there is a sense in which the 85 percent could be telling the truth. Different people define "athletic ability" differently, each defining it in a way that aligns with his or her strengths. The runner believes aerobic fitness defines the athlete; the weight lifter, strength; the golfer, coordination and consistency. Each can indeed be above average on the dimensions they honor most without diminishing others who value different competencies.

This sports analogy points the way to an organization in which everyone can have high status: Increasing the variety of scales on which status is measured will create an organization in which everyone is able to win. The ideal is many independent dimensions of recognized excellence in which everyone can be one of the best at something.

Free intraprise creates a system with many more high-status positions. Almost everyone can be part of a small team that is among the best in its area of expertise or service. Given freedom, an offering that aligns with one's core values, and enough customers happy with the results, everyone can feel special. Nothing kills the sense of self-respect more than having to repeatedly submit to another. As freedom increases, the total status available increases because domination by higher-ups, the ultimate status destroyer, decreases.

Make Membership a Source of Pride. When members are proud of their group, their sense of self-worth increases. When the mission and goals of the organization provide a sense of special meaning, when the way the group works together is satisfying and somewhat noble, simply being a part of the group satisfies some of the craving for status. More energy is thus available for raising the group rather than raising oneself relative to others within the group.

Territorial equals are in a more promising position for intelligent interaction than master and slave or boss and subordinate. Free intraprise can provide many organizational citizens with safe bases in intraprises whose balance sheets are strong and whose services are in demand. Free intraprise can stop there and just be a loose confederation of independent intraprises, or the people who have built a sufficient base of independence can then come together in the territory between all the intraprises to form a community with strong common purposes.

The basic error of Marxist-Leninist theory was not the assumption that community was a more satisfying and egalitarian way to live but the assumption that replacing individual territory with a central hierarchy was the way to get to it. In fact, just the reverse is true: For most of us, the security of one's own limited territory and possessions is a precondition to the generosity required to achieve a full spirit of community.

✳ A COMMUNITY OF COLLEAGUES

In *The Fifth Discipline*, Peter Senge describes dialogue as a form of discourse in which we work together to find the truth rather than fighting to make sure our ideas prevail. In dialogue, there is, as the quantum physicist David Bohm puts it, "a free flow of meaning between people, in the sense of a stream that flows between two banks."[19]

One of the essential conditions for dialogue is a degree of equality. Colleagues engage in dialogue; boss and subordinate do not. "Hierarchy is antithetical to dialogue," says Bohm, which gives us yet another reason to seek self-organizing forms of organization.[20]

The Butterfly Effect and Ambition

Because accomplishing anything significant in a bureaucracy seems to require getting promoted, people too often focus on rising to a position of power first, figuring they will worry about fixing the system once they get there. Only later in life do they discover that in a bureaucracy nearly everyone feels his or her hands are tied.

The belief that one is powerless because others are in charge destroys community. What builds community is the sense that everyone together is producing the organization's results. In the fluid self-organizing systems of an intelligent organization, we can never truly say one person alone caused something to happen. Because every event is the confluence of many different contributions and causes, it is more nearly correct to say that everyone caused it. If truth be told, even in a bureaucracy, the "lowly" often put things in motion that have unacknowledged systemwide consequences. Systems scientists talk about "the butterfly effect," the idea that in a chaotic system very small causes may have very big effects, that a butterfly moving its wings in Beijing could change weather patterns in Kansas from sunshine to tornadoes some months later. Of course, a second wing beat, or hot air from a speaker in Des Moines, might change it back. Because long-range weather patterns are so unstable that every tiny motion today changes the details of future weather patterns, everyone is in some sense causing those weather patterns. Who then is responsible? The only sensible answer short of God is that everyone who has lived shares responsibility for what is happening today.

Many aspects of organizational behavior are like the weather. They could go in any of several directions, and it may take only a very small push at the right time and place to nudge the system into a different outcome. If a team chooses a course of action, what earlier events conditioned their thinking? Many people caused each of those earlier events, so all of them had a role.

When the difficulty of assigning cause in an interlinked organization becomes obvious, we realize that there is in the end no way to keep score on who did best, who was most influential, who mattered the most. Personal ambition becomes a bit less important, and doing what one believes is right in the deepest sense — trusting to the wisdom of ethical principles that have survived the millennia — becomes the best guide for action. In virtually every religion and culture, these principles include treating others as having an intrinsic value. For example, we grew up learning "Rich and poor alike are equal before God," "Do unto others as you would have others do unto you," and "Love your neighbor as yourself." Other cultures say the same thing in different ways. All these principles urge us to see all people as equal in value and to create more opportunity for all of us to develop and express our potentials.

The collaborative action that develops when people begin treating each other as having equal value is nearly impossible in most bureaucracies. Bureaucracies rank people. Promotions are accorded to those who conform, who like to command, and who can approach the inevitable tough decisions with simple bureaucratic answers. The system can even favor those who are willing to harm others or put the future at risk in order to support the short-term interests of those in power above them. The level of responsibility and wisdom such a system brings forth is not enough for long-term success in this complex age.

The Power of Community

In the coming revolution in the workplace, only those organizations that decentralize, distribute power, and grow a community of differences will be able to embrace the breadth and speed of change.

Everyone needs the power to be heard and to influence the course of things.

The more diverse the group, the better and more widespread are the collaborative processes of self-management needed to integrate everyone into a true community. The more complex the challenges an organization must face, the deeper the commitment to common ethical principles and shared purpose must be. Just as individuals must let go of old patterns to achieve mastery in any field, so communities must let go of conformity to old hierarchies to achieve dynamic power and enjoyable community.

People can develop a sense of community that, with growing heart, crosses the divide between customer and supplier, company and larger community, and industry and the community of living things. When we reach across boundaries to care about all those affected by what we are doing, we better anticipate crises, provide authentic service, develop deeper loyalty, and create security for ourselves and those we serve.

Voluntary Learning Networks

The network form is designed to handle tasks and environments that demand flexibility and adaptability.... Unlike a bureaucracy, which is a fixed set of relationships for processing all problems, the network organization molds itself to each problem. Moreover, it adapts itself not by top-management fiat but by the interactions of problems, people, and resources; within the broad confines of corporate strategy, organizational members autonomously work out relationships.... The intrinsic ability of the network organization to repeatedly redesign itself to accommodate new tasks, unique problems, and changing environments enables such organizations to escape the plight of forms such as bureaucracy, which ossify and become incapable of change.

WAYNE E. BAKER

THE EMPLOYEES OF A DANISH COMPANY called Oticon, one of the world's largest hearing aid manufacturers, volunteer for tasks and projects all over the company. They have dissolved the bureaucracy by establishing a voluntary network within the organization based on the market choices of people and projects. Companies like Benetton are discovering that it pays to be the marketing arm for a complex network of smaller firms rather than trying to bring them under the direct control of the hierarchy. The structure of AT&T is beginning to move from the vertical silos of bureaucratic turf to a horizontal network created by choices between alternative internal providers of certain staff services.

For over twenty years, Lennart Boskjö, Sven Atterhed, and Gustaf Delin have run the Foresight Group, a worldwide consultancy without a central office or employees. Before fax and computer messaging, they used telephone answering machines and long rambling cassette tapes to keep in touch. Now new technology makes it even easier to have a big effect without retaining a shred of the old hierarchical model. They reach the majority of clients who benefit from their work through a larger network consisting of a number of consulting firms around the world who license their courses and processes. Their job at the center is to keep new ideas percolating through the network and facilitate everyone's sharing of expertise. The three partners add what they do best and let their collaborative network do the rest.

Even in large bureaucratic organizations, much of the real work is done through networks of voluntary connections. People share the details of an emerging technology with colleagues across organizational boundaries or give friends advice on how to steer a new idea through the politics of senior management committees. Almost no one's job description details the informal connections needed to integrate their responsibilities with the other viewpoints and sources of knowledge throughout the rest of the organization. Almost no one is told how to get his or her initiatives aligned with those in other parts of the organization. No one says whom one is to help and whom to brush off with a few names of other people to try. The decisions that create the informal organization are voluntary.

Informal networks are at work in all organizations, whether bureaucratic or more intelligent. Even in a bureaucracy employees are expected to develop a fair faculty for finding their way through the informal organization.

A business unit of a large computer industry firm was struggling with how to serve its customers from another industry (automotive) as they converted from a centralized computing environment to distributed processing. In particular they were wrestling with the future of client servers, those powerful computers that process data for other computers on a network.

So much depended on other parts of the company. Would people in engineering support their vision? Would the maintenance, repair, and software support services be there to help their clients implement the new systems? If they just forged ahead on their own, they figured the odds were poor that the rest of the corporation would be ready and willing to support their direction.

Rather than speculate about what others would support, or ask senior management to legislate, they called up people from every relevant function and group they could think of and asked for help. The groups these people belonged to were organizationally separate in the company's chain of command but were concerned with common issues of how the next big transformation in their industry could help their clients. They included representatives from

Several client server *product groups* using both Intel's 486 and Pentium processors

Several *operating systems groups,* including those working with UNIX and Windows NT

Marketing people interested in both local area networks and enterprisewide networks

Service organizations providing maintenance, installation, and system integration

Diverse geographic regions, including both the United States and Europe

Often members of such a group see one another as competitors, all hungry for the same investment dollars and head count allocations from the top. Each would fight to get as large a share as possible of the limited resources for their projects or their solutions. But in this instance they worked together well, and established a common vision.

As one member of the group put it,

If you want a high performance team, you have to make the whole greater than the sum of the parts. To do that we started out focusing on the whole we wanted to achieve and only later got to what role each of our organizations would play. We used a planning process that focused in turn on three questions:

What do customers want?

What would the customers have to implement to get what they want?

What do we or could we have that would support them in that implementation?

These questions prevented participants from concentrating on what each group had to offer until they had worked out which customer needs they most wanted to serve. For example, they concluded that customers wanted to reduce their "time to market." One major initiative to achieve this would focus on improving information flow so documents could be approved in days instead of weeks. Only after reaching this conclusion did the representatives talk about what each of their groups could offer to help automate the document approval procedure.

Because this was an informal team without much of a budget, one of the members who had been through the planning process many times acted as facilitator. After four months of occasional meetings, the group had developed client server strategies that people from every function could support.

After helping the automotive business unit develop the client server portion of its business, the group was expected to disband, but the connections that had formed were too valuable to drop. They were solving integration problems for the whole organization, not just fine-tuning one business unit's business plan. No one else was thinking as clearly and broadly about the company's client server strategy.

A portion of the group coalesced to promote continual lateral integration among their different units. Working informally, they developed a common view of the market, created a common look and compatible messages for their promotional materials, and improved interconnectivity between their systems.

Once the informal integration team had developed a common vision, each unit's piece of it naturally went up the chain of command as part of its contribution to the formal planning process. When the time came for the bosses to present their divisional plans to top management, everyone was pleased to find they were all singing out of the same book. Prior informal integration saved senior management time, avoided potential conflict, and prevented the last-minute compromises senior management would have had to make if they had been given a bunch of incompatible plans.

People who are empowered to work within the informal networks that cross all the boundaries of the organization make up the main nervous system of the modern organization. Like the human brain, the organization gets its intelligence from its rich interconnections — each individual and each team connected to many others. The informal network follows no organization chart; it is the sum of all the connections people make to get the job done.

Informal connections across organizational boundaries violate the basic operating principle of bureaucracy: namely, that all coordination should be done not by the people doing the work but by those a level or so above. In a bureaucracy, coordination is a boss's prerogative, and communications to another part of the organization should flow up to the boss and then across and down. But no modern bureaucracy lives by the formal pattern of communication bureaucracy prescribes, because if it did, the organization would become slow, simple-minded, unresponsive, and uncoordinated and soon die.

The Complexity of Interconnections

A network organization, like the human brain, is richly interconnected. Though each person may not have the ten thousand or more connections a typical nerve cell in the brain has, each knowledge worker in an organization keeps enough contacts to fill a good-sized Rolodex®. Perhaps the "real" organizational structure includes all the connections recorded in all the address books, pop-ups, and name files of everyone in the organization. If so, even a mid-sized organization is far too complex to draw: A big sheet of paper would be totally blackened by the connecting lines branching out in the hundreds from each person.

How does this complex structure come into being? It is not possible to make all the linkages across the organization that might be useful — there are too many possibilities. One solution would be to have a brilliant organizational architect figure out who should talk to and partner with whom and require them to do so, forbidding all other internal linkages. No one is smart enough to do this, so network organizations are grown rather than designed. In egalitarian network organizations, each person or team individually connects to the network and embraces or discourages the connections others want to make.

For every connection in a voluntary network, both sides must agree to connect. The two-way choice provides a discipline that screens out those connections that provide less value to the system and keeps in place those that prove fruitful in the eyes of the people engaged in them. The network of connections that people can develop on the basis of their own free choices will adjust to match the complexity of the jobs the organization is called upon to perform.

The rule that connections must be voluntary cannot be absolute — at some point, even in the most democratic societies, certain forms of misbehavior will get one dragged up in front of a judge and jury. Obviously every organization must at times limit choice to create a worthwhile culture. But in a free organization, we limit as little as we can and still keep the system orderly and productive. Put another way, an intelligent organization exists to create the conditions in which free choices lead to cooperation toward common ends — achieving the goal of the organization and being a good place to work.

Parallel Architecture

Intelligent organizations have to be networks because, in the jargon of computers, only a massively parallel architecture can get high-level intelligence from relatively slow devices. People communicate slowly compared to silicon chips, so systems made up of people can generate enough integrating communications to be smart only if a lot of meaningful conversations are going on at once across all the boundaries of the organization.

For these many simultaneous communications to be meaningful in an economic or moral sense, they must lead to action. If we try to funnel communications up the chain of command in order to make decisions at high levels, every manager will experience information overload, important information will not be passed on, and decisions will be made that ignore most of what the organization has already learned about the matter at hand. This level of performance is common enough, but increasingly it is not good enough.

✳ OTICON A/S

Oticon A/S, an eighty-eight-year-old Danish hearing aid manufacturer, was the third largest in the industry worldwide. According to its managing director, in 1987 Oticon was probably one of the world's most conservative and aristocratic companies, "with hardwood paneling on the walls and the steepest of hierarchies."[1] It was not working; in 1987 the company lost half of its equity. Clearly something had to change.

"We decided that we wanted to be the champions—to capture a larger part of the market," said Lars Kolind, a mathematician before he turned managing director.[2] "The goal was not just to slowly get better products and technology but to run ahead, to be markedly better than others."[3]

Oticon's competitors are large and very competent firms. According to Sten Davidsen, who was a project leader on the task of changing the company to a radically less hierarchical form, "It would be difficult for us to develop chips for digital sound processing better than Sony, but we had to try to do something better. What we could do was develop a unique organizational concept."[4]

To get beyond hierarchy, Oticon redesigned four key areas: jobs, the method of organization, the work environment, and methods of communication.

From Monojob to Multijob

People at Oticon do not have a job, they have a constantly changing portfolio of jobs that they choose for themselves. For example, an engineer might have a primary job designing new integrated circuits but also sign up to do a market study or prepare the company newsletter. The surprising idea is that, in addition to working at the center of their expertise, all workers do something they are not qualified to do. As a result of the job portfolio approach, the company benefits from the part-time use of many skills that would be unavailable in a more bureaucratic firm. A woman in accounting who happens to be fluent in Spanish serves as the company's contact for all Spanish-language calls. Spanish-speaking customers know whom to ask for and trust that she will see that the company tends to their needs. Between calls she continues with her normal accounting work. Even managing director Kolind signed up; he writes instructions for the hearing aids along with doing more traditional tasks like strategic planning. As he says about the work, "You have no idea how much more I learned about our products."[5]

Part of the philosophy behind the flexible job portfolio concept is fitting the work to the people rather than trying to change the people to fit the work. One brilliant product developer was having trouble in a project leader position because the administrative details of the project were not being handled. He advertised on the "Job Exchange" for a project manager to help him out and got an enthusiastic part-time volunteer from accounting eager to participate in product development. Lars Kolind explains that Oticon's job flexibility works because, "Everything is based on voluntariness—and this can be done because we have de-Stalinized the company and introduced a market economy."[6]

The rules have definitely changed. It is assumed that all employees are adults who can take care of themselves and their responsibilities. Employees set their own hours and vacations. Each person selects what he or she wants to do. Everyone can see how all the projects are doing and how much the company owes the bank and can compare actual financials with the plan. They go to the place where their talents are most needed. "Liberating people worked better than we ever expected," says Davidsen. "People manage themselves."[7]

Organization Almost Without Hierarchy

As part of redesigning jobs, Oticon began at the head office, eliminating the hierarchical departments that fragmented the organization. They eliminated all titles and created a structure with no bosses or managers. "Nothing is left but the teams that work for a common cause," says Davidsen. Kolind refers to their highly interconnected, nonhierarchical kind of organization as "the spaghetti organization."[8] He is referring to spaghetti that is well boiled and well tangled. Oticon uses a number of critical systems that keep the chaos under control without resorting to hierarchy:[9]

Everyone knows the strategies and policies. When everyone shares the same strategy and policies, the chances are far better that actions taken independently will align with and support each other. "This is a highly transparent organization which is good for some and not for others," says Kolind. "It is very demanding on management and managers. It is also necessary that all our development plans are known in the company. We are willing to take the risk of our competitors' getting hold of our plans."[10]

Project leaders ensure that the team working on a project stays coordinated. "We subscribe to the philosophy of a little management but a lot of leadership," says Kolind.[11]

A management group decides which projects to offer. This keeps work and related costs from ballooning out of control.

Project leaders set salaries in cooperation with the management group.

The Flexible Work Environment

The physical office layout at Oticon is one of its most charming features. Everyone has exactly the same amount of space, and in fact no one has a fixed desk. Everyone gets a caddy that is a low file cabinet with a desk drawer on wheels. To work together, a project team chooses a bunch of adjacent tables, and each member wheels his or her caddy up to one of the tables, which then becomes that person's "desk." On each table there is already a computer that gives whoever parks there and signs on access to all the personal files, E-mail, company databases, and common files to which people would have access if they stayed at a fixed location. The system could have created a problem with telephones, but everyone carries mobile phones that can reach them regardless of where they are.

This nomadic office system not only creates great flexibility for working arrangements, it is a strong builder of community. There are common areas such as conference rooms and a coffee bar on every floor. The cafeteria is open all day. "I encourage staff to take long lunch breaks because that is the way ideas develop," says Kolind.[12]

Another way that the layout creates community is through the equality it implies. One day when he was on a trip to Norway, Kolind's rolling file (no larger than anyone else's) was left pulled up in front of a desk that was needed by a project team. The team had heard him mention that he needed to spend more time in marketing, so they rolled his desk into a marketing area. Kolind is pleased by these sorts of liberties because he knows that if the employees feel free to move the CEO's desk when it gets in the way, the organization has moved a long way from hierarchy toward flexibility.[13]

Beyond Paperwork

One reason the flexible office layout works is that Oticon is a leader in the paperless office. In the cafeteria a huge glass pipe runs from ceiling to floor. When the mail comes in, it is immediately scanned into the computer, shredded, and thrown down the tube to "the general cheers of the employees."[14] Only about ten documents a day, items like legal contracts, escape the shredder. Having all mail and memos available only as computer files to be read on the screen makes it easy to dispense with large physical storage areas for people who work at desks. Instead, they have large private areas on hard disks.

Moving to the paperless office required a rapid increase in computer literacy, but rather than set up a corporate training program, they turned the problem over to employees. Eight months before the system was installed, they offered each employee a powerful personal computer for use at home in exchange for training themselves to use it. Over 90 percent accepted, and the employees organized "The PC Club" to help one another learn.

The big change was not the move from paper memos to computer messages. As a company devoted to hearing, Oticon realized that the more radical transformation is from written to verbal communication. For example, each coffee bar is the site of about twenty meetings a day averaging ten minutes and 2.7 participants each. That is several brief meetings per day per person in the headquarters building, a big improvement over memos and the occasional multihour sit-down meeting typical of the old culture. People do not send each other memos, they talk. As Davidson puts it, "We have jumped through the memo wall and gone right to action."[15]

On the eighth of August 1991, the headquarters left its old wood-paneled offices for the new building and the era of open communications. Since then they have cut in half the time to market on new products. In 1992, sales grew 13 percent more than ever before, and profits rose sixfold. The year 1993 is on track for a 15-percent growth in sales with profits up another twofold to fourfold. Are people happy with the change? Despite a downsizing of 15 percent, employee satisfaction is hitting record highs.[16]

Oticon has created an organizational pattern that supports great freedom of action for individuals and teams. They have tied it together with a minimum of hierarchy. The first clear results to show up were in the greater efficiencies generated by people spending less time in management activities. Less management is needed because when people have real choice in the nature of their jobs, they commit themselves to being responsible for their areas of choice and have some investment in the success of the project they choose. Oticon has succeeded in breaking the mold and taking a lead in nonbureaucratic organizational design.

✳ THE DRIVERS OF NETWORK STRUCTURE

Several different steering forces work together within organizations to guide the growth of voluntary network structures. Three of the most important are

Networks of barter

Free market networks

Networks of generosity and common purpose

The informal organization works on a combination of barter and the generosity of common purpose. Sometimes people exchange favors, and other times they just help out as a good member of the organizational community.

Networks of Barter

Part of the integrating structure of the informal network is created by people exchanging favors and making trades. Barter works easily between friends when useful items are exchanged. A quart of milk for a dozen eggs is an easy trade, as is straightening out a personal computer mess in exchange for painting windows. Barter works well for these sorts of widely useful services but gets complicated when the things to be traded are more specialized. Trades then become complex, with three-way and four-way trading required for everyone to end up with something he or she wants.

A Bottle of French Perfume. We own a small share of a Russian electronic scale company. They are a sophisticated company making their own chips and sensors, and their scales are amazingly accurate. Unfortunately they do not also make the light emitting diode (LED) readouts used to display the weight the scale is measuring and need to get them from other state industries.

In 1990 they needed another lot of LED displays to produce their scales. The Ministry of Electronics had not allocated any LEDs to their company, so they could not just buy them. Instead they began a "purchasing" cycle based on barter.

It began with a bottle of French perfume, whose origin is shrouded in mystery. Sasha, a political "fix-it" man and part of the team of venture capitalists who helped spin the company out of state ownership, gave the bottle of French perfume to the person who fixes the locks on doors. Sasha then asked him to help a person who controlled the distribution of automobiles allocated to a large firm—and who had a broken lock. Rather than waiting months for his lock to be fixed, the distributor got it fixed at once.

In exchange for this miraculous favor, the auto distributor agreed to move the head of a food cooperative up in the list for buying a new car. The head of the food cooperative was so pleased that he agreed to sell our electronics firm a truckload of food.

Sasha, having orchestrated each step in this elaborate chain of bartered favors, had converted rubles and perfume into something of universal value, food. He drove the truckload of food to the factory that made LEDs. The managers of the factory at once recognized a way to get around the old Soviet proverb, "They pretend to pay us, and we pretend to work": The managers offered a bag of groceries to each employee if production increased. The flood of extra LEDs went unreported, and a portion of them went into the back of Sasha's truck. Because of Sasha's "Olympic" scrounging ability, the whole transaction of buying the lot of LEDs only took a few months, and the firm was back in business.

In the Soviet Union in 1990, the Ministry of Electronics supposedly decided where every LED would go. Our little electronic scale company, though the only one in the country, was too small to enter into that planning process. The bureaucratic system did not have the detailed intelligence needed to make good decisions about small-scale uses, so they allocated the LED output to a few major users whose activities were considered strategic. It was left to the informal economy to correct any allocation errors that occurred.

The people at the Ministry of Electronics are not to be blamed. No one sitting in a Moscow office could effectively process all the thousands of potential uses for those LEDs and intelligently pick those whose benefit to the Soviet economy would be greatest. A free market would have been more efficient, but a huge network of contacts and skillful barter got the job done. Much of the informal network of any organization works on the friendly barter of favors. Rarely does it require barter of the level of complexity that was routine in the Soviet Union, where it was doubly handicapped by laws against free enterprise and the absence of a decent currency for underground transactions. Still, it is worth noting that both these impediments exist in nearly every bureaucracy.

Free Market Networks

As a flexible and self-adapting organization, [a network organization] is well suited to unique customized projects, close customer and supplier involvement in the production process, and complex turbulent environments.

WAYNE E. BAKER

Free markets create networks capable of dealing with a level of complexity that would baffle any system based on barter. If the LEDs in the story had been sold to the highest bidder, those manufacturers whose customers valued having a display most would have got the LEDs. No one in the ministry would have had to plan or decide; buyers and sellers in voluntary relationships would have worked it out among themselves.

The networks created by a free market system efficiently manage very complex exchanges. An aircraft manufacturer buys components from other manufacturers and assembles them into airplanes. The airlines who buy the planes made by Boeing or Airbus are also "systems assemblers," buying aircraft, computer systems, space in airports, prepared food, fuel, and a host of other items and services that they then assemble into a convenient system of transportation. Pratt & Whitney, General Electric, and Rolls Royce, suppliers of jet engines to aircraft manufacturers, are themselves just part of the endless chain. They offload much of the complexity of building jet engines onto their own network of vendors.

If we take this chain all the way back to the mine, we find mining companies relying on others for much of their machinery, for geological analysis and exploration, and even for maintenance of their machines. And these networks of vendors fold back on themselves when, for example, all the companies we have discussed buy air travel. Truly the network involved in air travel is too complex for any one firm to master.

The network of vendors supporting a company is a multitiered layer of suppliers that takes responsibility for big chunks of the whole system's complexity so that each individual group can maintain a simpler focus. The direct suppliers pass on big pieces of the complexity they have taken responsibility for to the second-tier suppliers who serve them. Second-tier suppliers perform some functions themselves, but pass on some of the job to third-tier suppliers, and so on forever.

For most large organizations, it is not feasible to push all the complexity onto external suppliers. Increasingly the organizations themselves will mirror the free enterprise networks they participate in through their own internal marketlike networks.

Mass Customization. The more complex a task, the more certain we can be that it will be performed by a network rather than a system integrated by a hierarchy of command. The movement for quality and continuous improvement struck a blow to traditional bureaucracy because it required copious horizontal communication. Now comes mass customization, the name given to production processes that can produce customized products and services at mass production prices. Contrasting mass customization with continuous improvement systems, authors B. Joseph Pine II, Bart Victor, and Andrew C. Boynton write in the *Harvard Business Review,*

> Mass customization, on the other hand, requires a dynamic network of relatively autonomous operating units. Each module is typically a specific process or task, like making a given component, a distinctive welding method, or performing a credit check. The modules, which may include outside suppliers and vendors,

typically do not interact or come together in the same sequence every time. Rather, the combination of how and when they interact to make a product or provide a service is constantly changing in response to what each customer wants and needs. From continually trying to meet these demands, the mass-customization organization learns what new capabilities it requires. Its employees are on a quest to increase their own skills, as well as those of the unit and the network, in a never-ending campaign to expand the number of ways the company can satisfy customers.[17]

How is all this to happen? How are the "autonomous operating units" motivated to learn? How will they reduce costs and increase efficiency when their patterns of work are continually changing? Without fixed patterns, how will they measure and motivate performance?

The autonomous operating units in this description will be most effective if they are intraprises disciplined by an internal marketplace. In the network, some intraprises deal directly with customers, figure out how to assemble what they want, and parcel out the pieces to different combinations of intraprises depending on what capabilities are needed. Intraprises that are responsible for big pieces will subcontract again and so forth as needed through a network disciplined by market choices.

In such a network, each intraprise looks ahead to acquire the new skills that will keep it in demand. Each buyer looks for the best deal to keep down the cost of supplying customers. For each outside order, a network of transactions produces profits and/or losses in many different intraprises, each of which learns from the experience.

Intraprises with orders parcel out each part of filling an order for a customized product or service to whomever can do the best and fastest job at the lowest price. If these networks of intraprises are linked with an effective computer system and have simple methods of billing one another, this system of distributing the work can be a remarkably fast and accurate way to find the best team for each part of the job.

Networks of Generosity and Common Purpose

A certain part of the isolation many people experience working in bureaucracies is self-imposed. Enterprising people discover that most people in the organization, even ones they have never met before, are reasonably generous when asked for advice, information, or minor assistance. This generosity is a manifestation of the fact that the organization is a community with common purposes and a shared sense of joint destiny and mutual survival.

Human beings have a propensity to give others something for nothing; some interpret it as generosity, and others as a desire for recognition and status as contributors. Whatever the deeper source of this behavior, generous support for common purposes is often underrated as a motivating force behind the formation and functioning of voluntary networks.

Lewis Hyde has written an intriguing book, *The Gift: Imagination and the Erotic Life of Property*, which shows that systems based on giving rather than exchange are more common than we might suspect.[18] In fact, in most tribal societies and in a number of institutions, giving rather than exchange is the predominant way in which things change hands.

Hyde contrasts societies based on two very different types of economy—the two-way exchange economies we are most familiar with, which are driven by barter and sale, and gift economies, in which things are given without thought of exchange. Many of Hyde's best examples of gift economies are from tribal societies like that of the Trobriand Islanders, who have elaborate rituals for giving one another gifts. For example, in gift economies it is the utmost in bad form to expect anything in return for the gift. As a Trobriand Islander gives an elaborate necklace to another, he places it on the ground in front of the recipient and says, "Here is some food I could not eat." By putting the necklace on the ground and calling it "food I could not eat," he makes it clear that the recipient owes nothing in return. How does this behavior make sense?

Status in Gift Economies. In a gift economy, status is accorded not to those who have a lot but to those who give a lot away. We see the extreme form of this in the potlatches of the Chinook, Nootka, and other Pacific Northwest coastal peoples. In these celebrations hosts vie with one another to see who can give the grandest gifts.

Though no modern industrial nation has a whole economy that follows the logic of gift giving, many of the institutions within our society are based on giving rather than on exchange. Before the grant game became all-consuming, science largely operated on the principles of a gift rather than an exchange economy. Others attending a conference at which Einstein presented a stunning paper did not owe him information of equal value; if he did well, he was admired and respected for having given more.

When a scientist *gives* a paper at a conference, he or she expects nothing in return from other scientists who receive valuable information. The act of *giving* a good paper raises one's status in the scientific community; scientists vie to see who can give the most valued papers (and sometimes, sadly, simply the most papers). The desire to be recognized for *giving* to the field more valuable theories, discoveries, and findings guides the scientist's choice of research in much the way the economics of the marketplace guides the entrepreneur. That economics, by the way, is often focused around giving one's customers something the entrepreneur wants to give, for *their* benefit. In addition, the entrepreneur often has the chance to give, and keep giving, another very important gift to others in the community: jobs.

It is not surprising that giving plays so large a role in science, because the logic of gift giving has significant advantages in an information economy. Whereas the logic of exchange, even in a refined market form, rewards intrapreneurial teams for withholding information until they can get customers to pay for it, the logic of the gift economy suggests giving it to anyone who could use it in any way. The more people receive and use the information, the more recognition one gets for providing it.

The logic of the gift economy is at work in nonprofit corporations, families, religious organizations, clubs, associations, and most healthy small groups. It is an honor to be appointed to a committee or a nonprofit board where you get to give more time and perhaps even more money.

Hyde points out that the gift economy is typical of our closer relations—family, tribe, guest-host, community. Good parents do not charge children for parental care. Friends do not charge friends for listening to their troubles. By contrast, the exchange economy tends to rule our relations with outsiders. Among tribal peoples, we often observe a society with a gift economy within the tribe and an exchange economy with more distant outsiders. What, then, are the appropriate boundaries of the group that define the limits of giving? For many kinds of information there may be no boundaries; all humanity gets it for free. For other kinds of information, such as trade secrets, the boundary may be defined by the limits of the whole organization.

To the degree that an organization becomes a strong community with shared purpose and vision, more of its work can be done without exchange and without paperwork. We often hear senior management asking for all members to realize they are on the same team. Implicitly they are asking for all relationships within the organization to be ruled by the logic of gift giving.

Why the Informal Organization Is Not Enough

Many of bureaucracy's deficiencies are compensated for by the informal organization, which works feverishly to make the connections across the boundaries of bureaucratic reality. Thus, many of the problems free intraprise resolves are also addressed by the informal organization. Can we keep the basic architecture of bureaucracy and simply fix it up by strengthening the informal organization? Probably not.

In advanced bureaucracies the informal organization is groaning and overloaded. As the world grows more complex, the informal organization can no longer perform on a volunteer basis all the tasks of integration that the hierarchy cannot provide. The informal organization is hitting a limit because the quantity of integration and information transfer needed exceeds what we can expect people to do on the basis of goodwill. In a bureaucracy, the people who cross boundaries to serve the needs of whole systems are not necessarily rewarded for doing so. They certainly are not given capital equipment and time to fulfill their informal roles more effectively.

When the interactions across the boundaries of the organization involve the transfer of not just information and casual help but complex and expensive components and services, generosity is not enough. People in a bureaucracy are not in a position to give substantial resources to projects that are not directly in service of the measurable output they are supposed to provide. Nor does generosity provide the guidance and controls that a free market does. In a free market, each intraprise can calculate whether the goods and services it provides are sufficiently valued by its customers to make it worthwhile to go on providing them. Intraprise members can invest in future capabilities to serve other internal units and calculate the quality of those investments. Networks of generosity are more vague, and they do not lead to accurate calculations of cost-effectiveness or to long-term planning of how each unit can develop additional capabilities.

Wherever complexity requires a network of skilled capabilities in a mutable architecture that changes as projects evolve, free intraprise will provide the intelligent self-regulating relationships needed to make the system respond cost-effectively to the needs of customers. All the things that build a stronger sense of community, including rights, justice systems, equality, and democratic participation, also create stronger and more principled voluntary networks.

The voluntary networks of the intelligent organization are driven by a mixture of free intraprise, barter, and generosity. A successful intraprise has a surplus of funds and discretion concerning how to spend it. If the culture of community is strong, intraprises are happy to help one another in many small ways without sending an electronic invoice. As members of the community, they raise their status by being generous. Even wearing the green eyeshades of an accountant, they know that being a good community member is also good business in the long run.

✳ HOW NETWORKS CREATE ORGANIZATIONAL LEARNING

Lateral network organizations—whether a network of market exchanges or an informal collaborative community—involve more people's thinking without slowing down the process of making a decision. The informal organization does this by voluntary consultations— by getting help without granting others veto power. The market does it by encouraging lots of consultation and mutual understanding between buyer and seller and by providing indirect systems information based on how much things cost.

Norbert Wiener, the mathematician behind the concept of cybernetics, suggested in 1964 that the technological revolutions encircling the globe would put supreme demands on our honesty and intelligence. "The future offers very little hope for those who expect that our new mechanical slaves will offer us a world in which we may rest from thinking. Help us they may, but at the cost of supreme demands upon our honesty and our intelligence. The world of the future will be an ever more demanding struggle against the limitations of our intelligence, not a comfortable hammock in which we can lie down to be waited upon by our robot slaves."[19]

An organization can only be smart, well-informed, and wise if its people are wise and interconnected. No fixed pattern of interconnection will do. The right combination of minds changes as fast as the organization can think through old problems and get on to the new ones. Each change requires learning new patterns and new competencies. Thus organizational learning in every conceivable sense is essential to our time.

Perhaps the greatest single advantage of network organizations over chain-of-command organizations is their ability to learn. Networks have more brains actively engaged in learning and more ways to implement learning in rapidly evolving organizational patterns.

In a voluntary network organization, learning takes place at several levels. First, each person learns and acquires better capabilities. Second, each person improves the number and quality of his or her relationships. Then, as the organization gets connected up in better ways, a type of learning occurs not so much in any one person as in the space between people.

In a hierarchical organization, many of the connections are designed from above with little knowledge of or time to think about the particulars of the jobs and people involved. Once the design is done, it is left in place for some time, making the organization static and inflexible.

In a network organization, the design of the organization changes as fast as people pick up the phone. With each sale in the internal market economy, the validity of old connections is tested against the challenges of competing vendors. Each variation in a customer's needs creates the opportunity to broaden the pattern, look up old friends, or discover some person or intraprise with the competencies one needs to satisfy a customer's dreams.

Scientists who study the brain believe that changes in the way the nerves are connected happen at least in part by change in the anatomy of the connections. In the growth of intelligence in the human brain, the Yale research scientist and neuroanatomist Steve Senft says, "We now believe that the interesting question is not how each nerve cell gets connected to about ten thousand other nerve cells. That may happen almost at random. It now appears that the interesting question is how a nerve cell gets disconnected from those cells that are producing less useful or less relevant information. At the age of six we have half as many connections in our brains as we did at two."[20]

This speculation leads to the interesting idea that we need to put as much attention into how to create networks that can selectively turn off information sources as into finding ways to get networks more connected. In a bureaucratic organization, we often receive more information and briefings than needed on some subjects and too little on others. (It is dangerous to tune out messages from the chain of command.) In a voluntary network organization, people create new connections, but they also hang up the phone and cease to buy. Connections can easily end, and vendors can be put on file until their special talents are needed.

Voluntary networks have this characteristic: We can choose whom to receive information from and whom to ignore or shut out. Free intraprise and the informal organization both provide such choices, which helps to explain why they lead to greater organizational intelligence. Bureaucracies tend to demand information that is not used; withhold other information; and force meetings, memos, and reports on people who do not need them.

If the nerve cell analogy is meaningful, intelligent organizations will slowly gain intelligence as the nodes in the network (people and intraprises) learn more precisely whom to count on for what and how to work with them most productively. Then a few quick phone calls or E-mail messages may be all that is needed to make a good local decision on a relatively complex subject.

Inhibition

In the brain, nerves provide one another with messages of two kinds: those that excite the receiving cell into more activity and those that inhibit the recipient's activity. If it were not for the fact that inhibitory messages outnumber excitatory ones, the brain might spin out of control in a constant state of seizure.

In a bureaucracy there is plenty of inhibition for new ideas, but how will this important function be performed in a more liberated network organization? There are at least five answers:

Internal and external regulatory bodies enforce standards in areas such as safety and environmental impact.

More generally, the laws and policies of the organization inhibit what they proscribe.

The informal network of friends and other voluntary informants when appropriate may pour the cold water of reality on an idea with serious flaws.

Customers inhibit ideas they do not choose to buy.

Processes and operations that do not generate more revenue than they consume get strong negative feedback.

The quality of learning that goes on in the inhibitory connections of the network is just as important as the learning that goes on in the excitatory part of the network. Organizations that learn to inhibit a destructive or highly dangerous practice avoid disaster. Organizations that learn not to inhibit something useful can grow. As Peter Senge points out, the limits to growth are generally overcome not by pushing harder but by removing the thing that is stopping you from growing.[21]

In bureaucracies the inhibitory mechanisms are strong and often quite unselective. The power of inhibition is so strong that any one person above in the chain of command can stop an idea. It is strange to see people promoted whose general *modus operandi* is to resist any new idea that involves change. In an intelligent organization, by contrast, inhibition is far more sensitive. As in the brain, a single inhibitory message does not stop the process. Both inhibition and excitation are pluralistic, and each person or intraprise gradually learns whom to listen to about what.

Learning Through Action

Perhaps the most interesting kind of learning for organizations takes place when they try to do something new. Once the organization has a goal, people make plans. In making plans, they discover unanswered questions. They develop theories about what will work and how the environment will respond. They try the theories in action and get feedback. With new ideas, things do not generally work out as planned, so there is reflection about what happened and why. Then there are new plans and a new round of theories, new tests in action, new reflections on feedback, and so forth.[22]

According to Charles Handy, author of *The Age of Unreason,* an organization must be good at each of these steps to learn effectively. This active learning loop is seriously impaired in a bureaucracy and works much more effectively in a network. Bureaucracies do not support discussions of the uncertainties and how to test them—they generally invest only in things that are presented as near certainties. The process of moving a project forward focuses on getting approval, and a questioning mind does not sell well in a brief review meeting when the decision makers have other more important issues on their minds. Certainly a discussion of theories and how to test them is not the kind of thing encouraged by the average bureaucracy. In a network organization, most of the important people to be sold on an idea are peers. They can take the time to discuss the theory behind a project of mutual interest and to contribute to better or cheaper experiments for finding out what will work. They do not threaten the idea's champion so that he or she begins hiding inconvenient facts or worries.

Information Flow and Awareness

For an organization to be intelligent, it must be aware of its surroundings and aware of itself. Bureaucracies are often remarkably unable to sense what is going on around them. Front-line employees' awareness is focused on the rules and the chain of command, with customers being a distant inconvenience. As information travels upward in the chain of command, each level sugarcoats or hides what it thinks might be politically sensitive information or conclusions until what reaches the top does not reflect reality. Because thinking and doing are separated in a bureaucracy, the "thinking" part of the organization is generally unaware of what the doing part has observed. This defect can make an organization composed of smart people look stupid.

In a bureaucracy it is not polite to undermine the authority of the existing structure. Unless the actions suggested by a piece of information fit the current form of the organization, the current strategies and current procedures, the bureaucracy will resist the information itself.

A market research study done some years ago by a consultant concluded safety would become a larger issue with customers of the auto industry. Safety, the report went on, would be a better focus for advanced technology than, for example, offering more exotic dashboard instrumentation. This conclusion did not fit with the company's strategy. Once the middle management client saw the results of the study, he chose to suppress the information. The manager forbade the consultant to discuss it with anyone else or show it to anyone and personally confiscated all copies of the report the consultant had provided. He certainly did not want to be a bearer of bad news for a corporate strategy based on the assumption that safety was a moral responsibility and a legal liability issue, not a potential source of significant competitive advantage.[23] If the organization had been able to get the information it had to those making the decisions, it could have gained a head start on the rest of the industry.

The problems with information flow in bureaucracies are not just about upward flow; lateral information flow is also restricted. The principle of coordination from above means that open coordination across boundaries is a way of stealing the bosses' jobs. Of course, the coordination takes place informally to a degree, but the fact that it is dangerous reduces the level of communication and cooperation.

Networks can learn faster both because they are more highly interconnected and because pluralism, choice, and greater equality of the units create a hunger for new ideas and allow less fearful and therefore more honest dialogue. When the information gleaned by one member does not fit the existing structure of connections, members of the network are motivated to form new ones in which they play a larger role. The network is thus more likely to pursue, learn from, and act on new information and new ideas.

Organizational Memory and Recall

Bureaucracies are passably good at remembering lessons that can be codified as rules and written procedures. Beyond that, bureaucracies can have amazingly short memories. They forget promises to employees and repeat the same mistakes with monotonous regularity.

Often job rotation robs the organization of access to other kinds of memories and lessons learned. In one case we worked with three successive generations of new venture managers in a large packaging firm. The company had unrealistic expectations for the speed at which substantial new ventures could be created. Each of the previous two attempts at creating a new ventures system had ended in a declaration of failure and punishment of all involved because no new $50-million businesses appeared in the first two years.

Given where they were starting from, which was a broad survey of opportunities, the expectation of such rapid progress guaranteed failure each time. Though others had, to their sorrow, learned this, the information was never communicated to the new team, so the exact mistake was repeated.

One of the two previous new venture managers had been fired, the other "put in the penalty box." No one who had been involved in the two earlier attempts ever talked to anyone else in the company about what they had learned. To admit association with the ill-fated earlier tries was to be labeled as "having failed," a label that, if it stuck, would mean a severe career setback. So everyone left in the company who knew anything was keeping quiet. All we could do once we saw the identical pattern developing a third time was to advise the team to polish up their résumés.

Internal Publishing Intraprises. One of the primary ways in which civilizations remember the past and spread learning from one part to another is through the institution of publishing. Since the invention of printing, the sum of human knowledge has exploded exponentially. The institution of publishing is used poorly inside bureaucratically structured organizations. For internal consumption they publish company newsletters, but these official bulletins are heavily biased by the need to promote the official line and to buck up company morale. They bear little resemblance to the rough-and-tumble world of free market publishing, where the readers get to choose among many competing publications that are supported by subscription.

An internal free press does not just mean that people are not forbidden to comment. It also requires that they are allowed to set up intraprises in the internal publishing business, to charge for information, and to distribute information internally with a minimum of interference from "organizational security officers." A thriving bunch of information suppliers selling well-sorted information to internal customers is part of the nervous system of the intelligent organization. In the information age, gathering, sorting, combining, and explaining information is a lot of work, not something done off the side of the desk by operating intraprises. An organization without independent information suppliers would be like a human body that had to do all its thinking with muscle and liver cells.

What will this informational nervous system look like? It is too soon to tell. There will be internal specialty journals, many of which contain confidential information. E-mail, bulletin boards, and conferencing systems will become systems both for free sharing and for buying and selling information. There will be internal consulting and "multiclient studies" for a small but very interested group of internal customers.

Organizational Creativity

Creativity generally consists of combining a number of existing ideas, technologies, and systems in new combinations. The need for inputs from other schools of thought often requires us to combine information from many different parts of the organization. Bureaucracy is not good at this, because its rules of communication keep things separated. Furthermore, bureaucracy does not like the result of creativity if it changes any of the boundaries between the existing zones of power. Though it can be reawakened, people working in bureaucracies often forget that they have much creative capacity.

Networks have the rich interconnections to generate better new ideas and the flexible structure to make good use of more of them. The intelligent organizations of the future will support the "idea brokers" who see the value of new interconnections and find ways to hook disparate parts of the organization together to create value in new ways.

Resolving Conflict and Dilemmas

In a complex world, the priorities of different people and different parts of the organization conflict. These conflicts often reflect real dilemmas: An engineering group sees a way to make a design better; a manufacturing unit has just barely learned to make the old design and does not want any more changes. Both viewpoints have merit.

Organizational intelligence means dealing effectively with dilemmas to come up with solutions that honor both sides.

The monopoly structures of bureaucracy tend to search for and support the one right answer and then avert conflict by suppressing all other ways of thinking. By contrast, the voluntary network structure creates a pluralistic system in which both sides of a dilemma are likely to be represented. For example, when there is choice between two technologies, specialty intraprises will emerge to represent each of them. In an advanced free intraprise network, the person seeking information or buying a service is likely to find well-developed representations of both horns of any important dilemma.

Even when monopoly suppresses conflicting opinions within a function, conflict can arise between functions. In a pure bureaucracy we experience this not so much as conflict as the inefficiency that occurs when a project is transferred from function to function. For example, without cross-functional design, much of the thinking of R&D is wasted when Manufacturing begins the design process over again to create a product that is cost-effective to manufacture and service. The design may not incorporate many key lessons learned during the research phase.

Rather than suppress our capacity to form self-organizing networks, or limit it as bureaucracy too often does, we can work to create opportunities for effective self-organizing networks to come into being. Humans have been given the instinctual equipment to build cultures that rise above pettiness to satisfying collaboration. We also have been given a potential for nastiness that was less of a threat when we lived in smaller tribes. Intelligent organizations create cultures that keep people focused on collaborative activities and constructive competition so the potential for nastiness does not come into play. Attempting to prevent nastiness through bureaucratic restraint only brings out more of it.

Learning Responsibility for Relationships in the Whole System

Bureaucracy embraces reductionist thinking as its fundamental principle of organization: The world is divided into tiny pieces, each a specialty and so not at all representative of the whole. Bureaucracy is based on the idea that if you perform each specialty professionally, the overall result will be good. As it becomes more evident that nearly everything is connected to everything else, having nearly everyone thinking only about his or her part makes less sense.

Systems thinking teaches us that the whole is different from the sum of the parts. Systems take on "emergent properties" of their own that do not seem to follow directly from considering the parts they are made up of. In the case of bureaucratic systems, the whole is often less than the sum of the parts.

Systems thinking focuses on the relationship among parts rather than on detailed analysis of each part. The whole behavior of a system can be altered by changing key relationships, which is why systems scientists look to relationships to find the key leverage points for changing system performance. Thus building a better system begins with improving the quality and productivity of the relationships in it. This does not mean just being nice. One way to improve the average quality of relationship in the system is to disband many of the less productive ones. This selectivity for productive relationships is one of the primary properties of voluntary networks disciplined by internal markets.

In bureaucracies the relationships among people are defined from above. They are not continually redesigned as the work evolves; rather, they are left constant and then changed abruptly, often by terminating one relationship and starting another. The result is that relationships in a bureaucracy often rely on rather basic aspects of human nature, such as fear and submission, rather than on learning how to fine-tune a sophisticated relationship to the personalities, talents, and tasks at hand.

In voluntary networks people take care of the relationships in the system. If they do not, their networks vanish. Suppliers and subcontractors take an intimate interest in what matters to their customers and, by extension, to their customers' customers. This means many people are working on figuring out how to shorten cycle times, speed up feedback, and keep the system under control.

When each team in the system thinks about the systems effect of their actions, dynamic performance improves. The next chapter deals with how to use the intelligence of everyone in the system not only to design and manage their immediate relationships but also to design the context in which the free people and intraprises of the system operate.

14

Democratic Self-Rule

Once authority is out of the bottle and has seeped through the organization, people do not want to return to the old days of drops of authority from a single, tightly regulated spigot.

PETER B. VAILL

THE POWER SHIFT toward greater freedom and responsibility in the workplace can be sustained only by introducing democratic processes at the various levels of coordination. The most natural democracy is direct and readily occurs in self-directed work groups where decision making is shared among people working closely together. Whether or not teams have a formal leadership structure, their collective intelligence relies on making collaborative decisions on matters such as allocating resources and responsibilities.

This is democracy at its simplest level, democracy within a team or small intraprise that involves everyone in working out together the best way to do their shared work. The Work-Out processes within General Electric go a step further, because the work group more formally solicits the participation and support of supervisors in their decisions and plans.

At the next possible level of self-rule are the connections among work teams, which have been traditionally been coordinated by management. Teams linked in free intraprise networks gain much of their coordination from market forces. Federations of teams also need to create focus and coordination. For alignment of the day-to-day decisions that take place in the work groups, everyone needs to create or at least buy into long-term visions of their mutual projects and see how the projects fit the changing environments within which they operate. They need to define the appropriate rules, regulations, and institutions for the intraprises to operate freely within.

The most ambitious direct democracy processes are "future search" conferences, which can involve as many as several hundred employees, often most of a large work group, in figuring out where they are and what is going on around them that is relevant and then in designing ways to meet the future. This level of democracy is certainly input from "the many, not the few" into the visions, policies, and institutions within which the teams and network structures form.

Democratic processes that allow self-rule in a team or small intraprise are different in kind from those through which people select representatives and leadership by majority rule, and it is important to distinguish between them. Processes through which representatives are selected make up only a small portion of the participation needed for democratic self-rule but do provide important symbolic ownership, an indirect voice, and the potential for real influence and control.

The most democratic forms of representative management are found at worker-owned companies, such as Polaroid, with steering committees of management and nonmanagement personnel overseeing participation and reviewing proposals from member teams.[1]

Robert Dahl, our favorite democratic theorist, argues that democratic processes—most simply, the rule of the many, in a context of constitutional rights—are needed to give everyone as much freedom as possible while still achieving coordinated action.[2] Democracy is any system in which the people rule themselves by creating a context for freedom and collaboration in the areas they share. Doing this was simpler in small, isolated villages, when the scope of actions that affected everyone was small. Today, democracy in nations and the workplace must involve people on multiple levels, from the small community to multinational collaborations, because the scope of actions that affect us all has become global in nature.

✳ THE DEMOCRACY IN FREE INTRAPRISE

The greatest power individuals have in democratic organizations is not their vote for representatives. Nor is it the influence their ideas have in conferences. Their greatest power is in making free choices as individuals and as small teams. These choices include whom to partner with, what products and services to buy from internal and external vendors, how to spend discretionary time, and what projects, causes, and customers to serve with what sort of offerings. They have the power to choose what to do with their lives.

A system of free intraprise is generally more democratic than a system of bureaucratic control. In market-mediated networks, more of the relationships that create the structure of the organization and its means of production are selected and maintained by the ordinary members of the organization; fewer relationships are dominated by bosses backed up by a centralized hierarchy telling everyone what to do.

Viewed in this light, there is an important overlap between the concept of self-organizing systems and the concept of democracy in its broadest sense. To the degree that the system puts ordinary people in control of structure and event, it is democratic. But that might also be a reasonable definition of self-organization: To the degree that people are in control, they are organizing themselves.

Collaborative self-management is the method of direct democratic self-rule characteristic of effective small intraprises. If external systems do not get in the way, human beings in groups of two to twenty-five seem to have a built-in capacity for collaboration. It seems likely that human beings evolved working in relatively small groups, and that our natural capacities for communication and collaboration are attuned to teamwork in relatively small and mutually supportive tribes and work groups. To the degree that work systems make use of this capacity for teamwork rather than pushing bureaucratic patterns all the way down to the level of the working team they give people much more control over the design of their own work lives and may rightfully be called democratic.

At the next level of structure—collaboration among teams—the best means of self-management mirror the ways the informal organization has facilitated people's doing things effectively together. There tends to be more cooperation and less conflict when the more formal roles and cooperative processes coincide with natural work relationships.[3] Yet free intraprise networks cannot be wholly marketled: For an organization to be more than the sum of its parts, people must share a vision of where they need to go and of the most beneficial and ethical ways to get there.

❊ DISCOVERING SHARED FOCUS

To create a competitive organization, Drucker (among others) warns, there must be a simple, single-minded mission to help members stay aligned as they share complex tasks.[4] Finding a single-minded mission can be relatively easy at the intraprise and business unit levels. Both smaller numbers of people and a narrower scope of activities make defining a meaningful vision easier.

Creating a single meaningful vision is far more difficult for large and diversified organizations. Free intraprise organizations can combine the virtues of sharp focus with diversity of enterprise. A network of intraprises, each with its own sharp focus, can work together in different combinations to produce different products and services and serve different customers. Despite the flexibility of the system's output, the intraprises remain focused on delivering their distinct competencies. The system, using the organizational power of a market-based network of subcontractors, can rapidly align diverse intraprises to focus on what needs to be done.

Rosabeth Moss Kanter says any business should be focused on what the members are good at doing and on avoiding distractions.[5] An organization is an evolving set of agreements, some more negotiable than others. Together members make binding decisions about obvious issues like the business they are in, who owns what, what jobs each person and group does, and which customers are served and how.

Future Search Conferences

Marvin Weisbord reports on one restructuring based on a series of democratic planning processes. R. R. Donnelley's Hudson Division, which prints software manuals, had been restructured into self-managing work teams. With the help of Dick Axelrod, they began a collaborative planning process with 75 percent of the workforce, some 150 people. The "future search" process, modeled on the pioneering methods of Fred and Merrelyn Emery in Australia,[6] involved Hudson's customers, suppliers, eventually all the employees, and even the wider community. Specific changes resulting from the first three-month search process included the reorganizing of twenty departments into four, better teamwork across the organization, and new focus on customers and quality.[7]

Axelrod set up and ran the future search processes at Hudson Division to give "choice in the whole design of the organization — who does what, the kind of jobs there are." His summary appraisal:

> Everyone was involved in the redesign; the search process enabled self-management and self-design from the outset. As a result, choice has been permanently infused into the organization; bureaucracy is not accepted the way it was before. Everyone is much more willing now to identify issues and talk about them.
>
> Within three weeks of the conclusion of the first search conference, people either observed or experienced the following emerging changes in the workplace culture: more opening up to each other and helping one another; more teamwork; doing more with less; focusing on the problem, not the person; more patience with one another; trying to listen more, communicate better; yearning to learn more; departments asking for help; fewer negative attitudes and complaints.[8]

There is a growing history of creating successful mission statements and planning strategies, and the action plans that accompany them, through participatory processes modeled on futures search conferences. Margaret Wheatley, in *Leadership and the New Science,* calls these "search" processes "the most exciting and richly textured organizational events I have participated in recently."[9]

Weisbord reminds us that all participation takes place in the context of large-system realities. Without big-picture participation, he says, the small groups may honor democracy but not systems thinking. "In short, if you have too narrow a group of people [participating], you miss the big picture. If you seek only to solve problems and manage conflict, you miss the common ground."[10] Weisbord and his partners at Block•Petrella•Weisbord have run future search conferences with as many as three hundred people, though more commonly with thirty to sixty-five people. Their normal search conference runs about two and a half days. All participants contribute to a common picture of the organization: where it has been, the world it is operating in, its future, and what it takes to get there.

There are some basic principles that make future search conferences work:

Get the whole system in the room. Search conferences are large because you can get better answers when people representing all viewpoints relevant to the issues to be addressed are present.

Search for common ground. Do not focus on resolving disagreements. Just make sure people appreciate one another's positions and the logic behind them and go on to find what people can agree on. Keep building lists of agreement on commonly held ideals and common future aspirations; list them on charts, and post these on the walls. These agreements and ideals then become the basis for new, creative solutions and strategies that avoid fortified positions.

Move from the outside in. Begin with the big picture of what is going on in the world. Work down to the specifics of what is happening in the company (past, present, and future). Beginning with the big picture and the distant past allows one to build common ground before getting to the more personal issues, where positions are entrenched and defended. It also avoids the classic error of hitting a fly with a sledgehammer by using good participative techniques to solve a smaller problem while the most significant big-picture issues that determine the future remain unaddressed.

Consider everyone a peer. Democratic processes to search out common futures demand fully egalitarian participation. "Everybody puts in information, discusses it, decides what to do." Outside experts, if any, participate rather than pontificate.

Break out into participative work groups. The tasks of the search are divided among mixed groups of about eight people each who report their work to the whole conference. Everything is posted where everyone can see it.

Follow a planned sequence. The conference follows a planned sequence of the tasks needed to produce a collaborative product in the limited time.

An early instance of a future search process was a meeting of the Bristol Siddeley Aircraft Engine Company on July 10–16, 1960, facilitated by Fred Emery and Eric Trist. Bristol Siddeley was created when the British government forced a merger between two aircraft engine companies, Armstrong Siddeley, which made piston engines, and Bristol Aero Engines, which made jets. The two cultures were incompatible, and the result was contempt and stagnation. Trist and Emery conducted a week-long inquiry into the merged companies' history, current environment, and possibilities. Outside experts were invited, but the focus was on dialogue among the eleven top executives of the merged company. They emerged with breakthroughs in technical, social, and business strategies and the design for a new airplane with four small engines that drew on the strengths of both companies and became the highly successful BA 146. According to Emery, "By the end of the week they were certainly thinking like one group, and not at all like Siddeley or Bristol men."[11] Trist and Emery "invented a new group orientation to help people integrate economics and technology—the whole open system—in a fast-changing environment" and turned around a serious crisis.[12]

Emery, in collaboration with his wife, Merrelyn Emery, began a long process of refining theory and practice by applying the approach to many hundreds of organizations worldwide. In Australia, where they are part of the staff of the Department of Continuing Education at Australia National University, their processes of democratic self-management have been used in most of the government service organizations and many commercial firms.

Learning Through Democratic Self-Rule

What leaders are called upon to do in a chaotic world is to shape their organization through concepts, not through elaborate rules or structures.

MARGARET WHEATLEY

The more freedom an organization wants to have for its individual and team participants, the better its systems of what Margaret Wheatley calls "self-reference" must be — so that a free and self-organizing network of individuals can know itself and improve itself through integrating many points of view and many people's information. Reality is most trustworthy when it is constructed from multiple viewpoints that arise from actual hands-on involvement.[13] Through participative processes as diverse as future search processes or electronic polling of randomly selected issue teams, the members of an organization can exercise their leadership.

Network organizations gain cohesiveness and wider participation when everyone can sign on to and influence an organization's self-definition. Democratic self-rule requires the kind of shared leadership and visions found through the processes within teams, as the members hash out a common and changing reality to pursue together. Democratic self-rule also requires the processes above the team level for wider-system integration. A network organization of teams is more dependent than top-down organizations on a widely internalized common vision to focus the efforts of multitier networks. Shared visions, values, and constitutional rights create boundaries to freedom and thereby align to a loose network organization.

The integration needed in a free intraprise network organization, even with strong local communities, will rely on regular participative processes to gradually bring everyone into the functions of leadership and shared responsibility. An organization is not a mechanistic structure but a "living, open system capable of self-renewal," like a supportive, empowering extended family or a community.[14] Wheatley reminds us that the Second Law of Thermodynamics, which predicts the gradual descent of any closed system into lifeless sameness, does not apply to open systems. Until one thinks deeply about the nature of bureaucracy and what it does to people's curiosity and sense of adventure, it seems strange that almost all our organizations are designed as if everything and everyone in them must be continuously pushed or they will wind down and die. This, of course, is not so — except inside a bureaucracy. We need to be liberated and strongly interconnected. So what does leadership do to integrate the system? Get everyone thinking alike? No. Leadership keeps the system alive, open to energy and to ideas from inside and outside and thus to continual renewal.

Our nation's tradition of freedom has ridden on the backs of thousands of visionary leaders as they taught and facilitated democratic processes. Today, as nations worldwide turn toward greater freedom, those that lack experience and facilitative leadership in democratic processes are unable to coordinate individual and small group needs with the wider common good. Freedom works bet when a society has the capacity for collaborative vision and action.

The democratic processes that allow people to coordinate complex actions across work groups are also learned through facilitative leadership and experience. The high learning rates in democratic start-up teams provide evidence of the importance of democratic processes for organizational intelligence.

In most of our workplaces, especially in the larger bureaucracies, people lack experience in democratic participation. The voting rituals we go through every few years as citizens to select local, state, and federal representatives teach more cynicism than participation and do not prepare us for responsible corporate citizenship.

As organizations leave bureaucracy behind for better ways to express the intelligence of all their members, a crucial aspect of leadership will be to provide the initial education, mentorship, and facilitation needed for participative democracy. As skills and experience in direct democracy spread throughout the organization, so will the capacity and courage for widespread leadership. One of the blessings of participative high-tech companies has been entrepreneurial proliferation and job formation — witness the start-ups that grew from Intel, Hewlett-Packard, Apple, and other Silicon Valley companies. When some of the members eventually spin off and start their own companies, they may take with them technical, entrepreneurial, and social expertise, including an understanding of how to create democratic self-rule.

We can learn collaborative responsibility by taking responsibility for choices at a local level in our workplace teams. The free intraprise system teaches through experience (of both success and failure) responsibility to internal and external customers. Wisdom and judgment emerge from finding ways to pursue simultaneously the self-interests of the team members, the long-term viability of their intraprise, and the interests of partners and customers. With these experiences as a basis, people are capable of shouldering the responsibilities of wider-system democratic self-rule.

Working Smart, Not Hard

High work loads and information overloads discourage people from meeting to maintain a common focus on their future options and larger purposes. Yet these participative processes improve methods of work and information exchanges and thereby reduce the work load. Participative processes open up communication and share innovation so people do not have to do the same work over again in many different parts of the organization. They also create a simplifying focus that makes it less likely people will work at cross-purposes or on projects that later conflict and thus get killed. Having participated in developing a common ground drives stable stakes in the shared area, around which the information can be organized and prioritized. Taking the time for democratic processes seems to be a magic potion for integrating decentralized groups, improving efficiency, involving workers, and enhancing the quality of the work.

Democracy in its simplest form is a direct way for people to make collective decisions, to set goals and policies, and to work out the best ways to organize to get things done—while leaving large spheres for individual and group freedoms. Direct democracy turns bureaucracy on its head, giving employees as a group the big picture and the authority to plan and implement their roles in the shared future.

✳ PARTICIPATIVE DEMOCRACY

When most people think of democracy, they think of voting for representatives who then make laws and policies and put in place a bureaucracy to administer them. This combination of representative democracy and bureaucracy is greatly superior to bureaucracy put in place by a dictator or an autocratic CEO, but it still does not create intelligent organizations.

The participative democracy needed by an intelligent organization is any process that involves everyone's intelligence directly in anticipating, solving, and acting on the complex challenges any organization faces. Representative democracy does little to involve ordinary people in designing the organization or planning its strategy and tactics. Worker representation on boards of corporations helps establish progressive policies on issues like safety and vacations, but we now know it does little if anything to increase worker involvement.[15] Fred Emery, one of the originators of the organizational self-management movement, said, "When we are talking about the sort of personal commitment that carries over to the daily activity in the workplace then we can place into the waste basket such things as exhortations and glossy communications from on high, profit sharing, and advisory bodies such as joint consultative committees and Works Councils. Schemes for worker representatives on corporate boards deserve a special place near the bottom of the waste basket."[16]

The democratic system needed in workplaces today gives employees more control over their individual and collective work lives. Yet there are areas, such as protecting limited resources and the corporate reputation, where a loss of control by responsible corporate officers raises legitimate concerns. Are people ready for that level of responsibility? Does the organization have the leadership to educate and facilitate democratic processes and develop widespread leadership? Can we develop a cost-effective, responsible democracy in the workplace rather than the contentious partisanship we see in national politics, in which numerous interest groups compete for the benefits of handouts and special power? What if employees tipped the table in the direction of wages and benefits that would cost them their jobs? What if a level of entitlements were voted in that bankrupted the company? Democracy works best when a firm constitution guarantees the rights of individuals and groups and limits the voting-in of entitlements.

Thomas Jefferson believed that the experience of running a small enterprise such as a family farm was essential preparation for the responsibilities of participating in a democracy. In an advanced free intraprise system, most employees will get that experience as they participate in the management of their intraprises. Membership in self-managing intraprises will give people in the organization the sobering experience of managing the bottom line, meeting a payroll, and seeing the consequences of their decisions. As a result, they will bring more wisdom and financial conservatism to their participation.

In for-profit business organizations, there is a natural logic for establishing a system of checks and balances that will further ensure financial responsibility. It is logical to create systems that represent a variety of stakeholders, including not only employees but also other owners and investors. Things will work best when both owners and workers agree on the course of action. In organizations that continue to separate ownership and employeeship, there might be two "houses" that must both consent to major decisions—one to include both the owners and the investors, and the other composed of employees. "Major decisions" might be limited to borrowing, stock issues, the design of financial control systems, headquarters budgets, safety, and other issues that directly affect the solvency of the organization.

Robert Dahl, in his book *Democracy and Its Critics*, presents many legitimate concerns that democracy raises, but he argues throughout the book that real participative democracy is necessary to freedom: "Democracy tends to provide a more extensive domain of personal freedom than any other kind of regime."[17] Specifically, Dahl goes on, the advantages of the democratic process are threefold:

> It promotes freedom as no feasible alternative can; freedom in the form of individual and collective self-determination, in the degree of moral autonomy it encourages and allows, and in a broad range of...particular [rights].
>
> Second, the democratic process promotes human development, not least in the capacity for exercising self-determination, moral autonomy, and responsibility for one's choices.
>
> Finally, it is the surest way (if by no means perfect one) by which human beings can protect and advance the interests and goods they share with others.[18]

Democracy presupposes that people are intrinsically equal in their moral worth. To work in practice, democracy requires that people "perceive themselves as about equally qualified to govern."[19] This perception of equality grows from experience with taking joint responsibility. The experiments with empowerment and participation in workplace decision making are proliferating, the extent of participation snowballing as people strengthen their abilities to self-govern, get good results, and gain more trust of themselves and others.

Democracy addresses the paradox that every act of freedom takes place within the limits and opportunities of relationship. Within collective enterprises—families, neighborhoods, workplaces, joint ventures, networks—everyone must simultaneously pursue what will benefit them, their customers, colleagues, families, friends, workplaces, and communities. Nowadays, as people and the planet become more interdependent, we are forced to figure in a wider span of responsibility, adding to the equation the health of all the systems our work encompasses. As organizations work to promote everyone's freedom and opportunities while wrestling with complex challenges, democratic processes give more opportunity for everyone to contribute wisdom.

A pitfall of all these benefits of participative democracy, as Marvin Weisbord points out, is that we can be lured into laissez-faire management before people have the systems and experience to manage themselves. "[Managers] defer to participation, imagining a collective magic born of good intentions that absolves them of tough choices." The trick that leaders can learn by experience, Weisbord says, is to let teams gradually take on the responsibilities of self-rule.[20]

Flexible Work Designs from Democratic Teams

People can do most of their work in the ground level of workplace democracy, small egalitarian teams that are fully participative in figuring out how to do the work. Systems that involve everyone in the work design produce faster adaptation and more focused innovation and therefore end up with more effective systems of work than the ones designed by experts or bosses for more passive workers.

We get much better results when the people doing the work have an active hand in designing it.[21] Given the opportunity to participate in design and decision processes, people discover in themselves high levels of responsibility and effectiveness. This idea seems obvious today, but our bureaucratic institutions are based on the opposite principle, namely, that the best results are obtained when work is designed by supervisors who tell those below how to do their job.

In 1949, Kenneth Bamforth from the Tavistock Institute in London discovered self-regulating teams in a South Yorkshire coal mine. Rather than specializing in a single task, each team did a whole group of tasks, from shoring up the walls to extracting and moving coal. Each individual on each team developed all-around skills, and roles became interchangeable. After visiting the mine, Bamforth's mentor, Eric Trist, wrote that "cooperation between task groups was everywhere in evidence, personal commitment was obvious, absenteeism low, accidents infrequent, productivity high."[22]

The people doing the work can design a more effective system because they are closer to how it works and know what is needed to make it work better. They have among themselves a diversity of knowledge, approach, and experience. Being responsible for the local system design, they can adapt it as situations unfold. Doers respond with specific practical innovations and new collaborative associations; higher-ups tend to respond with broad-brush policies, simple structures, and rules that collectively restrict adaptability.

The processes of a business usually involve a number of people. If the many people involved have continual responsibility for the whole system, their job descriptions must at least overlap here, making each diverse individual both a specialist and an intrapreneurial generalist. Even without training, people in small teams can often find effective ways to work together; with a little training to erase the destructive beliefs inculcated by a history of bureaucracy, the chances are excellent that a self-managing team will perform well. Team participation is increased as people gradually develop their overlapping repertoires of skills and their understanding of one another's jobs and responsibilities. A multiskilled workforce has the ability to trade, redesign, eliminate, and fit jobs together more efficiently, and flexibly adapt to changing demands.

Rosabeth Moss Kanter describes a clash of traditions for organizing work when General Motors and Toyota set up a joint venture on the West Coast. To make the collaboration possible, GM had to get a major concession from the union to radically reduce the number of job classifications. "When GM ran the plant, there were 33 separate classifications; for a similar plant, Toyota had three. Consider the implications of 33 different jobs versus three. Toyota had people who thought more broadly, knew more things to do, and were more flexible."[23]

Because modern enterprises are flexible networks, ever responding to customers and other external sources of change, work systems must be redesigned constantly. Competition and rising standards of quality require continual improvement of all processes. Changing customer needs and specific service requirements call for a flexible response, customer by customer. This continual redesign of the connections in the intelligent network requires so much detailed first-hand intelligence that it will be done effectively only by the people involved. Only the people dealing directly with customers can immediately make the connections needed to work the system in the customers' interest. Only the people operating the system see and touch it enough to do a detailed job of adapting the processes and policies to a continually evolving task.

The payoff can be great, as Rosabeth Moss Kanter noted: "In facilities that are run by employee teams who manage them as though they were their own businesses, costs are half what they are in conventional factories, quality is higher, and flexibility is higher."[24] When people stick to narrowly defined roles that are rigidly defined by collective bargaining, there is little freedom for self-managing teams and thus little real workplace democracy of the kind that brings out a sense of being in control of one's own work life. Making job categories broader is a necessary precondition for self-selection of tasks and a sense of responsibility for the whole business. The unions of the future will demand freedom of action and the right to the fuller use of intelligence for all employees.

A Self-Managing Special Project Team

Sherritt, Inc., used the Canadian National Railroad (CN) to haul fertilizer, but they had a lot of complaints about the service CN provided. CN management listened and believed that unless they improved the quality of service provided to Sherritt, they would lose Sherritt's business. CN management decided to get a handle on the situation by meeting with Sherritt's management and listing all the problems Sherritt had with CN's service.

Once they had the list, CN management divided it into problems CN should handle internally and things that would best yield to Sherritt-CN collaborative problem solving. Working together, Cathy Hrudey, from the CN Quality at Work office in Edmonton, and Sherritt put together a joint quality action team of seven people, including

Len Lindsay, Locomotive Engineer/CN

Gary Morris, Coordinator Customer Service/CN

Ron Wells, Train Movement Clerk, Calder/CN

Darryl McBurney, Conductor, Scotford Yard Switcher, Assignment 601/CN

Bill Sudyk, Supervisor Feed Materials/Sherritt

Carl Dzwienko, Production Supervisor Fert I/Sherritt

Ken Witwicki, Production Supervisor Fert II/Sherritt

Cathryn Hrudey, Facilitator (Administrator, Quality)

The team took a two-day course in problem solving at the CN Quality at Work Center in Edmonton, including

♦ Defining problems

♦ Brainstorming causes (including cause-and-effect [fish-bone] diagrams)

♦ Gathering statistics on frequency of causes (Pareto diagrams)

♦ Analyzing the data

♦ Brainstorming solutions

♦ Planning

♦ Making recommendations

♦ Monitoring results

After they completed the problem-solving course at the CN Quality at Work Center, the joint quality action team went to work on the list of unsolved problems from the earlier joint CN-Sherritt management meeting. The team identified the root causes of operating problems. The most common, they discovered, was poor communications. Not knowing that Canadian railway regulations had safety rules that required mandatory rest for train crews after eight hours on duty, Sherritt people became frustrated and annoyed when incoming trains stopped for rest just a few miles from the terminal. They thought the crews stopped because they felt like it, and it seemed very inconsiderate that Sherritt had to wait for the trains to be delivered. Once Sherritt's people understood the safety rules, they were better able to predict and deal with the delays. CN, with a clearer understanding of Sherritt's concerns, focused on having fresh crews to meet its commitments.

A problem arose when Sherritt ordered extra unscheduled cars on short notice. Often the only extra cars CN had available had just carried something other than fertilizer, but Sherritt marketing people, determined to deliver their fertilizer according to their customers' needs, would accept the uncleaned, empty cars. However, sometimes the fertilizer ended up contaminated; for example, fertilizer stored in a car that has previously held wheat without first being cleaned will be contaminated. After studying numerous incidents of this kind, the team discovered that the most common problem was lack of communication between Sherritt marketing and Sherritt loading crews. The loading crews were not informed which cars were unclean. Sherritt put in procedures to make sure their loading crews were notified of dirty cars, and the problem cleared up.

Perhaps the funniest problem (after it was solved) occurred because the two teams spoke different "languages." One company called a huge depression in the ground near the entrance to the Sherritt facility "the valley"; the other called it "the hole." If one company called it the "south gate," the other company wondered why it came in from the north. Amid such misunderstandings, trains got misdirected.

Sherritt had ten sidings sensibly called number 1, number 2, number 3, and so on. For CN, the ten sidings were part of a much larger identification system, so they had odd names for them like VD58, VD67, and so on. Only experienced CN crew members knew that VD58 was number 3, VD67 was number 8, and so on. New train crews on rotation did not know Sherritt's system. As a result, when Sherritt asked for a car to be redirected to siding number 7, it often ended up on the wrong track.

The CN people explained that their track numbers were hard to change. But the Sherritt numbering system was uncomplicated and preferred by Sherritt people. The frustration on each side with the other's inability to adapt might have ended cooperation if a trained facilitator had not been there to defuse it. In the end the team found two solutions to the siding names problem:

> The buildings at the end of each siding were already labeled with the Sherritt number. They added the CN numbers to the ten sidings. Sherritt people thus could direct CN with CN numbers, and CN crews more rapidly learned the Sherritt system.

> Sherritt orders for cars were communicated by faxing a map clearly indicating where the cars were to be placed. The engineers took the map with them on the train and knew that they placed cars where Sherritt wanted them to be.

Soon the cars were arriving at the right siding, and the joint company quality action team went on to solving more problems.

Before the teamwork, the CN people were justified in fearing they might lose Sherritt's business if the problems were not solved. When the team finished its work, Sherritt gave CN more business. No management team working on all the problems occurring on those ten sidings would have had the time to explore every incident in detail and figure out root causes for every type of failure. Having less time for a thorough analysis of the problem, management would have guessed at the causes and ordered broad-brush solutions that probably would have infuriated the people in both companies who were actually doing the work. By contrast, the solutions the team found worked, in part because the people who came up with them were the people who implemented them.

As an outsider it is easy to criticize some of the solutions the team came up with as not being bold enough. Why couldn't CN change more, for example, by sticking a bright label on the dirty cars? This sort of second-guessing from a distance is exactly what management must learn not to do. Another example: Painting numbers on the sidings and faxing maps seems hokey. If a management team had been put on the job, with the power at their disposal they would have been tempted to order changes in CN's computer systems so the sidings could be renamed to fit Sherritt's numbers.

This kind of top-down solution would have cost more, taken longer, diverted limited information systems resources from other critical projects, failed to build friendships and the habit of problem solving between workers in the two companies, and thus failed to keep the Sherritt account with CN.

Team Training and Democratic Process. Canadian National Railway's Quality at Work office for Western Canada would like to train everyone in CN to work in teams to solve problems collaboratively. However, CN has learned that it works best to wait to train teams until just before they set out to solve a specific real problem. At CN all volunteers for quality action teams learn basics like brainstorming, list reduction, use of cause-and-effect diagrams, data gathering, and use of Pareto diagrams. They learn to work together through a more democratic process and to create common output from a diverse group better than what any one of them could have done alone. Immediately after the course, working with a trained facilitator, they practice what they have learned by addressing their real problems and concerns. This sort of training and experience builds the base of skills and attitudes needed later for broader adventures in democracy.

Overcoming Bureaucratic History. CN and Sherritt, as we have seen, were wise to use the intelligence of the people who had the problem to solve it. But given its history, it was not easy for CN to break with bureaucratic ways. As in many organizations tracing back to the dawn of the industrial era, relations between labor and management at CN are colored by what are seen as past betrayals by both sides. Even within management or within labor, historical functional "silos" left over from the heyday of bureaucratic industrial engineering keep people so separate that it remains harder to understand where a person from another function is coming from and easier to point fingers than to solve problems together.

Railroads, because they became huge early in the Industrial Revolution, were early pioneers in the development of the bureaucratic system. The rules of bureaucracy were necessary to coordinate a system too large for any one person to understand. They prevented wrecks, kept schedules, and organized relations with a huge labor force. Now, computers and other modern systems let us replace this rigid bureaucracy with more flexible systems, but the old ways are built into the system and die hard.

The rail industry has been downsizing for a long time, and downsizing makes it hard to create an attitude of trust and collaboration. The reasons for downsizing continue—for instance, stiff competition from the trucking industry, which is subsidized by government-provided roads. Yet relations between management and labor may be improving, and a more positive future for railroads developing, as people are trained to work together democratically toward the common objective of getting and keeping the business on which all their jobs depend.

✳ FREEDOM AND LARGE-SCALE COOPERATION

[Intelligent organization] flourishes under that type of democracy that accents freedom of opinion and dissent, and respect for the individual.
NEVITT SANFORD

One of the basic challenges of our time is to find more ways to organize the larger systems so teams can safely be given more control over their own destinies. Within a free intraprise system, teams skilled at democratic self-management can make many of the decisions that shape their contribution to the larger system. They can initiate and participate in many possible partnerships with other teams, formally as vendors and customers but actually as a network of friends. Having found customers, they can negotiate what they will deliver and use their own methods to produce it. It is a lot of responsibility for all, but it is also highly productive.

As the issues to be addressed involve more people and the size of the group participating in the design of work systems increases, more conscious technique and thoughtful structure are required. Future search conferences are a starting point in getting everyone focused on the big picture and pulled by the real challenges of the future into cooperative action. Large democratic systems are often made up of groups. If it is possible to imagine a search conference with representatives from sixty-five lead intraprises, each representing in a sense their supporting network of thousands of suppliers, it is possible to imagine a democratic process for a very large enterprise. The context set by common values and purposes can simplify the subsequent processes of collaborative decision making.

There are broad but specific issues needing binding decisions that everyone in an organization or department must agree on and, once determined, obey until they are redetermined. These common agreements address the many issues that cross boundaries between teams—for example, the multitude of decisions that must be made in developing a product or service. Then there are the wide issues of strategy and governance that affect everyone yet must be flexible and able to evolve—can these too be more democratically developed, with individuals and teams still retaining basic rights to manage themselves?

The Consent Model

Twenty-five years ago, a Dutch firm, Endenburg Electrotechniek, pioneered a surprisingly creative and specific way of increasing employee participation in decision making.[25] The system has since spread widely in Holland and made significant inroads in Canada, due to the work of Gilles Charest of Montreal. More recently it has begun to find application in Brazil and the United States as well as a few other European countries.[26]

The organization of Endenburg Electrotechniek is still hierarchical, but the way in which decisions are made differs considerably from practices in a traditional bureaucracy. The basic democratic principle of the Endenburg system is neither voting nor consensus but what Endenburg calls "consent." Consent occurs when no reasoned objection to a decision remains.

The consent process empowers even the last lonely voice, because as long as anyone can give good reasons against a decision favored by the majority or higher-ups, the system has to listen to the reasons for dissent. Dialogue on all reasoned objections usually leads to further creativity and better plans. Consent produces more intelligent decisions than either voting or decision by the chain of command because it takes into account more points of view.

Work Groups. In the "consent" system of participative democracy, every person is in one or more work groups. Each group has its own mission, produces an output, and measures and manages itself. Members of the group choose by consent strategies and policies appropriate to its mission and scope of authority. The mission and scope of authority are defined by a group one level up in the hierarchy of groups.

Double Linking. Endenburg Electrotechniek is a hierarchy of groups rather than a hierarchy of individual managers. Each group is linked to the group above it in the hierarchy with a double link. The group is represented in the meetings of the next level group by its "manager" and a representative from the group itself selected by consent. The manager is appointed by consent in the group above and consented to by the group he or she is to manage. This double linking of each group to the group above changes the character of hierarchy. Information a manager might choose to hide from his or her work group is carried freely by the representative.

Election by Consent to Tasks. In the consent system, people are not appointed or ordered to tasks by the manager. Tasks and jobs are distributed with the consent of all members of the group. Anyone may raise reasons why an assignment is inappropriate and suggest alternatives. If someone thinks the person suggested for a task is not the best suited, he or she can speak up, and the dialogue lasts until a candidate is found with everyone's consent.

The consent model may seem at odds with some aspects of a free intraprise network. For instance, the consent model makes the hierarchy work better rather than replacing it with an internal market discipline of free intraprise. But the hierarchy of groups that have links to both management and workers in the consent model is not exactly a hierarchy of command. We believe a version of the consent model can be useful in a free intraprise organization in these ways:

Use the consent model within intraprises

Use the consent model in the remaining "organizational government," which might otherwise be a more traditional bureaucracy

Use the consent model to find overall missions, strategies, and policies for the organization

Use the consent model to link the flexible hierarchy of supplier tiers in the network supporting a major project or enterprise

The consent model is just one of many ways to structure collective self-management with democratic participation. Workplace participation is inherently energizing—engendering learning and commitment. People try harder to make a system work if they have had a hand in designing it and guiding the day-to-day changes. As systems get bigger, maintaining a sense of coherence and common purpose without using authoritarian means requires more conscious effort to find the right democratic processes.

Voting from Ownership (ESOPs) and Worker-Owned Cooperatives

Employee ownership is a direct way to make networks of free intraprise teams and larger groups more democratic, because when owners and employees are the same, employees vote as stockholders.

"No other approach has succeeded in democratizing the firm so well" as employee ownership, say Corey Rosen, Katherine J. Klein, and Karen M. Young, coauthors of the 1986 book *Employee Ownership in America: The Equity Solution.*[27] Rosen is the executive director of the National Center for Employee Ownership, founded in 1981 to provide employee ownership information to its membership, which now numbers over seventeen hundred. Rosen and his colleagues have documented the expanding group of companies in which workers have an equity stake and also participate in some aspects of decision making. Gary B. Hansen and Frank T. Adams are also studying the growth of employee ownership in all its forms, whether the organization combines equity ownership with any direct participative democratic processes, has only limited representation for worker-owners on boards and councils, or has no democratic processes. They note that employee ownership "has increased over fifty times...since 1974." In their book *Putting Democracy to Work: A Practical Guide for Starting and Managing Worker-Owned Businesses*, they separate out the various areas of legitimacy for both democratic participation and ownership.[28]

They distinguish three areas of legitimacy for "rule of the many, not the few": shop floor/work group decision making; management level decision making; board level decision making. How much democratic influence is allowed in each organization or level? What is the legitimate domain of everyone's collaborative control? Do workers control their work? Can they become collectively self-managing between teams as well? Can they have influence on board missions and policies?

Adams and Hansen also distinguish two financial involvement approaches—sharing of rewards, and sharing of ownership. Do workers share the profits? Do they own equity that could grow as the company's value increases? Sharing profits or ownership may or may not include expanded rights to decision making. The combination of financial involvement (profit-sharing, ESOPs, or direct ownership) and democratic involvement (through rights and participative decision making) is becoming more common, with some big companies such as the Polaroid leading the way. It is a direct and important way to encourage participation and help guarantee the legitimacy of everyone's involvement in democratic self-management.

A smaller company, Web Industries, a $20-million contract manufacturer founded in 1969, began a program for all employees to acquire a 25-percent stake in the company funded from profits. Web had an employee stock ownership program for several years before they realized that the level of participation of the employee-owners did not necessarily change because they owned stock in the company. They began a series of changes to increase participation. The CEO meets with each employee-owner annually. Employees meet in small groups to openly exchange information. Self-managing teams are being organized.[29] The operations manager of the Framingham plant, Bill Holt, described the changes over the years in the managerial roles: "Nineteen years ago, when I came to work here, the plant manager was boss. He had the authority. You did what he said or you lost your job. He was in charge of all operational decisions. Today, I am an advisor. This is the way I like to work anyway. I have to accomplish my job through other people by teaching, by listening, by encouraging. I have to be about helping people to grow."[30] Bill Holt, like the other Web Industries managers, takes a turn at the switchboard every day— essentially doing his part to maintain the outside network connections for everyone else who works there.[31]

Leadership is at the core of the transformation of organization to a more democratic state. Rosen, Klein, and Young state,

There is often a strong, dynamic, charismatic leader who is making this egalitarian imprint on the company. One of our researchers reported that he felt as though he has been through a wind storm after an interview with one of these company's CEOs. This kind of dynamism is the extreme, but it is often present and is apparently inspiring. It inspires others to believe in and try to make ownership work. There is, of course, an irony here, for it seems that in some cases one of the best ways to create a more equitable workplace is to find a strong leader. When the inertia and habit ingrained in people's more traditional expectations about how work should be organized are considered, however, the usefulness of having such a strong, change-oriented leader becomes more obvious.[32]

✳ FULL PARTICIPATION

Both worker ownership and unions can be powerful tools to institutionalize effective democracy, or they can be irrelevant.

The modern purpose for a union will be to create a democratic system that uses everyone's input to make better decisions. Forget the old pattern, in which the union only fought for money, benefits, safety, and welfare issues. The modern union's day-to-day work is as part of the brain of the organization—an alternative route for communicating visions, ideas, and opinions. The genius of unions will be in creating systems that are participative, fast, and cost-effective, that have worthwhile destinations and contribute to the development of all their members. These tasks enter the territory of management prerogatives—how the system should work and what its priorities should be. If the union evolves to become the much-needed institution for bringing democratic input to business decisions, the old bargain in which the union left management to managers will end. With new responsibilities to ensure that every employee's voice is heard and respected, the union can cease adversarial protection of workers and help everyone participate in shouldering the burden of tough choices. This is a great opportunity for unions to reinvent themselves.

There is a parallel between workplace ownership and union membership—if we conceptualize both as vehicles for grounding the rights and responsibilities of democratic self-rule in the workplace. All employees, including management, can make their participation more concrete either through actual workplace ownership or as members of highly democratic unions. This system will work if everyone embraces the task of empowering every employee with a respect for reasonable profit and a drive to deliver the organization's mission.

The effectiveness and deep humanity of democratic self-management suggests a simple direction: To achieve high levels of responsiveness and responsibility in a workplace, put people in control. Engage the intelligence of everyone in the organization, and provide feedback that tests output against shifting realities. Put to work the inherent morality of democratic participation and self-rule.

15

Limited Corporate Government

That government is best which governs least.

THOMAS JEFFERSON

THE "GOVERNMENT" OF a traditional corporation consists of the board of directors and the chain of command. Traditionally that government is totalitarian, reserving for itself the right to make all the rules and business decisions. Freedom is an essential ingredient of organizational intelligence, and that freedom can exist only when the organization's government has a limited role.

The structure and method of operation of bureaucratic organizations more closely resembles the command economy of the former Soviet Union than the limited government and self-organizing systems of a free nation. In the bureaucratic system, the government of an organization may delegate some freedom of action to its divisions, but it is still in charge of them in the same sense that the Soviet ministries were in charge of that nation's nationalized businesses.

This chain-of-command relationship between the parts of a system and its center is not inevitable. Although it creates laws that they must follow, the U.S. government does not run General Motors or the National Audubon Society.

An emerging worldwide consensus holds that the government's role should be limited by civil rights, respect for the free market, and a bias against giving the government tasks that could be performed as well or better by independent groups. The basic impetus driving national economies toward free markets is the market's superior ability to foster productivity, innovation, and the efficient coordination of complex technologies. For this same reason, an intelligent organization limits the role of government and relies more on the power of internal markets and internal community to bring an effective order. Instead of directly managing the organization's many intraprises, a limited organizational government creates rules of the market that make the networks of independent intraprises effective.

The emerging worldwide consensus also holds that the legitimate source of governmental power is the will of the people. To most living outside of totalitarian states, this implies some form of democracy in which people are given ultimate control over the context of and limits to their collective freedom. The belief in democracy is driven by a popular distrust of power in the hands of the few and a strong egalitarian philosophy: All people are equally worthy of consideration and respect.

Democracy improves productivity because people work harder to make a system work if they have had a hand in designing it. Moreover, it seems that systems designed with a broad spectrum of voices at the table are often better attuned to the real world. For all these reasons, advanced intelligent organizations will use democratic processes to shape the decisions of their organizational governments.

✳ THE SOURCES OF LEGITIMATE POWER

Before the eighteenth century, those in charge of in Europe and its colonies conducted policy for the benefit of the king and his associates, not for the good of the common people.

In *The Work of Nations*, Robert Reich writes, "National wealth pertained only to the wealth of the sovereign—to the kings and queens and retainers who contrived, financed, and directed various schemes to accumulate foreign riches in order to wage wars and enhance their power and prestige—rather than to the well-being of ordinary individuals within the nation. Patriotism meant devotion to the monarch rather than to fellow citizens."[1]

Another view emerged in the eighteenth century. The policy and laws of the land had the welfare of the citizens as their purpose, not the enrichment of the king. Nations still sought a strong economy, and did so in part to support a strong military, but their reason was to remain free of foreign domination, not to support the glory of their sovereigns.

The eighteenth century saw a series of revolutions against aristocratic governments and in favor of governments of the people, for the people, and by the people. "Democratic patriotism proved a far more potent force than loyalty to a sovereign," Reich continues. "Sacrificing one's life and property to a monarch living luxuriously in a distant castle seemed far less inspiring (and less sensible) than sacrificing for one's nation."[2] Democracy built stronger nations. This same basic logic, along with the growing complexity and growing mobility of talent, will eventually lead to the growth of democracy in organizations such as businesses, nonprofits, and government agencies.

As society challenges the legitimacy of organizations along several dimensions of performance, they need the capacity for effectiveness while serving multiple ends.

Not long ago it was common for some managers, institutional investors, and even business school professors to say that the manager of a public corporation's sole responsibility was to get the best possible return for shareholders. Serving customers well or making a decent life for employees might be an effective strategy toward that end, but these things were legitimate for management consideration only as means, not as ends in themselves. Every humane breakthrough in business practices was legitimate only if one could *prove* it increased profits.

Today, with customer focus emerging as a new "religion," many managers see serving customers as the end and adequate profits as a necessary means. And as relationships in an organization become more collegial—or as high-value talent becomes the center of competitive advantage—the happiness of employees is emerging as a legitimate end as well. In explaining Federal Express's extraordinary success, James Brian Quinn says, "The Federal Express manager's manual states, 'People-Service-Profit [in that order] are the very foundation of Federal Express.'"[3] This is the exact reverse of the more traditional profit-customers-employees.

As the ends of organizational governance are changing to include more beneficiaries, the means will in time become more democratic as well. In a funny way, designing democratic systems for nations is easier than designing them for organizations that exist to fulfill a mission. Whereas a nation exists primarily for the benefit of one group of people, its citizens, a productive organization serves customers, working members, owners or trustees, and the communities in which it operates. There are many different types of formal stakeholders and many possible ways their interests and viewpoints can be represented.

We have discussed many of the processes by which multiple viewpoints will be integrated. They include recognition of rights, forming of self-managing teams, free intraprise, and the processes of democratic self-rule. In the next decades we will gain knowledge of how to apply democratic self-rule within larger organizations. Will we end up using representative democracy with separate "houses"—one for owners (the board), another for employees, perhaps including managers (the union?), and a third for the larger community? Can these groups work through collaborative processes to find wider common ground?

Will real-time systems of computerized voting be widely used? In *Democracy and Its Critics*, Robert Dahl suggests a way to deal with a very complex world.[4] For each major national issue, impanel a large (he suggests one thousand people), randomly selected group. Give them time (he suggests a year) to educate themselves and meet via telecommunication. Then take their informed opinion on the subject. A smaller and briefer version of Dahl's process might be used to extend democracy to organizations too large for more direct democracy. A major advantage of random as opposed to elected representatives is the time saved and the grandstanding and bitterness avoided by doing without elections and political parties. Of course, groups might spring up to lobby those selected, but those selected have no political debts to pay and no hope of reelection, so they can vote an educated conscience.

The experiments now being carried out are too new for us to know what forms will work best. What we do know is that those organizations that find efficient ways to get the widest variety of viewpoints integrated in creative solutions will have a significant competitive advantage.

✳ THE TASKS OF ORGANIZATIONAL GOVERNMENT

The word government is from a Greek word, which means to "steer." The job of the government is to steer, not to row the boat. Delivering services is rowing and government is not very good at rowing.

                                                                    E. S. SAVAS

In totalitarian bureaucracy the organizational government performs tasks such as

♦ Managing the business units via the chain of command

♦ Providing various staff services to the business units

♦ Promulgating and enforcing rules and standards

♦ Allocating resources to businesses and projects

♦ Developing and implementing visions and strategies for coordination among businesses

♦ Interfacing with external groups, such as investors and governments

In an intelligent organization, the tasks performed by the center are far more limited than the tasks of a totalitarian bureaucracy. In their book *Reinventing Government,* David Osborne and Ted Gaebler clarify what tasks a limited government should perform and what tasks it should leave for citizens, businesses, and other nongovernmental organizations. They build on Savas's distinction between rowing and steering. By rowing they mean managing and doing work; for example, sweeping the streets, building roads, providing counseling, building and managing low-income housing, housing the homeless, manufacturing, and policing. By steering they mean guiding the work of independent enterprises that do the work; for example, developing legal rules and sanctions; monitoring and investigation; licensing;

making tax policy; subsidizing, contracting, and creating public-private partnerships; rewarding; providing information, seed money, and encouraging volunteers; collecting impact fees; making equity investments; providing vision; and shaping the rules of the game to bend the system toward things that make it work for the good of the whole.[5] They summarize:

> Steering requires people who see the entire universe of issues and possibilities and can balance competing demands for resources. Rowing requires people who focus intently on one mission and perform it well. Steering organizations need to find the best methods to achieve their goals. Rowing organizations tend to defend 'their' method at all costs.[6]

When governments get involved in providing services, they get stuck in defending their methods and results rather than scanning the world for better ways to keep the system in balance. The result of a government too involved in rowing is often a slow boat headed in the wrong direction. Osborne and Gaebler conclude that state, local, and national governments should, whenever possible, get out of the business of providing services so they can concentrate on guiding the system and catalyzing action by others.[7]

With some exceptions, a similar logic holds for governments of intelligent organizations. Intelligent organizations operating complex enterprises will discover that the primary role of the center is to create a context for an effective free intraprise system, not to run the intraprises themselves. Only when no viable alternative exists should the organizational government enter into the business of producing products or services. This takes the headquarters largely out of the business of appointing, supervising, and rewarding the people who run the many enterprises of the organization. The operation of enterprises and internal services is generally better when disciplined by the self-organizing systems of choice than when given to bureaucracy's monopolies of power.

For national governments, defense is one possible exception to the warnings against rowing: Governments may buy the weapons, but they still direct their nations' forces in battle.[8] Similarly, the limited government of an intelligent organization may come to the aid of a business unit under concerted or "unfair" attack. In some cases the center will "row," for example by taking over the legal defense of a business unit being sued for amounts that threaten the whole organization. Whenever possible, however, the organization will defend using the tools of steering rather than direct participation in the battle. Central steering might include funding targeted intrapreneurial R&D, subsidizing heavy advertising or price cutting, and picking up legal expenses.

Few organizations today have their mature externally focused enterprises operating on a free intraprise system. The steps to a free intraprise system require letting go of the enterprises and trusting

■ THE ROLES OF ORGANIZATIONAL GOVERNMENT

	Bureaucracy	Intelligent Organization
Steering the system—e.g., vision and values, whole-system strategies, rules of the game, standards	SOMETIMES *top management may be too involved in crises to think deeply about these issues but unwilling to let go*	ALWAYS *this is the core job of the government but not a monopoly of government; leaders help everyone to steer*
Operating the enterprises *serving external customers*	ALWAYS *enterprises are run by the chain of command with corporate allocation of capital and approval of budgets*	SOMETIMES *leaders may be centrally appointed; when possible, intraprises run independently with employee intra-ownership and control*
Providing services *to its enterprises*	USUALLY *provides all services that are not outsourced through staff groups run by the chain of command*	ALMOST NEVER *are services to intraprises provided by any but free intraprises or outside firms*
Defending *against outside attack*	SOMETIMES *bureaucracies seem strangely willing to abandon businesses and competencies under attack; internal monopoly power is strongly defended*	SOMETIMES *the "government" may subsidize businesses under attack; it may protect or subsidize developing and strategic competencies*

them to internal "intrapreneurial" co-owners. As with privatization of state-owned industries, this process is bound to create some turbulent changes in the operation as the new "owners" cut out the fat left by years of bureaucratic administration.

"Intrapreneurialization" (the internal equivalent of privatization) of business units is far easier if the units are small in relation to the organization as a whole. In the case of a large functional organization with only one business unit, there may be no way the center can let go of the responsibility for managing the business directly. In such a case, the first step is decentralization by dividing the organization into business units. With demassifying markets and a new taste for buying services "unbundled," the marketplace often supports decentralization anyway.

Though intrapreneurialization of externally focused businesses may be a slow process, intrapreneurialization of corporate or "head office" services can proceed far more rapidly. Most services provided to the operating units of the organization can be put on a free choice basis. Many of these staff services are not highly capital intensive, so there are fewer difficulties with capitalizing the intrapreneurialization of a software function, for example, than there might be in an oil refinery or an integrated circuit fabrication plant.

The kinds of service that can be intrapreneurialized are diverse. The Maintenance Shop Renewal program at Union Carbide's Texas City plant encouraged maintenance personnel to run their area as if they were an independent entrepreneurship. They set their own prices, marketed their services, and bid for jobs against outside contractors.[9]

The machine shop learned that they could recondition the seals in the plant's approximately 2,200 pumps for less than half the cost of getting them rebuilt at the factory, a savings of $200,000 in 1992. Intrapreneur Bobbie Dillard saw the opportunity under the Maintenance Shop Renewal program to get more business for the machine shop and extend the savings to other plants. They bid on the overhaul of two hundred seal parts at the nearby Taft, Louisiana, plant. "The cost was less than a quarter of what Taft normally would have paid to its mechanical seal supplier to repair them."[10] What had been a maintenance cost center has begun to show revenue, give excellent customer service, and save the corporation money.

✳ STEERING THE SYSTEM

At a minimum, the center of an intelligent organization provides visionary leadership, justice, and the rules and boundaries of the game. These tools are used with an egalitarian bias, but this bias must be weighed against the need to govern with a light hand and leave as much freedom in the system as possible.

Organizational governments will, at least

♦ Guarantee the rights of people, teams, and intraprises

♦ Establish the institutions of the internal market

♦ Provide or charter system(s) of justice

♦ Provide limits that protect the reputation, integrity, and deep pockets of the corporation

♦ Intervene when a unit mistreats customers, the environment, or employees

♦ Provide an unemployment and health care safety net for all employees

♦ Support both the continuing education of employees and organizational learning

♦ Support organizational standards for accounting, product and service compatibility, and other common systems

♦ Foster dialogue on the vision for the long-term future of the organization

Frequently, organizational governments will also

♦ Guide and encourage a communications infrastructure

♦ Coordinate and fund strategies too large for any intraprise to take on

♦ Support marketing beachheads in new territories — nations, product categories, customer groups

♦ Foster the development of core capabilities

♦ Fund the defense of intraprises against unfair attacks

Finding a Common Vision

Declining bureaucratic organizations seek a shared vision as though it were a magical cure. This notion makes sense, because organizations with a shared vision need far fewer bureaucratic controls. It is easy to believe that "all we need is a compelling and inspiring vision of where we are going, and the troops will get out of bed in the morning eager to do or die."

The problem with this line of thinking is that it is difficult to find a shared vision that makes a common cause of all the disparate activities of a large organization—particularly if the vision is created without the involvement of those troops.

Some organizations are apparently lucky. Amnesty International has a clear and inspiring mission. The old AT&T found the goal of "Universal Service" guided everyone from a repairman climbing a pole at four in the morning in a storm to the negotiators working with regulators to establish rates high enough to cover the expense of running a cable several miles to serve a rural ranch. The mission drove whatever it took to get one black phone in every home and on every desk and keep them working continuously. This easily understood and worthwhile mission contributed greatly to AT&T's success until the world became more complex. Most organizations are not so fortunate.

For many diversified organizations with a breadth of different businesses, an overall mission would have to be so general that it would give little guidance on specific decisions.

How many times have we heard "missions" with themes like these:

We will provide our customers with the best products and services at a competitive price.

We will treat each employee with respect.

We will be good corporate citizens.

These are not missions, these are values.

In decentralized organizations each business unit often has a separate mission, so any overall mission would have to be so general it would not mean much. In a diversified organization what ties the organization together may be values, core competencies, and ways of doing business rather than a single common mission. 3M's intrapreneurial product development system and ability to apply coatings are core competencies that guide the system. Procter and Gamble's commonalaties include a package goods marketing and distribution capability and an early start in high performance teams for manufacturing. The commonalities of almost any intelligent organization include a belief in freedom and democracy, a spirit of cooperation and cross-boundary sharing, and a set of institutions and educational offerings supporting those values.

Top executives of an intelligent organization tiptoe out of strategy and operations and into the arenas of political science and education in order to create a constructive environment for the intraprises. If that task does not appeal, and for many it will not, the alternative is to remain in or return to an intraprise. The pay and even the status of a successful intrapreneur compares favorably with the status and compensation of a senior official in the limited organizational government of an intelligent organization. In an intelligent organization there is no "top." It is a game with many winners and many sources of vision. People can seek the positions that best suit their talents and interests.

The vision provided by the center of an intelligent organization is most effective if it does not merely echo the inspired imaginings of a brilliant leader but also captures a sense of what the group knows and believes. This creates a ticklish dilemma for leaders operating from the center, because they must pull the organization ahead by holding up pictures of how it could be more than it is today while simultaneously leaving plenty of room for others' creative imagination. Providing vision should not become more an exercise in the leader's own creativity than an act of creative listening. Great leaders sense vision circulating vaguely in the group consciousness and give it a form through participative processes involving a wide spectrum of stakeholders.

Brokering Collaboration

One obvious way to increase the alignment and integration of the organization without using command or force is to broker collaborations. "In Pittsburgh, the Advisory Committee on Homelessness, made up of government, university, community, and religious leaders, coordinates the city's response to homelessness. It uses federal, state, and corporate funds to fund dozens of food banks, soup kitchens, counseling centers, job training programs, and housing initiatives."[11]

According to the *Washington Post*, "This kind of broad-based response to homelessness has helped this city of 387,000 dodge the bullet that is crippling cities like New York, Chicago and Washington."[12]

Leaders inside an intelligent organization who see new ways the pieces could fit together can bring the relevant units together to build on what the leader has imagined. Seeing how the parts could combine forces to create superior value is a valuable leadership role requiring little exercise of power.

Defending the Rights of Members

As Supreme Court Justice Louis D. Brandeis said,

> Those who won our independence believed that the final end of the State was to make people free to develop their faculties. They valued liberty both as an end and as a means. They believed liberty to be the secret of happiness, and courage to be the secret of liberty. They believed that freedom to think as you will and to speak as you think are means indispensable to the discovery and spread of political truth; that the greatest menace to freedom is an inert people; that public discussion is a political duty; and that this should be a fundamental principle of the American government.[12]

The primary job of the central government of a free nation is to maintain a safe space for citizens to exercise their freedoms in constructive and courageous ways. The government helps the people defend their rights against any enemy of freedom, foreign or domestic. For example, in addition to repelling foreign attackers, governments of free nations guarantee free speech and take a dim view of any individual or local government that tries to suppress it.

The government of an intelligent organization has similar responsibilities. It defines the rights of its "citizens" and creates a system for defending them. If a unit tries to suppress the free speech of its people, the organizational government provides courts in which they may seek redress. If an intraprise tries to keep a member from leaving to join another intraprise, the government provides a process to examine the contract between the intraprise and the member and render a just decision.

The rights of the members of intelligent organization are spelled out in a constitution and bill of rights that all officials of the limited organizational government are sworn to uphold. This commitment probably requires an independent judicial system that balances the executive and legislative powers of the central government of the organization.

Creating Rules and Sanctions

We do not know how to make freedom in large systems without rules and regulations. The free enterprise system, for example, is as much a set of rules as it is a set of freedoms. The laws of free enterprise systems place fraud and false advertising outside the boundaries of legal behavior because systems that permit fraud and false advertising are less constructive than those that prevent them.

The real-world alternative to having laws or rules is not anarchy but rather a system in which the officials of the government decide what is acceptable behavior case by case. This system gives those subject to their decisions no ability to predict what will be acceptable, and thus no guaranteed zone of freedom. An intelligent organization gets around excessive reliance on administrative decision making by relying more on freedom within the bounds of rules or laws. Finding and fairly applying a good set of rules is a critical part of governing. A good set of rules leaves a wide latitude of freedom for all the players and at the same time creates boundaries and force fields that channel free choices toward the good of the whole.

It may seem ironic that a critical step in reducing bureaucracy is the creation of rules or laws. The difference is this: The rules of bureaucracy more often specify what is to be done or who has what powers over whom; the rules of a liberated organization define the boundaries within which there is free choice.

Intelligent organizations are flexible in part because the rules adapt over time. Many of the players are involved not only in playing within the rules but in getting the rules to evolve and adapt to a rapidly changing world.

Internal Justice

In 1980 just ten major companies provided employees with an internal court system. By 1992 the number had risen to seventy, including companies such as GE, Federal Express, Polaroid, GTE, Toledo Hospital, and Coors. Many of these companies use a model developed by GE in which employees present their grievances to a jury of five—three peers and two managers. Some common policies make these courts work.[14]

The jury's job is to determine if policy was broken, not to make new policies or set aside unpopular ones.

All jurors are volunteers and are trained for the job.

There are limits on the kinds of issues that can come to the court. Most companies allow promotions and disciplinary actions to be changed, but not wage rates or marketing decisions.

When the courts are fair, employees often prevail—one year, for example, employees won 40 percent of their cases at GE and 60 percent at Federal Express.[15] Having an independent court system makes managers careful to observe employees' rights. It gives employees a sense of fairness, win or lose. It begins the process of replacing strict hierarchy with pluralistic sources of power. "We're changing our paradigm of power," says John Fassnacht, director of Human Resources at Vista Hills Medical Center in El Paso. "We realize we're giving some power away. But the more we give away, the more we get back."[16]

As organizations move further away from hierarchy toward limited organizational governments, the caseload of their independent courts will change. Because self-management will play an ever larger role, fewer of the cases will be grievances against management. Instead, two intraprises may go to the justice system for a decision on an internal contract dispute. Because an intraprise exceeding allowable company limits on pollution has no boss to discipline it, the intraprise would be brought before the organizational court for charges of policy violation and be subject to fines or even in serious cases revocation of its charter or license.

One of the great liberating social inventions that took our civilization beyond the divine rights of kings was the system called the "rule of law." It limited the arbitrary power of kings and nobles. It gave people freedom within defined boundaries. Intelligent organizations rely heavily on the "rule of law" and thus need a court system independent of both the executive and the legislative functions.

Fostering New Core Competencies

The core competencies of an organization often cut across the lines of businesses. For example, in the 1980s Honda leveraged a core competence in designing and manufacturing small motors in many different businesses, ranging from motorcycles and small cars to lawn mowers, generators, and outboard motors.[17]

This sort of core competence that is not contained in any one business could be supported with a central research and development department that serves all the businesses. A drawback of this approach is that it puts the central government in the business of providing services. A bureaucratic central staff is unlikely to do well at providing services to operating units. In our experience with hundreds of successful new products in companies with large central research departments, discouragingly few of the innovations are the direct result of the efforts of central research. Often when central research gets its budget from headquarters rather than from the divisions using the research, the motivation to get technology transferred is insufficient, regardless of how brilliant the research may be.

Is there an alternative to centrally provided services when the government wants to influence the system to build, sustain, or grow a core competence? We believe several other paths are worth considering. As an example we will consider nonhierarchical ways of supporting technological research deemed strategic by the organizational government.

Support the Intraprises Embodying the Core Competence. If a core competence is currently providing competitive advantage, in a liberated organization there will be a cluster of intraprises embodying aspects of that core competence that compete with one another to supply the business units. Each will provide one or more of the technologies or skills that make up the constellation of technical, manufacturing, marketing, and administrative skills that underlie an enduring core competence. The providers of those capabilities may be in a position to invest in developing future technology and competence themselves, in which case little central intervention is needed. But the central government may want to subsidize the activities of those intraprises contributing developing or endangered skills and capabilities.

Fund Basic Research. Subsidies or grants are particularly appropriate in the case of basic research. Unless intraprises can afford to fund basic research, market reality may dictate a focus on immediate applications of a new technology rather than on advancing the state of the art. But advancing the state of the art may be the road to a long-term corporate competitive advantage. At times the center may need to focus support on more fundamental research in technologies deemed to be strategic.

Direct grants for specific research projects can go to any of the intraprises capable of doing the research. If the payments from the organizational government cover only part of the cost of any given research project, the R&D intraprise has to invest its intracapital or get matching support from an operating unit. The organizational government then gets the best of both worlds: a bias toward both basic research and eventual application. Similar strategies for joint funding could develop strategic capabilities in manufacturing and strategic beachheads in marketing.

Provide More Egalitarian Funding. The problem with grants for research is twofold: They pull attention off serving the marketplace, and they tip the balance strongly in favor of the winning intraprises. A more egalitarian scheme is to provide a matching subsidy to all those applying the technology. This puts funds behind the new technology but gives pluralistic control of those funds to all players proportional to their own commitment to the new technology.

Pay Royalties. How can we reward R&D's long-range thinking if their customers are focused on a shorter time horizon? Imagine that successful innovators or innovative units are given an extra budget calculated as a royalty payment for all the successful technologies they have developed in the past that are being used by the organization today. The business units paying those royalties pay only for what they are using today, but the effect in R&D is to create a pluralistic source of funding for long-range research in the hands of those who have the best track record for making good decisions about it. This system is particularly applicable to funding basic research in existing central research facilities, because it will rapidly lead to the formation of intraprises around every research group that has had enough past success to deserve a royalty stream. These intraprises can continue in the same building and ostensibly under the same management structure, but because they are now self-funding, they will in effect have moved out from under the hierarchical system into the world of free intraprise, with its advantages of flexibility, innovation, and market focus. Internal property rights must balance the desire to reward successful innovation with freedom and resources against the desire to rapidly apply new technology across the organization. We suggest inventors and developers be entitled to intra-money royalty but not entitled to prevent a technology from being used by another internal unit.

Establish Common Standards. Common systems, or at least common standards, often make communication and cooperation easier. There need to be protocols that make E-mail and groupware compatible across the organization. There is benefit in offering external customers turnkey solutions, in which the offerings of many intraprises fit together seamlessly, rather than bits and pieces customers must integrate themselves. Whole-systems compatibility may arise naturally in a network organization, but the center may lend a hand to accelerate the process of finding standards. In some cases the center will specify and pay for "infrastructure" used by all, much as the government of a nation pays for roads.

The appropriate degree of centralization for information technology solutions will continue to be a challenge for years to come. Clearly there is a major advantage in reducing the number of "platforms" to make interconnection easier. But we have all watched as mainframe-mentality central information technology groups got in the way of efficient use of the newer minicomputer and microcomputer technologies by trying to centrally control what could have evolved faster if users had had choice. From a static perspective, it appears to make sense to allow only one solution. In a time of rapidly evolving technology, however, it may be better to have some parallel development of different platforms so all the eggs are not in one basket—which sooner or later will become obsolete.

Though allowing diverse local solutions has obvious advantages, it remains necessary to have common communication protocols so that information may be exchanged. It may be fine for an intraprise to do its accounting on a microcomputer, but the result has to be delivered to the center according to the categories and formats that allow the center to rapidly aggregate it in the ways that are needed for various filings and reports. This kind of issue is better resolved by a standards committee defining communications protocols that meet the interests of all parties than by edicts from a powerful information technology monopoly.

Biasing the System Toward Serving the Larger Community

Society is holding organizations to increasingly high standards in a number of areas. Environmental standards will continue to get tougher. Communities expect organizations to be good neighbors. Minorities expect good jobs and promotions. How is a limited organizational government to make sure the organization meets its responsibilities in all these areas?

Managing Environmental Concerns. An intelligent organization strives to both produce an enviable environmental record and provide business units and intraprises with as much choice as possible in finding ways to reduce pollution.

At 3M, the 3P program (Pollution Prevention Pays) has been one of the most successful corporate pollution programs ever. In the last eighteen years, it has saved over $1 billion and 1.2 billion pounds of pollutants by cutting out pollution at the source.[18] The secret of their success? The corporate folks did not try to come up with ways to reduce pollution; they provided support and recognition to anyone in the company who had an idea for a way to pollute less. They increased the options for people with ideas who were stymied by the bureaucracy. If their bosses turned them down, they had another chance outside normal channels—apply to 3P for help. The results speak for themselves: Even in pollution control, choice in ways to implement change increases performance.

But there is still good reason to ask, Will free intraprise, with its focus on customers and direct costs, put enough emphasis on the costs to the environment? After all, though free enterprise societies may have done a better job of pollution control than the Communist countries, our record in resource use and habitat destruction is still cause for alarm and would be worse had the government not been involved.

There are some obvious tools to use:

Corporate regulations stricter than current government regulations. The Pulp and Paper Sector of the Weyerhaeuser Company has a "No-Effect" vision for their pulp and paper mills. In line with this vision, they have decided to eliminate chlorine bleaching, not only in any new mills, but as they modernize existing ones. Government regulations do not yet prohibit chlorine bleaching, but it is a major topic of environmental debate and a concern expressed by customers. Weyerhaeuser has discovered that they can modernize in such a way that they improve environmental performance, quality, costs, and productivity at the same time. This approach, which is stricter than government regulations, protects the company against possible problems in the future. But it is also more than just a way to deal with outside pressures. For many Pulp and Paper executives and employees the "No-Effect" vision is intrinsically worthwhile.

Corporate pollution taxes. When governments regulate businesses, companies use a good part of their creativity to argue that the regulations are too strict. When governments tax pollution and the use of nonrenewable resources, they not only raise revenues, they also focus creativity on reducing pollution to the lowest cost-effective level. What will be "cost-effective" for producers to do to avoid pollution is determined by their creativity and the pollution tax rate. Without telling companies what to do, the government, by setting pollution taxes, is able to adjust the system to reflect what society is willing to pay for pollution abatement.

As our current technology hits the limits of the world's carrying capacity, and the environmental consequences of current ways of doing business become more apparent, the percentage of GNP devoted to avoiding pollution will increase. Managing this area creatively will be a key strategic advantage, both to save money and to keep the loyalty of customers and employees. Creativity will increase if the corporation uses "force fields," like the 3P program and pollution taxes, that influence choices rather than simple do's and don'ts.

Supporting Equal Opportunity

Granting equal opportunity to all is not easy. It requires us to learn how to use the full potential of people with different backgrounds, values, and ways of solving problems. In a decentralized system, how can we make sure everyone gets an equal chance? Quotas will not work in intraprises that are too small for statistics to be meaningful. Education plays two roles, training in handling diversity and continuing education to move everyone to higher levels of productivity, flexibility, and creativity. Education pays unless your plan is to lay people off soon. Maintaining strong values and a strong community can help integrate those traditionally left out. People as community can rise to the challenge and make a place for women and minorities.

The center can help by

♦ Providing good diversity training for all employees

♦ Establishing and enforcing internal policies against discrimination

♦ Keeping track of the company's results in hiring and promoting women and minorities

♦ Requiring intraprises selling to external customers to report on the diversity of their networks

♦ Thanking those who do a good job of inclusion

Building a community of difference requires local initiative, many local acts of generosity of spirit and leadership. With enough of the people believing in it, an inclusive sense of organizational community can emerge.

✳ PROVIDING FOR DEFENSE AND COMMON SURVIVAL

In the lives of nations, common defense and just laws may be the most basic services citizens expect of their government. The organizational analogs of justice are obvious, the analogs of defense a bit less so.

Repelling Unfair Attacks

American industry suffered great setbacks when a number of Japanese firms adopted a strategy of targeting U.S. industries one by one. When several companies, each in many other profitable businesses, focused great resources and energy on penetrating the U.S. market in a targeted industry, the business units of U.S. firms operating in those industries began losing both money and market share. After a few years, their headquarters understandably concluded that their operations in the targeted industries were not good businesses, so they cut back their funding and resources. Sensible as this response seemed, what would we think of a general who routinely responded to the message that a section of the line he was defending was under heavy attack by cutting back the defending unit's ammunition and supplies instead of sending reinforcements?

As a result of the resource cutbacks, the targeted businesses fell further behind, starting a vicious cycle that in many industries — most of consumer electronics, for instance — eventually led the U.S. firms to exit the business. Emboldened by their success, the Japanese firms chose new strategic targets and began repeating the cycle.

A quite different outcome to this sort of story ensued when in 1981 Yamaha nearly took over as the world leader in motorcycle sales. Honda had long been the leader but had been neglecting investments in motorcycles to concentrate on building its car business. When Yamaha publicly announced a plant that, when operated at capacity, would give it world leadership in sales, Honda declared war. It cut prices, stepped up advertising, and launched 113 new models in eighteen months. By the end of what was known as the Honda-Yamaha war, Yamaha surrendered. Yamaha's president Eguchi publicly conceded: "We want to end the Honda-Yamaha war. It is our fault. We cannot match Honda's sales and product strength. Of course there will be competition in the future, but it will be based on a mutual recognition of our respective positions." (With Honda as number one.)[19]

Once Yamaha admitted defeat, Honda, which had been funding its motorcycle madness with car profits, went back to making money in motorcycles. Not only Yamaha but Suzuki and Kawasaki had been warned.[20]

Sometimes it pays to let others know that you are not an easy nut to crack. If people are afraid to attack, it saves you the trouble and expense of defending. Procter and Gamble, for example, has had a fierce reputation in the United States because it defends its key brands with great tenacity.

In a decentralized company, individual business units or intraprises may not have the resources to fight battles that establish a corporate reputation for invincibility. As in nations, there is in business a place for the common defense of the pieces of an organization lest they be bitten off one by one. How then can a free intraprise organization gather its collective will to defend its territory from being bitten away a piece at a time by more centralized competitors?

Democratic nations take the declaration of war seriously. In the United States, for example, declaring war is not a prerogative of the president; it requires an act of Congress. Similarly, in an intelligent organization, we cannot have every mismanaged intraprise receiving financial aid from the center in the name of defending the whole against common enemies. Informal support can come from symbiotic suppliers who individually give the threatened intraprise a break on pricing during tough times with the expectation of continued business on better terms once the battle is over.

However, if a division needs more than informal support, the organization as a whole must have a collective process for declaring the battle worth fighting. Though the center should not make these declarations unilaterally, at the very least, the center should coordinate the process by which the community makes the decision to send a message to competitors by pooling resources to defend a threatened intraprise. If this process signals intent to the attacker, so much the better—the attacker, knowing the organization's reputation for perseverance once "war" is declared, may choose to back off.

Applying Taxes, Tariffs, and Subsidies

Nations have long employed tariffs to help make their industries competitive. In the late nineteenth century, when rapid industrialization produced worldwide overcapacity in manufacturing, Germany, France, Russia, Italy, and the United States hid their industries profitably behind tariff walls and used those profits to drive low-cost exports to other nations. As a result, from 1870 to 1913, Britain, which was a pure free trade nation, saw its share of worldwide manufacturing decline from 31.8 percent to about 14 percent.[21] Japan and Korea have recently succeeded with modern versions of this strategy.

As headquarters moves from having absolute control of all enterprises within the organization and being internal monopoly providers of many services, they will often find it convenient to use temporary "intra-tariffs" and subsidies to protect their new intraprises that compete with outside competition to serve internal customers. There are several reasons to protect the new intraprises from outside competition. The first is humanitarian. Tariffs can help minimize the need for downsizing. Downsizing is painful, expensive, and bad for morale. As the welfare of employees emerges as a first-rank goal of the corporation, all strategies to provide gainful employment in the intraprises will gain legitimacy.

The second reason for erecting tariffs is that they may eventually lead the system to become more profitable. Tariffs are a way to fund the development of core competencies, though the aim is to develop a competitive capability. The danger, of course, is that some infant industries will never grow up and, through their uncompetitiveness, eventually drag down their internal customers as well.

Providing Job Security and Safety

Particularly before the current round of downsizings, employees were attracted to large bureaucratic organizations by the security of health plans, pensions, safe working conditions, and guaranteed employment. These things still matter, and providing members with higher levels of security can be a source of competitive advantage. Organizations wanting to use free intraprise and preserve a sense of community create a social net under their people that protects them from fear.

Job Security. One of the advantages of an intelligent organization is that resources move rapidly from job to job, with projects rather than functions being the basic unit of work. Such a system has the weakness that it does not guarantee stable work. For this reason, the government of the intelligent organization, like the government of a liberal democratic nation, will generally offer an internal equivalent of unemployment insurance.

Once "out of work," in a typical intelligent organization, an employee's salary will be paid by the organizational government, at first at 100 percent of the old salary, and after a few months at, say, 80 percent, until the employee gets another job in the organization or his or her "unemployment insurance" within the organization runs out.

One virtue of this system is that it helps the company to make better personnel decisions. The social and caretaking concerns of the company are held collectively, and each intraprise or business unit is allowed to do what is best for it without excessive concern for the fate of those who do not work out or are not needed. The system will take care of them, and those managing businesses can focus on results. Only those who fail to find any takers after months of assisted internal job shopping will have to leave the company.

In a well-established intelligent organization, downsizing will be uncommon. The company has the flexibility to reduce compensation to stay competitive if under attack and the effectiveness in innovation to create new businesses if the old ones are shrinking. However, if a company adopts free intraprise because it is in deep trouble, there may be a period of very painful downsizing as the free internal market declares many operations noncompetitive.

A good safety net reduces fear and so brings out more innovation, more ethical behavior, and a greater willingness to take chances. It creates a system that can respond rapidly to changing technology and other challenges without terrifying employees. It helps support the integrity needed to stay out of trouble as society discovers new ethical and environmental concerns.

At 3M, for example, experienced middle managers will have perhaps six months to a year to find a job elsewhere in the organization, and help and training to make themselves more attractive to other divisions. In addition, in some firms, to make the employees who remain unemployed more attractive, Human Resources may offer to pay a portion of their salary for the first year of their employment by an intraprise or business unit.

To feel relaxed about competition, we must remember that ideas, products, and, at worst, intraprises die in the competition of the internal market. People do not need to be seriously inconvenienced even if they have to shift to another intraprise. When the intraprise shrinks or fails, the central government of the intelligent organization provides "unemployment insurance," help finding a job elsewhere in the organization, and accelerated retraining.

Central Funding of Continuing Education. The only real guarantee of continued employment is continual learning and new skill development. Only with radically better education can the United States escape the conflict and economic decline that could be caused by a disenfranchised underclass too poorly educated to be allowed to work. The goal of having everyone in the organization flourish can be achieved only if each member of the organization keeps growing.

Though most organizations never hire the worst educated, the education that remains to be done after people are hired remains considerable. What does it mean when one of our best-managed and most highly technical companies, Motorola, sets a strategic goal of bringing every employee to the seventh-grade level?

Even if our public schools delivered 99.9 percent literate graduates, constant education is the only guarantee that members of the organization will remain employable. In an era of increased efficiency and technological sophistication, involuntary downsizing often seems inevitable. With well-educated employees and the ability to handle change that is inherent in the intelligent organization, it should be possible to create enough new sources of revenue to keep everyone working.

The freedom inherent in knowledge work—which includes most of the best jobs of the future—brings with it the responsibility for continual learning. Knowledge work is about changing knowledge; *speed* of learning and application is the competitive edge. All businesses, even service businesses, will increasingly demand greater technical skills—almost everyone will have to be computer-literate. A new level of human and business skills is required of self-managing employees—the skills to learn quickly and improve a particular assigned operation, as well as the skills of collaboration, teamwork, and whole-business judgment.

We cannot count on intraprises to supply the consistent training necessary for the best interests of the organization and its members. People may stay with an intraprise for a short while, so training does not necessarily pay there; the payoff may come later, when the person continues productive employment in other intraprises rather than becoming a human resource problem. For this reason, corporate headquarters will require and fund continual training for all employees.

Workplace Safety. Many large and bureaucratic organizations have achieved admirable safety records through carefully thought-out rules and procedures. Can a network of intraprises, each cutting costs to "win a contract," do as good a job with safety? The answer we suspect is yes, because the greater organizational intelligence of networks can be applied as well to safety as to any other issue. It is one of the organizational government's jobs to make sure it does.

Protecting the Integrity of the Whole

The organization exists as a whole rather than just a collection of legally separate enterprises because there is value in being together. The organizational government exists to defend the whole against outside threats and to create an environment that brings out the synergy among the parts.

One small intraprise has the potential to expose the whole organization to liability or serious loss of reputation. How can we manage these risks and still have great freedom for intraprises to take legitimate and moderate risks?

Above and Below the Waterline. Bill Gore, founder of Gore Associates, discovered how to bring out the responsibility that goes with freedom. One of his best tools was the "waterline" criterion. He told his associates (employee was a "no" word at Gore Associates) to ask two questions before beginning a task: If you do it and it works, will it be worthwhile? If the answer to that question was yes, the next question was the waterline criterion: If you do it and it fails, can we afford it? If the answer to both questions is yes, he would say, just go ahead and do it.

Gore explained the second question with a metaphor: "If you want to bore a hole above the waterline in the superstructure of the ship, go ahead—just do it. But if you want to bore a hole below the waterline, a hole through which water will pour in if you make a mistake, then check carefully with others before you go ahead."[22]

The great discovery Gore made was how well people understood this analogy. Once so instructed, they did not go boring holes "below the waterline" without checking with the appropriate people first. When they made mistakes interpreting the idea, it was generally to check when it was not really necessary.

Any effective system of freedom in a complex world begins with trusting people's integrity and educating them enough about the potential dangers so that they know when and where to go for a waterline check.

Commitments to Outsiders. The right to commit the organization to agreements with outsiders cannot be held too closely, or a slow and bureaucratic system will evolve. Intelligent organizations will evolve forms of "best effort" agreement that are binding on an intraprise but not on the organization as a whole should the intraprise prove unable to deliver. Of course the organization as a whole will need to back intraprises in keeping these agreements whenever possible, or the whole system will lose its reputation for reliability.

When the organization as a whole must make a commitment, there may need to be a formal system of approval limits. Each intraprise could earn the right to make larger commitments over time.

Ensuring Quality and the Reputation of the Whole. Keeping customers or clients satisfied is so central to the reputation and future of the organization that no organization will leave the matter entirely to the self-organizing systems of free intraprise and the good intentions of members of the organizational community. At a minimum, the central government should receive and monitor regular reports of customer satisfaction and inquire further whenever problems appear to be building up.

A major step toward ensuring customer satisfaction is to make sure everyone in the organization is trained in the basic attitudes, tools, and techniques of quality. In the interests of pluralism, there should be several vendors of quality within the organizations, with perhaps a single corporate exam for certification on the basics.

✳ A GREAT POLITICAL CHALLENGE

Intelligent organizations will for the foreseeable future be more centrally controlled, more guided by their governments, than the freest of nations. This will be so because the greater the complexity of a system, the more self-organization is needed to deal with it. The smaller and simpler a system, the greater will be the effectiveness of a combination of community spirit, generosity to all, and central coordination. Thus, because even the largest business organization is still far simpler than a nation, we find that the central governments of the most effective businesses, government agencies, and nonprofits are more interventionist than the central governments of the most effective free nations. In a surprising irony, executives who, on the one hand, complain bitterly about government intervention in their businesses, on the other hand, impose a style of government on the organizations they control that is far more interventionist and even "left wing" than the national government they complain about.

Seen as governments, the headquarters of corporations favor more centralized intervention in capital allocation, the selection of core technology, and other "industrial policy" issues. Though some nations still claim they cannot afford to do so, major corporations in the advanced nations almost all offer universal health care to their employees. For those who retire with enough years of service, they also offer good pensions. Intelligent organizations retain the "socialist" bias toward taking care of all employees but become less interventionist in the business decisions of intraprises and in the careers of their members.

In establishing systems of government for liberated firms, nonprofits, and government agencies, there is room to improve on the systems we now use in nations. For example, the justice system can surely be faster and less adversarial. In many cases, because of smaller size, the "government" of an organization can be more participative, less formal, less adversarial, and more efficient.

The design of systems of government for the liberated organization is one of the great political challenges of our time. It is worthwhile in itself because it addresses better government at every level of organization, in all the places where we work, in towns where we live, in schools that prepare the next generation. It is also possible that, working on the smaller and more easily controlled systems of governance appropriate to organizations, we may learn lessons useful for the governments of nations.

16

The Power of Freedom and Community

An emerging strategy that offers hope for better economic results, better control of technology, and dignity and meaning too [is] "getting everybody improving whole systems."

MARVIN R. WEISBORD

OUR THEME IN THIS BOOK is that today's challenges are too great for bureaucracy and can be met only with self-organizing systems such as free markets, self-rule, and an effective community. We believe these principles can greatly improve the intelligence, ethics, and competitive capacity of business organizations. We believe the principles of organizational intelligence can help government agencies find better ways to fulfill their missions and balance the needs of different constituents with many apparently conflicting objectives. We believe these principles can help nonprofits build collaborations with multiple stakeholders and mobilize an army of energetic volunteers to achieve their missions.

We have faith in the vitality and intelligence of a workplace where people have the rights and freedom necessary for effective self-organization. No one really believes that bureaucracy is the best solution, but changing from a system that has recently brought unparalleled prosperity and security to many is hard, especially when those with the most power to make the changes derive the greatest benefit from the status quo. Nonetheless, many courageous leaders are driving organizations to respond to the challenges of global competition, more limited resources, and new standards of organizational intelligence and commitment. There is a new level of awareness and responsibility in workplaces, driven by good news and bad—spreading layoffs and downsizing of the most elite bureaucracies, many successful models of greater freedom and participation in less centralized organizations. Even governments are exploring new private and nonprofit partnerships to overcome their monopoly inefficiencies.

How society defines the basic necessities for security is changing, and the focus of invention along with it. Rather than expanding industrial and military might for cold war security, the creative energy of our society is beginning to focus on ways to promote quality of life in the face of environmental limits to expanding population, energy use, and waste disposal.

✳ APPROACHING RADICAL DISCONTINUITIES

Free markets have given us the power to exploit our environment with unprecedented efficiency, but they have not given us the wisdom to establish a balanced relationship with nature. Our global civilization approaches a crescendo of species extinction, and we are using resources at increasingly unsustainable rates. Overcrowding and violence seem to be on the rise. Free markets will not provide the wisdom to deal with all these issues, because markets "love" the growth of consumption, which is near the root of the problem.

People who honestly look at where our world is headed in the decades ahead see some radical discontinuities in our way of living and working. Douglas C. Strain, the founder and CEO (retired) of ElectroScientific Instruments, served as the chairman of the Energy Policy Task Force, an extraordinary electronic conference that continued for most of a decade under the sponsorship of the Western

Behavioral Sciences Institute. The diverse group, including visionary army generals, CEOs, scientists, and academics, teamed up to examine whole-system issues of energy and resource use.

Strain, a successful entrepreneur-engineer, is in a position to see the direct relationship between energy policy and the business community. Many of our businesses have benefited from expanding markets that are gradually bringing the advanced nations' patterns of high resource use to the rest of the world. Strain's conclusion: If most of the growth of our businesses is dependent on expansion of population and resource use, we are heading for a fall. He says, "We have pressed beyond the limits of our sustainable resources and, like any other species which has overrun its resources, our continued existence is endangered."[1]

The patterns of energy consumption and population in different parts of the world have been plotted by Courtland L. Smith, an engineer-anthropologist. Every child born in the United States is scheduled to consume twenty times more energy in a lifetime than a child born in China and sixty times more energy than a child born in India.[2]

The United States cannot continue to consume more and expect the consumption levels of other nations to stay where they are. As third world countries abandon state-dominated economies they will grow. We are all in trouble if the U.S. industrial model defines prosperity and national security for these growing nations. A twentyfold increase in China's consumption of natural resources would be short-lived. But what happens when the population doubles again? And again? Too many curves that plot global growth have become exponential, and it is as certain as death and taxes that all exponential curves hit limits. Finding a soft landing as we approach the limits is the world's greatest challenge.

Talking with Doug Strain suggests an industrial transformation that we can scarcely imagine yet must prepare for. The organizational intelligence needed for riding through these discontinuities will require that everyone understand the limits and possibilities of the future and approach them with entrepreneurial ingenuity. Everyone will work together through pluralistic, decentralized collaborations and partnerships to influence wider systems. In the hopeful voice of an entrepreneur, Strain says, "We may find living within our resources more of an opportunity than a burden." For instance, "As a trans-portation-based society is not sustainable, we should be building the infrastructure for a sustainable information-based society... building fiber optical dataways instead of more super highways."

Businesses that see growth as an increase in customer satisfaction, knowledge, capability, responsibility, and sustainability will prosper. Businesses that see growth as shipping more pounds of goods and high-resource-use devices will not be around in the long run.

Making the organizational transformation to a low-resource, high-satisfaction world will require exquisite customer service, close attention to every detail, and constant flexibility to use the inputs available to produce the specific satisfactions customers demand. Each pound of material and each calorie of energy will carry more meaning, deliver more human satisfaction, and be designed to last longer and do more.

This move from the quantity of material things toward the quality of meanings and relationships depends on each worker developing greater heart and wisdom along with technical abilities to produce great value per unit resources used. Bureaucracy cannot bring out our highest humanity, because at some level it cannot abide the qual-itative, the nonnumerical, the strictly caring, or the spiritual. People are difficult to supervise in the bureaucratic sense when the primary value created is intangible.

Ways of living and working built up over generations will change in decades ahead whether or not people change their organizations. Improvement will depend on engaging the intelligence and wisdom of as many people as possible, not just to compete today but to develop ways of becoming more efficient, cooperative, and responsive tomor-row. The best companies are training everyone, not just management, in leadership, collaboration, business skills, and intelligent pre-paredness for the future as the idea spreads that everyone in an orga-nization can make a valuable contribution.

Ecological Partnerships

Dealing efficiently with resources cannot be accomplished by the kind of thinking that is confined within individual companies. Many of the most effective savings are made by thinking in terms of a web of enterprises with a common ecological vision, a cause that creates a community of enterprises.

Ernest Lowe, director of the Change Management Center and an expert advocate of industrial ecology, reports on the amazing collaboration in Kalundborg, Denmark.

> A web of multidimensional recycling has developed between an electric power generating plant, an oil refinery, a biotechnology production plant, a plasterboard factory, a sulfuric acid producer, cement producers, local agriculture and horticulture, and district heating utilities.
>
> In this man-made "ecosystem," water, energy (for both heating and cooling), chemicals, and organic materials flow from one company to another. Air, water and ground pollution is decreased, water and other resources are conserved, and "waste" materials generate revenue streams.
>
> As an added bonus, the power plant profits from a fish farm which plays an important part in the recycling processes.[3]

✳ DEALING WITH SOCIETY'S LARGER CHALLENGES

We realize that the organizational structures we have been advocating will not automatically lead to the solution of society's whole-system problems. Yet each organization that successfully gives people more control of their lives demonstrates a viable alternative to dependency on bureaucratic institutions. Every organization that thrives in the future by systematically conserving resources will show others a better way. Every business that flourishes through its members' expression of their deeper values and conscious ethical choices will give hope that humanity can make radical transformations in its social and economic life. James Robertson of the New Economics Foundation calls these changes in economic practices the beginning of a post-modern economics; by the end of the century, he says, they will spread as "political, business, and financial leaders everywhere...admit the scale and nature of the changes now needed" and begin a collective reinvention of economic reality.[4]

Intelligent organizations will help meet the larger challenges of the future in direct ways:

First, they will develop their people and their shared masteries within freedom and responsible community. Working in an environment of freedom and collaboration creates organizational citizens more experienced in whole-system responsibility, democratic process, and dealing with complex dilemmas. Organizations that use the intelligence of all their members will make human development issues a priority. They will invest in continual education and training, and that will create better citizens more prepared to initiate and control the necessary changes in the larger society.

Second, when a rich diversity of decentralized intraprises is interconnected in productive networks, organizations can develop the intellectual capacity to execute their missions efficiently while dealing effectively with additional issues such as sustainability, safety, and diversity. More intelligent organizations will allow us to avoid situations like what occurred when the U.S. automobile manufacturers were asked to make cars with higher mileage and less pollution or when the public schools were asked to be the primary agents for correcting society's deeply ingrained racism. Both the automobile companies and the majority of U.S. public school systems were too bureaucratic to carry out their original missions while also embracing the new challenge. The quality of their output fell on both measures. New ways to address complex challenges will use the intelligence of all the members of an organization.

Third, intelligent organizations—as communities of relatively autonomous stakeholders—can experiment with new forms of self-rule, new ways to guide markets, new ways to integrate complex objectives, new forms of organization, and new forms of democracy. In organizations, municipalities, and nations, we need better ways to unite groups of great diversity of purpose, talent, and culture to address systemwide problems. It should be easier for business organizations, nonprofits, and government agencies to experiment with new forms of direct democracy and participation than it is for whole nations to do so. Intelligent organizations can be pilot projects for the new, wiser institutions we will need in the twenty-first century.

✳ GETTING STARTED: A CHALLENGE TO THE LEADERS

Of the principles we have spoken about in this book, some are relatively easy for leaders at the top to implement systemwide; others are very hard to put into practice even when those at the top agree to do so. Some are virtually impossible for leaders below the top of a bureaucracy to implement without a serious commitment from those above; others can be implemented through informal activities open to all.

Establishing the Free Intraprise System

For those at the top, establishing a free intraprise system is a large but straightforward task. Establish the right to form an intraprise, the institutions of intra-ownership and justice, and a low-friction internal medium of exchange. Break up as many internal monopolies as possible. Use the external free enterprise system as a model to get started designing free intraprise institutions that fit your organization's character and needs.

Put a team together to establish the intracapital bank. Pull together another team to establish the internal rules and policies that will guide the free intraprise system.

As the system design evolves, invite many people, from intrapreneurs to accountants, to probe for flaws and suggest improvements, but do not hold up action until the system is perfect. Let volunteers form intraprises and coevolve the free intraprise institutions with the growing sophistication of the intraprises. Use the experiences of the early intraprises to detect parts of the bureaucratic immune system that will have to be changed if free intraprise is to flourish. Listen to your intrapreneurs.

Building the Confederation of Liberated Teams

Given that the institutions of a free intraprise system are in place, liberating teams may be the easiest of the seven essentials of organizational intelligence. Free intraprise gives teams a structure for establishing their independence. Serving customers gives a team more freedom and flexibility than following orders and pleasing a boss appointed without the team's consent.

The Environment for Effective Teams. We are social animals; a propensity for teamwork is naturally hardwired into the human species. Because teamwork is an innate capability of humans, if it is not happening in work teams, it is being prevented. It is a good idea to check all your systems to make sure they are not rigged against teamwork. Do controls frequently cause delay or focus more than 10 percent of people's time on preparing papers and presentations for the benefit of the approval systems? If so, ease off; people do not need that much supervision. Get rid of most paperwork, and go to a verbal culture. Face-to-face communication is more efficient than memo wars. Oticon may have combined the best of both worlds with its series of quick, small, stand-up meetings with a summary of decisions and commitments posted on the computer network for the participants to refer back to later.[5]

Those in a position to change the climate for teams in the organization can do a quick check of the current environment. Are there discretionary funds so teams can usually get what they need to be productive? Do the accounting and measurement systems keep up with teams and provide them with useful feedback on team performance? Do they pit one teammate against another? Do bosses external to the teams routinely second-guess the team's decisions? Are teams free to recruit and keep members who wish to join or stay? Charter a group to find out in what ways the organization supports and defeats teams.

Training for Teams. As teams move from a bureaucratic to a free intraprise basis, they become small businesses and therefore need basic business skills. In addition to the highly developed and presumably narrowly focused specialty that the team provides to its customers, it must also market its services, plan its finances, develop future offerings, and exercise business judgment. Bureaucracy ill prepares the great majority of its members for this sort of general management role; therefore, new intraprises will be more effective if the teams receive training in intrapreneurial business planning and management.

In an organization well steeped in total quality, many members will already be trained to use effective processes for team decision making, including brainstorming, statistical analysis, and project management. Teams will continue to benefit from such training and from facilitators who help them apply what they have learned.

Creating the Environment for Widespread Truth

It should be easy to create an organizational community in which everyone tells the truth, but the bureaucratic system of organization has a long history of shooting the messenger and otherwise discouraging communication of the whole truth. This is one way bureaucracies become shortsighted—they punish those who look ahead and sound warnings of approaching dangers.

Distribute all business information and strategies widely, and encourage freewheeling internal public debate. Train all members to understand the business and the ways it is measured, include training in how to read financial reports.

Establish and defend the rights of free speech, free press, and free electronic communication with great vigor. Create hotlines for members of the organization to call if they feel they are being squelched, and handle the complaints by opening the system more, not by punishing the people apparently trying to restrict the flow of information.

Do what you can to reduce fear of consequences for voicing opinions or telling the truth. React constructively when criticized, especially by those who are under your authority, so they are free to practice being outspoken safely. Never make "jokes" about cracking down on people if they say the wrong thing. These jokes get taken seriously.

Open up multiple new channels of communication, and tune each one for maximum truth. GE's Work-Out program is an example of a good start. Get a lively dialogue going on all the big issues on your electronic networks.

One strong signal to send is support for privacy, because privacy gives the safe space to test out new and potentially dangerous truths. Tune E-mail for maximum privacy—make sure the system automatically destroys all old copies of messages. Allow effective ciphers. Let people have private conferences. Provide do-it-yourself video and computer conferencing systems that are user-friendly. Encourage everyone who is willing to try to facilitate an issues conference.

Building Community

Building a context for the development of community is one of the hardest challenges leaders face. You do not "do" community as if it were an action; community, like trust, is the pattern of relationships

developed over time. In the case of community, the pattern of relationships emerges from a vast network of interdependency, caring,
and common purpose that bonds the whole system together.

Move the system toward equality, the foundation of participative
community. Remove every sign and symbol of rank. Look at what
Oticon accomplished in moving from a "hardwood on the walls and
Jaguars in the garage" kind of company to a place where the CEO has
no desk and his files get wheeled out of the way when he is out of
town. They got a sixfold increase in earnings the very first year, which
is a remarkably fast payoff on a system that required the discipline
of community to function. Of course they made investments in democracy, freedom, and computers all at the same time.

Help the group find a clear, uplifting common purpose. Learn to
state it in ways that are meaningful in all areas of the organization.
Walk the talk and get honest feedback from *all levels*. Financial goals
by themselves do not get people out of bed in the morning eager to
come to work and make a difference. Aim the organization at making
the world better in some focused way.

Help bring into being a strategic plan for the group as a whole. List
the core competencies, key market initiatives, and value propositions
needed to achieve your purposes. Then find creative ways to achieve
those objectives with the minimum use of central power needed to
be effective.

Get the organization to establish a human resource strategy and
"people development" policy. Find ways to ensure the continuing
education and growth of all working members and the growth and
effectiveness of diversity with the minimal use of central command
and policing. Let taking care of everyone become a manifestation of
healthy community.

Making Diversity a Competitive Strength

An intelligent organization makes diversity a competitive strength
by cultivating the wisdom of every member. A sign of effective leadership is that people feel united as one despite all differences. To move
beyond racism, we have to start working in early childhood. In addition, for generations to come, leaders in organizations will have responsibility for helping to heal the hurts of prejudice and develop the

potential of all their people. Hire, partner with, and reward diversity and divergent thinking. Be a leader by making friends across every barrier of difference you can find, whether of race, gender, function, age, product line, rank, or even Myers-Briggs type. Learn to enjoy, and be made richer by, diversity. Find effective ways to work toward easy acceptance of diversity, and find systems that allow a wide range of people to do their best work.

More Effective Democratic Self-Rule

Democratic self-rule begins within teams. Once people are successful with participative processes on a small scale, begin working on larger-scale planning and governance using the input of larger numbers of people. The challenge is to find processes that obtain inspired syntheses of the best thinking in the organization, not the least-common-denominator thinking. Intelligent organizations continually study and scan the environment for new means of facilitating large-group intelligence.

Building a Voluntary Learning Network

Imagine that the voluntary learning network is the brain of the organization, the people and teams are the nerve cells, and the relationships are the synapses. The number and quality of nerve cells are relatively fixed; what can change relatively rapidly are the relations between them—the synapses. For this reason, one might say that the leader's role in creating organizational intelligence is to improve the quality of relationships within the organization.

Celebrate acts of generosity and uncalled-for informal support. Broker collaborations. Extend the network beyond the organization. Demonstrate decency in your treatment of all the people you contact. Teach people to bring out the best in one another. Support institutes like internal publishing intraprises that spread information. Use the best "group ware" or social computing to connect people of like interests and diverse views.

Encourage and reward mentoring. Disseminate the lessons from group and team successes and failures. Import similar lessons from other organizations.

Building a Limited Organizational Government

Building a system of limited organizational governance means building a new set of liberating institutions and gradually turning over to them control of many parts of the organization. There is no preordained order in which things must be done, although recent national histories (Russia, China, Korea, Taiwan, Chile) suggest a slight edge for economic liberalization first, with political liberalization following as quickly as possible.

Establish free intraprise and begin testing it with services and lesser enterprises. Open up free speech, direct and electronic. Converse with all levels. Create randomly selected advisory panels to study key issues. Establish a bill of rights and responsibilities, and work hard to make it real. Create an independent internal justice system. Develop internal commercial law as democratically as seems prudent. As experience develops with both freedom and democratic process, increase the power of democratic institutions representing working members as well as owners or trustees. Study history and political science; create a constitution that defines the system of governance. Divide internal monopolies, fund intrapreneurialization of more businesses and internal services. Grant intra-ownership of intraprises to their workers and managers. Reduce the role of government. Set up employee equity plans. Encourage the constitution to evolve through democratic processes.

✳ A MESSAGE TO EVERYONE (YOU CAN MAKE A DIFFERENCE)

Change is very difficult to make in a bureaucratic organization because it seems almost no one has the power to make substantial changes. Nearly everyone seems to be waiting for the great "they" in the sky to act. The more interesting question is, What can ordinary people do right now?

Everyone is in a position to have a meaningful effect.

When you work with others across boundaries with the big picture in mind, you build community. When you raise the quality of your dialogue and interactions with others, you create a cascade of communication that ripples through the organization.

Experiments in greater choice, greater self-management, more effective networks, and more inclusive community are going on all around us. If an organization were not operating already with more freedom and community than the rules of bureaucracy permit, it would not be intelligent enough to survive in the late-twentieth-century maelstrom. The people who are influencing the system from below are strong, but not by virtue of their positions in the bureaucratic hierarchy. Many transcend that paltry dose of empowerment with their ability to get things done through their network of friends and co-conspirators. Eventually the people upstairs notice what is working, and it shapes new policy. Who is having more effect, the bureaucrats or the intrapreneurs? Who is having more fun?

Virtually all significant systemwide changes in a large organization are preceded by experiments that show the people on top new possibilities. Be an experiment worthy of copying. How many of the essentials of the intelligent organization can you put in place in some small way? Find other people in other workplaces who are also building better forms of organization. What can you learn from them? What can you teach?

Make the organization smarter all around you. Improve the quality of the dialogue between your group and others. Let your passions and values show. Connect the people you influence with others who can broaden their understanding of the larger system. Establish an organizational intelligence network. Never mind if the companywide body does not exist yet; start your own discussion group and link up with other groups interested in the issues of freedom and systemwide responsibility as those groups appear. Share learning, and build the sense of common cause that becomes the community of and for organizational intelligence.

Human systems change through courageous collaborations. Take care of one another: When the bureaucrats try to kill off an example of budding organizational intelligence, make sure they meet an immediate companywide protest. If a self-managing plant is about to be merged into a traditional hierarchical one, let the network send the CEO hundreds of letters asking for a reprieve. If a free-choice staff function is prevented from seeking customers across organizational boundaries, spring to its defense. Support good sponsors with a bar-rage of commendation letters.[6]

When you get together with others to discuss organizational intel-ligence, we urge you to take the long view first. What might the world look like in twenty-five or fifty years? What will the big changes be? What capabilities might the organization need? Get up in your "heli-copter" and view the situation from afar. Consider what the company has to be to flourish in the twenty-first century, what capabilities it has to acquire, what forms of intelligence it must have in high degree.

Once you have considered the big picture, it is time for practical dreaming and doing. As soon as you begin learning what works, drop us a note by mail, fax, or computer. In the matter of high levels of organizational intelligence, we are all beginners together.

A Free Intraprise Manifesto

WE COLLECTED our thoughts before writing this book by writing a fictional account of a company transforming itself from a firm with an aging entrepreneurial leader to an intelligent organization with widely distributed power and authority. A team of employees created a Free Intraprise Manifesto, which appears here edited to remove references specific to the company.

✳ THE LANGUAGE OF FREE INTRAPRISE

Freeholder

The individuals in a free intraprise system are not *employees,* a word that connotes and legally implies hierarchical subjugation to bosses. The word *associates* is not bad, but it lacks energy. Instead, we have decided to call ourselves *freeholders,* which implies independence, dignity, and responsibility.

In a traditional corporation, bosses have an almost absolute right to tell employees what to do as long as the action requested is legal. In a free organization such as ours, individuals make up their own minds what to do, limited only by general rules, the promises they make, and the need to sell their services internally or externally.

No one in a free intraprise system owns another's labor to do with as he or she pleases. In general, intraprises are mutually owned by all their full-time members, and they contract for results with others. An individual freeholder may contract with an intraprise for a relationship very similar to that of an employee to a corporation. Even in this case, an intraprise employee retains the rights of a freeholder, such as

♦ Freedom of speech
♦ Freedom of association
♦ Freedom to give reasonable notice to leave and take a job elsewhere in the organization
♦ Freedom to moonlight for other, noncompeting intraprises

Intra-property

Over the years civil rights, such as free speech and the right to own private property, have proven to be basic tools for defending the citizen against governmental tyranny. Similar rights are needed to protect freeholders against the potential tyranny of their corporate government. Many of these rights, like free speech, can be translated easily into the corporate realm; others, like property rights, need translation.

Workers own their tools; inventors own their inventions; intrapreneurs own their intraprises—what might these things mean? Our system will work better when freeholders have the right to go on controlling the assets they have created even when our corporate government would rather give them to someone else to manage. In a free corporation many things, such as tools, inventions, and businesses that are legally the property of the corporation are for most practical purposes "owned" by one or more freeholders. "Ownership" in this sense is the right to control and dispose of within the confines of the corporation. Although the freeholder may not use them for a purely private purpose, intra-ownership implies that their intra-owners may use what they own for any legitimate purpose of the corporate community. The rules we build up to govern such ownership are the rules of intra-property. Our internal property rights are protected by our internal justice system and its courts.

Free Corporation

A corporation organized by the free intraprise system is a "free corporation."

✳ THE MECHANICS OF FREE INTRAPRISE

We Build Our Organization by the Partnerships We Choose

Rather than top-down design, we employ bottom-up design. The organization as a whole has a mission. We are free to choose our own best way to serve that mission. Freeholders form associations, partnerships, and intraprises to get the work done. These patterns of voluntary association create the structure of the organization.

The Basic Building Blocks of the Corporation Are Intraprises

Intraprises are businesses within the organization that serve internal or external customers. They may have many members or consist of a single freeholder selling his or her services. It is the network of intraprises that creates the products and services of the company.

Everyone works as part of one or more intraprises. Each person may be his or her own intraprise, work as part of several intraprises, or work through a single intraprise. The intraprises take in revenues, pay other intraprises and outside vendors, and direct their payroll agents to issue compensation to the freeholders who work as part of the intraprise.

An intraprise may compensate its members by the hour or the month or for a contracted result. In professional intraprises, freeholders may receive what they bill minus overhead. Freeholders may own shares in an intraprise and share in revenues or profits as they come in. They may own shares in projects.

An Intraprise That Earns Revenue Has the Right to Decide How to Spend or Invest It

In a free organization, the primary source of power is not the hierarchy; instead, power comes from having customers and making a profit. Revenue received by an organization is deposited in its bank account and remains there until the intrapreneurs choose to spend it.

An Intraprise Is a Profit Center

The accounting system is designed to easily keep track of every intraprise as a profit center. The basic discipline of free intraprise is that each intraprise make ends meet. If the intraprise writes checks, it must have the funds to cover them. This requirement places responsibility for making the output of the intraprise valuable on the group of individuals forming it. It is possible for an intraprise to spend money it is not making only if it has savings or if someone is willing to invest in it.

Intraprises Own Things, Such as Machinery, Brand Names, Patents

Property rights protect citizens from excessive government power. If citizens cannot have property, then everything belongs to the government. As long as the government owns everything, we are little more than slaves. It does not help to say we all own everything collectively, because experience teaches us that collective property is controlled not by the people but by the bureaucracy.

In the creation of free organizations, the right of intra-property plays the same role as the right to property does in the creation of the free state. If the organization owns everything, our development is arrested by our enforced dependence on bosses. We can never develop the full flowering of capability that is the birthright of the adult freeholder. Ownership is the physical manifestation of a boundary that says, "I don't care what your rank is; within this territory, with regard to these things and relationships, you don't get to tell me what to do."

Intra-ownership allows intraprises to think long term. They can build up a position and manage it for long-term results without fear of having someone else take it over. For lack of better institutions, we are beginning with finding analogies to most of commercial law. For example, in order to give intraprises the motivation necessary to develop innovations and spread them to others, we define internal intellectual property rights to include the right to license innovations to other intraprises. This issue has engendered some debate; a strong contingent believes ideas do not belong in the exchange economy but fall in the domain of the gift economy, like ideas in science. One credits the earlier author, but one does not pay for ideas. So far this is a minority view, but already many of our more prolific inventors are saying enough is enough and giving away all but enough of their ideas to guarantee themselves sufficient capital to explore new ones.

Intraprises May Form Joint Ventures, Enduring or Project-Based

Many of the activities of a large free corporation cannot be done by small groups. Nonetheless it is natural for working human beings to form small teams. For this reason, the average large intraprise is made up not of individuals in a single intraprise but of numerous teams that are intraprises themselves. The intraprises making up a larger intraprise may be partners or subcontractors.

Much of the Company Is Organized in Intraprises That Solve Problems and Deliver Services Internally

There will be specialized teams providing many services to other intraprises, such as

- Certain types of skilled workers
- Graphics
- Programming
- Payroll processing
- Bookkeeping
- Purchase of components and materials at better prices
- Selling of products made by other intraprises

Whenever possible, teams will not be required to purchase services from any particular intraprise. Whenever possible, the system will provide choice, because only if customers have choice can the intraprise be evaluated fairly.

Free Intraprise Financial Institutions

If our system of free intraprise is to form the complex networks of a modern flexible business network, it will need fairly sophisticated financial institutions to represent the newly generated relationships. For this reason, we will continue to work in this area and maintain public dialogue concerning our internal financial institutions.

Intra-money. The most basic financial institution is money itself. We have created intra-money of two kinds. The first is created by the accounting system. Intraprises have bank accounts and can transfer intra-money funds to the accounts of other intraprises or ask Accounting to cut a check to an outside vendor. Internal transfers do not have to be reported to the external government, and external payments, whether to employees, outside persons, or firms, go through Accounting with all the normal controls.

In addition, we have created another system of paper intra-money in denominations from ten dollars to one thousand. These "bluebacks" are the final guarantee of the freeholder's right to an unencumbered medium of exchange.

Money is an essential part of the liberation of the small against the big. If there is no money, then the only thing that will keep ordinary members of the organization in the larger game is an internal gift economy. Relying exclusively on an internal gift economy would be fine if it were enough. Once we go beyond the level of technological sophistication at which gifts and barter can mediate all internal transfers, not having a medium of exchange causes dependence on hierarchy and reduces ordinary members to the role of employee. A flexible business network needs a medium of exchange.

Intracapital. Free intraprise, like free enterprise, depends on sources of capital. If intrapreneurs cannot store the fruits of past success to spend on innovative and even risky new projects, then they will exhibit some combination of shortsightedness and focus on the hierarchy that controls the long-term money. Capital is one of the essential forms of ownership. *Capital* is a name for the ability to store value for a period of time as well as the ability to gather resources from a number of people in hope of reaping a greater return in the future.

In large late-twentieth-century bureaucracies, it is customary to berate managers for their short-term focus and the risk-averse nature of their decisions. This behavior is not surprising if these managers have no capital to spend on their own say-so.

If, despite their past success, they have no inalienable right to commit resources to the future they see, then their caution is very sensible. No matter what their past successes are, they own nothing; the state (corporation) owns it all and must be petitioned for the next allotment of capital. If things go poorly for a while as a result of having taken a risk, then they have no savings within the corporation to guarantee their survival or pay their people until things look up. It is prudent for them not to take risks.

The Central IntraBank. Being able to store the surplus of one's past successes to bridge through hard times and to invest in new ideas allows freeholders and intraprises to take risks and manage for the long run. Intracapital banks are the place where this intracapital is stored and accounted. In addition, the intracapital bank is a clearinghouse for economic transactions. It provides a mechanism for one intraprise to conveniently pay another for services rendered. It provides a mechanism for an intraprise to convert intra-money into outside currency in order to pay outside vendors.

The first intracapital bank is the Central IntraBank of the free corporation, which provides banking services until banking intraprises take over and then remains as a clearinghouse and regulator of the intra-banking system.

Each intraprise has an account in an intra-bank, because banking is necessary to an intraprise. It need not be the Central IntraBank if other banking intraprises have grown up. In the beginning, however, it will be the central bank because no other exists.

Each individual has an intracapital account, which, as it grows, provides security and freedom. An individual with a year's salary in the intracapital bank has little to fear except permanent disability.

Dollars received from outside customers are deposited in the intra-money account of the relevant intraprise. The intra-money in individuals' or intraprises' accounts is theirs. They may write checks requesting the intra-bank to transfer funds to another intraprise or to pay an outside vendor for goods or services. Requests to pay individual freeholders what the IRS would consider to be compensation must be paid through the payroll intraprise selected by the freeholder. The payroll intraprise will accumulate all compensation from various intraprises, withhold the appropriate taxes and insurance premiums and savings, and otherwise make sure that all requirements of law and good bookkeeping are followed.

Venture Intracapitalists. Venture intracapitalists are individuals who have earned more intracapital than they care to spend on their own ideas. They therefore invest in the intraprises of others. Their existence creates a market in which there are many potential capital sources for an intrapreneurial team looking for backing.

If an intraprise requires capital, it may seek it from

♦ The central bank
♦ Any of the intraprises that act as banks in competition with the central bank
♦ Any of the venture capital intraprises
♦ Any other intraprise

Corporate Government

Managing a free intraprise system has costs, and we imagine certain functions will remain with a skeleton headquarters staff. The right to enforceable contracts between intraprises requires a system of justice. Though there may be arbitration intraprises competing with this aspect of corporate governance, the corporation provides the justice system of last resort.

The communities and governments of the states and municipalities in which we operate must be respected; thus there are some costs associated with ensuring that they are. Concern for the environment has long been one of our core values, and we are maintaining our corporate environmental monitoring and research function.

The corporation also provides a safety net and will pay half of any education costs if an intraprise or individual will agree to pick up the other half.

Protecting the image of the corporation and its guiding focus is also a corporate issue. We are seeking ways to achieve these objectives.

To fund all the activities of the "government" of the company, the government will levy three classes of taxes:

A gross revenue tax on external sales not to exceed 5 percent (internal sales will not be taxed, to avoid double taxation and needless bookkeeping)

A payroll tax not to exceed 5 percent above and beyond external payroll taxes, health insurance, and pensions to fund the job insurance and training functions

A pollution tax designed to encourage intraprises to achieve the highest standards of environmental protection (this tax will be charged on the whole-system costs of an enterprise's activities, so pushing dirty processes out to external vendors will not escape the tax)

The corporate government will not charter monopolies of any kind without submitting them for approval to the antitrust committee, which will examine critically the contention that a monopoly in any particular instance is necessary or highly beneficial. Unless a monopoly has been declared, which is unlikely, any intraprise may enter any business it chooses.

Appendix B

Bill of Rights and Responsibilities of the Intelligent Organization

RIGHT TO	RESPONSIBILITY TO
I. Freedom of Expression	

Freedom of speech
Freedom of press and E-mail
Freedom of the arts
Privacy in communications
	Tell the truth, the whole truth, and
	    nothing but the truth
	Appreciate and bring out the many
	    sides to every issue
	See the good in others and express it

II. Freedom of Learning	

Freedom of inquiry
Full business information
Develop one's knowledge and
    competence
	Be curious, persistent, and aware
	Learn from past failures and
	    successes
	Develop multiple skills
	Keep learning and growing

III. Freedom of Work	
Choice of projects and teams Choice of customers Intra-ownership of tools	Commit to something worthwhile Act with courage and integrity Respond to the needs of the whole system
IV. Freedom of Intraprise	
Live by customers' decisions Intra-ownership of intraprises An internal medium of exchange	Live within your means Give fair measure Work for the good of the larger system Deliver on promises
V. Freedom to Work as Teams	

Freedom of team decisions
Freedom to choose teammates
Joint intra-ownership
Joint responsibility and rewards
	Achieve team goals
	Make good team decisions
	Care for teammates
	Recruit and treat teammates without
	    bias
	Build the capabilities of every
	    member

RIGHT TO	RESPONSIBILITY TO
VI. A Community of Differences	

Full membership in the organization
A community that cares for your welfare
An ethical organization
	Neither show nor tolerate bias or
	  prejudice
	Balance self-interest against the
	  common good
	Work toward worthwhile common
	  vision and values
	Find value in diversity

VII. Justice and the Rule of Law	
Freedom within the law Due process An independent judicial system A jury of peers	Obey the law Work to establish good law Avoid self-serving rules and entitlements Fight injustice
VIII. Democratic Self-Rule	

Local self-management within bounds
Participation in designing the larger
  system
	Listen to others
	Educate oneself on whole-system
	  realities
	Stand for what one believes

IX. Freedom of Network Connections	
Freedom of association Freedom of choices Freedom to make and honor commitments	Make commitments wisely Deliver on one's commitments Use others' time wisely Serve the larger community
X. Limits on Internal Government	

Support the rights of every member
Constitutional limits on internal
  taxation
A government that guides the system
	Use incentives, not mandates,
	  whenever possible
	Be farsighted
	Reward service to the whole
	Push decisions to the lowest possible
	  level

Notes

Preface

1. Norm Macrae, who said, "The corporation of the future is a confederation of entrepreneurs." *Intrapreneuring* was dedicated to him for issuing this challenge to our thinking. (In "The Coming Entrepreneurial Revolution: A Survey," *The Economist*, December 25, 1976.)

2. "The Internal Entrepeneurs," *UC World Magazine*, Fall 1993, p. 5.

Part I. The End of Bureaucracy

Epigraph: Warren Bennis, *Beyond Bureaucracy* (San Francisco: Jossey-Bass, 1993 [reprint of 1964 edition]), pp. 3–4.

Chapter 1. Organizations That Engage Everyone's Intelligence

Epigraph: Jack Welch, quoted in Noel M. Tichy and Stratford Sherman, *Control Your Destiny or Someone Else Will* (New York: Doubleday, 1993), p. 251.

1. Carol J. Loomis, "Dinosaurs?" *Fortune*, May 3, 1993, p. 37.

2. Rogier F. van Vlissingen, "Beyond Democracy, Beyond Consensus," *At Work*, May/June 1993, pp. 11–13.

3. Personal observations.

4. Michael Janofsky, "Parks Workers with Fewer Rules Test Stereotype About Public Jobs," *New York Times*, November 16, 1992.

5. Many of these basic ideas became familiar to business readers in this country via Marvin R. Weisbord's *Productive Workplaces* (San Francisco: Jossey-Bass, 1987).

6. Julie Pitta, "It Had to Be Done and We Did It," *Forbes,* April 26, 1993, p. 151.

7. Ibid., p. 152.

8. Ibid., p. 153.

9. Interview with Rick Belluzzo, Hard Copy Products Group, Hewlett-Packard, March 17, 1993.

10. William McKnight, quoted in Virginia Huck, *The Brand of the Tartan: The 3M Story* (New York: Appleton-Century-Crofts, 1955), p. 239.

11. Edward O. Welles, "Least Likely to Succeed," *Inc.,* December 1992, pp. 74–86.

12. Ibid.

13. Karl H. Mettke, "Reinventing Government: A Case in Point," *Tapping the Network Journal* 3:2 (Fall 1992), 14.

14. Personal conversation with Max Peterson.

15. Joseph F. McKenna, "Empowerment Thins a Forest of Bureaucracy," *Industry Week,* April 5, 1993, p. 64.

16. Butch Marita, quoted in Mettke, "Reinventing Government," p. 15.

17. Jim Carlyn, quoted in Ronald E. Yates, "Total Quality Management a Forest Service Resource," *Chicago Tribune,* February 15, 1993.

18. Randall Johnson, "Beating Bureaucracy: Team-Based Power Structure Cuts Waste, Improves Service," *Total Quality,* December 1992, p. 5.

19. McKenna, "Empowerment Thins a Forest of Bureaucracy," p. 64.

20. Mettke, "Reinventing Government," p. 14.

21. Yates, "Total Quality Management."

22. Presentation by Jack Pandole, Jr., at the Ecological Farming Conference, Asilomar, California, January 1992.

Chapter 2. The Rise and Fall of Bureaucracy

Epigraph: *The Dakota Farmer,* February 28, 1938, p. 94, quoted in Catherine McNicol Stock, *Main Street in Crisis: The Great Depression and the Old Middle Class of the Northern Plains* (Chapel Hill: University of North Carolina Press, 1992), p. 111.

The epigraph under "Why Bureaucracy No Longer Works" is from Wolfgang J. Mommsen, *Political and Social Theory of Max Weber* (Chicago: University of Chicago Press, 1989), p. 113.

1. Wolfgang J. Mommsen, *Political and Social Theory of Max Weber, p. 112.*

2. R. H. Hall, "The Concept of Bureaucracy: An Empirical Assessment," *American Journal of Sociology* 69 (1963): 33. See also Warren Bennis, *Beyond Bureaucracy* (San Francisco: Jossey-Bass, 1993), p. 5; and Gerald Zaltman, Robert Duncan, and Jonny Holbeck, *Innovations and Organizations* (Malabar, Fla.: Robert E. Krieger Publishing, 1984), pp. 122–123.

3. Fred Emery, "The Management of Self-Managing Groups," unpublished paper, November 1989.

4. Weisbord, *Productive Workplaces,* p. 24.

5. William Blake (1757–1827).

6. John Case, "A Company of Business People," *Inc.,* April 1993, p. 81.

7. Peter Drucker, *Post-Capitalist Society* (New York: HarperBusiness, 1993), p. 64.

8. Alvin Toffler, *The Third Wave* (New York: William Morrow, 1980), p. 45.

9. D. Keith Denton, "Multiskilled Teams Replace Old Work Systems," *HR Magazine*, September 1992, p. 49.

10. As Fred Emery has pointed out, no system can exist without redundancy to provide reserve capacity when something does not exactly follow the plan.

11. Denton, "Multiskilled Teams Replace Old Work Systems," p. 49.

12. Ibid., p. 48.

Chapter 3. Clues to Bureaucracy's Successor

Epigraph is from Margaret J. Wheatley, *Leadership and the New Science: Learning About Organization from an Orderly Universe* (San Francisco: Berrett-Koehler, 1992), p. 95.

1. This story is based on interviews with Al Boese, Pat Carey, Paul Hansen, and Art Fry.

2. This is not to deny the inequities and iniquities of the movie business. Market freedoms are but half the answer. The other half, the institutions of community, are less well developed in the cutthroat world of moviemaking.

3. Private interviews.

4. Robert Mamis, "Apple Tree," *Inc.*, August 1993, pp. 72–76.

5. Erich Jantsch, *The Self Organizing Universe* (Elmsford, N.Y.: Pergamon Press, 1980), p. 40.

6. Peter Senge, *The Fifth Discipline* (New York: Doubleday, 1990).

7. Brian Moskal, "Donnelly Manages for the Future," *Industry Week*, February 1, 1993, p. 28.

8. Ibid.

9. Consultants and trainers take note: There will be a growing market in training all employees in basic business analysis and business judgment. These courses will be customized to reflect the realities of the specific markets, technologies, and business practices the companies operate in. Simulations and experiential learning will be necessary.

Chapter 4. The Seven Essentials of Organizational Intelligence

Epigraph: David Nadler, quoted in Michael Finley, "Smaller(er) Is Beautiful," *Business Ethics*, January-February 1993, p. 32.

1. Max DePree, *Leadership Is an Art* (New York: Doubleday, 1989), p. 147.

2. Senge, *The Fifth Discipline*, pp. 236–237.

3. Private conversations.

4. Hazel Henderson, *Paradigms in Progress: Life Beyond Economics* (Indianapolis: Knowledge Systems, 1991).

5. Fred Emery, *Toward Real Democracy* and *Toward Real Democracy: Further Problems*, Ontario Quality of Working Life Centre, Ontario Ministry of Labour, 1989. (Study from a grant from the Centre for Continuing Education, Australian National University.)

Part II. Creating Freedom of Choice in Organizations

Epigraph: Willy Brandt, from *My Life in Politics*, quoted in "A Man for Peace and Multiple Freedoms," *U.S. News and World Report*, October 19, 1992.

Chapter 5. Widespread Truth and Rights

Epigraph: James P. Womack, Daniel T. Jones, and Daniel Roos, *The Machine That Changed the World* (New York: Macmillan, 1990), p. 99.

The epigraph under "The Right to Privacy" is from a private conversation between R. Buckminster Fuller and Gifford Pinchot.

1. Will Schutz, *The Truth Option: A Practical Technology for Human Affairs* (Berkeley, Calif.: Ten Speed Press, 1984), p. 283.

2. Stratford P. Sherman, "Inside the Mind of Jack Welch," *Fortune,* March 27, 1989, p. 38.

3. "For here we are not afraid to follow truth wherever it may lead"—the words of Thomas Jefferson, from a book of quotations, *The Best of Success,* compiled by Wynn Davis (Lombard Ill.: Great Quotations Publishing, 1988), p. 318.

4. Sherman, "Inside the Mind of Jack Welch," p. 38.

5. Noel M. Tichy and Stratford Sherman, *Control Your Destiny or Someone Else Will* (New York: Doubleday, 1993), pp. 195–197.

6. Thomas A. Steward, "GE Keeps Those Ideas Coming," *Fortune,* August 12, 1991, pp. 40–46.

7. Ibid.

8. This is a fictitious name because this story is not about who made the mistake.

9. Robert L. Schwartz, who was at the dinner where Abraham Maslow told this story, reported it during a personal interview.

10. Value as of July 21, 1993, per ConAgra public relations department.

11. "The ConAgra Philosophy," brochure published by ConAgra, Inc., Omaha, Nebraska, 1993, pp. 8–9.

12. Max DePree, *Leadership Jazz* (New York: Doubleday, 1992), p. 147.

13. Tom Ehrenfeld, "The Productivity-Boosting Gain-Sharing Report," *Inc.,* August 1993, pp. 87–89.

14. "The ConAgra Philosophy," p. 8.

15. Timothy W. Firnstahl, "The Center-Cut Solution," *Harvard Business Review,* May-June 1993, p. 71.

16. Ibid., p. 65.

17. "Building a Customer-Driven Company: The Saturn Story," an interview with Richard G. Le Fauve, president, Saturn Corporation, *Forum Issues* 14 (Boston, Spring 1993), p. 1.

18. Other rights will be discussed in later chapters. For the complete Bill of Rights, see Appendix B.

19. "The ConAgra Philosphy," pp. 9–10.

20. Tom Peters and Nancy Austin, *A Passion for Excellence* (New York: Random House, 1985), p. 213.

21. Conversation with Karl Mettke, March 31, 1993.

22. Jack Stack, *The Great Game of Business* (New York: Doubleday, 1992).

23. John Case, "A Company of Business People," *Inc.,* April 1993, p. 86.

24. Gifford Pinchot, *Intrapreneuring* (New York: Harper & Row, 1985), p. 185.

Chapter 6. Freedom of Enterprise Inside Organizations

Epigraph: Louis V. Gerstner, quoted in Judith H. Dobrzynski, "Rethinking IBM," *Business Week*, October 4, 1993, p. 92.

1. By contrast, Ford and Chrysler remained longer as simple monarchies with each function reporting directly to the CEO. GM won that round; in fact, it got in real trouble only when all the divisions became little more than marketing hype because they shared the same basic automobiles dressed in different upholstery and grills.

2. Jon R. Katzenbach and Douglas K. Smith, "The Discipline of Teams," *Harvard Business Review* 71:2 (March-April 1993), pp. 111–120.

3. Firmware is software burned permanently into chips.

Chapter 7. Rights and Institutions for Establishing an Internal Free Market

Epigraph: Fernand Braudel, *Civilization and Capitalism, 15th–18th Century;* vol. 2, *The Wheels of Commerce* (New York: Harper & Row, 1979), p. 600.

1. Hernando de Soto, *The Other Path* (New York: Harper & Row, 1989), pp. 133–134.

2. Ibid.

3. Ibid., p. 98.

4. *The Employee Ownership Casebook* (Oakland, Calif.: The National Center for Employee Ownership, 1992); revised annually.

5. De Soto, *The Other Path*, p. 93.

Chapter 8. Corporate Financial Systems for Free Intraprise

Epigraph: Braudel, *The Wheels of Commerce*, p. 555.

1. Intraprises should not be charged for intracapital saved by the intraprise or its intracapital investors.

2. Constance L. Hays, "Girl's Plan to Save for College Runs Afoul of Welfare Rules," *New York Times*, May 15, 1992.

3. For more discussion of the whys and wherefores of team rewards, see Chapters 9 and 10 in Pinchot, *Intrapreneuring*.

4. In practice, a total run on the intracapital bank is unlikely because there is no currency to convert intracapital into except for investment and for funding losses.

5. Perhaps the absorption of intracapital in downturns can be further cushioned by doing something like treating intracapital as a contingent liability as it is accumulated and an extraordinary expense as it is drawn down.

Chapter 9. Outsourcing and Insourcing

Epigraph: Robert Reich, "Brainpower, Bridges, and the Nomadic Corporation," *New Perspectives Quarterly*, Fall 1991, Los Angeles.

1. James Brian Quinn, *Intelligent Enterprise* (New York: Free Press, 1992), p. 45.

2. Ibid., p. 41.

3. Ibid., p. 91.

4. Ibid., p. 37.

5. Microsoft Financial Department figures.

6. Loomis, "Dinosaurs?" p. 42.

7. Dobrzyinski, "Rethinking IBM," p. 88.

8. This is a composite of many conversations from a number of clients in different industries.

9. C. K. Prahalad and Gary Hamel, "The Core Competence of the Corporation," *Harvard Business Review*, May-June 1990, p. 84.

10. Charles Handy, *The Age of Unreason*, (Boston: Harvard Business School Press, 1990), p. 114.

11. Prahalad and Hamel, "The Core Competence of the Corporation," pp. 82, 84.

12. Tim Raymond in *Our Story So Far: Notes from the First 75 Years of 3M Company* (St. Paul, Minn.: Minnesota Mining and Manufacturing Company, 1977), pp. 112–113.

13. Quinn, *Intelligent Enterprise*, p. 41.

14. Ibid.

15. Many of the world's most productive research units long ago found that a few talented "gatekeepers"—exchanging information with dozens of outside sources—generate a huge percentage of their implemented ideas (from C. Gronroos, *Service Management and Marketing* [Lexington, Mass.: Lexington Books, l990], p. 118). Quinn, *Intelligent Enterprise*, p. 376.

16. Milt Freudenheim, "Speeding New Drugs to Market," *New York Times*, November, 22, 1992.

17. Machiavelli, *The Prince*, translated and edited by Robert M. Adams (New York: W. W. Norton, 1977), p. 41.

18. Quinn, *Intelligent Enterprise*, p. 79.

19. This story is based on the experiences of several companies in several industries but told as if it all occurred in a single firm.

Chapter 10. Liberated Teams

Epigraph: From Brian Dumaine, "Who Needs a Boss?" *Fortune*, May 7, 1990, p. 52; also quoted in Kimball Fisher, *Leading Self-Directed Work Teams: A Guide to Developing New Team Leadership Skills* (New York: McGraw-Hill, 1993), p. 95.

Epigraph from Petronius found in Tom Brown, "It's One Thing to Reorganize," *Industry Week*, May 4, 1992, p. 17.

1. Richard J. Schonberger, *Japanese Manufacturing Techniques: Nine Hidden Lessons in Simplicity* (New York: Free Press, 1982), p. 184.

2. Edward Lawler III, Susan Albers Mohrman, and Gerald Ledford, Jr., *Employee Involvement and Total Quality Management: Practices and Results in Fortune 1000 Companies* (San Francisco: Jossey-Bass, 1992).

3. Pitta, "It Had to Be Done and We Did It," p. 152.

4. Kevin G. Salwen, "Labor Letter" *Wall Street Journal*, August 31, 1993, p. 1.

5. Schonberger, *Japanese Manufacturing Techniques*, p. 183.

6. Randall Johnson, "As Work Becomes More Complex, Teams Become More Necessary," *Total Quality*, February 1993, p. 3.

7. Ibid.

8. Judith M. Bardwick, *Danger in the Comfort Zone* (New York: AMACOM, 1991), pp. 38–39.

9. Ibid., p. 29.

10. Ibid., pp. 163–164.

11. David T. Kearns and David A. Nadler, *Prophets in the Dark* (New York: HarperCollins, 1992), p. 80.

12. Personal conversations.

13. Personal conversations.

14. Carl Larson and Frank M. J. Lafasto, *TeamWork* (Newbury Park, Calif.: Sage Publications, 1989), pp. 31–33.

15. Katzenbach and Smith, "The Discipline of Teams."

16. Ibid.

17. Ibid., p. 115.

18. Larson and Lafasto, *TeamWork*, pp. 124–125.

Part III. Ensuring Responsibility for the Whole

Epigraph: William Van Dusen Wishard, "The American Future," *World Business Academy Perspectives* 6, no. 3 (1992): 35.

Chapter 11. Community in the Workplace

Epigraph: Theodore Roszak, from *Where the Wasteland Ends*, 1972, quoted in Edward Goldsmith, *The Way: An Ecological World-View* (Boston: Shambala, 1993), p. 376.

1. Senge, *The Fifth Discipline*.

2. Kazimierz Gozdz, "Building Community as a Leadership Discipline," in *The New Paradigm in Business*, edited by Michael Ray and Alan Reinzlen (Los Angeles, Tarcher/Perigee, 1993), p. 113.

3. Andrew Bard Schmookler, *The Illusion of Choice* (New York: State University of New York Press, 1993), p. 25.

4. Charles Hampden-Turner and Alfons Trompenaars, *The Seven Cultures of Capitalism* (New York: Doubleday, 1993), p. 163.

5. Ibid., pp. 195–196.

6. J. Nelson-Horchler, "The Magic of Herman Miller," *Industry Week*, February 18, 1991, pp. 11–17.

7. Max DePree, *Leadership Is an Art* (New York: Doubleday, 1989), p. 16.

8. Nelson-Horchler, "The Magic of Herman Miller."

9. DePree, *Leadership Is an Art*, p. 17.

10. Ibid., pp. 7–9.

11. Ibid., p. 9.

12. Schmookler, *Illusion of Choice*, p. 46.

13. Hampden-Turner and Trompenaars, *The Seven Cultures of Capitalism*, p. 234.

14. Ibid., p. 168. Numbers are taken from *USA Today*, March 24, 1991, Leisure Section.

15. Hampden-Turner and Trompenaars, *The Seven Cultures of Capitalism*, p. 169.

16. The word search here is noteworthy. It has become the identifying nomenclature for an increasingly common process, pioneered by Fred and Merrelyn Emery of Australia, that allows small and medium-sized work groups to find their common ground through processes of collective self-management. See *Productive Workplaces*, by Marvin Weisbord, and *Common Ground*, by Marvin Weisbord and 35 international coauthors.

17. Cited from Edward B. Lindaman and Ronald Lippitt, *Choosing the Future You Prefer,* 1979, p. 4, in Weisbord, *Productive Workplaces,* p. 281.

18. David Osborne and Ted Gaebler, *Reinventing Government: How the Entrepreneurial Spirit Is Transforming the Public Sector* (Reading, Mass.: Addison-Wesley, 1992), pp. 65–70.

19. Ibid., pp. 66–70.

20. Barbara Presley Noble, "Dissecting the 90's Workplace," *New York Times,* September 19, 1993.

21. Ibid.

22. Doug Pasternak and Peter Cary, "A $200 Billion Scandal," *U.S. News and World Report* 113, no. 23 (December 14, 1992).

23. One organization is the Human Economy Center based at Mankato State University, Mankato, Minnesota. Their slogan is "Economics as if people mattered."

24. Andrew Stark, "What's the Matter with Business Ethics," *Harvard Business Review,* May-June 1993, pp. 38–48.

25. Laura L. Nash, *Good Intentions Aside: A Manager's Guide to Resolving Ethical Problems,* quoted in Stark, "What's the Matter with Business Ethics."

Chapter 12. Equality and Diversity

Epigraph: Private conversation. Virginia Satir's books include *Peoplemaking* (Palo Alto, Calif.: Science and Behavior Books, 1972), *Conjoint Family Therapy* (Palo Alto, Calif.: Science and Behavior Books, 1983), *Making Contact* (Berkeley, Calif.: Celestial Arts, 1976).

1. Rollo May, Carl Rogers, Abraham Maslow, and other humanistic psychologists, *Politics and Innocence* (Dallas: Saybrook Publishers, 1986), p. 41. Throughout this section we are indebted to Maurice Friedman, "Community of Otherness," pp. 32–42.

2. Sharif Abdullah, private conversation. See also Sharif Abdullah, "Building a Compassionate Workplace," *AHP Perspective,* July/August 1993; and Robert Gilman, "Values at Work: Transforming Workplace Culture with Compassion: An Interview with Sharif Abdullah," *In Context* 33 (Fall 1992), 26–31.

3. Abdullah, "Building a Compassionate Workplace."

4. May, Rogers, Maslow et al., *Politics and Innocence,* p. 41.

5. "The Melting Pot Bubbles Less," *The Economist,* August 7–13, 1993, p. 63.

6. Ibid.

7. Richard G. "Skip" Lefauve, "Building a Customer-Driven Company: The Saturn Story," *Forum,* Summer 1993, p. 3.

8. Ronald Henkoff, "Companies That Train Best," *Fortune,* March 22, 1993, p. 62.

9. Ibid., p. 75.

10. William Wiggenhorn, "Motorola U: When Training Becomes an Education," *Harvard Business Review,* July-August 1990, pp. 71–83.

11. Merrelyn Emery, "Searching: For New Directions, in New Ways, for New Times," *Occasional Papers in Continuing Education,* no. 12 (Canberra, Australia: Centre for Continuing Education, Australian National University, April 1982), pp. 27–39.

12. John W. Gardner, *Excellence: Can We Be Equal and Excellent Too?* (New York: Harper & Row, 1961), p. 142, quoted in *Managing as a Performing Art,* by Peter B. Vaill (San Francisco: Jossey-Bass, 1989), p. 127.

13. Kahlil Gibran, *The Prophet* (New York: Knopf, 1923).

14. Donella Meadows, Dennis L. Meadows, Jorgen Randers, and William W. Behrens III, *The Limits to Growth* (New York: Universe Books, 1974).

15. Donella H. Meadows, Dennis L. Meadows, and Jorgen Randers, *Beyond the Limits: Confronting Global Collapse, Envisioning a Sustainable Future* (Post Mills, Vt.: Chelsea Green Publishing, 1992), pp. 233–234.

16. Donella H. Meadows, Dennis L. Meadows, and Jorgen Randers, "Love and the Revolution," *In Context* 32 (Summer 1992), p. 13.

17. Keith Johnstone, *Improv: Improvisation and the Theatre* (New York: Theatre Arts Books, 1979).

18. James Gleick, *Chaos: Making a New Science* (New York: Viking Penguin, 1987).

19. Senge, *The Fifth Discipline*, p. 240.

20. Ibid., p. 245.

Chapter 13. Voluntary Learning Networks

Epigraph: Wayne E. Baker, "The Network Organization in Theory and Practice," in *Networks and Organizations: Structure, Form, and Action,* edited by Nitin Nohria and Robert G. Eccles (Boston: Harvard Business School Press, 1992), pp. 397–398.

Epigraph under "Free Market Networks" is taken from the same source, p. 422.

1. Conversation with Sten Davidsen, Oticon.

2. Ulla Plon, "Thinking the Unthinkable," *Ex* magazine, March-April 1992.

3. Ibid., p. 21.

4. Conversation with Sten Davidsen, who led the team responsible for organizational change.

5. "Eliminating Paper and the Organizational Structure," *Denmark Review,* January 1993, p. 3.

6. Plon, "Thinking the Unthinkable," p. 22.

7. Sten Davidsen.

8. Lars Kolind, CEO, Oticon, in a speech in Stockholm, June 1993.

9. Ibid.

10. Plon, "Thinking the Unthinkable," p. 22.

11. Ibid.

12. Ibid.

13. Sten Davidsen.

14. Plon, "Thinking the Unthinkable," p. 23.

15. Sten Davidsen.

16. Sten Davidson.

17. B. Joseph Pine II, Bart Victor, and Andrew C. Boynton, "Making Mass Customization Work," *Harvard Business Review* (September-October 1993), p. 109.

18. Lewis Hyde, *The Gift: Imagination and the Erotic Life of Property* (New York: Vintage Books, 1979).

19. Norbert Wiener (1894–1964) from *God and Golem, Inc.,* 1964. Taken from *Bartlett's Familiar Quotations,* 15th edition.

20. Private conversation. Dr. Senft hastens to point out that he was not the first to observe this.

21. Senge, *The Fifth Discipline*, p. 95.

22. See Charles Handy, *The Age of Unreason* (Boston: Harvard Business School Press, 1989), pp. 76–80, for a clear explanation of something like this.

23. Private conversation.

Chapter 14. Democratic Self-Rule

Epigraph: Peter B. Vaill, *Managing as a Performing Art* (San Francisco: Jossey-Bass, 1989), p. 13.

The epigraph under "Learning Through Democratic Self-Rule" is from Wheatley, *Leadership and the New Science*, p. 133.

1. *Employee Ownership Report* 11, no. 6 (November-December 1991), National Center for Employee Ownership, Inc., Oakland, Calif.

2. Robert A. Dahl, *Democracy and Its Critics* (New Haven, Conn.: Yale University Press, 1989), p. 89.

3. Paul Maggio, "Nadel's Paradox Revisited: Relational and Cultural Aspects of Organizational Structure," in *Networks and Organizations*, edited by Nohria and Eccles, pp. 118–142.

4. Peter F. Drucker, *Post-Capitalist Society* (New York: Harper Business, 1993), p. 53.

5. Rosabeth Moss Kanter, "Mastering Change," *Executive Excellence* 10, no. 4 (April 1993), p. 12.

6. Marvin R. Weisbord and thirty-five international coauthors, *Discovering Common Ground: How Future Search Conferences Bring People Together to Achieve Breakthrough Innovation, Empowerment, Shared Vision, and Collaborative Action* (San Francisco: Berrett-Koehler, 1992).

7. Marvin Weisbord, "New Paradigm Planning," *At Work*, November-December 1992, pp. 15–16.

8. Dick Axelrod, personal communication, 1993.

9. Wheatley, *Leadership and the New Science*, p. 66.

10. Weisbord, "New Paradigm Planning," p. 9.

11. Ibid., p. 30.

12. Weisbord, *Productive Workplaces*, p. 282, and *Discovering Common Ground*, pp. 19–38.

13. Wheatley, *Leadership and the New Science*, pp. 62–73.

14. Ibid., pp. 77–78.

15. Emery, *Toward Real Democracy and Toward Real Democracy: Further Problems*, p. viii.

16. Fred Emery, "Human Resources Management," White Paper, July 1990.

17. Dahl, *Democracy and Its Critics*, p. 89.

18. Ibid., pp. 311–312.

19. Ibid., p. 31.

20. Weisbord, *Productive Workplaces*, p. 328.

21. Weisbord, *Productive Workplaces* and *Common Ground*.

22. Weisbord, *Productive Workplaces*, p. 151.

23. Kanter, "Mastering Change," p. 11.

24. Ibid, p. 12.

25. Our discussion of this case is based on the work and research of Rogier Fentener van Vlissingen of Millennium Management, Inc., 40 Rampart Road, South Norwalk, Conn. 06854.

26. Rogier F. van Vlissingen, personal correspondence.

27. Frank T. Adams and Gary Hansen, *Putting Democracy to Work*, rev. ed. (San Francisco: Berrett-Koehler, and Eugene, Ore.: Hulogosi Communications, 1992).

28. Ibid., p. 9.

29. *The Employee Ownership Casebook*, 1992, p. 46.

30. Gary B. Hansen and Frank T. Adams, "Web Industries: Tapping the Talents of Everyone," *At Work*, September-October 1993.

31. Ibid.

32. Corey Rosen, Katherine J. Klein, Karen M. Young, *Employee Ownership in America: The Equity Solution* (Lexington, Mass.: Lexington Books, D.C. Heath and Company, 1986), p. 168.

Chapter 15. Limited Corporate Government

Epigraph following "Tasks of Organizational Government" is from E. S. Savas, as quoted in Osborne and Gaebler, *Reinventing Government*, p. 25. Permission granted by Professor E. S. Savas, Department of Management, Baruch College, New York, N.Y.

1. Robert B. Reich, *The Work of Nations* (New York: Knopf, 1991), p. 13.

2. Ibid., p. 17.

3. James B. Quinn, *Intelligent Enterprise* (New York: Free Press, 1992), p. 138.

4. Dahl, *Democracy and Its Critics*, p. 89.

5. Osborne and Gaebler, *Reinventing Government*, pp. 25–36; samples are from list on p. 31.

6. Ibid., p. 35.

7. Ibid., pp. 25–36.

8. Hierarchy was designed for battle, and it may be its last stronghold, though even there it is challenged by guerrilla forces that operate with great local autonomy.

9. "The Internal Entrepeneurs," *UC World Magazine*, Fall 1993, p. 5.

10. Ibid.

11. Osborne and Gaebler, *Reinventing Government*, p. 40.

12. Ibid.

13. From an opinion by Supreme Court Justice Louis D. Brandeis, as quoted in *Breaking New Ground*, by the original Gifford Pinchot (1947; reprint Washington, D.C.: Island Press, 1974), p. 507.

14. Sherwood Ross, "More Companies Giving Workers Their Day in Court," *San Francisco Chronicle*, May 6, 1992, and Dick Grote and Jim Wimberly, "Peer Review," *Training*, March 1993, pp. 51–55.

15. Ibid.

16. Grote and Wimberly, "Peer Review," p. 55.

17. Quinn, *Intelligent Enterprise*, p. 57.

18. The public relations department at 3M.

19. George Stalk, Jr., and Thomas M. Hout, *Competing Against Time*, (New York: Free Press, 1990), pp. 59, 140.

20. Ibid., pp. 58, 59.

21. Reich, *The Work of Nations*, p. 29.

22. Paragraph from memory of personal conversation.

Chapter 16. The Power of Freedom and Community

Epigraph: Weisbord, *Common Ground*, p. 3.

1. Douglas C. Strain, "The Endangered Species—Homo Sapiens," paper of November 12, 1992, Box 749, Grand Lake, Colo. 80447.

2. Courtland L. Smith, "Growth in Population and Energy Consumption: More Than a Matter of Interest," *IEEE Technology and Science Magazine*, June 1983, pp. 9 ff. Smith's work suggests another way to look at the twin problems of population growth and resource use growth: Imagine a society with a 2-percent population growth over the lifetime of one of our children, say, seventy-five years. (The United States has around a 1-percent growth rate; some countries, higher.) In the unlikely event that the population uses no more resources per capita in that time and the resources are equally abundant over that time (also unlikely), there will be one-fourth as much in energy resources to go around. And what if energy use expands—as it has—at, say, 5 percent a year over the lifetime of the child: Energy use alone might be forty times as great, and taking into consideration population growth, energy use per capita could climb to two hundred times as great. This cannot happen in the world as we know it. At some point we will have to give up the model of growing wealth through expansion of markets for energy-dependent products and services.

3. Private communication from Ernest Lowe based on materials included in *Applying Industrial Ecology*, 1994, Cypress Communications, 6757 Thornhill Drive, Oakland, Calif. 94611.

4. James Robertson, "Seven Years On: The Other Economic Summit Begins Its Second Seven Year Cycle," *The Human Economy Newsletter* 12, no. 3 (September 1991). Robertson is the author of *Future Wealth: A New Economics for the 21st Century*.

5. Private conversation with Sten Davidsen, Oticon.

6. You have our permission to photocopy a few pages at a time of this book if it supports your view and you want to include highlighted pages in your message to another in the organization. For broadcast or training purposes, please contact the publisher.

Index

Permissions

GRATEFUL ACKNOWLEDGMENT is made for permission to reprint excerpts from the following:

Chapter 1

Adaptation of quotation in *Control Your Destiny or Someone Else Will* by Noel M. Tichy and Stratford Sherman (Doubleday Currency). Copyright © 1993 by Noel M. Tichy and Stratford Sherman. By Permission of General Electric and Stratford Sherman.

New York Times: "Parks Workers Challenging Stereotype of Public Jobs." Copyright © 1992 by The New York Times Company. Reprinted with permission.

Epigraph for Part II

Viking Penguin: *My Life In Politics* by Willy Brandt; translated by Anthea Bell. Translation copyright © 1992 by Anthea Bell. Original copyright © 1989 by Verlag Ullstein. Used by permission of Viking Penguin, a division of Penguin Books USA Inc.

Chapter 5

Harvard Business Review: Reprinted by permission of *Harvard Business Review*. "The Center Cut Solution" by Timothy W. Firnstahl, May/June 1993. Copyright © 1993 by the President and Fellows of Harvard College; all rights reserved.

Rawson Associates, an imprint of Macmillan Publishing Company: *The Machine That Changed the World* by James P. Womack, Daniel T. Jones, Daniel Roos, and Donna Sammons Carpenter. Copyright © 1990 James P. Womack, Daniel T. Jones, Daniel

Roos, and Donna Sammons Carpenter. Reprinted with permission.

ConAgra Philosophy, ConAgra, Inc. One ConAgra Drive, Omaha, Nebraska. Reprinted with permission.

Inc.: "Gainsharing." Reprinted with permission, *Inc.*, August 1993. Copyright © 1993 by Goldhirch Group, Inc., 38 Commercial Wharf, Boston, Massachusetts 02ll0.

Chapter 7

HarperCollins: *The Structures of Everyday Life: Civilization and Capitalism 15–18th Century, Vol. II* by Fernand Braudel. English translation copyright © 1982 HarperCollins Publishers, Inc. Reprinted with permission.

Chapter 8

New York Times: "Girl's Plan to Save for College Runs Afoul of Welfare Rules." Copyright © 1992 by The New York Times Company. Reprinted with permission.

Chapter 9

Harvard Business Review: Reprinted by permission of *Harvard Business Review*. "Core Competence of the Corporation" by C. K. Prahalad and Gary Hamel, May/June 1990. Copyright © 1990 by the President and Fellows of Harvard College; all rights reserved.

New Perspectives Quarterly: "Brain Power, Bridges, and the Nomatic Corporation" by Robert Reich, Fall 1991. Copyright © 1991 by the Center for the Study of Democratic Institutions. Reprinted with permission.

Chapter 10

Harvard Business Review: Reprinted by permission of *Harvard Business Review*. "The Discipline of Teams" by Jon R. Katzenbach and Douglas K. Smith, March/April 1993. Copyright © 1993 by the President and Fellows of Harvard College; all rights reserved.

Rawson Associates, an imprint of Macmillan Publishing Company: *The Machine That Changed the World* by James P. Womack, Daniel T. Jones, Daniel Roos, and Donna Sammons Carpenter. Copyright © 1990 James P. Womack, Daniel T. Jones, Daniel Roos, and Donna Sammons Carpenter. Reprinted with permission.

Sage Publications, Inc.: *Teamwork* by Carl E. Larson and Frank M. J. LaFasto. Copyright © 1989 by Sage Publications, Inc. Reprinted with permission of the publisher.

AMACOM Books: *Danger in the Comfort Zone: From Boardroom to Mailroom—How to Break the Entitlement Habit That's Killing American Business*. Copyright © 1991 Judith M. Bardwick, Ph.D., Inc. Published by AMACOM, a division of the American Management Association. All Rights reserved. Reprinted with permission of the publisher.

Doubleday, a division of Bantam Doubleday Dell Publishing Group, Inc.: *The Seven Cultures of Capitalism* by Charles Hampden-Turner and Alfons Trompenaars. Copyright © 1993 by Charles Hampden-Turner; all rights reserved. Reprinted with permission.

Epigraph for Part III

World Business Academy Perspectives: "The American Future" by William Van Dusen

Wishard. *World Business Academy Perspectives* Vol. 6 No. 3. Berrett-Koehler Publishers, Inc. Copyright © 1992 by World Business Academy, Ltd. Reprinted with permission.

Chapter 11

Addison-Wesley Publishing Company: *Reinventing Government* (Excerpt from pp. 66–70). Copyright © 1992 by David Osborne and Ted Gaebler. Reprinted by permission of Addison-Wesley Publishing Company.

New York Times: "At Work/Dissecting the 90's Workplace" by Kazimierz Gozdz. Copyright © 1993 by The New York Times Company. Reprinted with permission.

Jeremy P. Tarcher: "Building Community as a Leadership Discipline" by Kazimierz Gozdz in *The New Paradigm in Business*. Copyright © 1992. Reprinted with permission..

Chapter 12

Association for Humanistic Psychology: "AHP Perspective" published by the Association for Humanistic Psychology. Copyright © 1993. Reprinted with permission.

Chelsea Green Publishing Company: *Beyond the Limits*, by Donella H. Meadows, Dennis L. Meadows, and Jorgen Randers. Chelsea Green Publishing Company, Post Mills, Vermont. Copyright © 1992. Reprinted with permission.

Chapter 13

Harvard Business Review: Reprinted by permission of *Harvard Business Review*. "Making Mass Customization Work" by B. Joseph Pine II, Bart Victor, and Andrew C. Boynton, September/October 1993. Copyright © 1993 by the President and Fellows of Harvard College; all rights reserved.

Harvard Business School Press: Wayne E. Baker, "The Network Organization in Theory and Practice." Pages 397–398 in *Networks and Organizations: Structure, Form, and Action*, edited by Nitin Nohria and Robert G. Eccles. Copyright © 1992. Reprinted with permission.

Chapter 14

The Forum Corporation: Interview with Skip LeFauve, "Building a Customer-Driven Company: The Saturn Story." Reprinted by permission of Richard G. (Skip) LeFauve, President, Saturn Corporation, Springhill, Tennessee.

Executive Excellence: "Mastering Change" by Rosabeth Moss Kanter. Copyright © 1989 Rosabeth Moss Kanter. Reprinted with permission. Rosabeth Moss Kanter is Class of 1960 Professor at Harvard Business School. She is author of *The Challenge of Organizational Change* (1992, coauthored with Barry Stein and Todd Jick); *When Giants Learn to Dance* (1989); *The Change Masters* (1983); and *Men and Women of the Corporation* (revised 1993).

Yale University Press: *Democracy and Its Critics* by Robert A. Dahl. Copyright © 1989 by Yale University; all rights reserved. Reprinted with permission.

Macmillan Publishing Company, a division of Macmillan, Inc.: *Employee Ownership in America: The Equity Solution* by Corey Rosen, Katherine J. Klein, and Karen M. Young. Copyright © 1986 by D.C. Heath and Company. Reprinted with permission.

Chapter 15

Acknowledgments

Steven Piersanti, founder of Berrett-Koehler Publishers, Inc., ferreted out the larger issues surrounding the small book we had written and insisted we dare to write about them, even if the scope of the book exceeded our certainty. In a series of all-day meetings, he stood with us in front of a flipchart rethinking the focus and organization of this book. When following the vision that emerged sent us back to reading, research, and a complete rewrite, he put his young company on the line by letting us finish three months late.

Many thanks to Alis Valencia, our transcontinental editor via phone, fax, and modem. Letting us do it over again, cheering on the better directions, slashing the beloved garbage, insisting on logic and the resolution of apparent contradictions, holding firm in her taste — Alis was everything one could hope for in a collaborative editor. Alis also drew on her knowledge and contacts gained from being editor of two periodicals, *At Work: Stories of Tomorrow's Workplace* and *World Business Academy Perspectives*, to provide us with leads and stories.

Linda Desrosiers and Kathy Markle Doheny have worked with us at Pinchot and Company for nearly a decade, running the finance, operations, and training curricula that animate this company. They worked with tenacious love to research and prepare this manuscript and get this book to press. Also thanks to Keith Desrosiers and Matthew, Arnie, and Allison Doheny, who bore with them during the months of the long final crunch.

Ron Pellman kept Pinchot and Company going while we worked on the book. Years ago Ron taught us and many others the basics of the consulting business. In the last years he has provided continual guidance, wisdom, stories, ideas, and critiques as the book evolved.

Yel Hannon created the original versions of many of the graphics used in both this book and *Intrapreneuring,* as well as pitching in at some memorable after-hours deadline sessions. Naomi Schiff did the gorgeous layout and design and the final renderings.

We want to acknowledge the extraordinary staff at Berrett-Koehler, including Pat Anderson, Valerie Barth, Mark Carstens, Valerie McOurt, Liz Paulus, Kristen Scheel, Elizabeth Swenson, and Steven Zink, as well as the network of independent suppliers that helped us put the book together, including Naomi Schiff and the staff at Seventeenth Street Studios (design and production), Virginia Rich (copy editor), Janja Lalich (proofreader), and Earline Hefferlin (indexer).

The quality of the collaborations among the members of this network and Pinchot and Company was a delightful illustration of the teamwork, speed, intelligence, and fun that emerge from a network organization, even among people in diverse locations and different types of businesses. We are proud to report that a dozen people or more in the two organizations and some of the independent contractors will share any profits from the book.

Our heartfelt thanks to our children, Marco, 17, Marianna, 10, Alex, 13, who once again took the disappearing parent act with sudden leaps forward in responsibility and the savoring of life. Anna Wannstrom, Anne Coon, Deva Khalsa, and Jeff Vibert in various ways have helped keep a home together for us all.

Jim Bolt, Peter Beinetti, and Kathy Gillam and all the folks in the Executive Development Associates network supported us, challenged us, and made us grow. Ken Shelton at *Executive Excellence* drew out our ideas, encouraged us, and visited us with sage advice.

The community in and about Wightwood School showed us the future of education in a child- and family-centered community. There we first experienced cross-functional teamwork in a democratic setting. Over a decade we participated in many planning and governance processes that had to respect the freedom of a number of strongly diverse groups of stakeholders. At the same time, a community was being built and strengthened and renewed that nurtured the institution to do the impossible on limited resources.

Chris Allen of Consensus Development let us use a beta version of Infolog™ to keep track of all the articles, quotations from books, and other research materials. The ability to find an old clipping at once even though someone else filed it was invaluable.

Thanks to Meg Wheatley, Dick Leider, Jim Thorpe, Jane Mulder, Otis Wollan, John Michels, Lise Dondy, Frank Van Haste, Geralyn White, Joy Sweet, Victor Budnick, Kevin Lezak, Dana Naumann, Bill Kaplan, Marianna Kastner, José Salibi Neto, Deva Khalsa, Roger Terry, Neal Jenson, Chris Allen, Peter Kindlman, and Guy Kawasaki, who read early drafts of the book and steered us away from a number of blind alleys.

We thank the many people who made and told the workplace stories that give substance to our speculations. We are also grateful to those who wrote the books in the Notes and hope we have introduced some of them to new readers.

And so hundreds share the credit — including the friends and business associates listed alphabetically below who helped toward our researching, writing, and producing this book. Most contributed within the pressure of a tight deadline, going out of their way to help get this work out to the readers. We have a sense of good fortune at having been part of an intensely productive project network spread across the country and abroad.

Steve Aaronson
Sharif Abdullah
Jerry Acuff
Rod Allen
Otto Andresen
Cindy Andrews
Marcia Arko
Sven Atterhed
Jim Autry

Dick Axelrod
Joe Balazs
Steve Barber
Steve Beitler
Rick Belluzzo
Warren Bennis
Dale Bernstein
David Bickett
Walter Bloch

David Boghossian

Lennart Boksjö

Bob Brightfelt

Frances Brody

Mae Brown

Edson de Godoy Bueno

Nigel Bufton

Gene Callahan

Pat Carey

Bill Clack

Cherrie Clay

Tom Cochrane

George Cofrancesco

Napier Collyns

Ann Coon

Ed Corboy

Stephen R. Covey

Barry Crook

Sarah Davison

Gustaf Delin

Eileen Drysdale

Martin Edelston

Dave Edison

Merrelyn Emery

Dick Erickson

Coleman Ferguson

Marilyn Ferguson

John Fischer

Andrea Forte

William E. Franklin

Will Fraser

Art Fry

Joseph L. Galarneau

Lynn Galligan

R. Donald Gamache

Charles Garfield

Robert George

Julia Gippenwriter

Marianne Glynn

Jon Goldstein

Barbara Graham

Len Groszek

Robert E. Gubrud

Sandrine Guillot

Jack Harnard

Dyer Harris

Ron Harrison

Susan and Bruce Harvey

Hazel Henderson

Donald Holmes

Joanna and Lee Jacobus

Beth Jarman

Wes Jarrell, Ph.D.

Howard Kahn

Pat Kazmierski

Rocky Kimball

Charlie King

George Land

George Lange

Michael Lanning

Jean Pierre Laroche

Ernest Lowe

Gloria Maddox

Jane Markle

Trevor May

Herman Maynard

Mariam McGlone

Bill McGlynn

Ronan McGrath

Ron Meeks

Alan Mendelson

Phil Meredith

Karl Mettke

Lorraine Mnich

Karen Muth

Peg Neale

Howard Newstadt

Sara Norton

Mike Nunan

Deborah Palermini

Emmett Parnell

Anne and Hank Patton

John Pearson

Norcott Pemberton

Cindy Pinchot

Peter Pinchot

Brian Piper

Nancy Pittman

Vladimir and Zareena
   Preobradzensky

Jack Rakusin

Lew Randall

Erik and Lucinda Redlich

Alex Rudakov

Will and Anita Sawyer

John Schiller

George Schoonmaker

Mary Schoonmaker

George Schrieber

Robert L. Schwartz

Florence Sender

Steve Senft

Norihiko Shimizu

Carlos Silvestrini

Mark Spivak

Ken Stahl

Joseph Steed

Suzanne and Stanley Steirs

Ray Symmes

Richard Tait

Matt Taylor

Jim and Diantha Thorpe

Alex Tilles

Edward Tokarsky

Mitsuru Tomita

Lenora Vesio

Rogier F. van Vlissingen

Bill Volkers

Rein Vosari

Kate Warich

Michael Winston

Bruce and Betsy Woolpert

Neils Young

All our friends at the Office
Network and many others
who chose not to be named
because they know that publicity often triggers the organization's immune system.

THE AUTHORS

Conversations with Elizabeth and Gifford Pinchot twist and turn
unexpectedly. In their Guilford, Connecticut, home, conga drums
share space with the electric piano, kids and dogs run in and out,
rock-climbing gear and old candle holders made during the blacksmithing days form a durable backdrop for Marco, 17, Marianna, 10,
and Alex, 13. The home swirls with visitors: a Russian psychologist and
her mathematician husband, a carpenter who teaches yoga and paints,
a high school science teacher, a series of exchange students, and this
year a seventh grader from Moscow, living with the Pinchots while
going to the local school where they are both board members.

Across the driveway, up a narrow staircase and overlooking a hay
field and pond, is their home office, a small loft over a workshop. The
workshop is crammed with lathes, anvils, and welding equipment.
The office above it, filled with computers, high-speed modems, and gra-
nola bars, is wired up to the information superhighway.

Gifford and Elizabeth (whom everyone calls Libba) were married
eleven years after they met while he was studying physics and economics at Harvard and she was studying philosophy and political
philosophy at Wellesley College. Gifford graduated with honors in

economics, attended Johns Hopkins in sociology, and received a masters degree in neurophysiology from the Johns Hopkins School of Environmental Medicine and Public Health. Libba transferred to Stanford University, graduated with a degree in philosophy, and received two masters degrees, one in human development from the University of Oregon and one in systems psychology and constructivist philosophy from Goddard College. Both are thinking of going back to school.

Libba and Gifford were each initiated into the business world by participating in small, university-affiliated research and training organizations between stints at graduate school. When they got together, they were both ready for "real work for a change." They bought a farm adjoining a relative's dairy in upstate New York and started a business making decorative iron plant hangers and fireplace tools. This craft enterprise achieved national distribution and produced enough former employees who made good as independent blacksmiths that some people in the state still talk about the "Silent Steam" school of artist blacksmiths. While at the forge they learned basic lessons about many aspects of business, from manufacturing efficiency to distribution, from collecting bad debts to keeping good customers, from training and motivating employees to dealing with international competition. They sold that business in 1978 and prepared to enter the twentieth century, but stumbled into the twenty-first almost by mistake.

That was the year Gifford coined the word *intrapreneuring,* and they made it the basis of a joint article and subsequent book introducing a new framework for freedom and innovation in the workplace. Their current venture, Pinchot and Company, is the fourth enterprise started by Gifford and Libba. Over the past eleven years the company has worked with over half of the one hundred largest companies in the United States and many abroad, including AT&T, Banco de Brasil, the Canadian National Railroad, DuPont, Ford, Hoechst Celanese, Kodak, Motorola, the New York Stock Exchange, 3M, and the U.S. Forest Service.

Bill Kaplan
Head of Wightwood School, Branford, Connecticut